PLAY ROCK KEYBOARDS

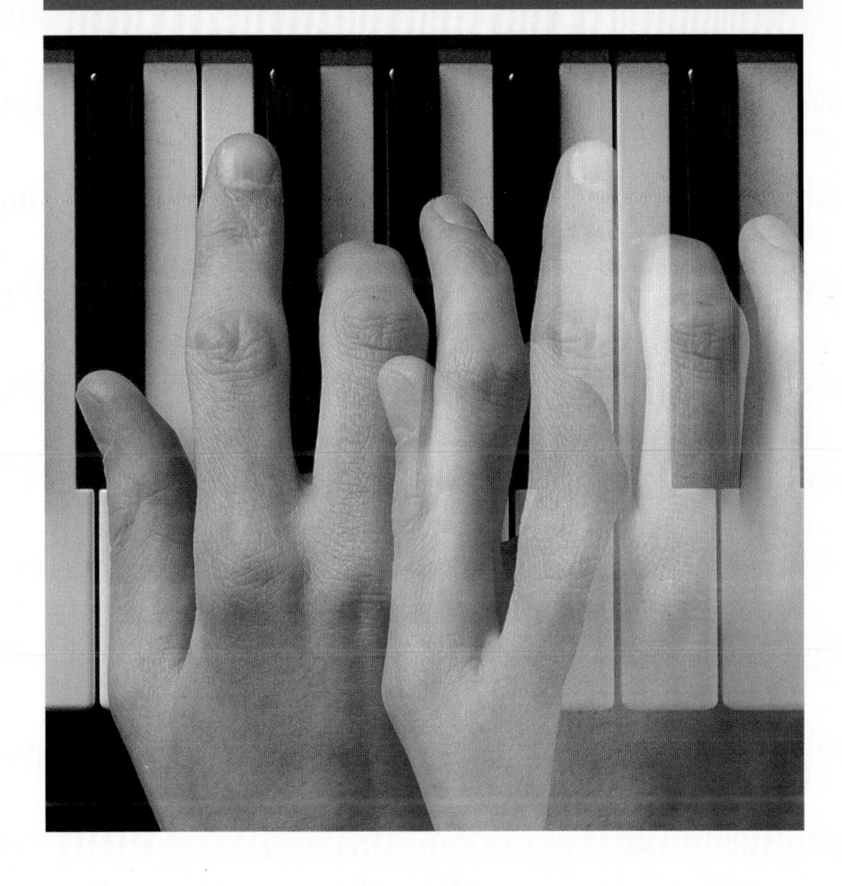

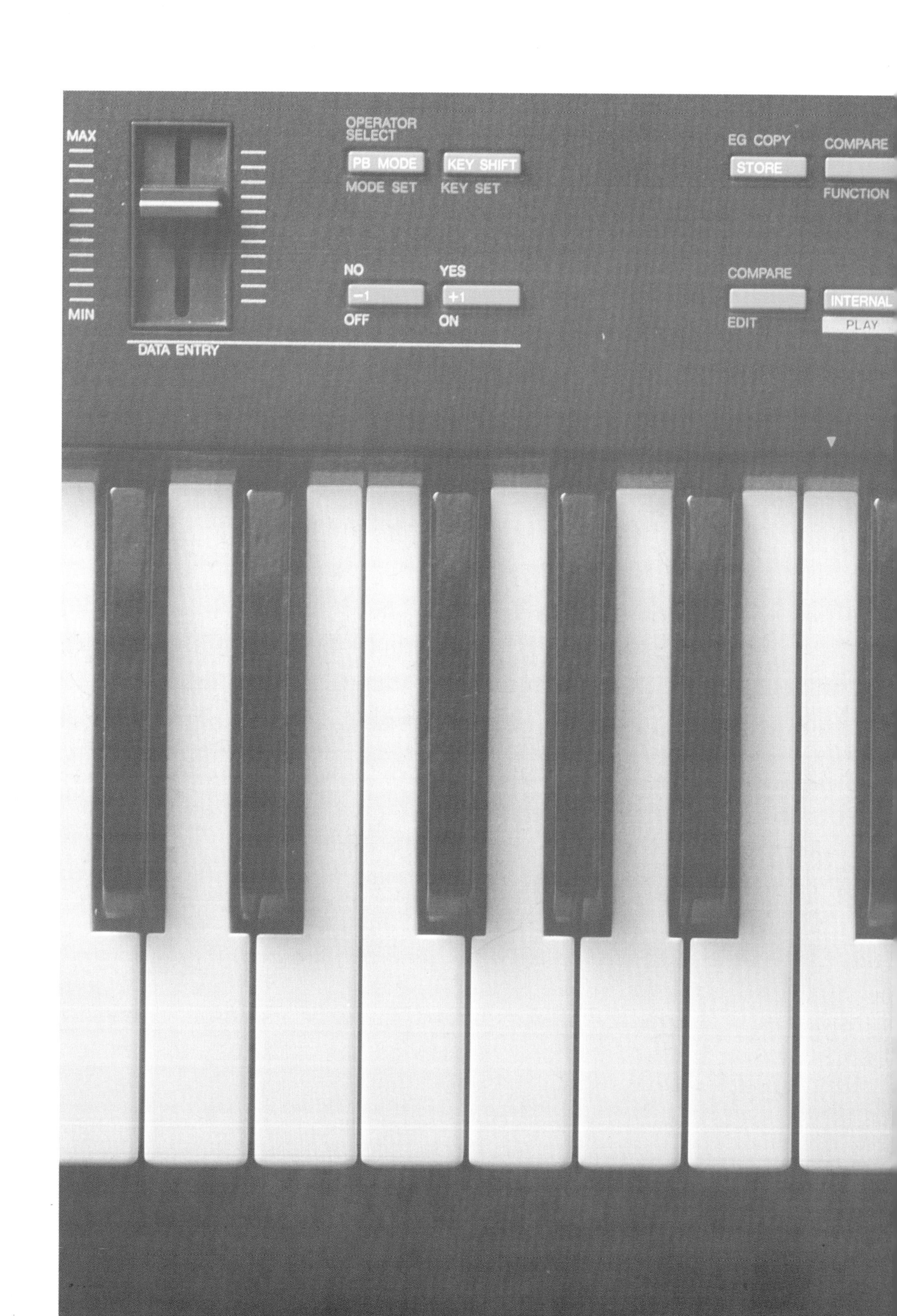
MAX
MIN
DATA ENTRY
OPERATOR
SELECT
PB MODE
MODE SET
KEY SHIFT
KEY SET
NO
−1
OFF
YES
+1
ON
EG COPY
STORE
COMPARE
FUNCTION
COMPARE
EDIT
INTERNAL
PLAY

PLAY ROCK KEYBOARDS

LEARN TO PLAY STEP BY STEP • USING MAJOR HIT SONGS
KEYBOARD BUYER'S GUIDE • A–Z OF KEYBOARD PLAYERS • HOW TO BREAK INTO THE MUSIC BUSINESS

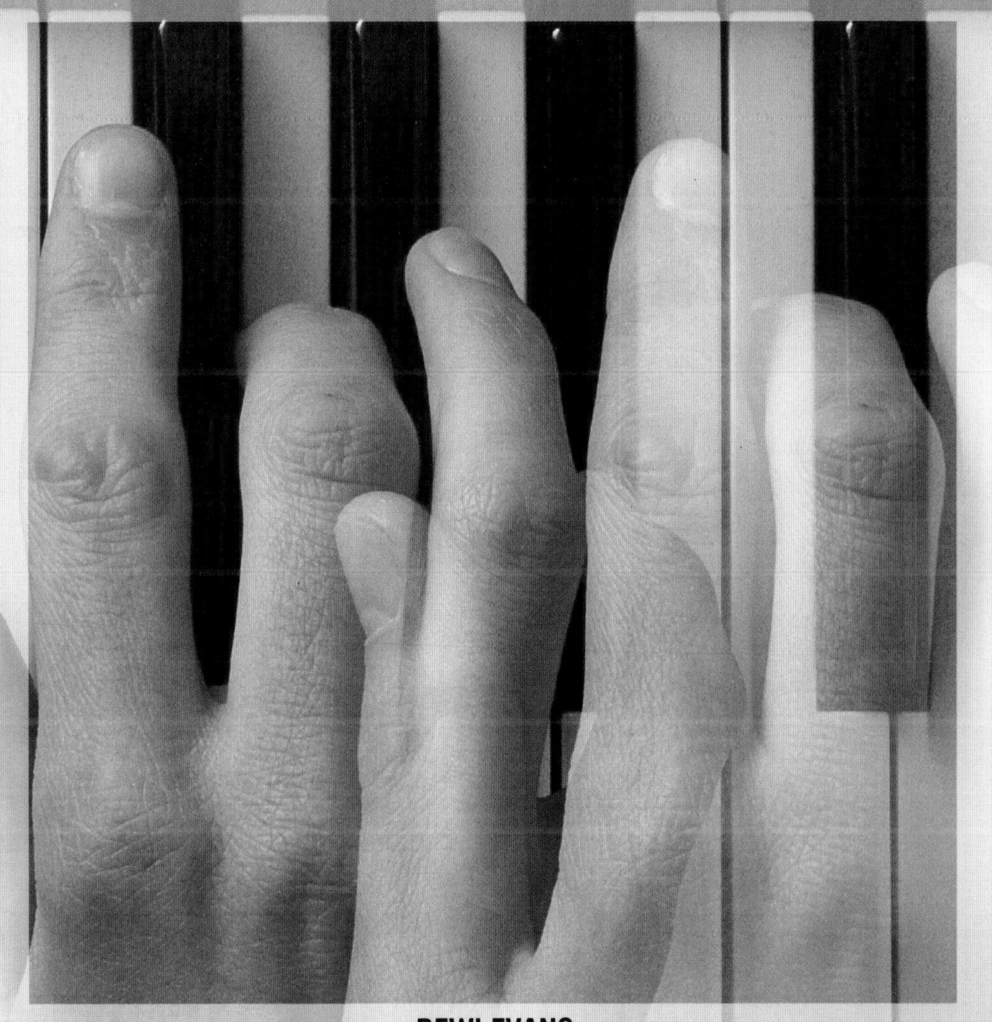

DEWI EVANS
CONTRIBUTING AUTHORS: TONY MITCHELL • CHRIS TRENGOVE • PHIL McNEILL
SPECIAL CONSULTANT: MIKE LINDUP

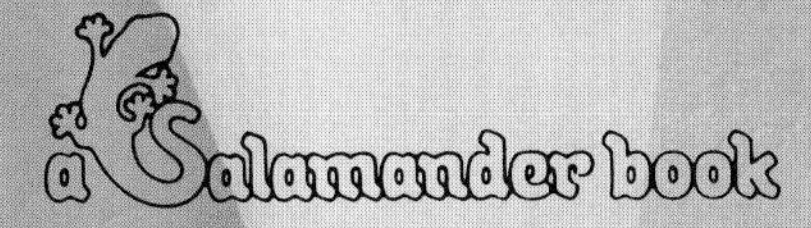

Amsco Publications

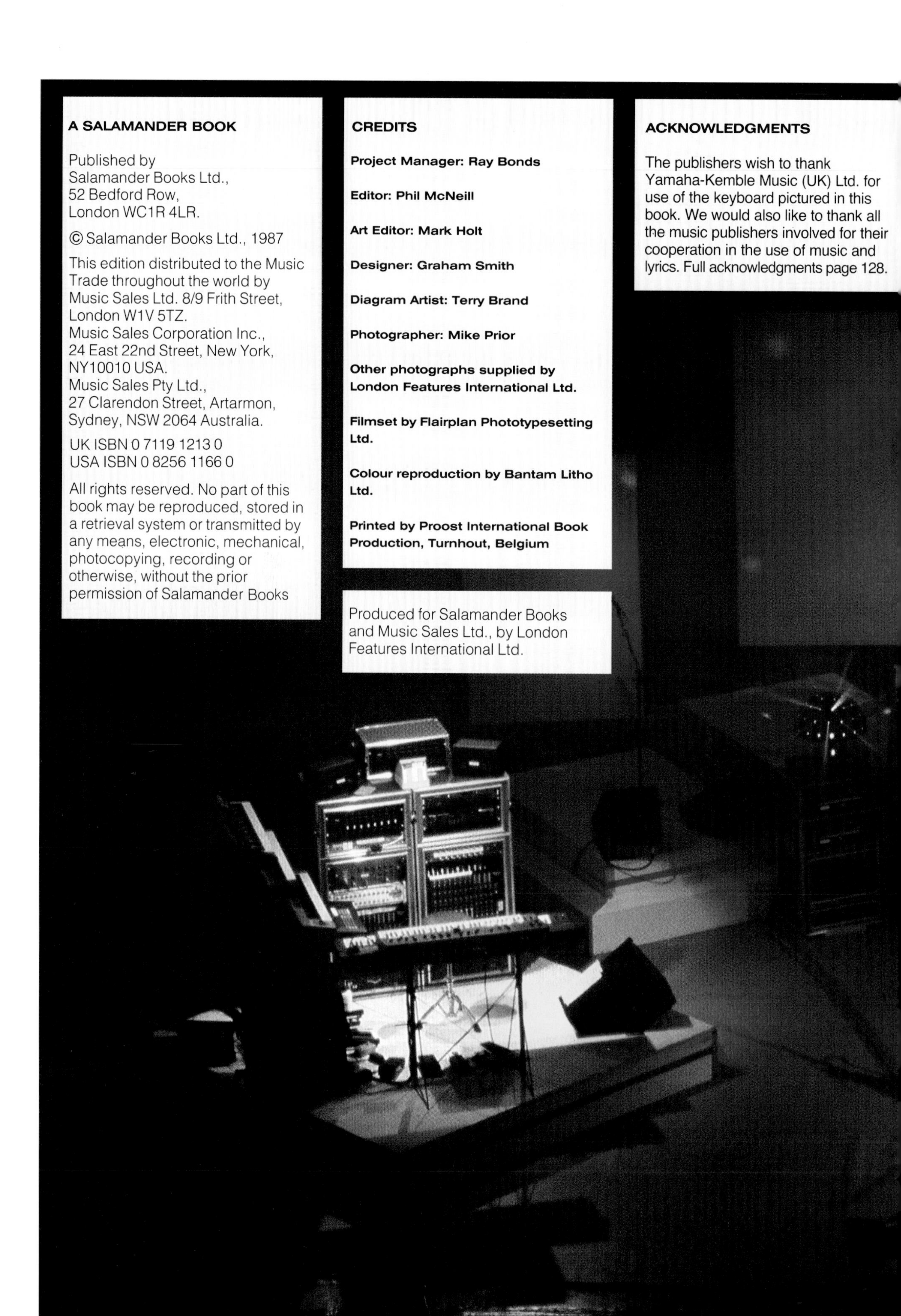

A SALAMANDER BOOK

Published by
Salamander Books Ltd.,
52 Bedford Row,
London WC1R 4LR.

This edition distributed to the Music Trade throughout the world by Music Sales Ltd. 8/9 Frith Street, London W1V 5TZ.
Music Sales Corporation Inc., 24 East 22nd Street, New York, NY10010 USA.
Music Sales Pty Ltd., 27 Clarendon Street, Artarmon, Sydney, NSW 2064 Australia.

UK ISBN 0 7119 1213 0
USA ISBN 0 8256 1166 0

CREDITS

Project Manager: Ray Bonds

Editor: Phil McNeill

Art Editor: Mark Holt

Designer: Graham Smith

Diagram Artist: Terry Brand

Photographer: Mike Prior

Other photographs supplied by London Features International Ltd.

Filmset by Flairplan Phototypesetting Ltd.

Colour reproduction by Bantam Litho Ltd.

Printed by Proost International Book Production, Turnhout, Belgium

Produced for Salamander Books and Music Sales Ltd., by London Features International Ltd.

ACKNOWLEDGMENTS

The publishers wish to thank Yamaha-Kemble Music (UK) Ltd. for use of the keyboard pictured in this book. We would also like to thank all the music publishers involved for their cooperation in the use of music and lyrics. Full acknowledgments page 128.

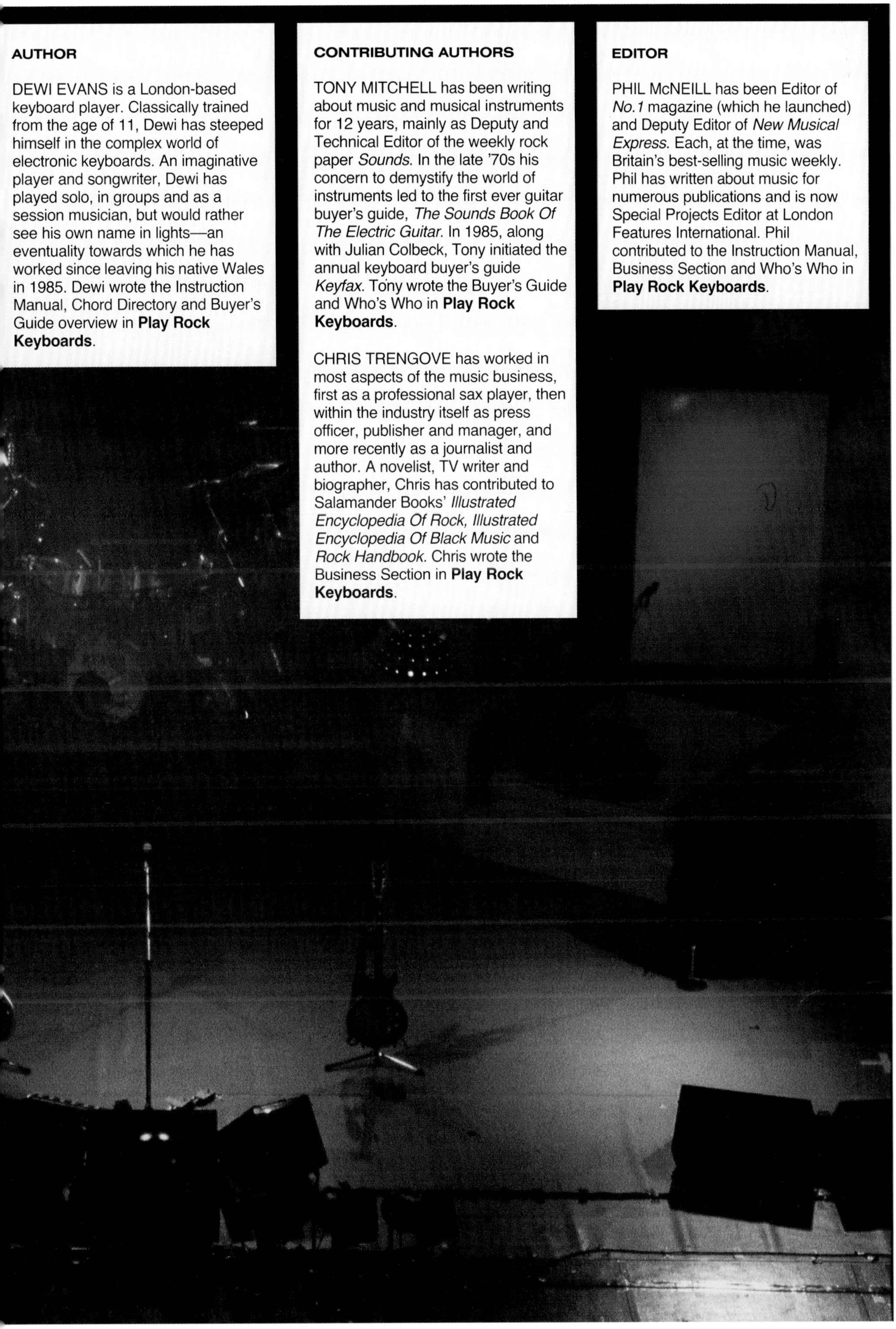

AUTHOR

DEWI EVANS is a London-based keyboard player. Classically trained from the age of 11, Dewi has steeped himself in the complex world of electronic keyboards. An imaginative player and songwriter, Dewi has played solo, in groups and as a session musician, but would rather see his own name in lights—an eventuality towards which he has worked since leaving his native Wales in 1985. Dewi wrote the Instruction Manual, Chord Directory and Buyer's Guide overview in **Play Rock Keyboards**.

CONTRIBUTING AUTHORS

TONY MITCHELL has been writing about music and musical instruments for 12 years, mainly as Deputy and Technical Editor of the weekly rock paper *Sounds*. In the late '70s his concern to demystify the world of instruments led to the first ever guitar buyer's guide, *The Sounds Book Of The Electric Guitar*. In 1985, along with Julian Colbeck, Tony initiated the annual keyboard buyer's guide *Keyfax*. Tony wrote the Buyer's Guide and Who's Who in **Play Rock Keyboards**.

CHRIS TRENGOVE has worked in most aspects of the music business, first as a professional sax player, then within the industry itself as press officer, publisher and manager, and more recently as a journalist and author. A novelist, TV writer and biographer, Chris has contributed to Salamander Books' *Illustrated Encyclopedia Of Rock, Illustrated Encyclopedia Of Black Music* and *Rock Handbook*. Chris wrote the Business Section in **Play Rock Keyboards**.

EDITOR

PHIL McNEILL has been Editor of *No.1* magazine (which he launched) and Deputy Editor of *New Musical Express*. Each, at the time, was Britain's best-selling music weekly. Phil has written about music for numerous publications and is now Special Projects Editor at London Features International. Phil contributed to the Instruction Manual, Business Section and Who's Who in **Play Rock Keyboards**.

HELLO
RON DeVOUS
YAMAHA DX7
TOP POP
BOY
moog

CONTENTS

Opposite: some of rock's foremost keyboard players in action. From left, from the top: Jean-Michel Jarre, Kraftwerk, Lionel Richie, Daryl Hall, Mags Furuholmen of A-Ha, Tony Banks of Genesis, Devo, Pet Shop Boys and Billy Joel.

THIS IS an exciting time to be a keyboard player. There are so many new keyboards coming out every year, and so many new sounds to be used, the role of the keyboard player is more important than ever before.

That's where this book comes in, because it puts learning to play keyboards into the context of today's technology and today's music.

Keyboards, and especially synthesisers, are not like any other instrument. It's not just a question of playing the chords or the part: keyboards can create atmospheres. Magic, if you like.

I grew up in a musical family, and I had piano lessons from an early age and then went on to a specialist music school. That was fine if you wanted to be a classical musician, but I found the approach to music very blinkered and disciplinarian. There was 'proper music' and 'not proper music'. Rock wasn't proper music.

I think a lot of young keyboard players experience that. They don't feel inspired to explore keyboards for themselves, so they stop having lessons.

One thing I like about **Play Rock Keyboards** is the way it encourages you to find out about the keyboard for yourself. It gives you a starting point.

But you must understand that in order to get the best out of the book, you've got to practise, and you have to stick with it. Some of the exercises might not be too exciting, but it will reward you at the end of the day, so it's worth persevering.

The best way of learning is by playing with other people—even one other person, whether they're singing or playing another instrument. But even if you're only playing on your own, this book will help you an awful lot. It will give you an idea of where things are—a kind of map of the keyboard—so that you can go on to make your own music.

HAVING SAID that, exactly how does a keyboard player make his or her own music?

It's not so easy for a keyboard player to forge a 'personal' style as it is for a guitarist, because the instruments are different in nature. So you have to work towards two things: creating your own sounds, by programming them into your synthesiser or sampler, and creating your own musical identity in the approach you take to each song.

You should try to give each song, or each part, a different sound and a different musical style, so they don't all sound the same. If you can do that and retain a consistent overall approach, then you're beginning to create your own identity.

The important thing is to keep your ears open. As a keyboard player you have to fulfil a role within the music, and hopefully add something original to it.

SOME PEOPLE suggest that, with so many highly developed keyboards available, the modern keyboard player needs to know more about technology than about music. In fact, of course, it's both—and I'm pleased to see that **Play Rock Keyboards** covers both the music and technology equally well.

Sometimes, I know, it seems like there's so much technology that the music is being lost. As a keyboard player, you have to remember that the technology is there to serve *you*. There are a lot of excellent keyboards on the market, and it's a question of exploring them, testing them out and finding the one you like.

You need an instrument that you can grow and develop with, and with so much available, there must be something to suit any taste.

As for what instrument you should start on, that's a difficult one because it's always different strokes for different folks. For me, the most exciting keyboard I discovered in the early days of Level 42 was Sequential Circuits' Prophet 5, because it was a polyphonic synthesiser capable of a wide variety of sounds. That really served me in good stead, and I still use it onstage.

But someone starting out now migh

prefer a digital synthesiser such as the Yamaha DX7, Roland D-50 or Casio CZ-1.

All of the instruments I've mentioned so far are synthesisers—and ideally, as a modern keyboard player, the synthesiser is likely to be your main instrument. But if you're just starting out, home keyboards are a good, inexpensive option. They make good sounds and they have built-in drum machines, so you can create a kind of band effect on your own, and then play over the top of it. That's good practice for playing in a band.

In fact, in a way that's how I started. My dad had a Philacordia organ—it was a very basic electronic organ, but it had about eight different stops to give you different sounds, and the last ten notes at the bottom of the keyboard were chords, so you could actually play a chord and then jam around at the top.

But really, there isn't any keyboard instrument that isn't good to start on, because just playing a keyboard—finding out what it can do, pressing all the buttons and exploring the possibilities—is all part of the process of learning.

WHEN YOU get a synthesiser, you'll find that you can either use the 'pre-set' sounds it comes with, or create your own sounds by a process known as programming.

I find programming a keyboard very stimulating, because I find a sound and then the sound suggests something, and an idea for a song can often come from that. In fact, I find it hard to concentrate on programming because if I find a good sound I'll start jamming away and stop programming!

On the other hand, I do use pre-set sounds a lot. There are some really good sounds that have been programmed as pre-sets, and they're there to be used. You just have to make sure you don't use them in the same way they've been used before.

I think a lot of the criticism about keyboards sounding computerised and synthetic is because the same pre-set sounds turn up on so many different records. That's where your individual identity comes in.

But in the early days there's no point in worrying about trying to sound like 'you'. That's something that can only come with time anyway.

SO PROGRAMMING is inspiring: there is a magic about creating a new sound.

At the end of the day, however, the most important thing is the music. The quality of the song is what's going to last, rather than the sounds that were used on a particular record.

If a song becomes a classic, it's because of what the singer is singing about, how it's sung, what sort of atmosphere the song has and what emotions it conjures up in the listener's mind.

For that reason, you should listen to as many different keyboard players as you can, because you'll find that different players will approach the same thing in different ways—there's so much you can learn just by listening to records.

From now on, when you listen to records, listen analytically—and make sure you take in a broad span of music. You shouldn't ever limit yourself to listening to one style.

ONE LAST point: this book will, if you use it well, show you how to play keyboards. But one thing about modern equipment such as sequencers and synthesisers is that you don't have to be a 'proper' musician to use them. You can compose on them and you can program them without having lots of certificates and so on.

And I think that's great, because music is for everyone. It's a universal language, a language that everyone in the world understands. Music isn't the property of musicians alone.

So if that's your aim, fine. I think you'll still find this book very useful.

FOR THE rest of you, the ones who want to become fluent keyboard players and discover the world of music which that opens up, you've got some hard work ahead.

There are no shortcuts to becoming a good keyboard player, but I hope that Play Rock Keyboards will make it a rewarding experience. It's an original book, and I think it's a good one.

So read it carefully . . . enjoy it . . . and get practising!

BORN IN London in 1959, Mike Lindup formed Level 42 in 1980 with three musicians from the Isle of Wight—bass player Mark King, guitarist Boon Gould and drummer Phil Gould. With Lindup and King sharing vocals, they rapidly became Britain's top jazz-funk band, with hits such as 'The Sun Goes Down (Living It Up)', 'The Chinese Way' and 'Hot Water'. The turning point came in 1985, with two albums—'Physical Presence' and 'World Machine'—which established them as a major force for the future, highlighted by classic singles such as 'Something About You' and 'Lessons In Love'. 1987's 'Running In The Family' album was equally successful, both commercially and artistically. Level 42 are now one of the world's most respected live groups, a fact emphasised when Mark and Mike joined the all-star 'supergroup' assembled for the 1987 Prince's Trust concert.

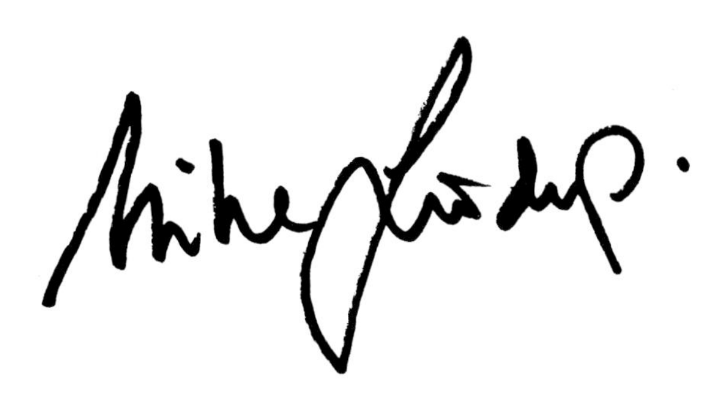

MIKE LINDUP (SPECIAL CONSULTANT)

THERE IS more demand for keyboard players in rock now than ever before. It may not always be obvious, but almost every record in the charts these days is dominated by digital keyboards. Synthesisers, samplers and sequencers are the new sound of music.

Yet, as anyone forming a group will tell you, competent keyboard players are surprisingly thin on the ground. That's where **Play Rock Keyboards** comes in—if you want to play current keyboard styles, using the keyboard instruments of today, this book is for you.

Play Rock Keyboards isn't just a series of piano lessons. Having been through quite a few years of formal music training myself, I know it's hard going, and I wouldn't wish the same on any aspiring rock or pop keyboard player.

As for other 'teach yourself' type books, it has to be said that most of them look so complicated and unappealing that they can put you off learning altogether.

Hopefully, **Play Rock Keyboards** will have the opposite effect. With its simple step-by-step approach, supported by clear, colourful diagrams and pictures, plus extracts from some of the best keyboard songs of the '80s, this book should make learning a pleasure, not a chore.

That doesn't mean that **Play Rock Keyboards** takes short cuts. Some elements of formal music training are essential, and you'll find them all here.

Please don't expect to become a good keyboard player overnight, and don't expect a kind of music-by-numbers approach. At every stage, we encourage you to understand what's going on, and you'll only get as much out of it as you put in in terms of practice and experimentation.

Obviously, we can only take you so far. But once you've mastered the basics which **Play Rock Keyboards** gives you, hopefully you'll find that you can progress further under your own steam.

Your ultimate object should be to develop a style of your own—and that can only come through a combination of the knowledge you take from this book, and your own instincts and talent.

Incidentally, don't think that you *have* to be a synthesiser player to read this book. Pianos, synths, organs, samplers, harpsichords . . . whatever the keyboard, **Play Rock Keyboards** can teach you how to play it.

Obviously, certain songs sound better on certain instruments. But theoretically you can play any keyboard part on any keyboard instrument. So it doesn't matter whether you're sitting at a Steinway grand or a Casio pocket synth. As long as it has a keyboard we're in business.

Dewi Evans

DEWI EVANS

From the acoustic roots of rock and roll to the remote master keyboards and digital synthesisers of today—from Little Richard ('50s) to Bryan Ferry ('70s) and Howard Jones ('80s)—the story of rock keyboards and how to play them is all here. You can use the techniques shown in Play Rock Keyboards as a jumping off point for any keyboard style and any keyboard instrument.

INSTRUCTION MANUAL

This is our step-by-step guide to keyboard playing. Take it gradually, and by the time you reach page 70 you'll be a useful performer.

To make the most of this section, concentrate on one double-page spread at a time. Make sure you've taken it all in, and practised all the exercises, before turning the page.

Each page has a top section giving you the basic theory behind the music you're learning, and below that the exercises, chords and scales you need to take you to the next step. If you find the theory hard to grasp, don't worry too much about it—you can still learn to play simply by following the exercises in the bottom part of each page.

Along the way, you'll find a number of major hit songs to play, including The Human League's 'Don't You Want Me', Berlin's 'Take My Breath Away', and the *Beverly Hills Cop* theme 'Axel F'. You won't need to read music to play them, because we've got our own easy system. But we've also printed the music for anyone who can read it. And if you want to learn to read music, there's a section for that too.

CONTENTS

THE KEYBOARD

A MUSICAL keyboard consists of a number of white and black 'keys'. Keyboards can vary in length from 25 to 88 keys—the average is 61.

Press any key and your instrument will make a sound, called a 'note'. Like most musical instruments, the keyboard is tuned to produce 12 different notes.

So why does a keyboard have up to 88 keys, when it can only produce 12 notes? Because each note appears more than once.

This illustration shows how the arrangement of the keys follows a set pattern across the keyboard. The keys are divided into five identical groups of 12—seven white and five black.

These 12 keys play the 12 different notes your instrument can produce. And those 12 notes are the basis of music.

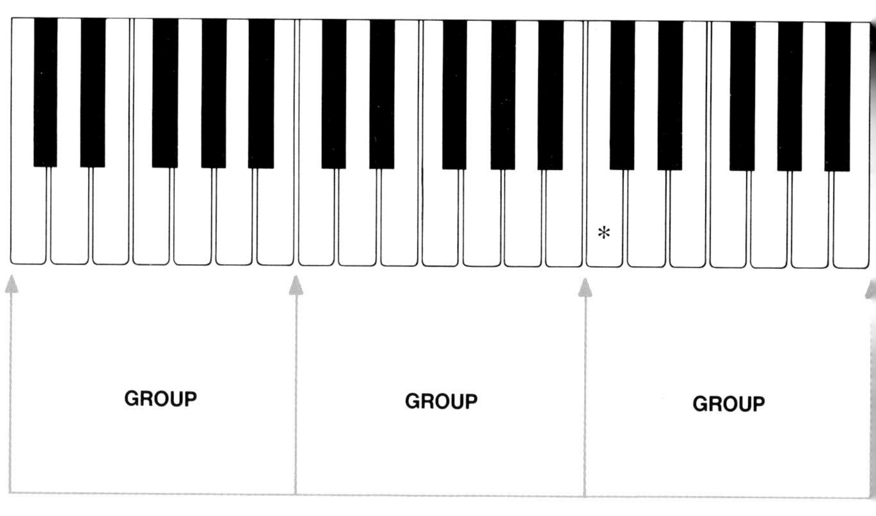

*=Middle C

THE HANDS

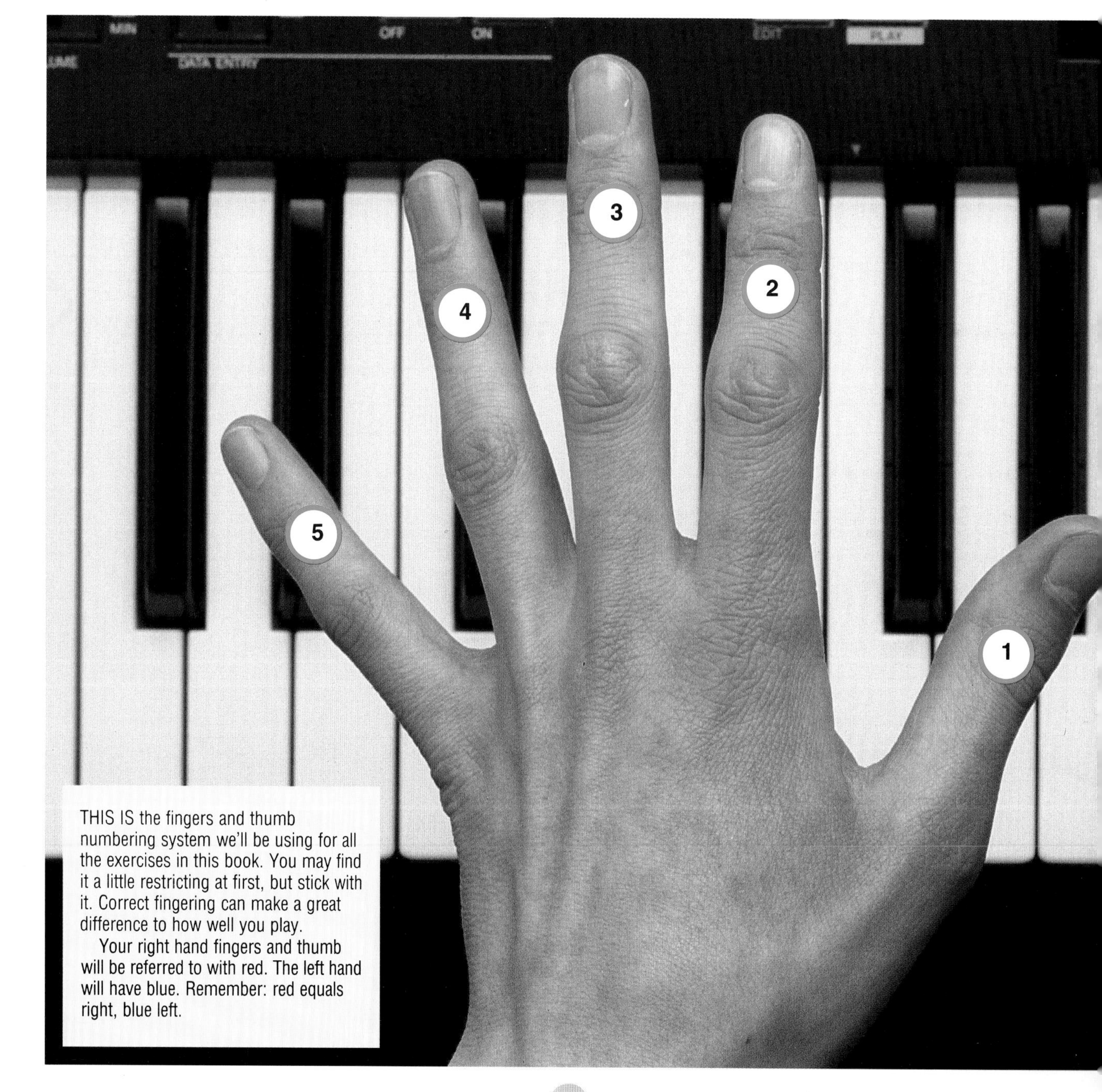

THIS IS the fingers and thumb numbering system we'll be using for all the exercises in this book. You may find it a little restricting at first, but stick with it. Correct fingering can make a great difference to how well you play.

Your right hand fingers and thumb will be referred to with red. The left hand will have blue. Remember: red equals right, blue left.

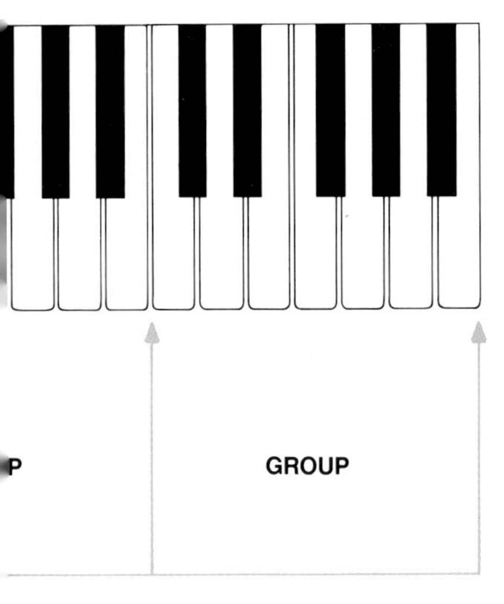

ON THE right we see one group of 12 keys in isolation. The seven white keys play the notes named **A**, **B**, **C**, **D**, **E**, **F** and **G**.

You may be wondering why the group starts with a **C** and not with an **A**.

Well, apart from the fact that the group looks clearer like this, **C** is generally regarded as the most important note on the keyboard—especially the **C** note called Middle **C**.

As far as sound is concerned, Middle **C** is a note like any other. But it has an extra function as a reference point. Middle **C** is the **C** note nearest the centre of your keyboard (probably left rather than right of the centre).

In this book you'll find Middle **C** is always marked with an asterisk (*). Most of the exercises you'll be doing are based around this note.

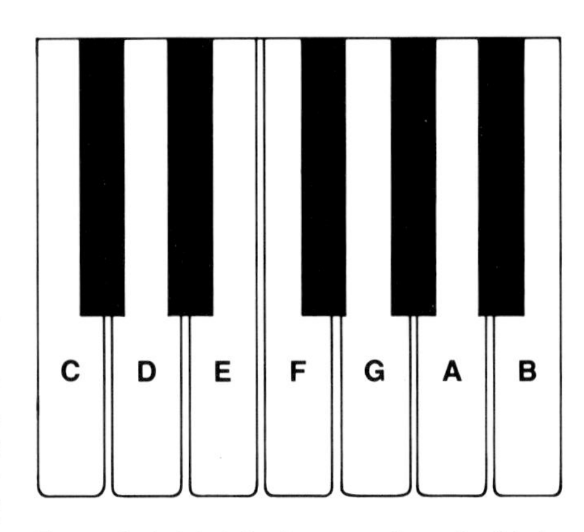

The musical alphabet only goes as far as G – this is how the letters appear on the white keys of a keyboard. The seven white keys (C, D, E, F, G, A, B) and five black keys play the 12 different musical notes. More on the black keys on the next page.

THE HANDS

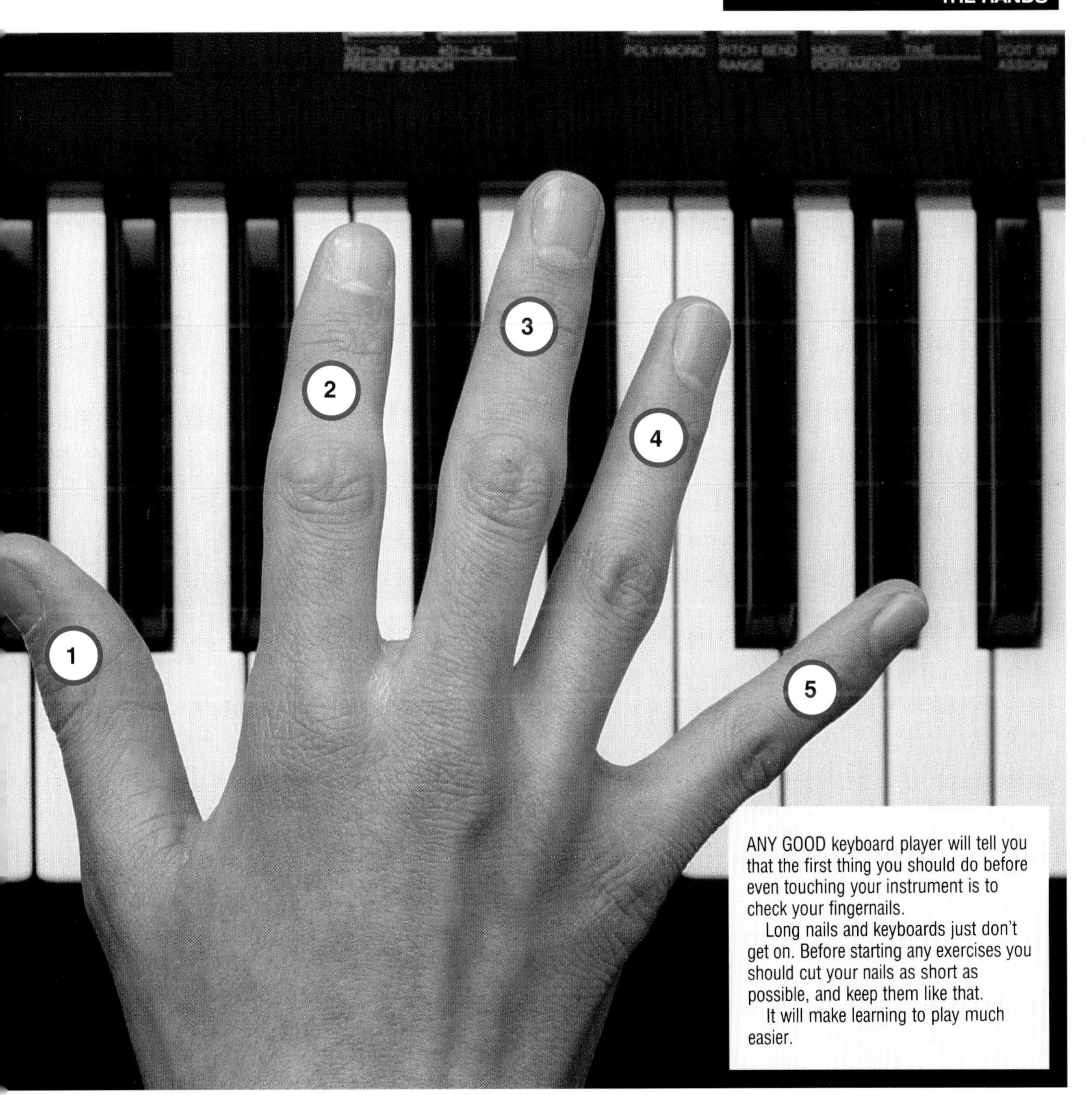

ANY GOOD keyboard player will tell you that the first thing you should do before even touching your instrument is to check your fingernails.

Long nails and keyboards just don't get on. Before starting any exercises you should cut your nails as short as possible, and keep them like that.

It will make learning to play much easier.

OCTAVES

IN LOCATING Middle **C** on your keyboard, it may help to know that the note is in the middle not only in position but also in sound: not too high and not too low.

If you're not sure what we mean by high and low notes, try playing two keys at opposite ends of your keyboard. The further to the right, the 'higher' the pitch.

Try playing Middle **C** and then the **C** notes in the groups immediately above and below it (to the right and left respectively). You will hopefully hear that they are the same note, but at different pitches.

The distance between a note in one group, and the same note in the next group, is called an 'octave'. Just as an octopus has eight arms, so an octave has eight notes.

An octave can start on any note. If it starts on a **C**, it will finish on the **C** above.

Between the start and finish notes there are eleven other notes, six of which are part of the octave. Which notes are in the octave depends on what the starting or 'root' note is.

We'll talk about this in more detail as we go along. But for the moment, it's time to try the exercise below which is the first of many 'scales' you'll be learning.

Don't be put off by the word 'scales'. They are essential to both understanding and playing the keyboard.

If the keyboard is a kind of musical map, scales are your means of transport.

A SIMPLE scale is the eight notes of one octave played in succession, starting at the bottom, working your way to the top, and back down once again.

The simplest scale of all is this one, starting on **C**, because there are no black notes in it.

When playing a scale you should start on the lowest note of the octave, work your way up to the top note, and then back down to the bottom note again.

In other words, all the notes are played twice—once going up and once on the way down. Except one. The top note is only played once. When the scale is played as it should be, in one continuous motion, playing the top note twice would give a 'slowing down' effect.

AS YOU play each note, try to release its key at the same moment that you press the next key, so that there are no gaps between notes. Otherwise your scale will sound 'plodding'. Try to play each note for an equal length of time.

C

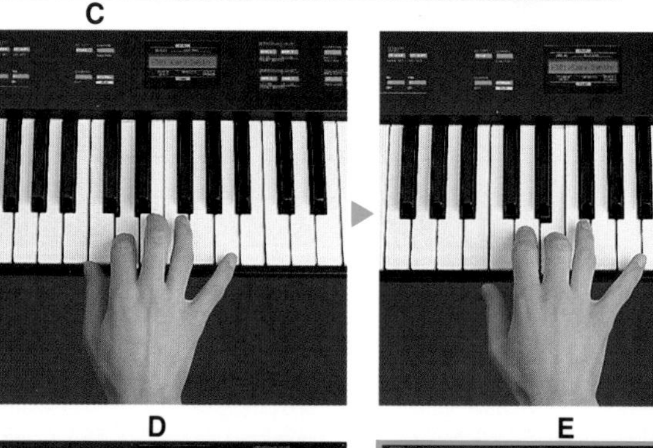

D E

F

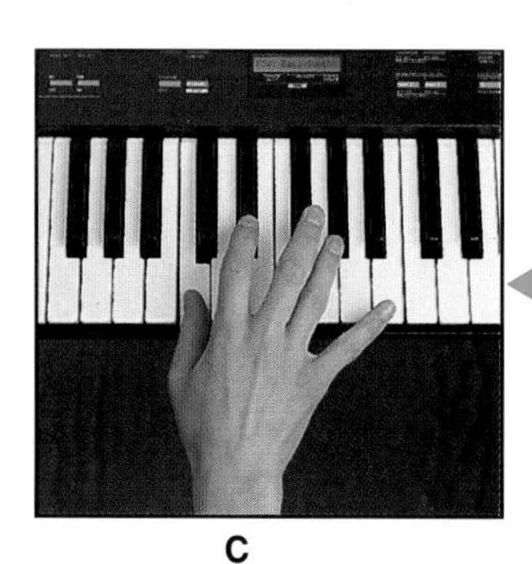

C

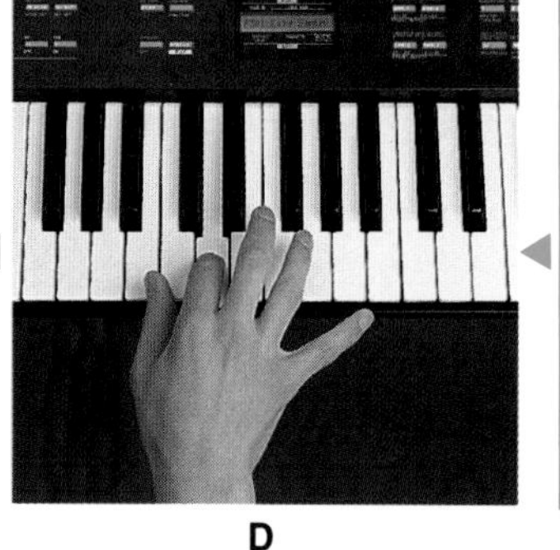

D

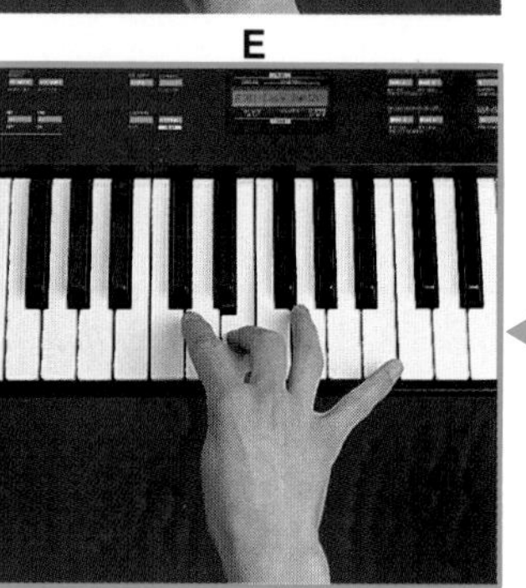

E

F

ʼhen playing a scale, keep the back of your hand nd forearm horizontal. Your fingers should be rched, not angled, with only your fingertips uching the keys. Your thumb, however, should be at, with the side of the thumb as far as the joint esting on the key.

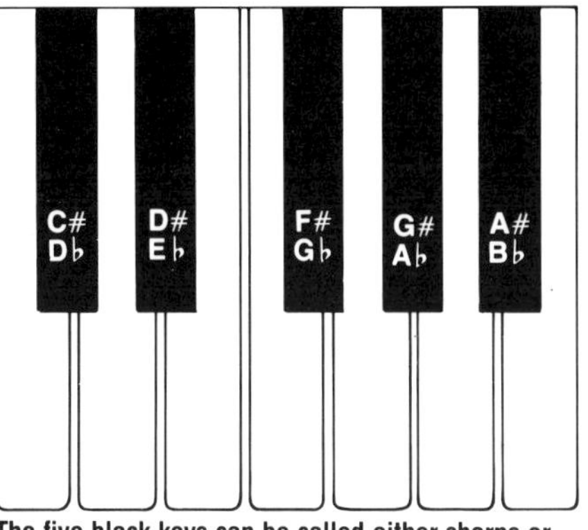

The five black keys can be called either sharps or flats. C# is also known as D♭. D# is also E♭. F# is also G♭. G# is also A♭. And A# is also known as B♭. There is no black note between the white notes B and C, or between E and F. So there is no such thing as B#, C♭, E# or F♭.

SHARPS AND FLATS

BY NOW you should be fairly familiar with the white keys on your keyboard, so let's turn our attention to the black keys and the notes they produce.

As you can see, the black notes also take their names from the first seven letters of the alphabet, but they are known as 'sharp' and 'flat' notes. Hence the symbols # (meaning sharp) and ♭ (meaning flat).

Basically, 'sharp' means *one note above* and 'flat' means *one note below.*

Look at the black key marked **C#/D♭**. Because this black key comes between the white keys **C** and **D**, it can be called either **C** sharp (**C#**) because it's one note above **C**, or **D** flat (**D♭**) because it's one note below **D**.

Whether you call it **C#** or **D♭** depends on what 'key' the piece of music is in – as we'll explain on the next page.

SCALE OF C MAJOR

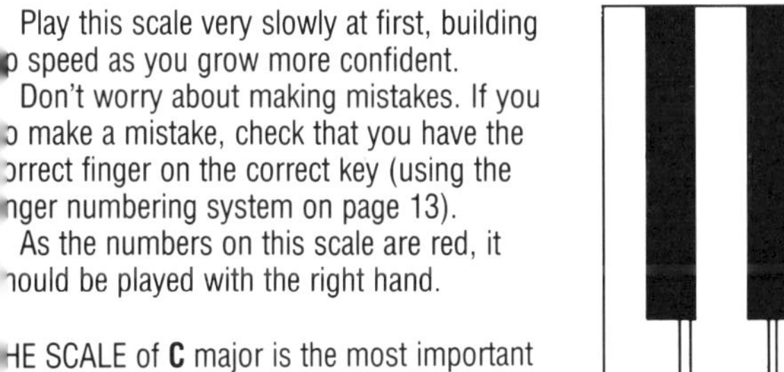

Play this scale very slowly at first, building p speed as you grow more confident.

Don't worry about making mistakes. If you o make a mistake, check that you have the orrect finger on the correct key (using the nger numbering system on page 13).

As the numbers on this scale are red, it hould be played with the right hand.

HE SCALE of **C** major is the most important ou'll ever learn, because it gives you the ap of the white keys. As you play each note, y to memorise its name—**C, D, E, F, G, A, , C, B, A, G, F, E, D, C**.

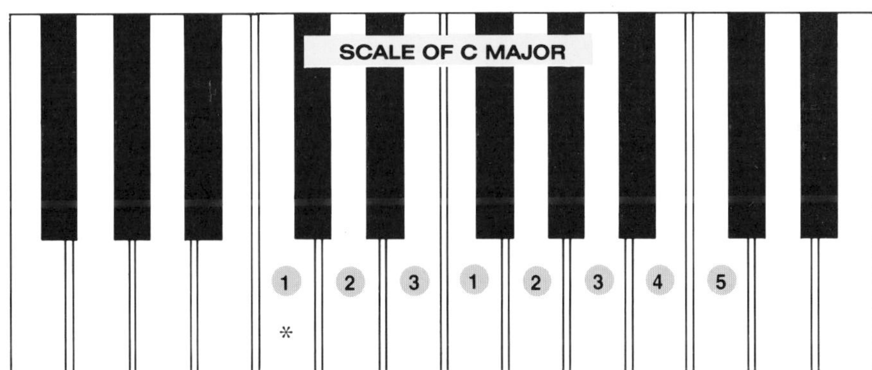

Note how the thumb slides under the middle finger (3) when playing F on the way up the scale. The middle finger (3) crosses over the thumb to play E on the way back down.

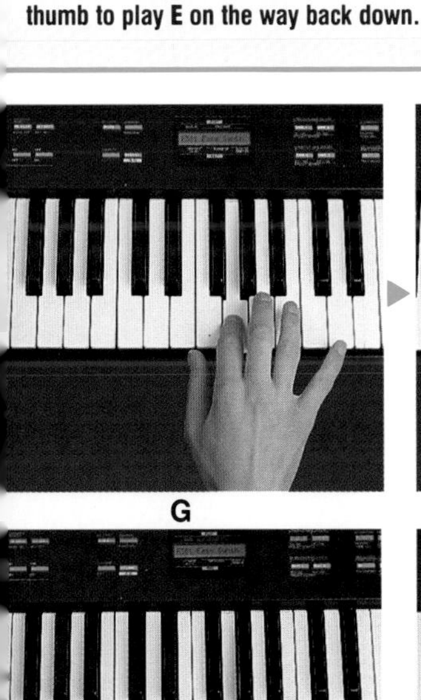

G

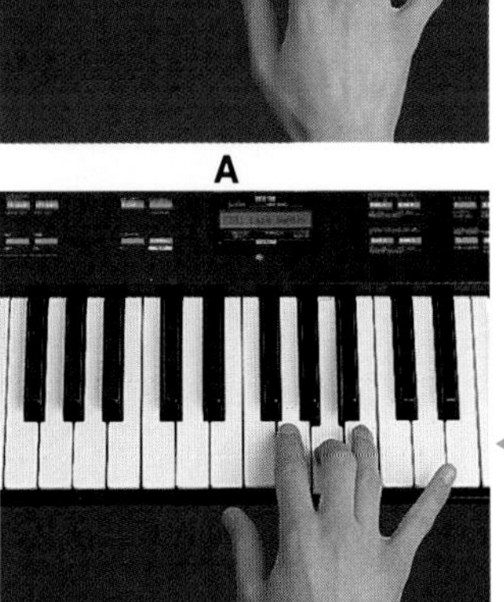

A

B

C

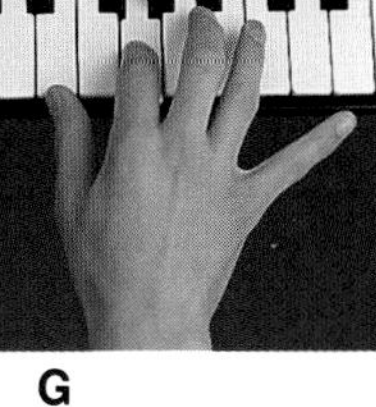

G

A

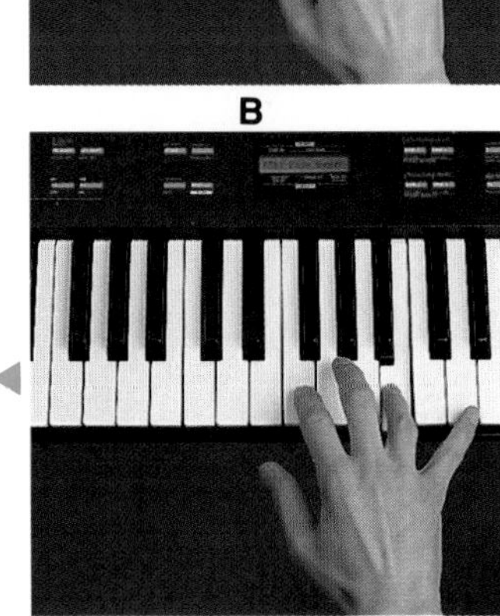

B

KEYS

WHEN A MUSICIAN asks, "What key is this song played in?", he or she is asking what note it is based on. This tells them all the other notes they can play.

If the piece is in the key of **C** major, like the scale on the previous page, you can safely play the root note (**C**) plus the six other notes related to that key—namely **D**, **E**, **F**, **G**, **A** and **B**.

Each of the 12 notes on the keyboard has its own major key, of which it is the root note. Each major key has its own scale, which tells you which seven notes 'work' in that key.

It's possible to add unrelated notes to any key, but this should be done sparingly and certainly not yet.

C MAJOR is the only major key which contains no black notes. As you know, it uses all the white notes: **C**, **D**, **E**, **F**, **G**, **A**, **B**.

One of the simpler black-and-white keys is **G** major. It contains the root note **G**, plus **A**, **B**, **C**, **D**, **E** and one black note, **F#**.

This note is called **F#** and not **G♭** because there is already a **G** white note present—and you can't have two notes with similar names in one key.

NOW LET'S look at the key of **F** major. This scale contains the root note **F** plus **G**, **A**, **B♭**, **C**, **D** and **E**.

In this case, the one black note is called **B♭** and not **A#** because there is already an **A** white note in the key.

So as you can see, we always name the black notes so that they can't be confused with the white notes in the key.

Incidentally, no key contains both sharps *and* flats. It's one or the other, never both.

WHY BOTHER WITH SCALES?

SCALES ARE often associated with tedious classical piano lessons. Here's why you need them too:

Scales improve your playing technique by encouraging you to use all your fingers all the time.

They show in a very practical way—with hands on keyboard—the six notes related to the root note on which the scale starts. As you practise, you'll soon learn this by heart—which will save you the trouble of referring back later.

When you play with other people, you'll need to know what notes are in each 'key'. As you now know, the scale will tell you which notes to use.

Jogging keeps legs fit and helps you run faster. Scales keep hands fit and help you play faster.

G MAJOR AND F MAJOR SCALES

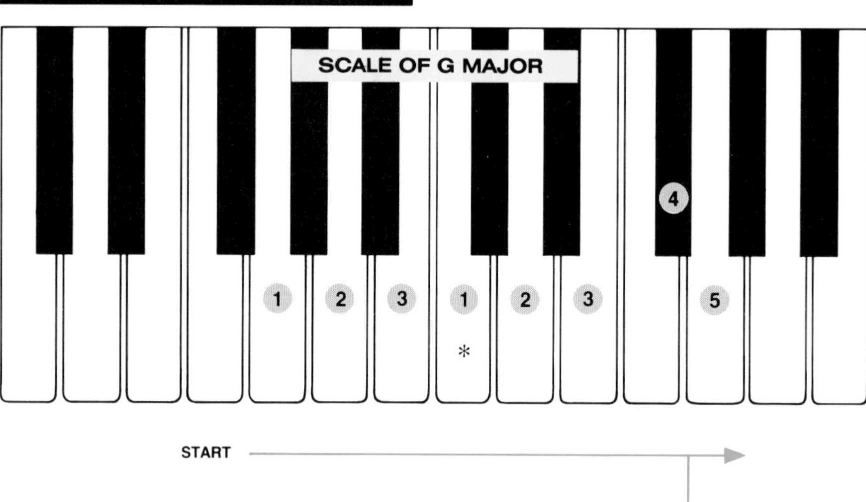

Fourth finger (4) playing F# in the scale of G major.

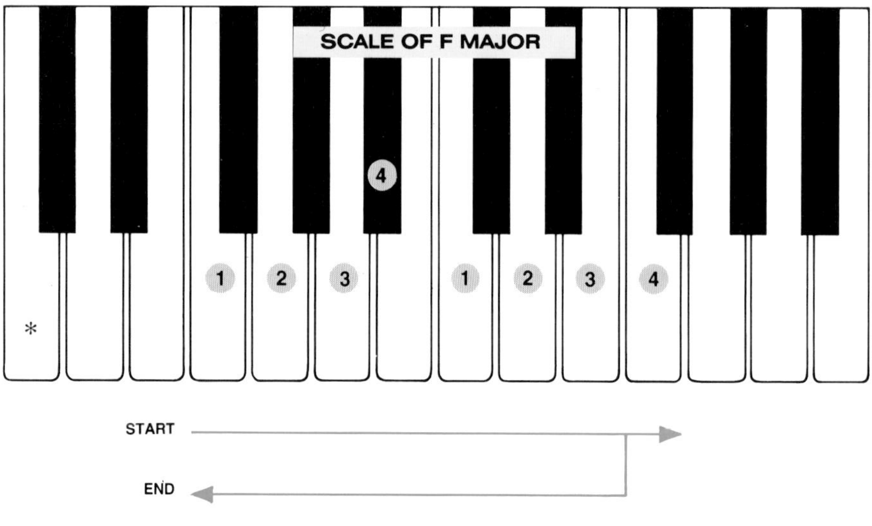

Fourth finger (4) playing B♭ in the scale of F major. Play the black key dead centre or your finger may slip.

Note that the scale of G major has one sharp (F#), whereas the scale of F major has one flat (B♭). Try to incorporate these black notes into your scale as smoothly as if they were white notes.

TONES AND SEMITONES IN THE SCALE OF C MAJOR

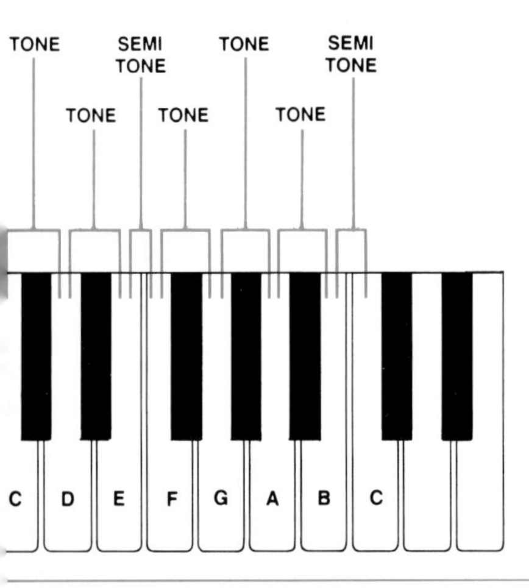

THESE DIAGRAMS show how the notes in a major key relate to one another.

In **C** major we step up two notes from **C** to **D**, then two (**D** to **E**), then one (**F**), two (**G**), two (**A**), two (**B**) and finally one (to **C**).

What we've been calling 'notes' here, we should properly refer to as 'semitones'. In other words, from **C** to **C#** is one semitone.

Two semitones equals one tone. So from **C** to **D** is one tone. So the scale of **C** major moves up the keyboard in jumps of *tone, tone, semitone, tone, tone, tone, semitone.*

Look at the scale of **G** major. That also progresses in jumps of tone (**A**), tone (**B**), semitone (**C**), tone (**D**), tone (**E**), tone (**F#**), semitone (top **G**).

Bearing this in mind, you can work out any major scale for yourself. Start with your root note, and climb in steps of *tone, tone, semitone, tone, tone, tone, semitone.*

TONES AND SEMITONES IN THE SCALE OF G MAJOR

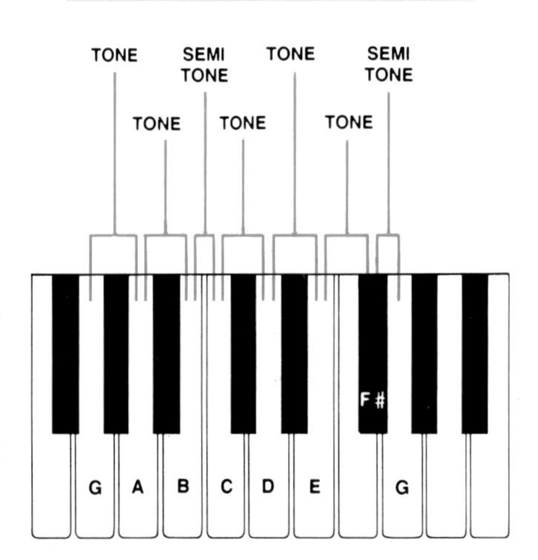

WHO PICKS THE KEY?

A GOOD keyboard player should be able to perform any song in any key. Not so a singer or a guitarist.

In groups it's often the singer who dictates which key a song is played in. If he's forced to sing too high or low, he's in trouble.

Morten Harket of A-Ha has a greater range than most singers. A song like 'Take On Me' seems to take his voice into the stratosphere. But even an accomplished singer like Morten will find that he can sing more easily or more expressively in a certain key. The key may vary from song to song.

So he will have first say as to which key A-Ha songs are played in.

After him it'll be guitarist Pal Waaktaar, because unlike keyboards, the key can make a drastic difference to a guitar part.

The sound of the guitar changes according to where on the neck it's played and whether strings are open or fretted. And a line that's easy to play in one key can be nearly impossible in another.

Keyboards are a much more scientific instrument. Any song can be transposed to another key. The only difference you'll hear is in the pitch.

So when it comes to what key he plays in, A-Ha's Mags Furuholmen probably has to like it or lump it.

MINOR KEYS

IN MUSIC there are two types of key: major and minor. Either type of key can be based on any note.

We've seen how a major scale is constructed, starting with the root note and climbing up the keyboard in steps of *tone, tone, semitone, tone, tone, tone, semitone.*

In a minor key, the third, sixth and seventh notes of the major scale are moved down (flattened) by one semitone. So the minor scale goes up by *tone, semitone, tone, tone, semitone, tone, tone.*

Let's look at one example. The scale of **A** major consists of **A**, **B**, **C#**, **D**, **E**, **F#**, **G#**, **A**. The third, sixth and seventh notes are **C#**, **F#** and **G#**. We flatten them by one semitone, giving **C**, **F** and **G**. So the scale of **A** minor runs **A**, **B**, **C**, **D**, **E**, **F**, **G**, **A**.

We've used **A** minor as our example because it happens to be the only minor scale with no black notes. You will remember that **C** major is the only major scale with no black notes. This is no coincidence.

A minor is known as the 'relative minor' to **C** major. This is because it uses the same notes in its scale, although the scale start on a different root note.

Every major key has a relative minor— minor key that is so closely related, shares the same notes. **A** minor is th relative minor of **C** major.

Going up the scale, **B♭** minor is th relative minor of **D♭** major. **B** minor is th relative minor of **D** major. And so on up th scale.

You will find it very useful to know whic minor keys relate to which major keys— and indeed, it will soon become instinctive

MAJOR AND MINOR SCALES							
C MAJOR	**C**	**D**	**E**	**F**	**G**	**A**	**B**
C MINOR	C	D	E♭	F	G	A♭	B♭
A MAJOR	A	B	C#	D	E	F#	G#
A MINOR	**A**	**B**	**C**	**D**	**E**	**F**	**G**

RELATIVE MINORS												
MAJOR KEY	C	D♭	D	E♭	E	F	F#	G	A♭	A	B♭	B
RELATIVE MINOR KEY	A	B♭	B	C	C#	D	D#	E	F	F#	G	G#

The root note of any minor key is three semitones below the root note of its relative major.

THREE MINOR SCALES

THE THREE major scales you've learnt so far are **C** major, **F** major and **G** major. These are their three relative minor scales: **A** minor, **D** minor and **E** minor.

Like **C** major, **A** minor has no sharps or flats. Like **F** major, **D** minor contains one flat note (**B♭**). Like **G** major, **E** minor has one sharp note (**F#**).

Don't forget to give each note equal weight, so that your scale becomes one smooth, flowing motion.

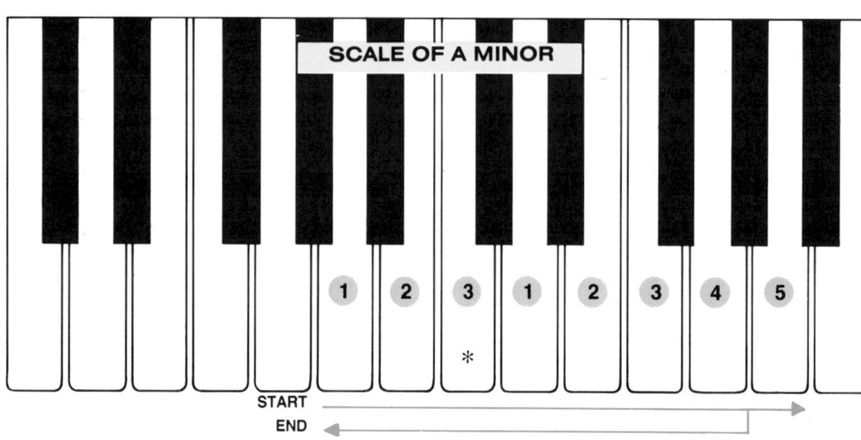

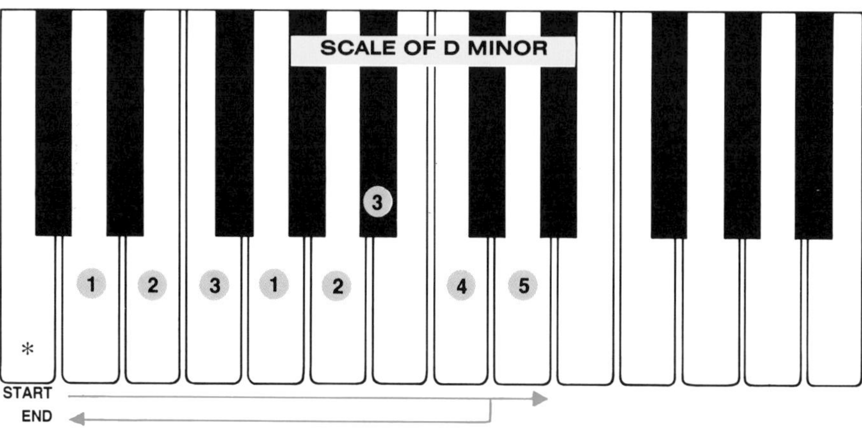

Thumb sliding under third finger (3) to play G going up the scale of D minor.

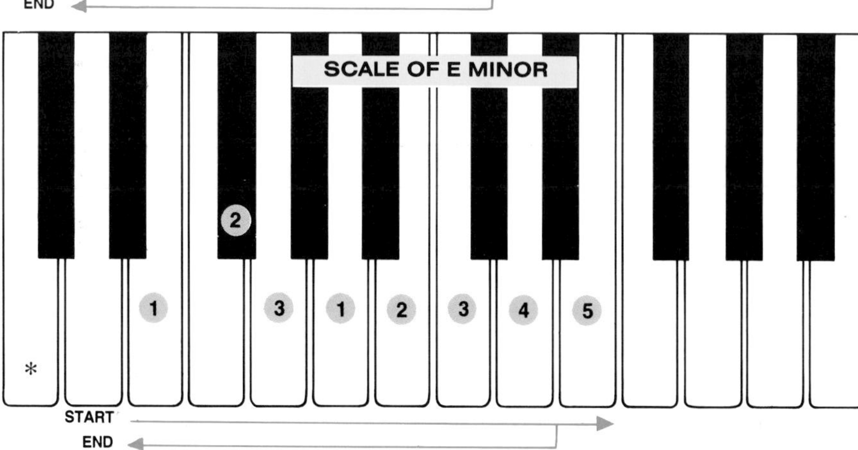

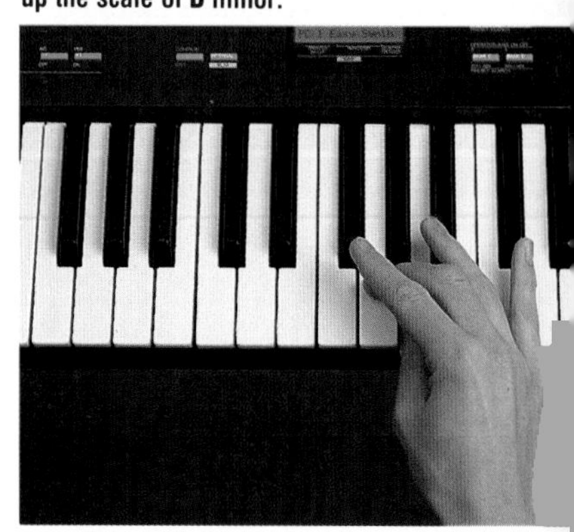

Third finger (3) crossing over thumb to play G, going down the scale of E minor

T'S HARD to explain why major and minor :eys sound different, but they do.

Music in a major key tends to sound appy and positive, whereas minor key nusic often sounds sad, serious or drama-ic. Nobody knows why this should be—it's ıst the way human beings respond.

Hopefully you can hear the difference as you play the minor scales below. Certainly you'll hear it when we get on to learning some chords.

There are, of course, plenty of exceptions to this major-minor rule. On the next page you'll get a chance to play the theme from *Beverly Hills Cop*—a minor key tune which on the face of it could hardly be happier.

If you've seen the film you'll know it makes you feel good—with a little help from Eddie Murphy of course.

On the other hand, a mournful lament like Sting's 'Russians' could never have been written in a major key. His stern thoughts on how anxieties are shared by people on both sides of the world's nuclear divide are reinforced by the sad sound of a minor key.

The part of 'Russians' which best demonstrates the doomy sound of a minor key wasn't actually written by Sting himself—he borrowed it from the Russian classical composer Prokofiev. It's a morbid little keyboard refrain which you might like to try for yourself.

bove: Sting's video for 'Russians'—a major xample of a minor key mood. The video was shot n black and white to heighten the bleakness.

MINOR KEY MOOD

HINK OF this excerpt from 'Russians' as a :ind of scale. We've transposed the tune into **A** ninor so there are no black notes (Sting's :eyboard player Kenny Kirkland actually plays it n **C** minor).

Start on the **A** below middle **C**, and work 'our way up and down the keyboard playing the otes shown. Make sure you use the right-hand ngering marked on the keys.

When you reach the end, simply start at the eginning again. By the time you've played it a ew times, you should be able to hear the wind noaning across those lonesome Siberian teppes . . .

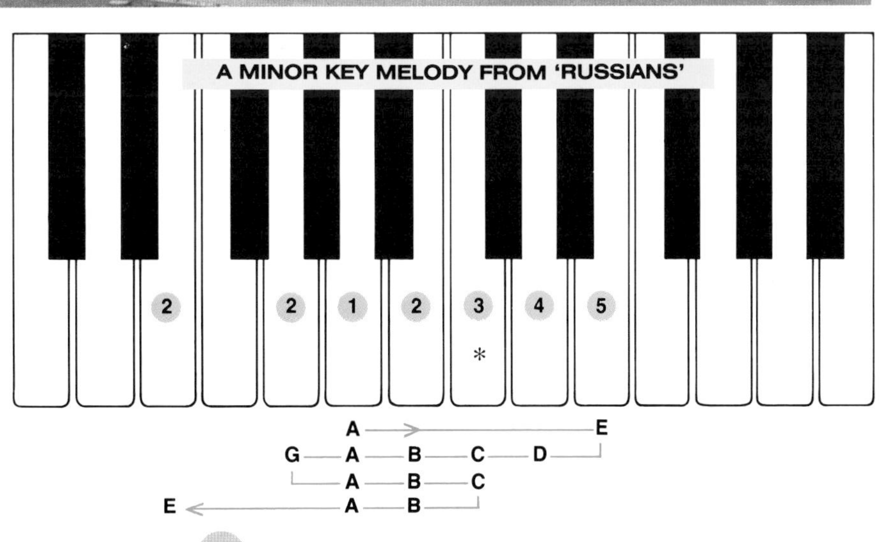

RHYTHM

THIS IS the big moment. We're about to play our first song.

Your work on scales has shown you how to play notes in a set order, and should help you sort out the tune we've chosen.

But there's more to a tune than knowing the notes. You also need to know when to play each note, how long for, and when to stay silent.

That, in a nutshell, is rhythm.

ALL MUSIC is divided up rhythmically into 'bars'. Each bar consists of a set number of beats, as in the beat of a drum.

The number of beats in a bar varies from song to song, and even from style to style.

Songs with two beats to the bar often have a marching rhythm (left-right, left-right, 1-2, 1-2 . . .). Songs with three beats to the bar are often said to be in waltz time (oom-pah-pah, oom-pah-pah, oom-pah-pah, 1-2-3, 1-2-3, 1-2-3 . . .).

Jazz musicians and pomp rockers sometimes use an odd number like seven beats to the bar, resulting in a complex rhythm for their sometimes complex tunes.

Most rock songs use four beats to the bar. With a drummer or drum machine counting out the main beats, this sets a solid groove for dancing, headbanging, swinging or swaying. It's the language of pop.

ONE OF the hardest things about playing and learning on your own is keeping time.

One simple way is with a metronome—a device which gives out constant and regular clicks or bleeps, not unlike the tick-tock of a clock. These clicks can be speeded up or slowed down to suit your requirements.

If you can afford it, a drum machine will serve the same purpose and a lot else besides. For learning purposes it's probably best to programme in a simple regular hi-hat beat.

If you have a home keyboard, such as a Casio, it will probably have a built-in drum machine with a number of rhythm patterns. Set it to the simplest 'rock' beat.

When learning a new song, you should set the metronome or drum machine to a very slow rhythm at first, taking one click as one quarter of a beat. If you don't own either, try to count out regular beats with your foot.

When you feel you can play a piece confidently like this, you can then take one click (or one tap of the foot) to be one beat rather than one quarter-beat—which should bring the song up to its correct speed ('tempo').

THE FIRST SONG

RATHER THAN trying to teach you how to read music, we've devised a system which—for our purposes at least—does the job just as well, but should be easier to understand.

If you already read music, you'll see that we've reproduced the music to this song at the bottom of the page—as we will do throughout the book.

If you want to learn to read music, there's a section that will help you do just that starting on page 68.

The song below is a nursery rhyme chant called 'Off We Go'. As you can probably guess when you play it, the words go: *"Off we go/ Off we go/ Off we go together . . ."* So off we go . . .

HOW TO READ THE GRID

Each row represents one bar of music. Each bar is divided into beats—in this case four to the bar. The beats are numbered 1–4.

Each beat is divided into quarters. In other words, each panel on the grid equals a quarter of a beat. This may sound a little tricky, but if you work it out slowly at first you'll soon get the hang of it.

Notes are represented by their letter names, with numbers to indicate fingering. So the first note is **C**, played by the thumb (1) of your right hand, because it's in red.

Blank panels represent quarter-beats where you don't play. So your first two beats go **C**-click-**D**-click-**E**-click-click-click, **C**-click-**D**-click-**E**-click-click-click.

The arrows tell you whether to go up the keyboard (to the right) or down (left) to play the note in that panel.

TITLE	KEY	TEMPO	STARTING NOTE
'OFF WE GO'	C MAJOR	MODERATE	MIDDLE C (*)

1				2				3				4			
C 1		↑ D 2		↑ E 3				C 1 ↓		↑ D 2		↑ E 3			
C 1 ↓		↑ D 2		↑ E 3		↑ F 4		E 3 ↓				D 2 ↓			
D 2		↑ E 3		↑ F 4				D 2 ↓		↑ E 3		↑ F 4			
↑ G 5		F 4 ↓		E 3 ↓		D 2 ↓		C 1 ↓				C 1			

MUSICAL NOTATION FOR 'OFF WE GO'

SYNTH HITS

THE TOP FIVE SYNTHESISER INSTRUMENTALS OF ALL TIME

1. CHARIOTS OF FIRE Vangelis (1982)
2. MIAMI VICE THEME Jan Hammer (1985)
3. AXEL F Harold Faltermeyer (1985)
4. MAGIC FLY Space (1977)
5. OXYGENE Jean Michel Jarre (1977)

AS YOU can see from our chart, Harold Faltermeyer's theme from the *Beverly Hills Cop* movie is one of the best-selling synth instrumentals of all time. But prize for the world's No.1 synth hit goes to Vangelis with the *Chariots Of Fire* movie theme.

GOT THE hang of 'Off We Go'? OK, now let's get onto something a bit more interesting . . . and, it has to be said, rather more difficult. Because you are about to learn to play one of the best selling keyboard instrumentals ever: the *Beverly Hills Cop* theme 'Axel F'.

Just apply the same methods you learned on 'Off We Go', and it should come right. Take it slowly at first, picking it out note by note.

If you have trouble with the rhythm, try to catch a listen to the record. If you're still not getting it, don't worry—the important thing is to get the notes right. Go on to the next page, and come back to 'Axel F' later.

Sound advice: If you're playing this on a synthesiser or home keyboard, try using a sharp brass sound.

Eddie Murphy—Axel F in the *Beverly Hills Cop* movie—a man with no hang-ups

TITLE	KEY	TEMPO	STARTING NOTE
'AXEL F' (MAIN THEME)	A MINOR	QUITE FAST	A ABOVE *

1				2				3				4			
A 1				C 3			A 1		A 1	D 4		A 1		G 2	

1				2				3				4			
A 1				E 4			A 1		A 1	F 5		E 4		C 3	

1				2				3				4			
A 1		E 3		A 5		A 1	G 3		G 3	E 1		B 2		A 1	

MUSICAL NOTATION FOR 'AXEL F'

NUMBERING THE NOTES

IT'S COMMON practice to refer to the notes in a scale numerically.

For instance in the key of **C** major, **D** is the second note in the scale, **E** is the third, **F** the fourth and so on.

The only note in a scale which isn't referred to by a number is the root note, **C** in the case of **C** major. It's always called the root note.

Perhaps we seem to be stating the obvious, but it's a system you should learn to use. When you play with other musicians you'll find that many refer to notes by number rather than name.

When playing scales, try to think of each note by number as well as name as you play it. And watch the notes in the chords you play.

NUMBERS OF THE NOTES IN THE SCALE OF D MAJOR

D	E	F#	G	A	B	C#	D
Root	2	3	4	5	6	7	Root

NUMBERS OF THE NOTES IN THE SCALE OF B MINOR

B	C#	D	E	F#	G	A	B
Root	2	3	4	5	6	7	Root

WITH THE addition of **B** minor, you nov know the scales for four minor keys: **Am Em, Dm** and **Bm**. However, they aren't the only scales that can be applied to those keys. There are in fact other types of mino scale.

The minor scale we've shown so far - which uses all the same notes as its relative major scale – is called the pure mino scale. Because it is so closely related to it major key, we believe it's by far the mos useful minor scale for rock players.

However, there are a couple of alterna tive minor scales which you may want to tr out: the melodic minor scale and the har monic minor scale.

The diagrams on the right show you hov to play them in the key of **A** minor. You'l notice that they both introduce notes which are not related to the key.

SCALES OF D AND Bm

UP TO NOW the six scales you've learnt have been comparatively easy—two with no flat or sharp notes (**C** major and **A** minor), and four with one sharp or flat each (**G** major along with its relative minor **E** minor, and **F** major along with its relative minor **D** minor).

So now it's time to move on to something a little more complicated: scales with two sharps, in the form of **D** major and its relative minor **B** minor.

In these scales there are two sharp notes, **F#** and **C#**.

You'll notice that your second (2), third (3), and fourth (4) fingers are all required to play black notes in the course of these two scales. This will be good practice in coordination.

Thumb sliding under the third finger (3) to play G on the way up the scale of D major.

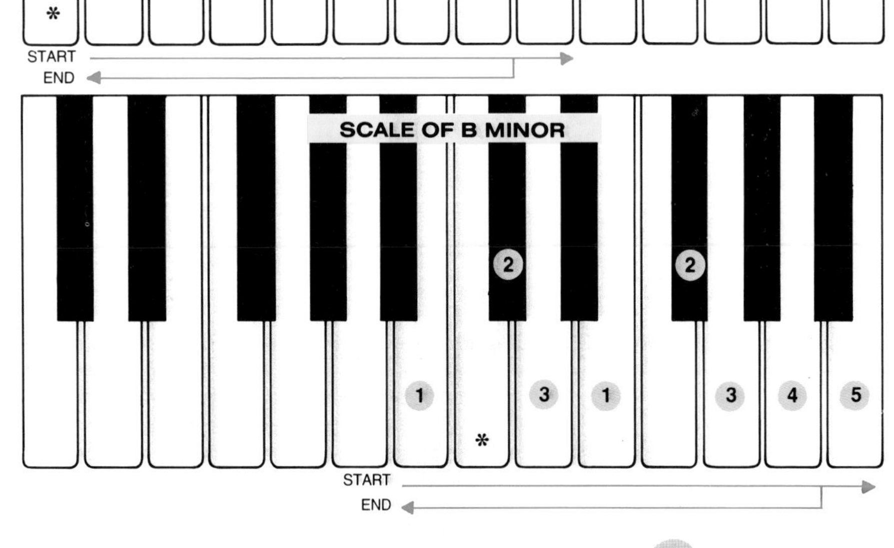

ON THE right is another tune to try—the introduction bassline to The Human League's famous 1981/2 hit 'Don't You Want Me'.

Although basslines are usually played with the left hand—and indeed you'll be playing this with your left hand later—you'll find it excellen practice for your right hand too.

This tune is played in a different part of the keyboard to 'Axel F', almost an octave lower to give it a 'bassier' sound. The key we've chosen is **B** minor—a little trickier than **A** minor, as there are two sharps in the key, **F#** and **C#**, and both are used here. Just take care that you have the correct finger on the correct key.

The rhythm is fairly straightforward. Like 'Axel F', there are four beats to each bar. Take i slowly at first, building up speed as you grow more familiar with it.

Note that, unlike 'Axel F', you don't just play the bars one after the other. There is a running order, with certain bars repeated. When you ge to the end of the running order, either stop or go back to the beginning again.

HOW TO READ THE GRID

YOU'LL NOTICE that the music grid differs slightly in appearance from 'Axel F'. This is because we've added more of the rhythm element to it.

A dark red square indicates, as before, where a note should be played.

A pale red square indicates that you should hold or 'sustain' the note played on the previous dark square. In other words, keep your finger on the key after it is pressed.

Each square is a quarter beat, so if a dark rec square is followed by 15 pale squares, the note is held for a total of 16 quarter beats—or four beats.

A blank square indicates a silence or 'rest', where you don't play anything.

The music for each bar is on the right.

KEY TO COLOURS
- **A NOTE PLAYED**
- **A NOTE HELD**
- **A REST (SILENCE)**

TWO ALTERNATIVE MINOR SCALES

The harmonic minor scale is almost the ame as the pure minor scale, except that ne seventh note is sharpened by one emitone. So in the key of **A** minor, **G** is eplaced by **G#**.

The melodic minor scale is also similar to ne pure minor scale, except that the sixth nd seventh notes are sharpened *on the vay up the scale only*. You come back lown the scale as if it was a pure minor cale. So in the key of **A** minor, **F** and **G** are eplaced by **F#** and **G#** on the way up, but 'ou play **F** and **G** on the way down.

It's quite possible that you will never ieed either of these scales. But they are vorth bearing in mind, especially when olaying lead solos (which we'll come to ater), because they give you extra notes nd different sequences of notes to use.

The harmonic minor and melodic minor scales are also good for practising. If you want to use them, go ahead – now that we've shown them in **A** minor, you can apply them to any other key by taking the pure minor scale and sharpening the sixth/seventh notes. But for the rest of the book we'll be sticking with pure minor scales – and as long as you know them, you should be OK.

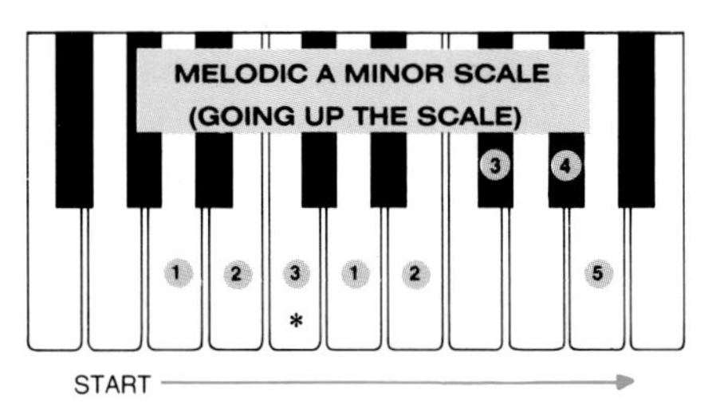

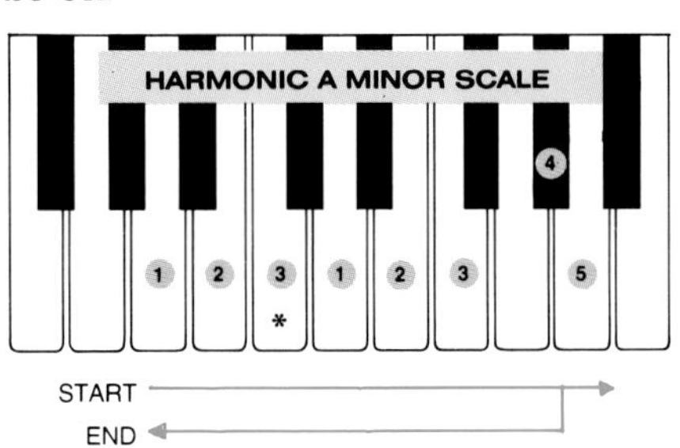

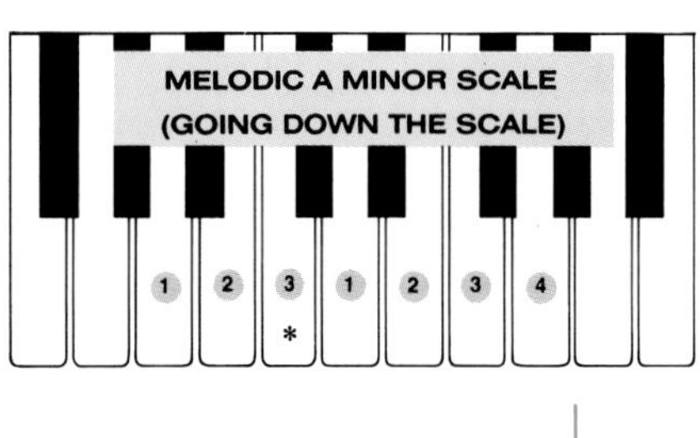

'DON'T YOU WANT ME'

TITLE	KEY	TEMPO	STARTING POINT
'DON'T YOU WANT ME' (INTRO BASSLINE)	B MINOR	QUITE FAST	B BELOW *

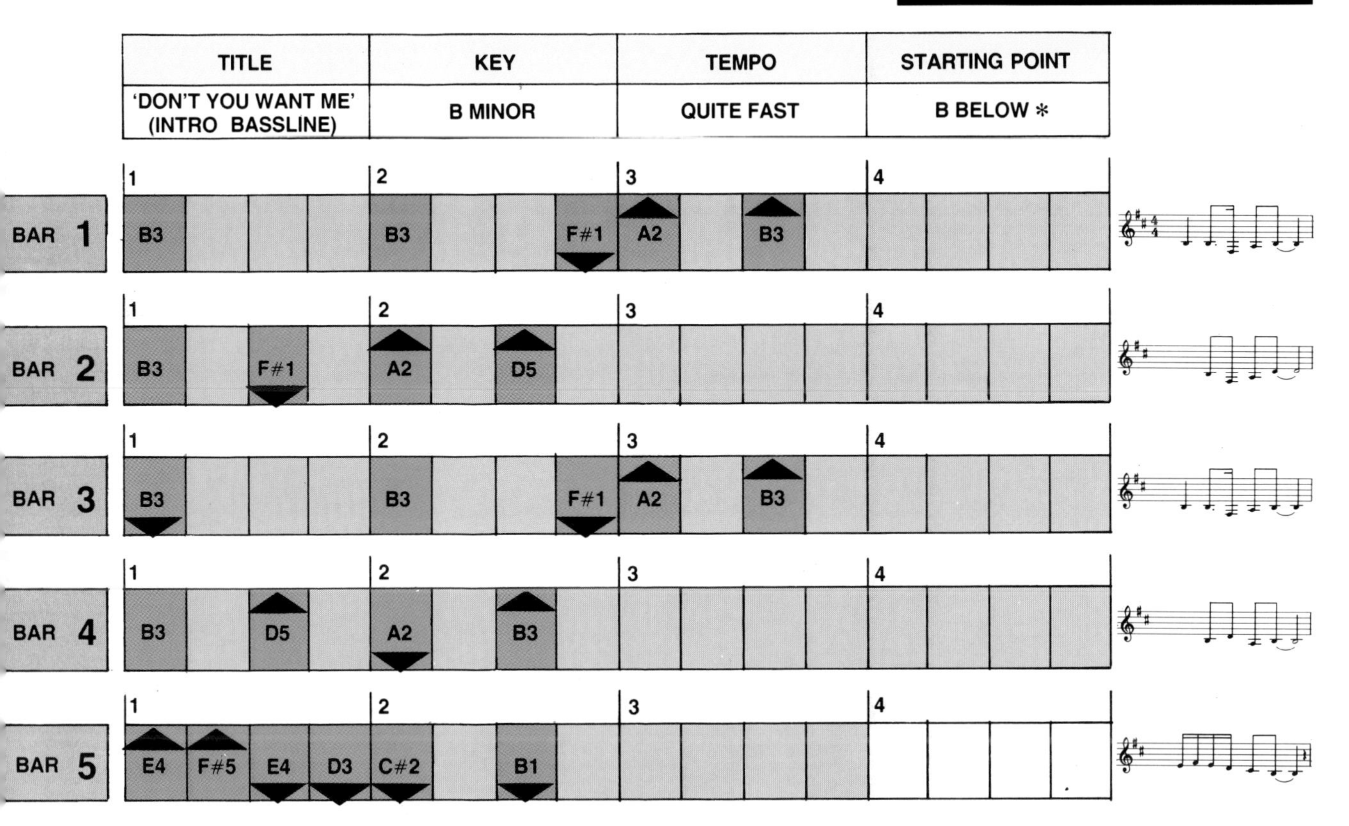

RUNNING ORDER

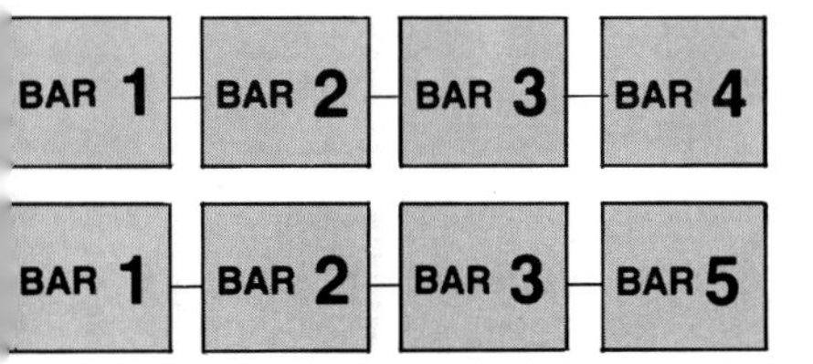

The Human League at the time of 'Don't You Want Me', from left: Phil Oakey, Susanne Sulley, Adrian Wright, Jo Callis, Ian Burden, Joanne Catherall.

SOUND ADVICE

If you're playing this on a synthesiser, try using a 'fat' bass sound. A home keyboard should have a 'brass' sound that fits the bill.

PRIMARY CHORDS

WE HAVE now looked at two of the three main elements of music: melody (single notes) and rhythm. The third element is harmony.

Whenever you have more than one note played or sung together, that's harmony.

We tend to think of harmony as a vocal skill, whether it's The Jacksons singing together or Todd Rundgren multi-tracking himself. But nearly all music involves instrumental harmony.

That can mean two or more instruments playing together. Or just one instrument playing several notes at once . . . a chord.

A CHORD is a number of notes which sound good (harmonious) when played together. They are used to fill out the sound of a song, and to provide the support or launch-pad for a melody line.

A chord always contains at least two notes. In theory it's possible to add an infinite number of notes, as long as they harmonise.

In practice you're limited by your instrument and your own physical capabilities. So a guitar chord, for instance, usually has six notes (one on each of the six strings).

Keyboard chords rarely have more than five notes, played by the four fingers and thumb of one hand.

The vast majority contain three or four notes, and it's these we'll be looking at in detail.

THE SIMPLEST chord in every key is called the **primary triad**. As the name suggests, this chord is made up of three basic notes.

These are the root note of the key, plus the third and fifth notes in the scale of that particular key.

So the primary triad in **C** major will contain the root note **C**, the third note **E** and the fifth note **G**.

Similarly the primary triad in **C** minor will contain the root note **C**, the third note **E♭**, and the fifth note **G**.

The table opposite gives you the basic information and a few examples. You can work other primary triads out for yourself.

IF YOU want to know other primary triad chords—or check whether you've worked them out properly yourself—turn to the Chord Directory, pages 71–84. The primary triad for each chord is the one marked 'BASIC'.

The three notes to use are marked with a solid red circle. Ignore the rest for now!

THE FIRST TWO CHORDS

HOW TO PLAY CHORDS

1 Try to play all the notes in the chord at exactly the same time. If one note is slightly earlier or later than the others, it will sound messy. Obviously this may take a little practise, so don't worry if you don't get it right first time.

2 Keep the back of your hand and forearm almost horizontal.

The fingers you use to play the chord should be arched—not straight or angled. Only your fingertips should touch the keys.

The thumb should be straight, with its left side as far as the knuckle joint resting on the key.

The fingers you are not using should be kept fairly straight, and lifted clear of the keyboard.

3 Watch the finger numbers! Make sure you have the correct finger on the correct key.

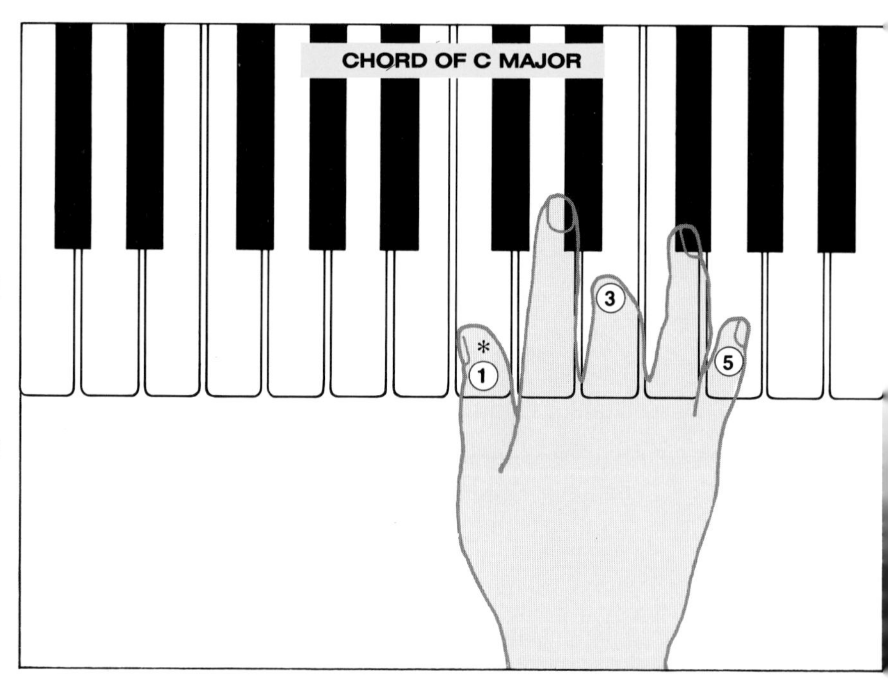

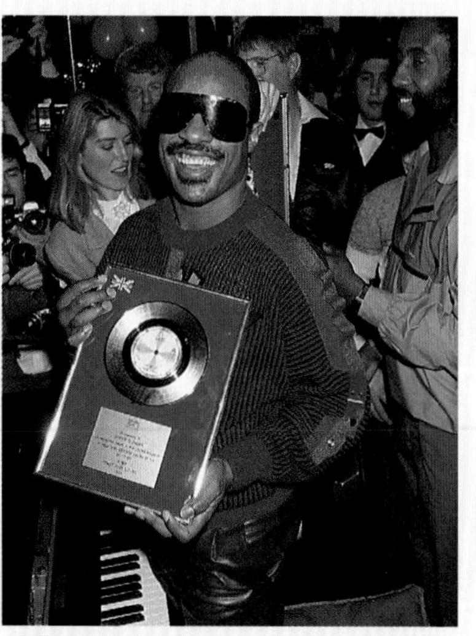
This one obviously struck a chord: full time superstar Stevie Wonder with his silver disc for 'Part Time Lover'.

Make sure your fingers are in the middle of each key.

THE THREE NOTES IN A PRIMARY TRIAD CHORD			
ALL KEYS	FIRST NOTE IN SCALE (Root)	THIRD NOTE IN SCALE (3rd)	FIFTH NOTE IN SCALE (5th)
MAJOR CHORD	Root note	Two tones up from root note	Three semitones up from 3rd
MINOR CHORD	Root note	Three semitones up from root note	Two tones up from 3rd

Don't forget: a semitone is one note. Two semitones = one tone.

EXAMPLES			
ALL KEYS	ROOT NOTE	3rd	5th
C MAJOR	C	E	G
C MINOR	C	E♭	G
A MAJOR	A	C#	E
A MINOR	A	C	E

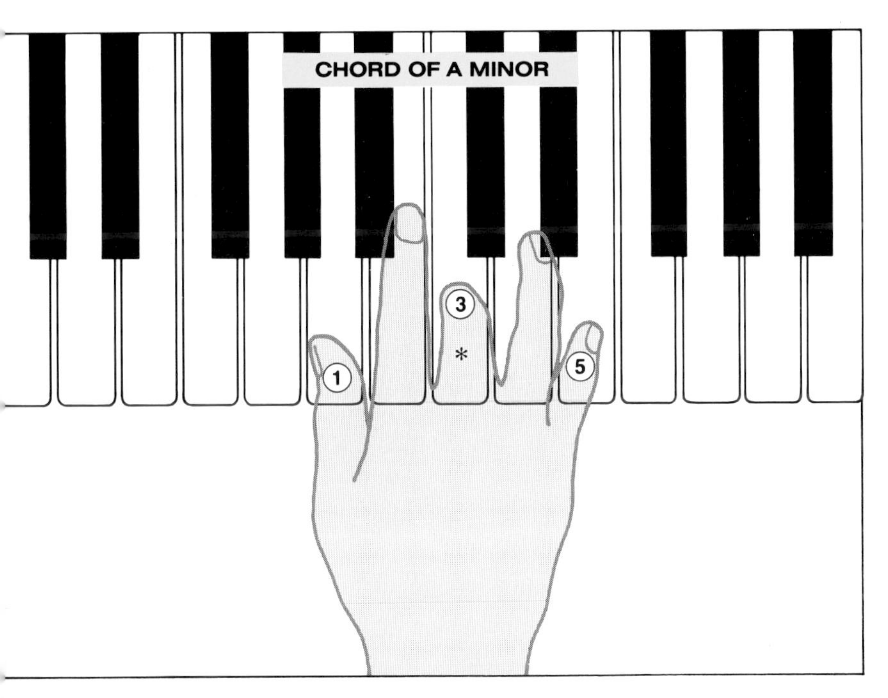

The chords of **C** and **Am** sound great together, especially with an organ-type sound.

BEST SELLING ROCK KEYBOARD INSTRUMENTALS IN AMERICA

1. TELSTAR
   The Tornadoes (1962, organ)
2. OUTTA SPACE
   Billy Preston (1972, organ)
3. GREEN ONIONS
   Booker T & The MGs (1962, organ)
4. SPACE RACE
   Billy Preston (1973, organ)
5. CHARIOTS OF FIRE
   Vangelis (1982, synthesiser)
6. MIAMI VICE THEME
   Jan Hammer (1985, synthesiser)
7. TIME IS TIGHT
   Booker T & The MGs (1969, organ)
8. 2001
   Deodato (1973, electric piano)
9. TUBULAR BELLS
   Mike Oldfield (1974, synthesiser)
10. THEME FROM HILL STREET BLUES
    Mike Post (1981, piano)

Multi-talented Billy Preston was known for guesting with The Beatles and Stones, yet he sang on two US No.1 hits ('Will It Go Round In Circles' and 'Nothing From Nothing')—and made two of the top keyboard instrumentals.

Stax Records band Booker T & The MGs played on many '60s soul classics by singers like Otis Redding, but guitarist Steve Cropper (top left), bassist Duck Dunn (top right), organist Booker T Jones (bottom right) and drummer Al Jackson became legends for instrumental hits such as 'Green Onions'—their first and greatest.

Czech-born Jan Hammer has recorded with Jeff Beck, Mick Jagger, John McLaughlin and many others. He wrote all the music for the glossy *Miami Vice* TV series.

CHORDS TO USE IN C MAJOR

TRY PLAYING the chords of **C** major, **F** major and **G** major in succession. If it sounds familiar, that's because it is sometimes known as the 'three-chord trick'. In any key there are three major chords which 'work', and in the key of **C** they are **C** major, **F** major and **G** major.

The reason is perfectly logical. The chords of **C**, **F** and **G** work in the key of **C** major because the notes in those chords all appear in the scale of **C** major.

The scale of **C** major includes the notes **C**, **D**, **E**, **F**, **G**, **A** and **B**.

The chord of **C** major consists of the notes **C**, **E** and **G**.

The chord of **F** major consists of the notes **F**, **A** and **C**.

The chord of **G** major consists of the notes **G**, **B** and **D**.

There are no other major chords which can conventionally be used in the key of **C** major, because you'd need notes from outside the scale of **C** major.

AS YOU KNOW, the scale of **C** major includes exactly the same notes as its relative minor key, **A** minor (**A**, **B**, **C**, **D**, **E**, **F**, **G**). So chords which work in **C** major also work in the key of **A** minor.

There are in fact six primary triad chords which work in both **C** major and **A** minor:

- **C** major (notes **C**, **E**, **G**),
- **D** minor (notes **D**, **F**, **A**),
- **E** minor (notes **E**, **G**, **B**),
- **F** major (notes **F**, **A**, **C**),
- **G** major (notes **G**, **B**, **D**),
- **A** minor (notes **A**, **C**, **E**).

As you learn these six chords, try them in different orders – before you know it you'll be writing songs!

CHORD SYMBOLS

UP TO now we've called all our major chords by their full name—**C** major, **G** major and so on. In fact, major chords are usually known by their letter alone—**C**, **G**, etc.

So if someone asks you to play an **F** chord, it's safe to assume they mean an **F** major. And similarly, if you're told that a song is in **C**, that means the key of **C** major.

In speech, if people mean minor they always *say* "minor". But on the page the term 'minor' is often abbreviated to just 'm'. So **A** minor becomes **Am**, whereas **A** major becomes plain **A**.

We'll be using these shortened terms frequently from now on.

G MAJOR AND F MAJOR CHORDS

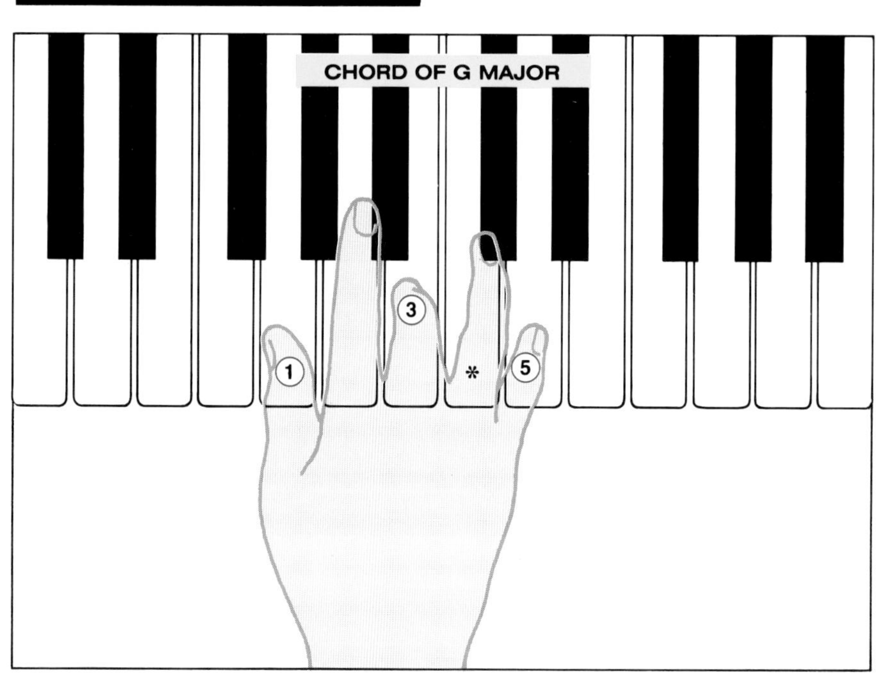

The chord of G major is the second most important chord in the key of C major, after the C major chord itself.

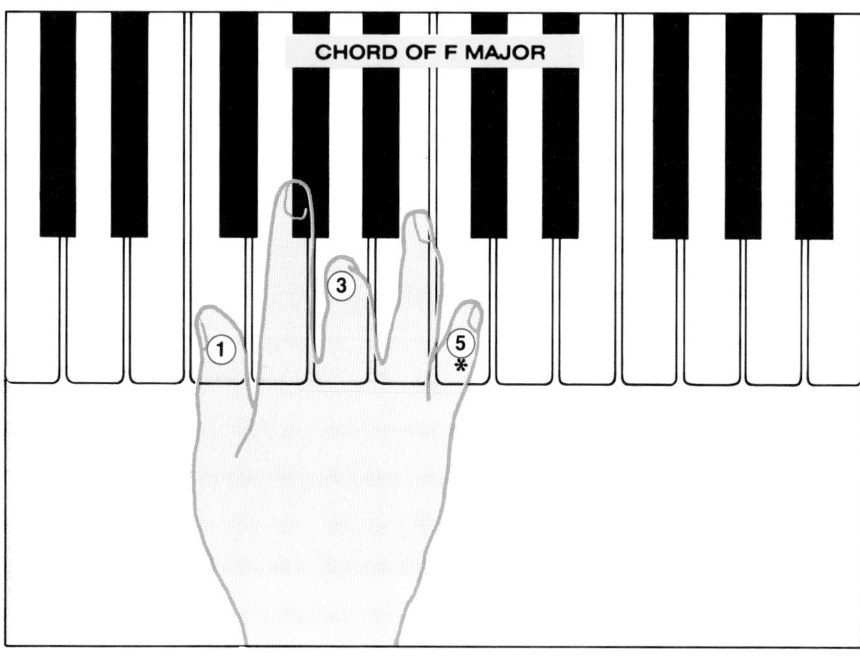

The chord of F major sounds good followed by G major. You can play C, F and G by moving your hand along the keyboard with almost no adjustment.

MONOPHONIC KEYBOARDS

EYBOARDS ARE either monophonic or olyphonic. Monophonic instruments can nly play one note at a time (hence the ame mono-phonic).

This makes it impossible to play chords.

However, it doesn't mean that you can't arry on learning if you've got one. You ave a keyboard in front of you, even if you an't hear what you're playing, and you nay buy a polyphonic keyboard later.

If you're lucky enough to own a good nonophonic synthesiser, don't get rid of it nless you have to. Although few are made nese days, the monophonic still has its ses—as we'll see later.

If you're planning to buy a polyphonic eyboard, check how many notes it plays t once. The ideal is at least eight; some ynthesisers and home keyboards offer less.

Rick Wakeman gets round the Minimoog's one-note limitation by playing two at once.

KEEP YOUR CHORDS CLEAN

YOU WILL notice that most of our chord exercises are based in the middle part of the keyboard. Chords sound best here, with a middle-ish sort of sound.

Chords played in the lower part of the keyboard sound muddy and harsh. Chords played towards the top end can sound thin and grating.

Higher register chords can also clash with a vocal line.

When playing in a group, it's important for the keyboard player to know his or her 'area'—too high can clash with vocals, too low can clash with the bass guitar.

This doesn't mean you should avoid high chords altogether. High sounding chords in particular can work well if played at the right time, especially with a brass sound. Chords like this are sometimes known as 'stabs'.

E MINOR AND D MINOR CHORDS

CHORD OF E MINOR

* 1 3 5

Don't forget that the relative minor key of G major is E minor. So this E minor chord is the relative minor of the G major chord opposite.

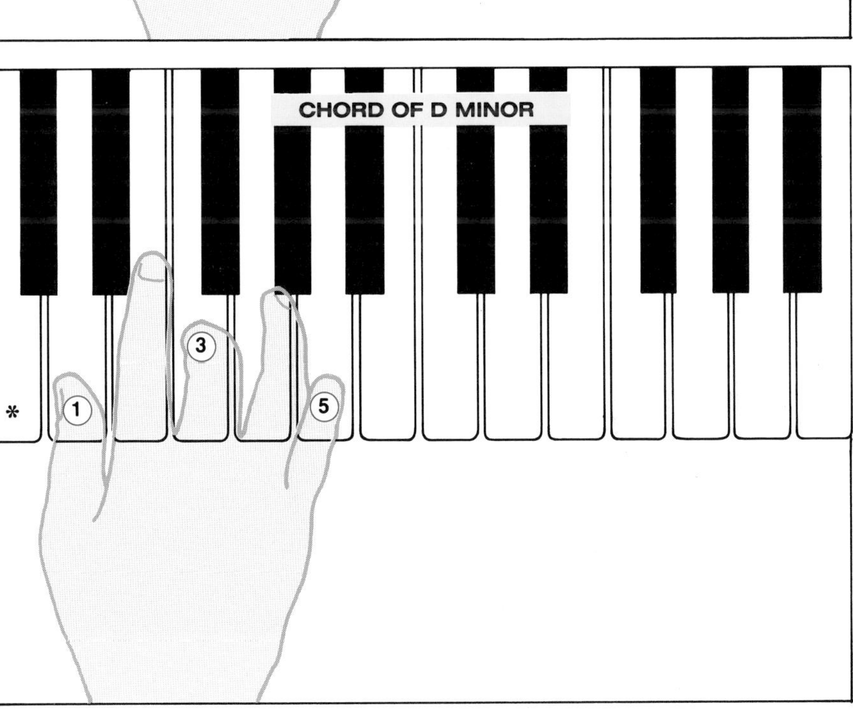

Try this D minor chord in combination with the chords of A minor and E minor. It's a simple movement, because the fingering stays the same.

CHORD PROGRESSIONS

NOW THAT you've learnt six primary chords, what can you do with them? The answer, as many songwriters have proved in the past, is quite a lot.

Indeed, some great songs have been written using as few as two or three chords. 'Mull Of Kintyre', Britain's best selling single before Band Aid, can be played using just **C, F** and **G**. Dozens of early rock hits by the likes of Buddy Holly and Chuck Berry relied on the same three chord trick. So it's obvious that six simple chords that work together can offer you a lot of scope when writing.

Chords arranged in a particular order are known as a progression. Many songs have similar chord progressions – it's the melody and rhythm that makes them sound different.

Here are a few well-known progressions for you to try, using the six chords you've learnt so far.

As with our music grids, the arrows indicate whether you move up or down the keyboard to play that particular chord. Don't worry about rhythm – just listen to the sounds of different progressions. Try playing each one over and over again.

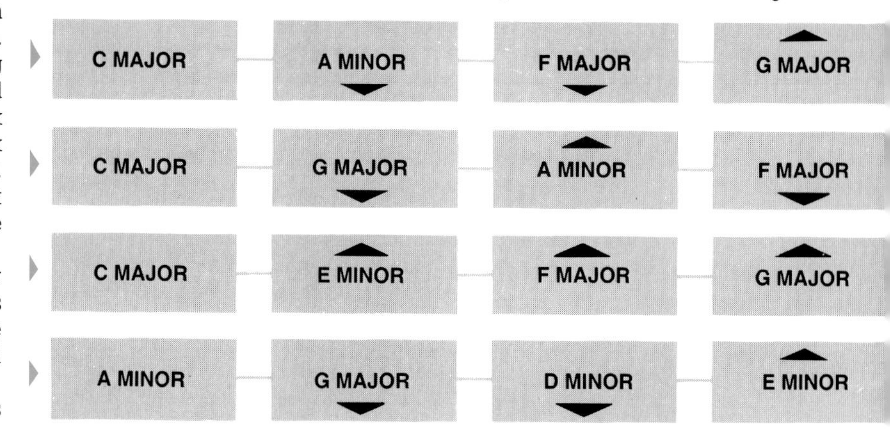

'DON'T YOU WANT ME' (VERSE)

HERE'S A MORE familiar chord progression for you to learn – the verse of The Human League's 'Don't You Want Me', which like the progressions above uses simple primary triads.

The chords used are **C** major, **F** major, **G** major and **A** minor. If you managed to play the rhythm patterns above, you shouldn't find this too difficult.

Note that there are four beats to the bar and that the progression doesn't start until the fourth beat of the first bar.

This is the progression for a single verse. If you want to go round and round continuously, just go directly from the third beat of the last bar into the fourth beat of the first.

To help you pick your way through it, we've printed the lyrics below, along with the vocal melody (above the lyrics) and chords (below the lyrics). The full words of the song are printed opposite, because we'll be returning to 'Don't You Want Me' later in the book.

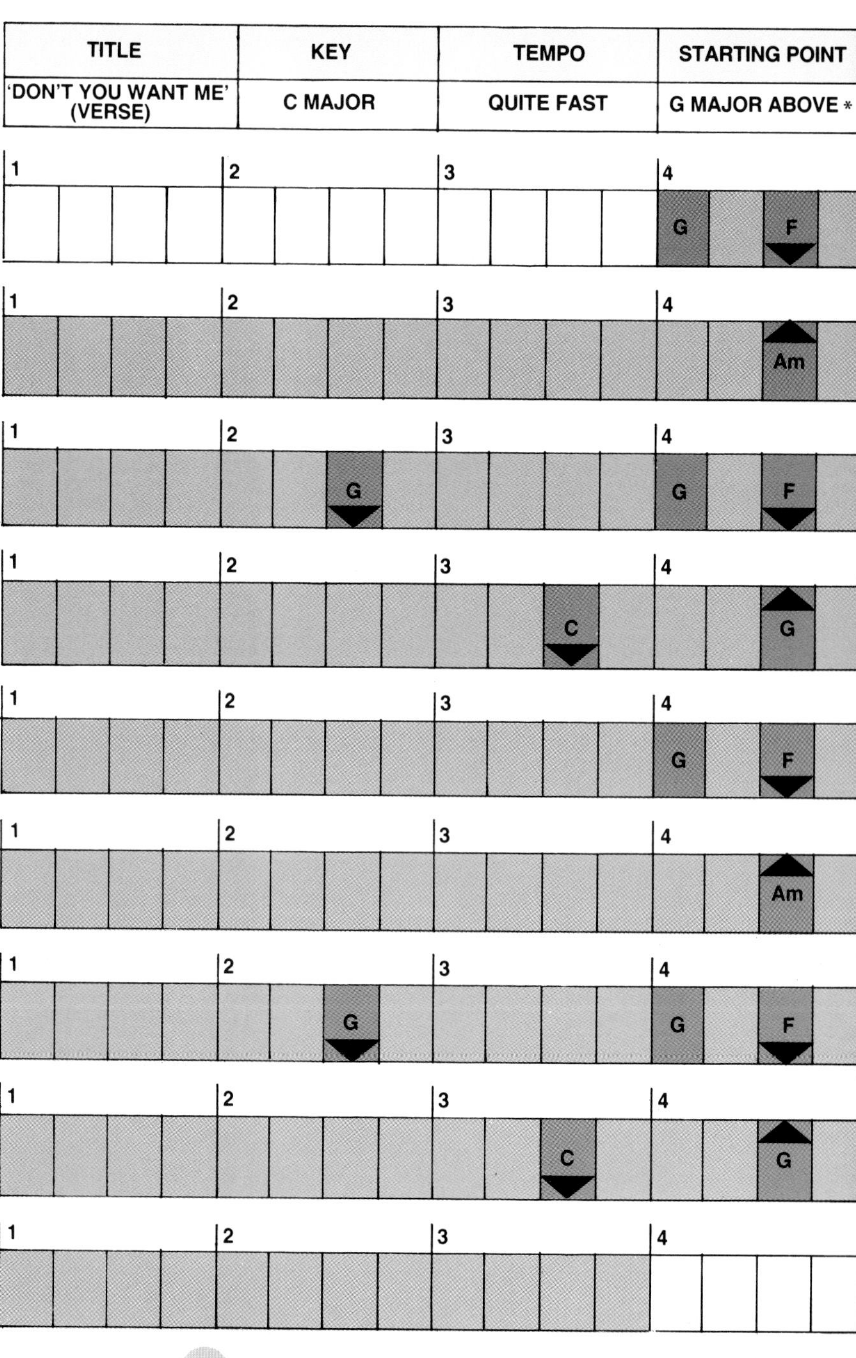

TITLE	KEY	TEMPO	STARTING POINT
'DON'T YOU WANT ME' (VERSE)	C MAJOR	QUITE FAST	G MAJOR ABOVE *

'DON'T YOU WANT ME' MELODY LINE WITH CHORDS

VERSE 1

C A C A C A C A C A
You were / work-ing as a wait-ress in a /
G F / Am/

E F E D E A C A G A
cock-ta-il ba-ar / When I met yo- / -ou.
G G F/ C G /

A C A C A C A C A
I / picked you out, I shook you up and /
G F/

E F E D
turned you a-round, /
Am G

C A C A C A G A
Turned you in-to some-one ne- / -ew.
GF C G /

KEY TO COLOURS
■ A NOTE PLAYED
▩ A NOTE HELD
□ A REST (SILENCE)

NCE YOU'VE decided on a chord prog- ssion that you like, you've then got to ink about how you want to play each iord – that is, what rhythm to use.

Should they be long and sustained or ort and rhythmic? Fast or slow? bviously, it depends on the song, but sing these progressions you can experi- ent with different rhythms for yourself.

Here are some examples of one-bar iythm patterns which can be applied to e chord progressions opposite. Make ach chord last the length of one of these ars.

Try keeping to the same rhythm pattern iroughout at first – then chop and change bit: one chord with one rhythm pattern, nother chord with a different rhythm pat- rn, and so on.

There's far more to playing keyboards than just knowing which notes to play – if you can't keep to a steady or difficult rhythm, knowing the notes will get you nowhere. From now on, as you learn new chords, put them together into progres- sions of your own and then exercise your rhythmic capabilities. And listen to the keyboard rhythms used on records.

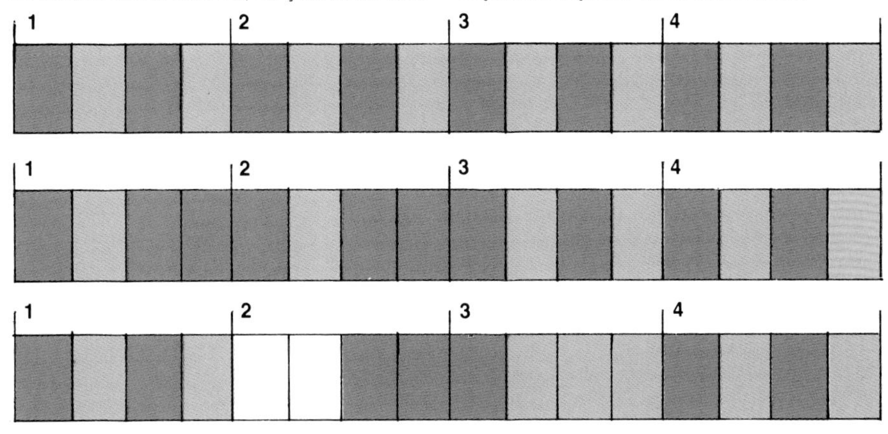

he Human League in action on Britain's top pop TV show *Top Of The Pops* – from left: Phil Oakey, Joanne atherall, Jo Callis, Adrian Wright. Oakey, Wright and Callis composed 'Don't You Want Me', which shot iem to No.1 in Britain over Christmas and New Year 1981/2, and later knocked Paul McCartney and Stevie Vonder's 'Ebony And Ivory' off the top spot in the States. In both cases the timing was symbolic, because ne record seemed to usher in a new era of electronic pop. Produced by Martin Rushent, 'Don't You Want le' had many traditional pop virtues such as an imaginative plot and song structure, memorable melodies nd melodramatic emotions, but it combined them with the synthesiser sound of the '80s.

MUSICAL NOTATION FOR 'DON'T YOU WANT ME' (VERSE)

'DON'T YOU WANT ME' (LYRICS)

RUNNING ORDER AND LYRICS

INTRO
VERSE 1

VERSE 2
Now five years later on you've got the world at your feet:
Success has been so easy for you.
But don't forget it's me who put you where you are now
And I can put you back down too.

BRIDGE 1
Don't, don't you want me?
You know I can't believe it when I hear that you won see me.
Don't, don't you want me?
You know I don't believe you when you say that you don't need me. It's

BRIDGE 2
Much too late to find when you think you've changed your mind,
You'd better change it back or we will both be sorry:

CHORUS
Don't you want me baby?
Don't you want me? Oh . . .
Don't you want me baby?
Don't you want me? Oh . . .

VERSE 3
I was working as a waitress in a cocktail bar,
That much is true,
But even then I knew I'd find a much better place
Either with or without you.

VERSE 4
The five years we have had have been such good times:
I still love you.
But now I think it's time I live my life on my own,
I guess it's just what I must do.

BRIDGE 1
BRIDGE 2
CHORUS
INTRO
CHORUS (Repeat to fade)

HOW CHORDS WORK TOGETHER

FOR EVERY major or minor key, there are six primary triad chords which can be used without sounding discordant. Using the table opposite, you can find out which chords 'work' in any key.

The top half of the table concerns major keys. Minor keys are in the bottom half.

Take the first key in the table: **C** major. Read down the scale from **C**. The second note is **D**, and the primary triad chord is minor. So a **D** minor chord will sound good in a song in **C** major.

Reading on down the scale of **C** major, the other primary triads that work in the key of **C** major are **E** minor, **F** major, **G** major, and **A** minor.

Take another example, at the right-hand end of the table: **B** major. The primary triads which sound good in this key are **B** major, **C#** minor, **D#** minor, **E** major, **F#** major, and the relative minor **G#** minor.

Now look at the lower table—the minor keys—and read down the sixth scale along, that of **D** minor. You can see that the primary triad chords which sound right in **D** minor are the relative major **F** major, plus **G** minor, **A** minor, **B♭** major and **C** major.

DON'T WORRY if all this seems a bit complicated. We'll be giving you most of these individual chord shapes in due course, and you can ignore the table if you want to.

But if you want to race ahead, using this table and the primary triads table on page 25 you can work out all the primary chords you can use in any key.

Treat this table like the Chord Directory—as a reference. If you want to write songs you'll find it invaluable.

Who's that guy . . . and is he sneaking a quick look at his trusty *Play Rock Keyboards* scales and chord chart? Billy Joel plays an innocent man.

CHORDS THAT WORK IN G

WE'VE SEEN how there are six primary triads which 'work' in each key. The ones that work in **C** major are **C**, **Am**, **G**, **Em**, **F** and **Dm**. The chart above page 31 shows which primary triads you can use in each key.

The next key we want to look closely at is **G** major. The chords that we can use in **G** are **G** major, **A** minor, **B** minor, **C** major, **D** major and **E** minor. Of these, we've already learnt **G**, **Am**, **C** and **Em**. Now we can learn **D** and **Bm**.

You'll remember that on page 22 we learned to play the scales of **D** major and **B** minor. As you know, the primary triads for these chords are constructed from the first, third and fifth notes of their scales.

Try using various combinations of the six chords together. It will show you instinctively how they relate to one another.

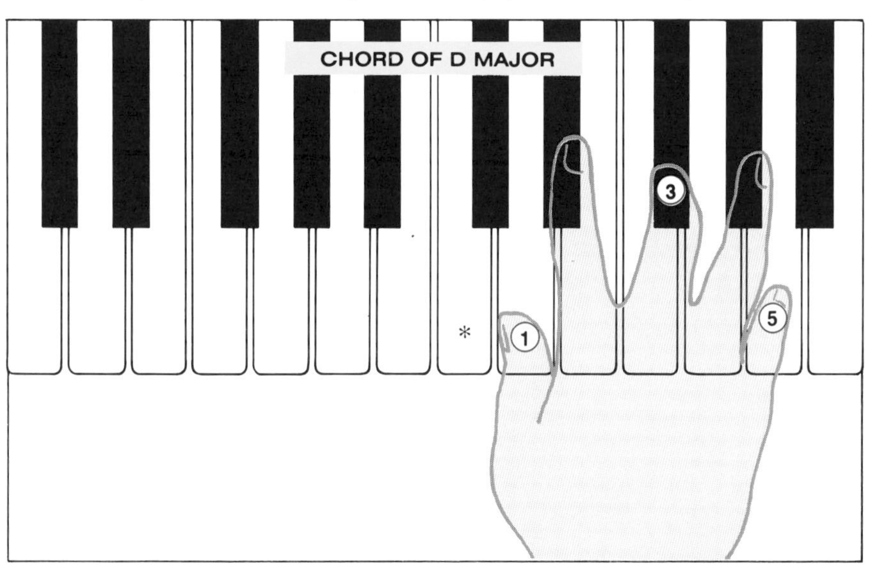

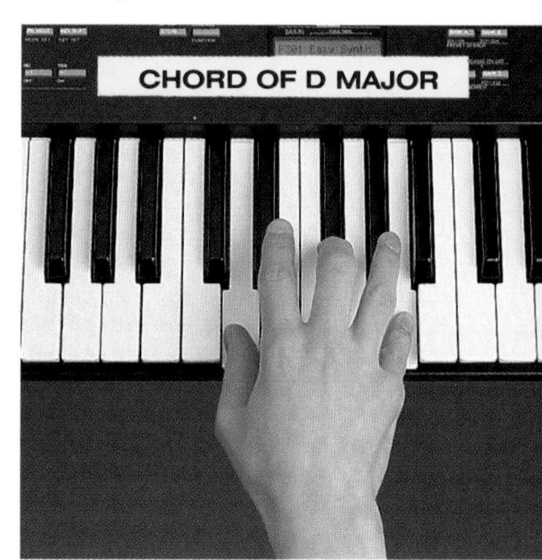

When playing a black note, remember to keep your finger in the centre of the key.

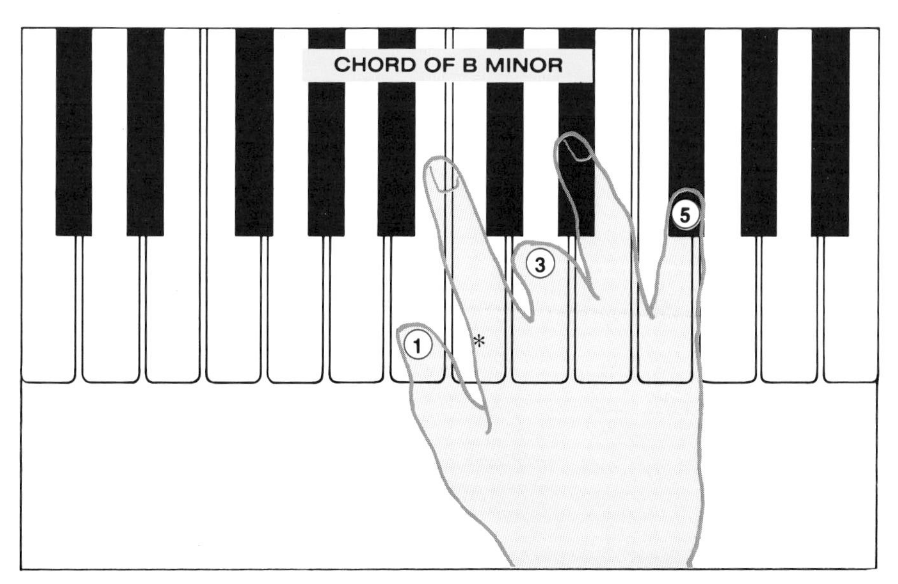

Like D major, Bm has an F# black note, but it's played with the little finger.

	NOTE IN SCALE	PRIMARY TRIAD CHORD	SCALE (READ DOWN FROM ROOT NOTE)											
MAJOR KEY	**Root**	**Root major chord**	**C**	**D♭**	**D**	**E♭**	**E**	**F**	**F#**	**G**	**A♭**	**A**	**B♭**	**B**
	Second	Minor chord	D	E♭	E	F	F#	G	G#	A	B♭	B	C	C#
	Third	Minor chord	E	F	F#	G	G#	A	A#	B	C	C#	D	D#
	Fourth	Major chord	F	G♭	G	A♭	A	B♭	B	C	D♭	D	E♭	E
	Fifth	Major chord	G	A♭	A	B♭	B	C	C#	D	E♭	E	F	F#
	Sixth	Relative minor chord	A	B♭	B	C	C#	D	D#	E	F	F#	G	G#
	Seventh	----	B	C	C#	D	D#	E	E#	F#	G	G#	A	A#

MINOR KEY	**Root**	**Root minor chord**	**A**	**B♭**	**B**	**C**	**C#**	**D**	**D#**	**E**	**F**	**F#**	**G**	**G#**
	Second	----	B	C	C#	D	D#	E	E#	F#	G	G#	A	A#
	Third	Relative major chord	C	D♭	D	E♭	E	F	F#	G	A♭	A	B♭	B
	Fourth	Minor chord	D	E♭	E	F	F#	G	G#	A	B♭	B	C	C#
	Fifth	Minor chord	E	F	F#	G	G#	A	A#	B	C	C#	D	D#
	Sixth	Major chord	F	G♭	G	A♭	A	B♭	B	C	D♭	D	E♭	E
	Seventh	Major chord	G	A♭	A	B♭	B	C	C#	D	E♭	E	F	F#

You'll notice that in the key of F# major and its relative minor D# minor, there is a note named E#. Although this is a sharp, it's actually a white note—the one usually named F. It can't be called F because there is already an 'F' note in the key (the root note F#). This is the only time this happens, and nobody will object if you decide to call it F.

HOW RELATIVES WORK TOGETHER

NATURALLY, ALL the chords you can use in **G** major may also be used in its relative **E** minor, because the notes in both scales are the same.

The six chords we can use in **G** are in fact three pairs of relative majors and minors: **G** major and its relative **E** minor; **C** major and its relative **A** minor; and **D** major and its relative **B** minor.

Similarly, the chords that work in **C** major are all pairs of relatives: **C** major and its relative **A** minor; **G** major and its relative **E** minor; and **F** major with its relative **D** minor.

If you look at the chart above, you'll see that this holds true throughout. If any major chord 'works' in a certain key, so will its relative minor.

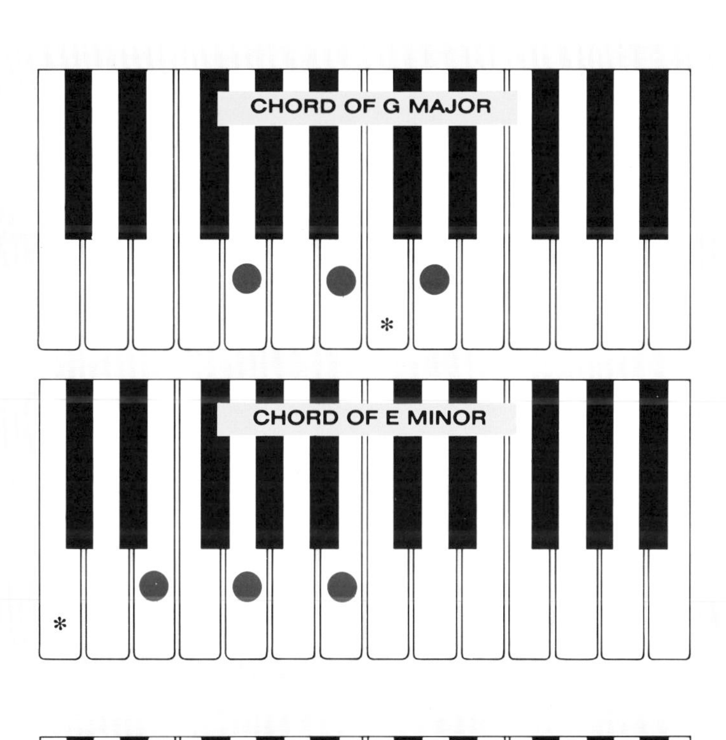

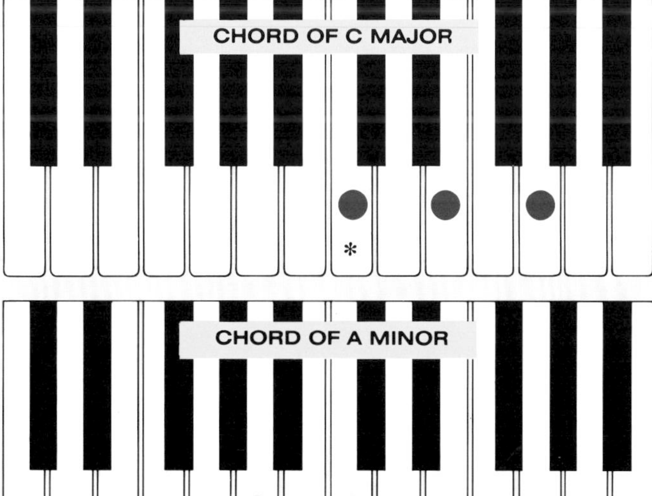

What an artist: even lying on his back Elton John always remembers to keep his forearms horizontal whilst playing . . .

TRANSPOSING KEYS

WE'VE LEARNT to play 'Don't You Want Me' in the key of **C** major. Now we're going to try it in the key of **D** major.

Moving a song from one key to another like this is called transposition—we're transposing the song from **C** major to **D** major.

If you work with other musicians or singers, you may need to know how to transpose keys for yourself.

Maybe your singer can't handle a song in a certain key, or your guitarist finds it easier in another key. It will help if you can change keys to suit.

TRANSPOSING IS easier than you might think. It just takes a little time and common sense.

In a case like 'Don't You Want Me', where we're transposing from the key of **C** major to the key of **D** major it's simple.

The new root chord **D** major is one tone higher than the original root chord **C** major. So it stands to reason that any other chords or notes will be one tone higher than in the original.

The chords in **C** major are **C**, **F**, **G** and **Am**. We move them all up one tone. So **C** becomes **D**, **F** becomes **G**, **G** becomes **A** and **Am** becomes **Bm**, giving us **D**, **G**, **A** and **Bm**.

THAT'S ONE method of transposition—and it works well if you're transposing to a key quite close to the original.

But if we wanted to transpose 'Don't You Want Me' into, say, **G** major it wouldn't be so easy. From **C** to **G** is a gap of eight semitones—and that can get pretty complicated.

You might find it easier to transpose each note or chord by checking its relationship to the original root chord, and working out what the equivalent would be in the new key.

Take the case of 'Don't You Want Me'. In the key of **C** major we use **C**, **F**, **G** and **Am**. These are the primary chords formed from the root, fourth, fifth and sixth notes in the scale of **C** major.

If we want to transpose the song to **G** major we need to find the primary chords formed from the root, fourth, fifth and sixth notes in that scale.

If you don't remember the scale of **G** major, refer to the chart on page 31. It will tell you that the chords you need are **G**, **C**, **D** and **Em**. To show how to use the table we've reprinted the section on major keys (see opposite).

CHORDS OF A MAJOR & F# MINOR

TO PLAY 'Don't You Want Me' in the key of **D** major, you will need to play an **A** major chord. Here is **A** major with its relative minor **F#m**—probably the trickiest so far.

Not only does **F#m** contain two black notes—**F#** and **C#**—but they are positioned on either side of the single white note, **A**.

You play the **F#** with your thumb (1) and the **C#** with your little finger (5). But it's the middle finger (3) that's the difficult part.

When playing chords like this, you'll probably find that you have to angle certain fingers, rather than arch them—and that's how you play the **A** in **F#m**.

The smaller the keys on your keyboard, the more you'll have to angle your finger.

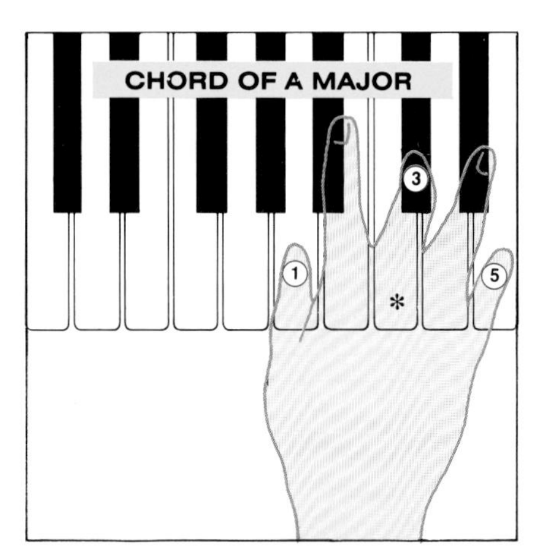

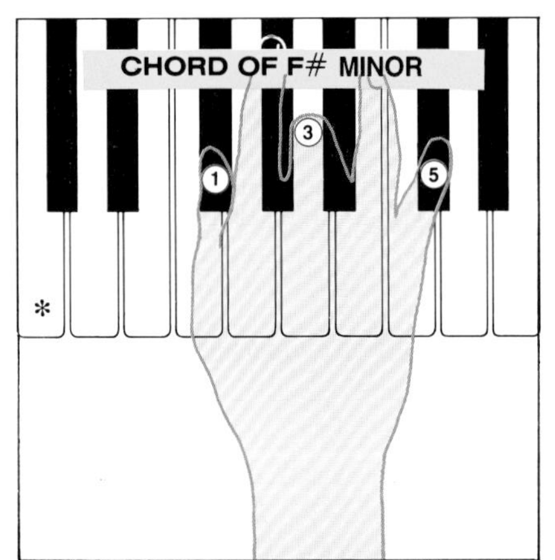

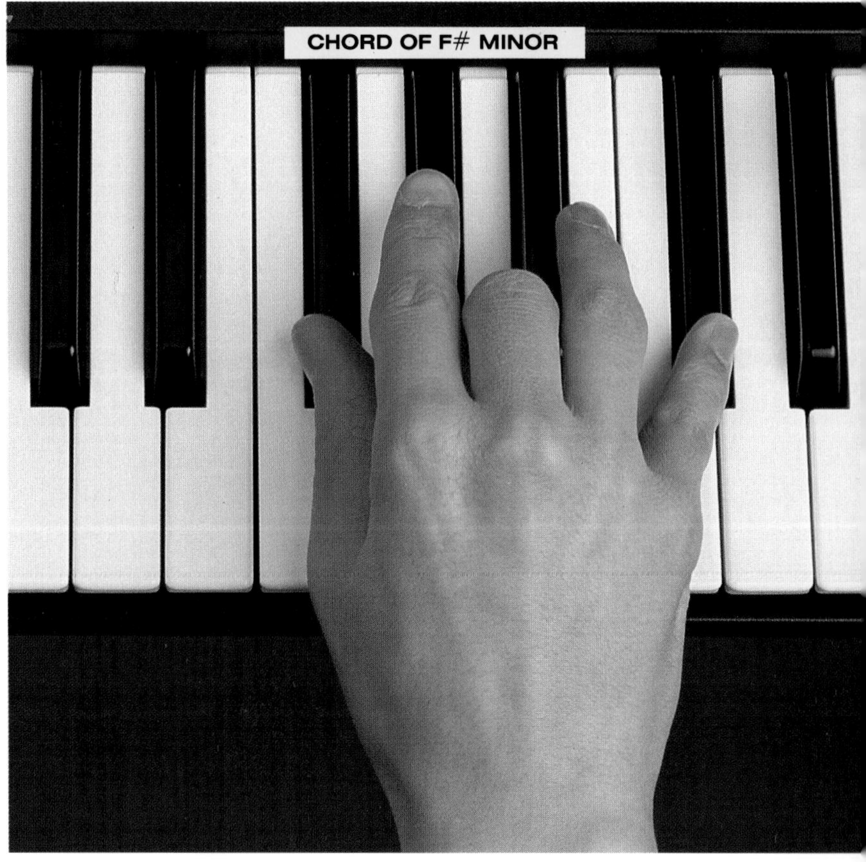

One of Casio's many home keyboards, the MT-520 can be a useful instrument to learn on, but the keys are so small that it's very hard to use the correct fingering, especially on chords such as F# minor which have two black notes which happen to fall either side of a white note.

ɔU CAN transpose keys easily by using e primary triads chart on page 31. 'hether you want to transpose chords or ɔtes, it works the same way.

In our example we want to transpose a ›ng in **C** major into **G** major. The chords in **C** major are **C**, **F**, **G** and **Am**.

First locate the scale of the original key, **C** major. Then refer across to the scale of the new key, **G** major.

You'll see that the notes **C**, **F**, **G** and **A** in the **C** major scale line up with **G**, **C**, **D** and **E** in the scale of **G** major. So you simply replace the chords derived from **C**, **F**, **G** and **A** in **C** with those derived from **G**, **C**, **D** and **E** in the key of **G** major.

So the chords of **C**, **F**, **G** and **Am** become **G**, **C**, **D** and **Em**.

	NOTE IN SCALE	PRIMARY TRIAD CHORD	SCALE (READ DOWN FROM ROOT NOTE)											
MAJOR KEY	**Root**	**Root major chord**	**C**	**D♭**	**D**	**E♭**	**E**	**F**	**F#**	**G**	**A♭**	**A**	**B♭**	**B**
	Second	Minor chord	D	E♭	E	F	F#	G	G#	A	B♭	B	C	C#
	Third	Minor chord	E	F	F#	G	G#	A	A#	B	C	C#	D	D#
	Fourth	Major chord	F	G♭	G	A♭	A	B♭	B	C	D♭	D	E♭	E
	Fifth	Major chord	G	A♭	A	B♭	B	C	C#	D	E♭	E	F	F#
	Sixth	Relative minor chord	A	B♭	B	C	C#	D	D#	E	F	F#	G	G#
	Seventh	----	B	C	C#	D	D#	E	E#	F#	G	G#	A	A#

'DON'T YOU WANT ME' IN D MAJOR

'E ARE going to transpose 'Don't You Want e' from its original key **C** major into the new ›y of **D** major.

As we explained above, this is simple. The stance from **C** to **D** is one tone. Therefore all e chords are raised one tone.

Previously we used **C**, **F**, **G** and **Am**. Now we ɜe **D**, **G**, **A** and **Bm**. It's a little more difficult, ; you've now got three chords with black ɔtes: **D**, **A**, and **Bm**.

NCE YOU'VE learnt this thoroughly you might ‹e to try putting it together with the intro assline which you learned on page 23.

That was in the key of **B** minor. Here we have the verse in the relative major key, **D** major—the song cunningly changes keys between major and minor, giving an ominous mood to the intro and a more carefree mood to the verse. But because the two keys are related, the two passages work together quite naturally.

To play both parts one after the other, just refer back to page 23. You'll see that the final bar there is BAR 5—which happens to be the first bar here. Overlap the two BAR 5's, and you can run straight from the intro into the verse.

If you want to play the chords over and over, just play the second line (9,6,7,8) repeatedly. If you want to return to the intro, just go from BAR 10 to BAR 1. For the lyrics, see page 29. And if you want to stop, finish on BAR 10.

RUNNING ORDER

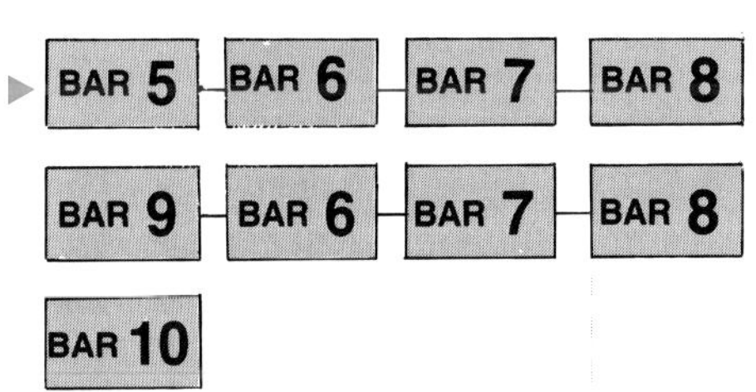

TITLE	KEY	TEMPO	STARTING POINT
'DON'T YOU WANT ME' (VERSE)	D MAJOR	QUITE FAST	A MAJOR ABOVE *

	1	2	3	4
BAR 5				A, G
BAR 6				Bm
BAR 7		A		A, G
BAR 8			D	A
BAR 9				A, G
BAR 10				

CHANGING KEYS

WE'VE SEEN how to take a song and set it in a different key. There's another good use for transposition—and that's to change keys within the song itself.

Key changes are often used towards the end of a song, because it feels like you are suddenly shifting up a gear.

Two great examples that spring to mind are Berlin's 'Take My Breath Away' and Bon Jovi's 'Livin' On A Prayer'. They are very different records—Berlin's in a romantic vein, Bon Jovi's in rock—but they both derive an extra boost and added tension from the key change.

The most common key change is the one that takes you up one tone, for instance from **A** major to **B** major.

Obviously, if you're changing keys from a minor key it must be *to* a minor key, and from a major key *to* a major key.

CHANGING KEYS

NOW LET'S try changing keys in a song in practise. Here we have the *Beverly Hills Cop* theme 'Axel F' in the key of **A** minor—as we learned it back on page 21—and, opposite, in the key of **B** minor.

This gives us the chance to play the classic key change—up one tone. First refresh your memory by playing the **A** minor version a few times. It should be a lot easier now than when you first struggled to master it.

Then move onto the version in **B** minor. Practise that on its own until you can play it fluently in either key.

Finally try playing them one after the other—first in **A** minor, then without a pause in **B** minor.

You should hear the music 'change up a gear' as you change key . . . an effect that reinforces the cliffhanger mood of Harold Faltermeyer's tune.

IF YOU COMPARE this music grid to the one on page 21, you'll see that we've added the rhythm element, with notes marked in different shades.

The 'old' version was fine for you to learn on, but now that you're playing faster, the 'old' version with all notes held for just one quarter beat will sound too clipped. This version, with the notes held for the correct time, will flow better.

IF YOU'RE still having trouble with the rhythm of this tune, don't worry. As long as you get the notes in the right order, it'll make sense—and you'll be able to appreciate the key change.

Harold Faltermeyer, composer of 'Axel F'.

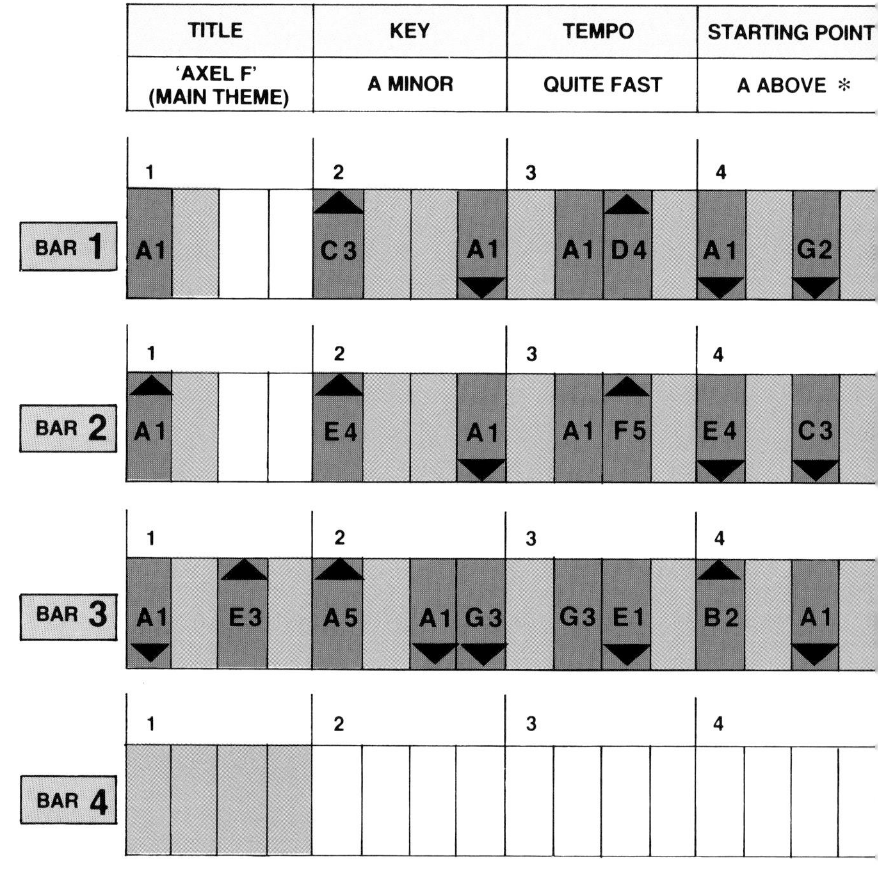

TITLE	KEY	TEMPO	STARTING POINT
'AXEL F' (MAIN THEME)	A MINOR	QUITE FAST	A ABOVE ✻

KEY TO COLOURS ON GRID: ■ A NOTE PLAYED ■ A NOTE HELD □ A REST (SILENCE)

MUSICAL NOTATION FOR 'AXEL F' IN THE KEY OF A MINOR

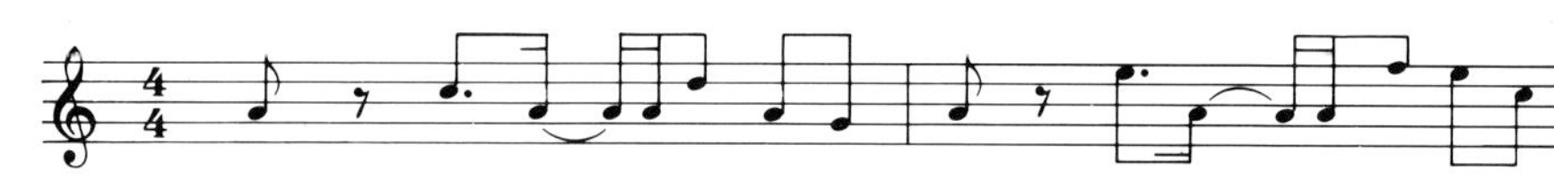

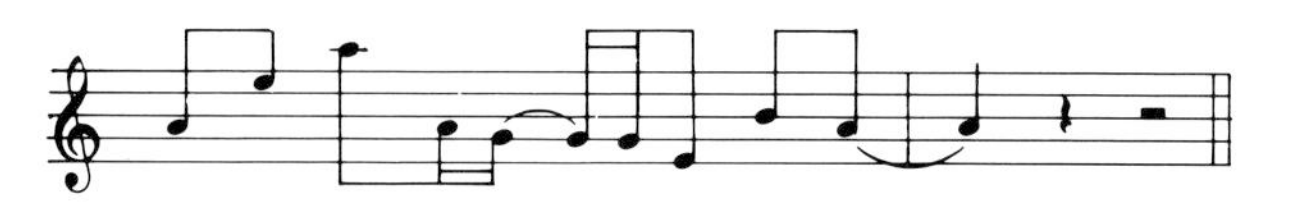

eft: Jon Bon Jovi,
ad singer with Bon
ovi. 'Livin' On A
rayer' gave them a
nash hit around the
orld, and went to the
p of the American
harts in the footsteps
the LP it came from,
lippery When Wet',
'80s rock classic.

ight: Terri Nunn, lead
nger with Berlin.
'ou Take My Breath
way', the theme from
op Gun, was a
umber one in several
ountries including the
SA and UK.

TITLE	KEY	TEMPO	STARTING POINT
'AXEL F' (MAIN THEME)	B MINOR	QUITE FAST	B ABOVE ✻

	1	2	3	4
BAR 1	B1	▲D3, B1▼	B1, ▲E4	B1▼, A2▼
BAR 2	▲B1	▲F♯4, B1▼	B1, ▲G5	F♯4▼, D3▼
BAR 3	B1▼, ▲F♯3	▲B5, B1▼, A3▼	A3, F♯1▼	▲C♯2, B1▼
BAR 4				

MUSICAL NOTATION FOR 'AXEL F' IN THE KEY OF B MINOR

UK TOP TEN

BEST SELLING ROCK KEYBOARD INSTRUMENTALS IN GREAT BRITAIN

1. TELSTAR
   The Tornadoes (1962, organ)
2. MOULDY OLD DOUGH
   Lieutenant Pigeon (1972, piano)
3. NUT ROCKER
   B.Bumble & The Stingers (1962, piano)
4. MAGIC FLY
   Space (1977, synthesiser)
5. OXYGENE
   Jean-Michel Jarre (1977, synthesiser)
6. POPCORN
   Hot Butter (1972, organ)
7. MIAMI VICE THEME
   Jan Hammer (1985, synthesiser)
8. FANFARE FOR THE COMMON MAN
   ELP (1977, organ)
9. 2001
   Deodato (1973, electric piano)
10. THE LIQUIDATOR
   Harry J & The Allstars (1969, piano)

Inspired by a space satellite, 'Telstar' by Billy Fury's Tornadoes was the first record by a British group to rocket to the top in the USA.

'Oxygene' turned composer Jean-Michel Jarre into a superstar. Now he lights up entire cities with his spectacular events.

From left: Keith Emerson, Greg Lake and Carl Palmer, whose one UK hit single went to No.2 on the charts and gets them into our all-time chart.

THE STORY SO FAR

LET'S JUST recap on what you should be able to play by now.

In the key of **C** we've had the scale, and all the chords that work in **C**.

In the key of **Am** we've had the scale, and all the chords that work in **Am**.

In the keys of **G** and **Em** we've had the scales, and all the chords that work in **G** and **Em**. We've had the scales of **D** and **Bm**, and the chords that work in **D** and **Bm**.

Now we've got the scales of **A** and **F#m**. And when you've taken in the chords of **E** and **C#m**, you'll be equipped with all th chords that work in **A** and **F#m**.

So you now know enough primary triad to operate in eight different keys.

On the opposite page we catch up o the 'flat' scales and chords.

SCALES AND PRIMARY TRIAD CHORDS LEARNT TO DATE

Scale of C	C	D	E	F	G	A	B
Chords that work in C	C	Dm	Em	F	G	Am	
Scale of G	G	A	B	C	D	E	F#
Chords that work in G	G	Am	Bm	C	D	Em	
Scale of D	D	E	F#	G	A	B	C#
Chords that work in D	D	Em	F#m	G	A	Bm	
Scale of A	A	B	C#	D	E	F#	G#
Chords that work in A	A	Bm	C#m	D	E	F#m	

Scale of Am	A	B	C	D	E	F	G
Chords that work in Am	Am		C	Dm	Em	F	G
Scale of Em	E	F#	G	A	B	C	D
Chords that work in Em	Em		G	Am	Bm	C	D
Scale of Bm	B	C#	D	E	F#	G	A
Chords that work in Bm	Bm		D	Em	F#m	G	A
Scale of F#m	F#	G#	A	B	C#	D	E
Chords that work in F#m	F#m		A	Bm	C#m	D	E

SCALES OF A AND F#m

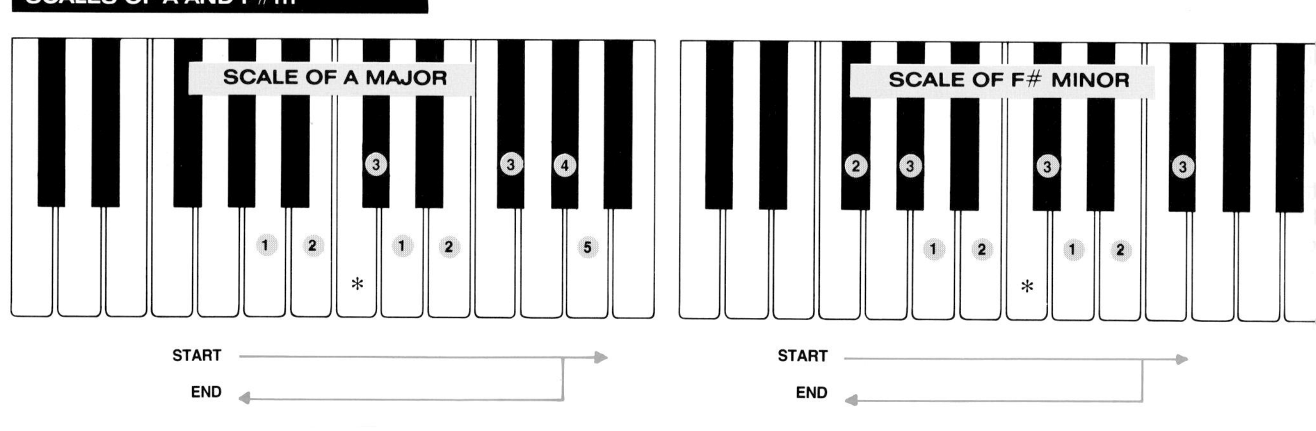

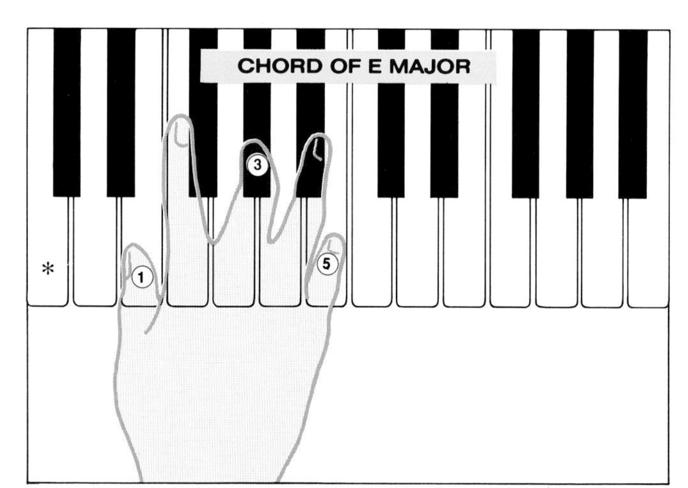

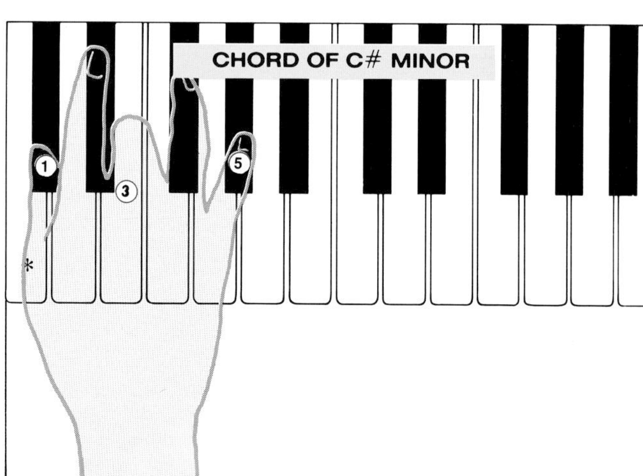

THE CHORD of **C#** minor is another of those awkward 'back-to-front' chords like **F#** minor, where your outside fingers stretch up to the black notes whilst the middle finger is pulled back on a white note.

You should play chords like this in the way that suits you best. If you find your middle finger (3) sliding up the white note to a position alongside the black note **D#**, don't worry—but make sure you only play the **E** note, and not the **F**.

The **E** major chord (left) is a more familiar shape, with the thumb and little fingers playing the white notes **E** and **B**, and the black note **G#** played by the middle finger (3).

Try going from one to the other.

JP TO NOW we have concentrated on ɛeys which contain sharp notes. This doesn't mean they're more important or easier than keys with flat notes.

Maybe your singer can't handle a song n E minor (which has one sharp note)... naybe the key which suits him or her best s C minor, which has three flat notes... Obviously you need to know that key.

Flat notes are just like sharps. But in concentrating on the sharps we have followed a logical progression from one key to he next.

C major has no sharp notes.

G major has one: F#.

D major has two: F# and C#.

A major has three: F#, G# and C#.

And of course their relative minor keys follow the same progression, as they share the same notes.

THERE IS a similar progression from one flat key to the next—again beginning with C major, which has no sharps or flats.

We've looked at the scales of F major and its relative D minor, which contain one flat note, B♭. The chords that work in these two keys are F major, D minor, C major, A minor, B♭ major and G minor. Of these, only two are new to you: B♭ and its relative Gm. These two chords are shown below.

THE SCALES of B♭ major and G minor are also shown below. They contain the notes B♭, C, D, E♭, F, G, and A.

The chords that work in these two keys are B♭ major, G minor, F major, D minor, E♭ major and C minor.

There are two new chords in that list: E♭ major and its relative minor, C minor. They're shown below. So now you're a flat *and* sharp operator!

Scale of F	F	G	A	B♭	C	D	E
Chords that work in F	F	Gm	Am	B♭	C	Dm	

Scale of Dm	D	E	F	G	A	B♭	C
Chords that work in Dm	Dm		F	Gm	Am	B♭	C

Scale of B♭	B♭	C	D	E♭	F	G	A
Chords that work in B♭	B♭	Cm	Dm	E♭	F	Gm	

Scale of Gm	G	A	B♭	C	D	E♭	F
Chords that work in Gm	Gm		B♭	Cm	Dm	E♭	F

SCALES AND CHORDS WITH FLATS

ОТЕ THAT in the scales of F# minor and B♭ najor, your second finger (2) plays the first ote, not your thumb (1). Take particular care ith the fingering in these scales.

The scale of F# minor is the trickiest you've ttempted to date. Although there are only three harp notes in the key, there are four black otes in the scale. Why? Because the root note # is played at both ends of the scale.

F# minor is an important key, so keep at it ntil you're really fluent.

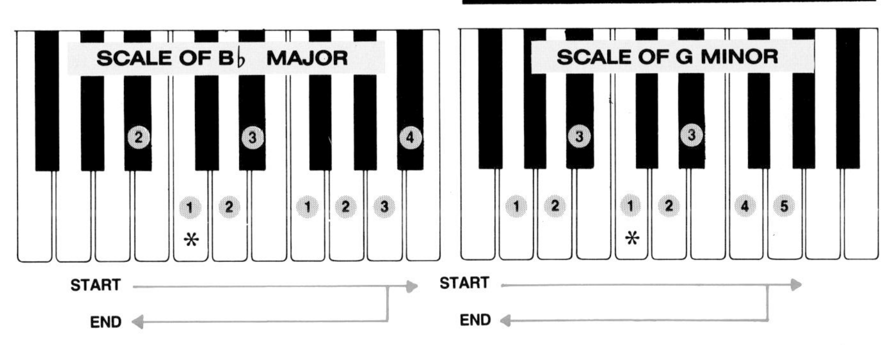

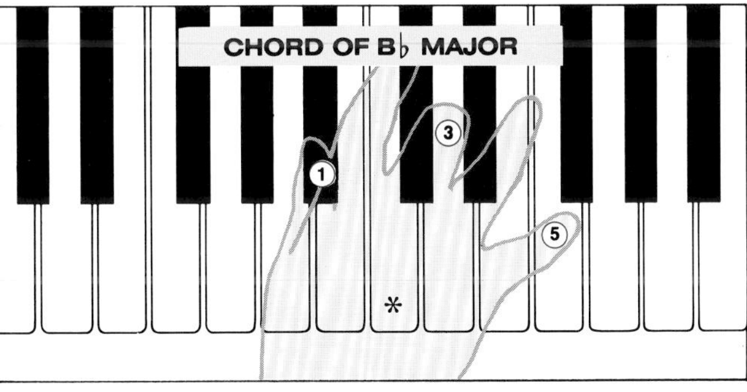

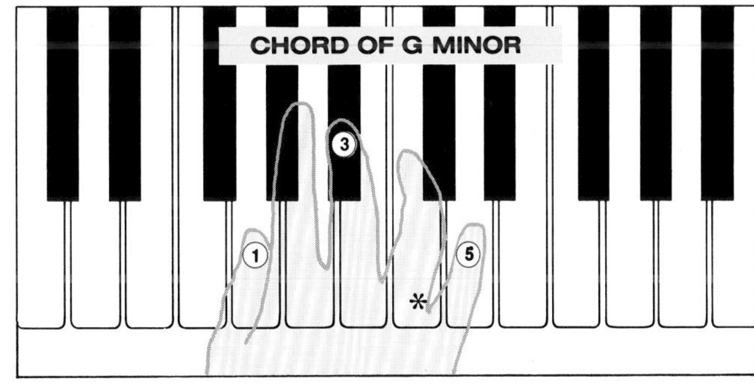

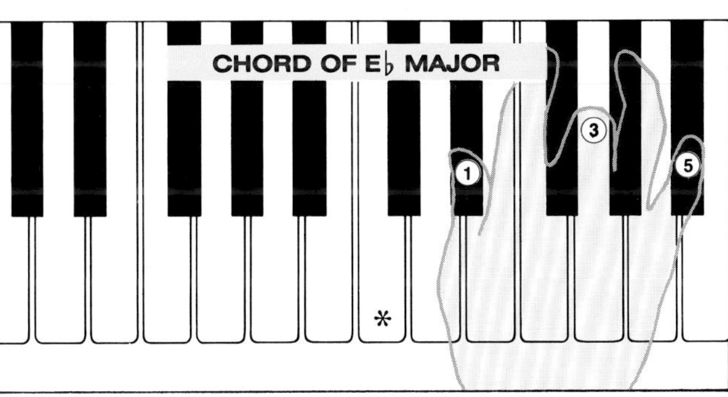

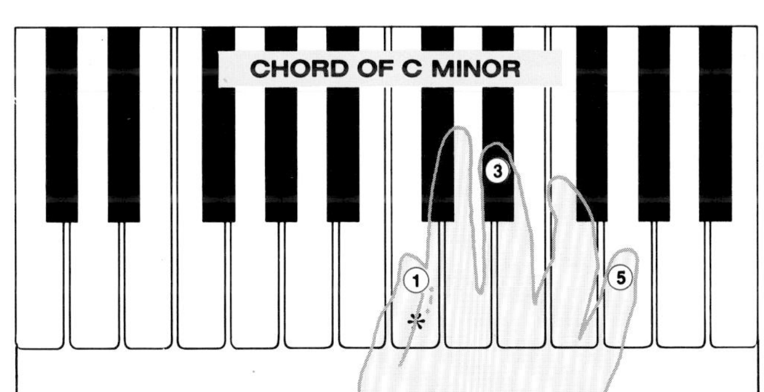

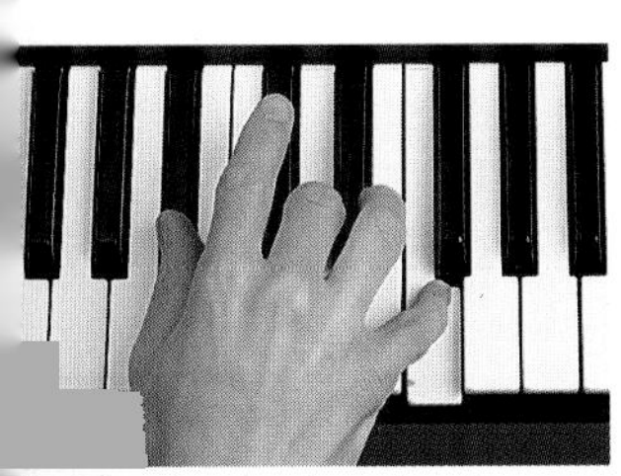

he B♭ major chord employs the same 1), (3), (5) fingering used for all rimary triad chords.

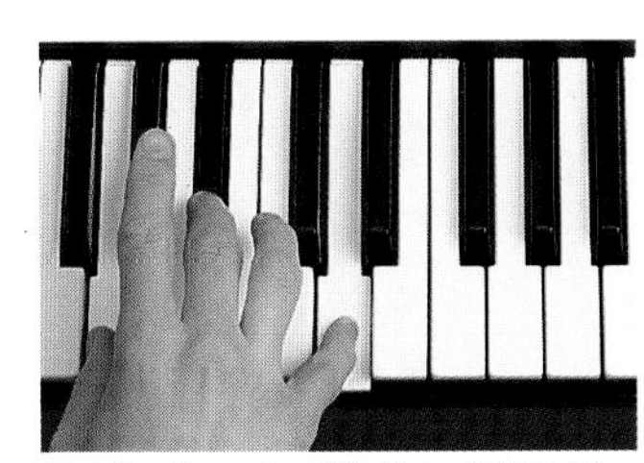

The G minor chord is the relative of the B♭ major on the left. E♭ major and C minor are also relatives.

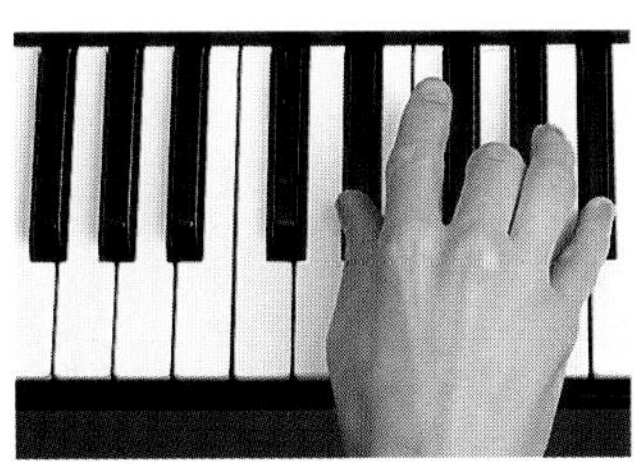

The E♭ major chord has two flats. Keep your thumb and little finger dead centre on the black keys.

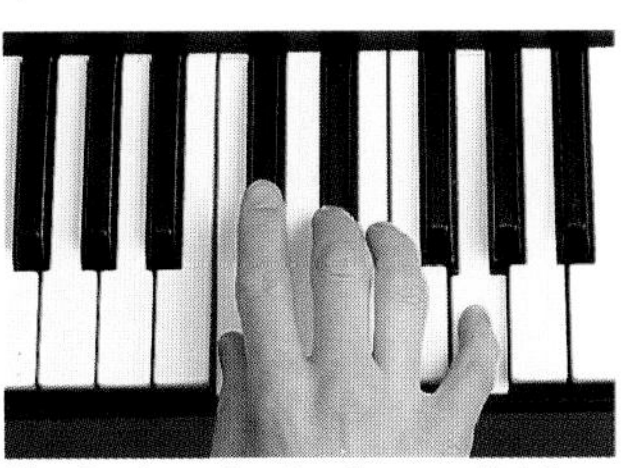

The C minor chord – fingers slightly arched, back of hands and forearm just about horizontal.

CHORD INVERSIONS

ALL PRIMARY triad chords contain the root, third and fifth notes in a scale.

So far, we've learnt these chords with the three notes arranged in the same way:

Root note at the bottom (thumb);
Third note in the middle;
Fifth note at the top.

However, this isn't the only way to play those three notes together. Move your hand slightly to the right, and you could play the chord like this:

Third note at the bottom (thumb);
Fifth note in the middle;
Root note (next octave) at the top.

Move your hand to the right again, and you could get this:

Fifth note at the bottom (thumb);
Root note (next octave) in the middle;
Third note at the top.

Each new way of playing the same chord is called an inversion.

Our original *root/third/fifth* combination is known as the 'basic' primary triad.

The *third/fifth/root* combination is called the 'first inversion' **(i)**.

The *fifth/root/third* combination is called the 'second inversion' **(ii)**.

When combined with basic chords, inversions can add variety and make for smoother chord progressions.

Instead of having to move along the keyboard from one chord to the next, you may find a handy inversion that means you hardly have to move at all.

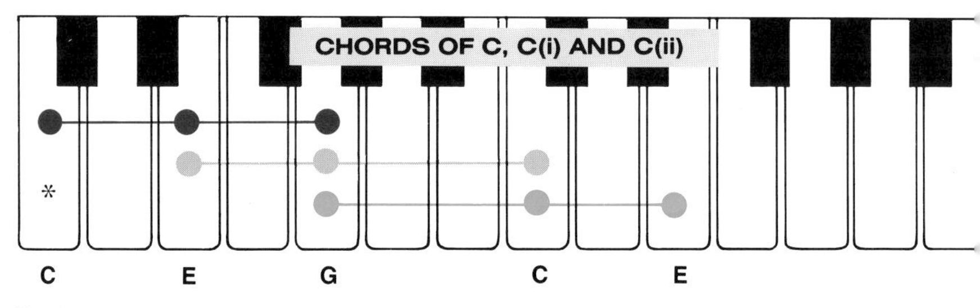

The three inversions of the C major primary triad— basic, first inversion (i) and second inversion (ii)— seen in relation to each other on the keyboard.

CHORD INVERSIONS

THIS EXERCISE shows you how to play the primary triad of **C** major in its basic form, then its first and second inversions, and finally in its basic form one octave above the original.

Play the basic: **C**, **E** and **G** notes as usual.

Then move to the right: you play them in the order **E**, **G**, **C**. This is the first inversion **(i)**.

Then move right again to play the same notes in the order **G**, **C**, **E**. This is the second inversion **(ii)**.

Then right again, to play the basic version once more: **C**, **E** and **G** one octave above your starting point.

Each time you are playing the chord of **C**.

ONCE YOU can move along the keyboard playing basic, first inversion, second inversion and then basic again, try it in reverse. Start at the top and work down through the second and first inversions, to the basic.

Then try going up and down in one movement as if playing a scale.

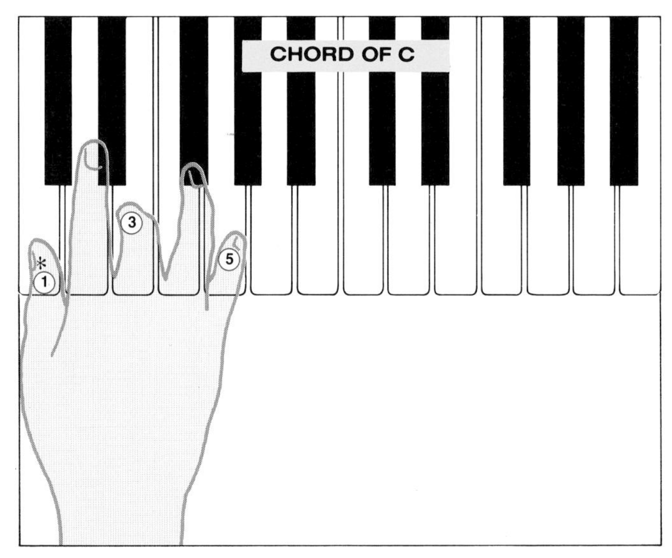

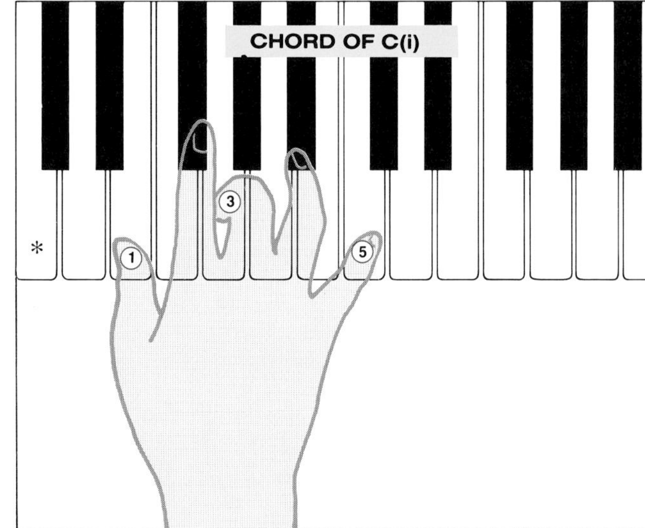

Whenever you play the notes C, E and G together, you're playing the chord of C major: an inversion is just another way to do it.

'ROM TIME to time from here on, we'll)e looking at different keyboard instru- nents in detail – beginning with the)iano.

Of all the keyboards you're ever likely) play, the acoustic piano (as opposed to s electric counterpart) will probably be ne oldest.

The most common type of acoustic)iano is the 'upright'. Compared to most nodern keyboards it's large and heavy,)ut it's positively light in comparison with ne other type of acoustic piano – the grand'.

Of the two, the grand tends to sound ıller and more dynamic, which is why it's nore often used in concert – and, of ourse, it tends to look somewhat more npressive.

Roxy Music pose in the grand manner, with Bryan Ferry in the driving seat as ever.

CHORDS OF C, C(i) AND C(ii)

HE BASIC, first and second inversions below re essentially the same chord, in that they are l made up of the same notes. Nevertheless, ach has its own character, which can give your hord progressions added variety.

You may also find situations where you know hich chord you want to use in a progression, but the basic primary triad doesn't sound right. Try the first and second inversions, because you can often find that one of them works better.

DON'T FORGET the essential rules for playing chords, which apply as much to inversions as to basic chords.

Play all the notes at exactly the same time, and keep the back of your hand and forearm almost horizontal, with fingers arched.

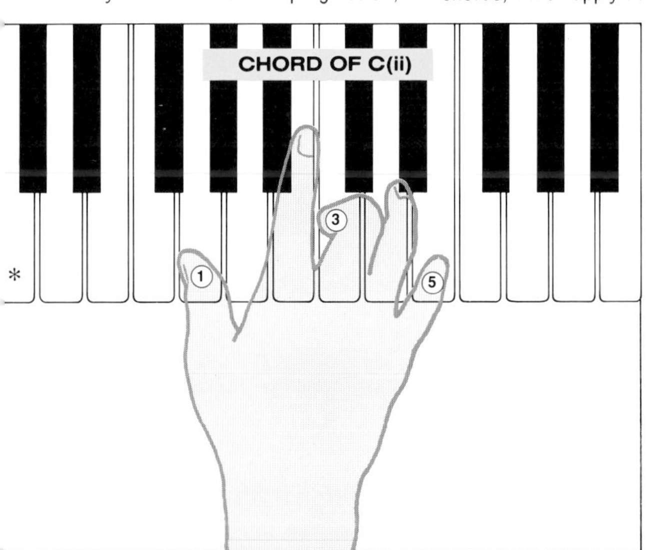

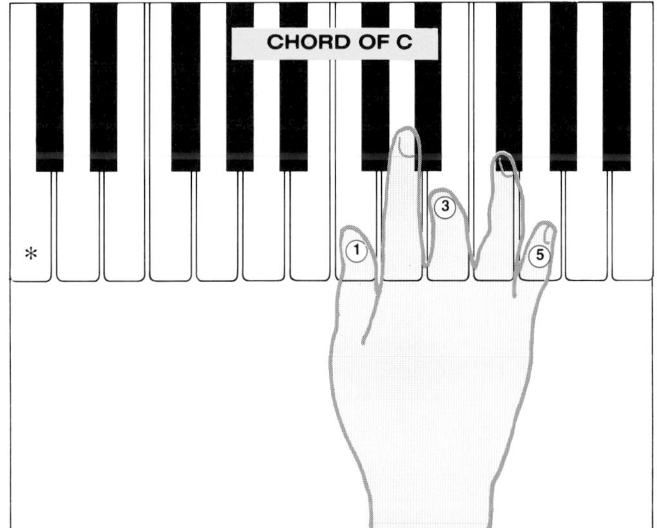

Each inversion has a slightly different character, depending on which notes are highest and lowest in the chord.

Mike Barson of Madness finds a new use for his grand piano—inspiration from above.

FOR EVERY key on an acoustic piano, there is a soft 'hammer' inside. When you press the key, the hammer strikes a metal string, which then sounds the note.

The piano's full name is pianoforte, derived from the Italian words for soft (*piano*) and strong (*forte*) – and although the piano has one basic sound, it can range from softness to strength, depending on how it's played. The slightest change in pressure on the keys can alter the sound dramatically.

This is why it is so difficult to find a convincing acoustic piano sound on an electronic keyboard. Even when it gets a good acoustic sound, it can rarely be as expressive.

Many people think of the piano only as a classical music instrument. But it's also an established rock instrument, used b '50s rock and rollers such as Jerry Le Lewis and Little Richard, and moder pop stars like Elton John, Billy Joel, an Bruce Hornsby (on 'The Way It Is').

If you want to play piano in a banc you've got problems. Pianos are difficu to transport, and sensitive to knocks an changes in temperature. Of course, club may have its own piano, but you can be sure what condition it'll be in – an they're not easy to amplify.

So if you really want an acoustic pian sound, you may have to compromise b using an electronic keyboard with decent piano sound.

This doesn't necessarily have to be synthesiser. It could be an electric c electronic piano.

USING INVERSIONS

THERE ARE three types of primary chord—basic, first inversion **(i)** and second inversion **(ii)**. These two exercises show how they can be used together in one piece of music.

The first exercise uses the chords of **G** and **C** in all their three versions—basic, first inversion **(i)** and second inversion **(ii)**. The chords are arranged to make a smooth and melodic chord progression.

The second exercise uses all three versions of **Em** and **Am**—basic, first inversion **(i)** and second inversion **(ii)**.

Take care to finger the chords correctly.

You'll notice that the fingering for each chord happens to be exactly the same: thumb (1) on the lowest note, middle finger (3) on the middle note, and little finger (5) on the highest note.

ONCE YOU feel you can play both exercises fairly confidently, try playing one after the other without a gap between them—the **G/C** version followed by the **Em/Am** version.

You'll notice that when you do this, finishing on the **Em (ii)** makes it sound incomplete. Try replacing the final **Em (ii)** with **G (i)**. It should round the tune off nicely.

WHEN YOU'RE familiar with the three varieties of primary triad, try listening out for them on records to hear how other musicians use inversions.

Keyboard-based songs where primary triad inversions stand out include 'Jump' by Van Halen, 'Everybody Wants To Rule The World' by Tears For Fears, 'Silent Running' by Mike And The Mechanics, and 'Obsession' by Animotion. All use inversions to very good effect.

You'll soon find inversions just as useful as basic primary chords.

EXERCISE SHOWING THE BASIC, FIRST INVERSION (i) AND SECOND INVERSION (ii) CHORDS OF G AND C

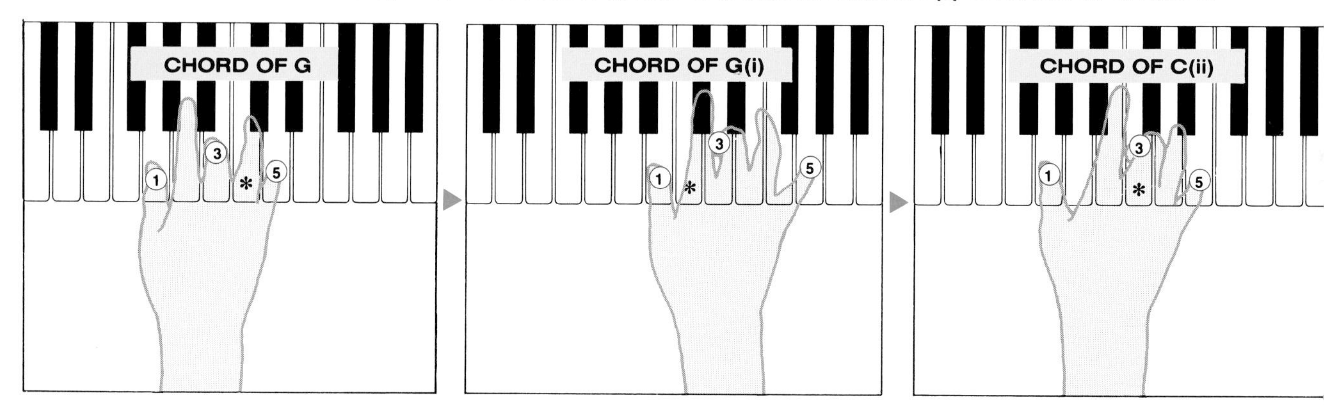

EXERCISE SHOWING THE BASIC, FIRST INVERSION (i) AND SECOND INVERSION (ii) CHORDS OF Em AND Am

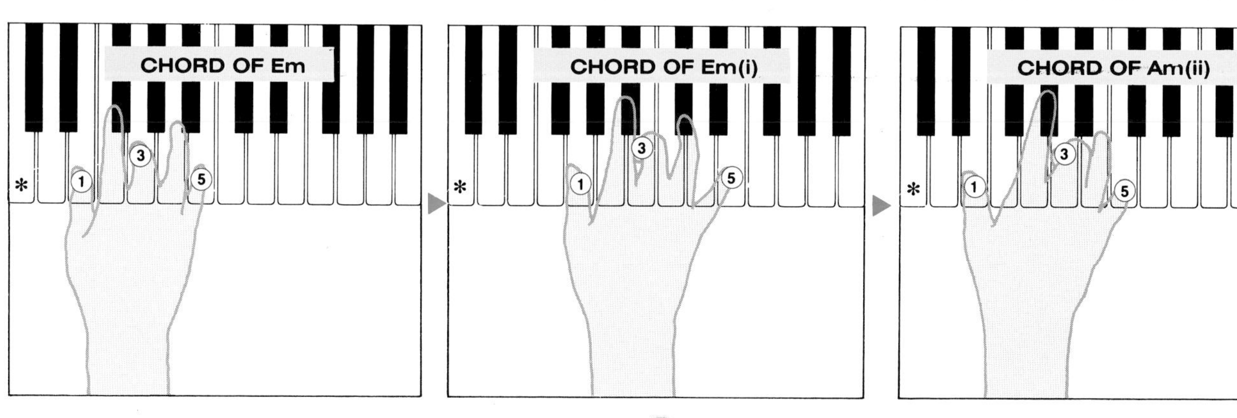

AN ELECTRIC piano is similar to an acoustic piano in that it has moving mechanical parts inside, but the sound of the hammer hitting the strings or reeds can be amplified.

In simple terms, the electric piano is to the acoustic what the electric guitar is to its acoustic counterpart. And just as the two types of guitar sound different, so do the two pianos. With one or two exceptions – notably the Yamaha CP70/80 'electric grands' – the electric piano cannot match the sound of an acoustic.

Not that electric pianos necessarily sound bad. Electrics such as the Fender Rhodes and the Wurlitzer sound as unique as an acoustic, though less versatile. Check out Stevie Wonder's 'Sunshine Of My Life' or Billy Joel's 'Just The Way You Are' to hear the Fender Rhodes at its best – and you'll hear a Wurlitzer on nine out of ten Supertramp songs.

Although not an electric 'piano' as such, another instrument along the same lines is Hohner's Clavinet. Based on a very old instrument called the clavichord, the funky sounding Clavinet was immortalised on Stevie Wonder's 'Superstition'.

Electric pianos do have problems.

Because of their mechanical parts, electric pianos tend to be heavy to transport. And like acoustic pianos, they can easily go out of tune.

In any case, most synthesisers feature a very convincing electric piano 'sound' – and faced with the choice of lugging a heavy instrument or pressing a button on your synth, which would you choose?

Stevie Wonder—early '70s style—at the Hohner Clavinet which he immortalised on 'Superstition'.

USING INVERSIONS

CHORD INVERSIONS OF G MAJOR, A MINOR AND E MINOR

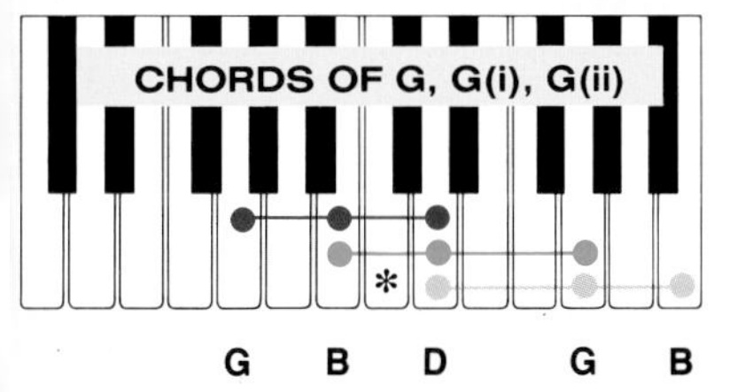

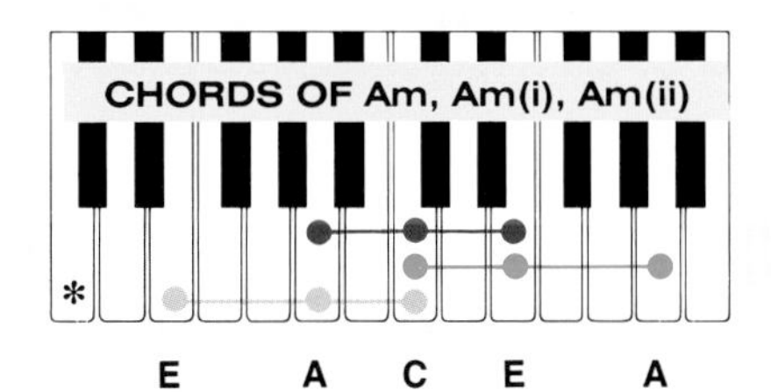

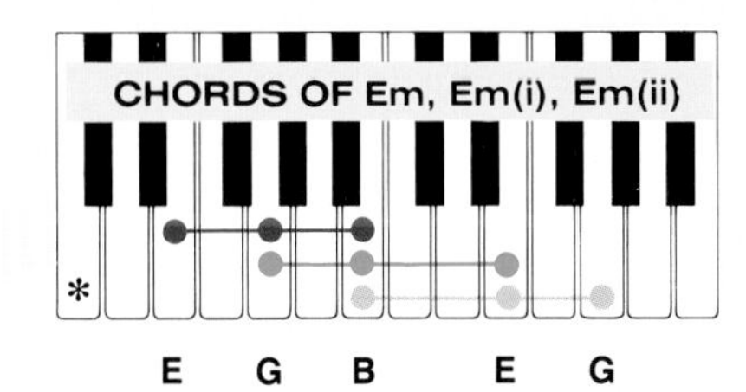

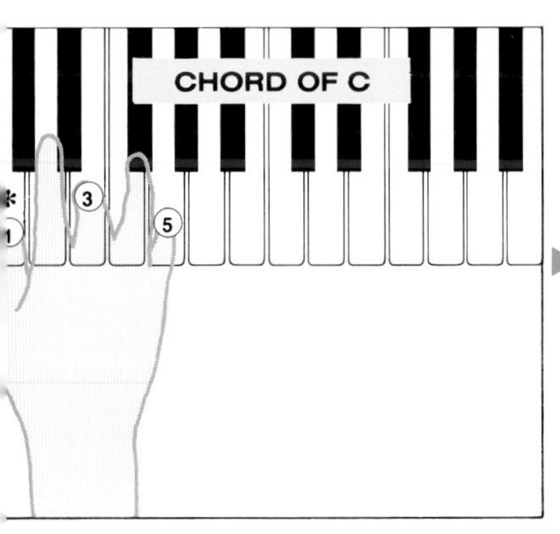

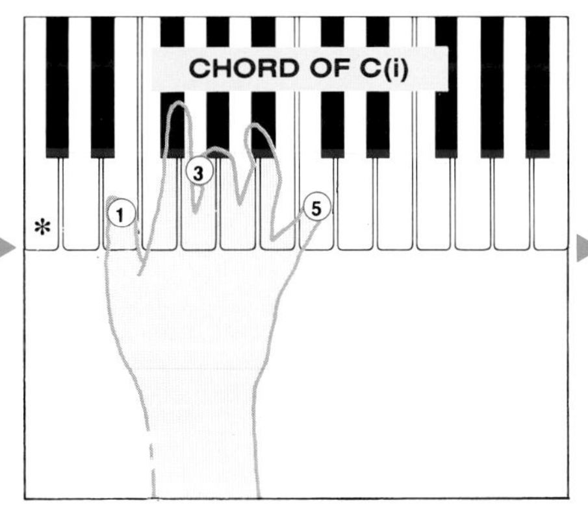

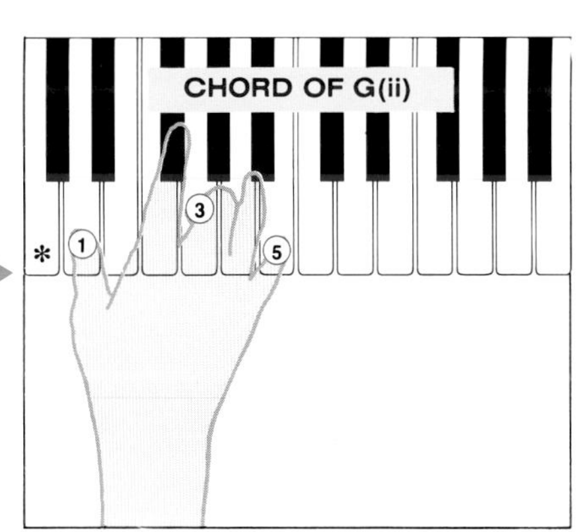

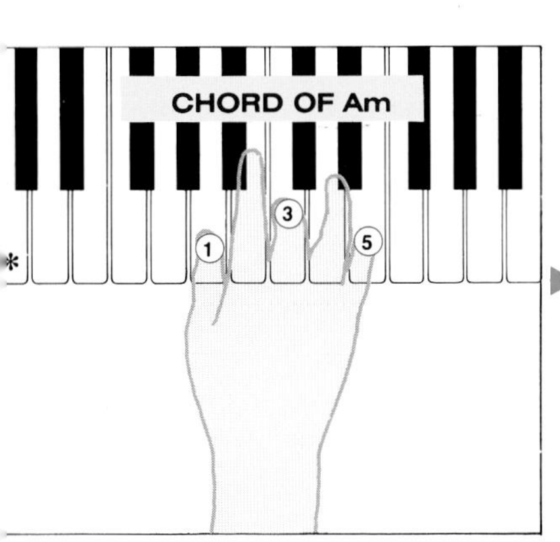

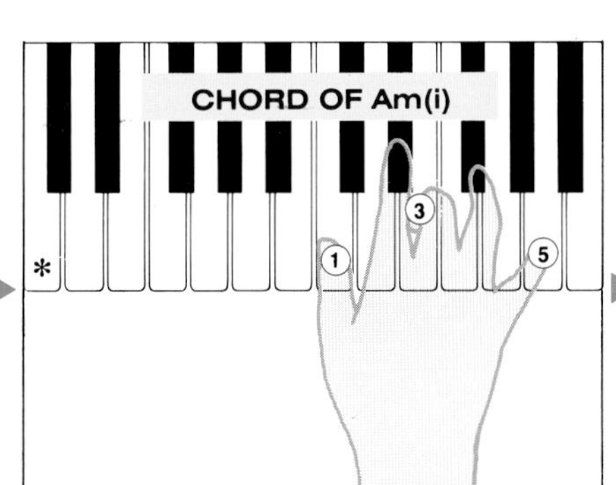

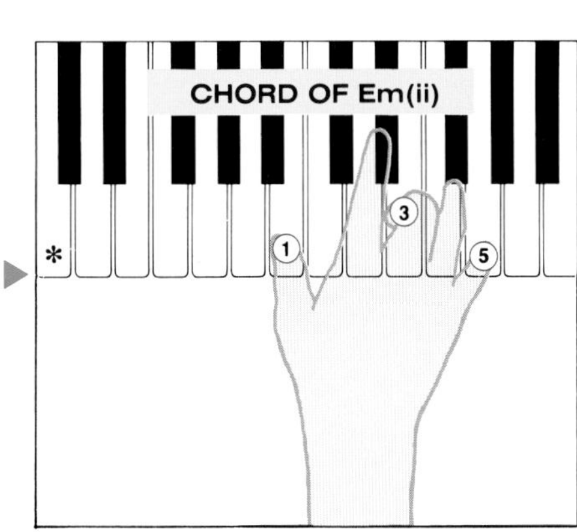

ELECTRONIC PIANO

AN ELECTRONIC piano has no moving mechanical parts, because the sound is originated electronically.

In the past electronic pianos were considered a poor second to the electric. As well as having a thin, clinical sound, they also lacked the dynamic response of an acoustic or electric piano. However, they were usually compact and stayed in tune, and so were much used.

Recent electronic pianos have good electric and acoustic piano sounds, and weighted keyboards for a firmer action.

Electronic pianos do tend to be quite expensive for the number of different sounds they produce – especially when many synths give you similar sounds plus much more – and you should think very carefully before getting one.

Michael McDonald's Fender Rhodes electric piano left its mark on many Doobie Brothers hits.

'TAKE MY BREATH AWAY'

TITLE	KEY	TEMPO	STARTING POINT
'TAKE MY BREATH AWAY' (VERSE AND CHORUS)	G MAJOR	SLOW	G(i) ABOVE *

	1	2	3	4
BAR 1	G(i)			
BAR 2	Bm			
BAR 3	Em(i)			
BAR 4	Bm(ii)			
BAR 5	Am(i)			
BAR 6	C			
BAR 7	D(i)			
BAR 8	D(ii)			
BAR 9	C(i)			
BAR 10	D(i)			

KEY TO COLOURS ■ A CHORD PLAYED □ A CHORD HELD

SOUND ADVICE

If you're playing this on a synthesiser or home keyboard, try using a strings type sound.

'OU'VE LEARNT the inversions of **C** ıajor, **A** minor, **G** major and **E** minor. Here re the inversions of **D** major and **Bm**.

As you know, each of these contains one ›lack note, **F#**. So as you change from one ıversion to the next, the finger which plays ıe black note has to change.

For each inversion, the fingering emains the same: thumb (1) on the lowest ote, middle finger (3) on the middle note, nd little finger (5) on the highest note.

You now have all the chords you need to ›lay the verse and chorus of Berlin's 'Take Ay Breath Away'—a song which uses ıversions in a very clever way. If you ompare the vocal melody to the chords ısed, you'll notice that the first note sung in ach bar matches the highest note in that ›articular chord. This gives the effect of the :hords 'ghosting' the vocal line.

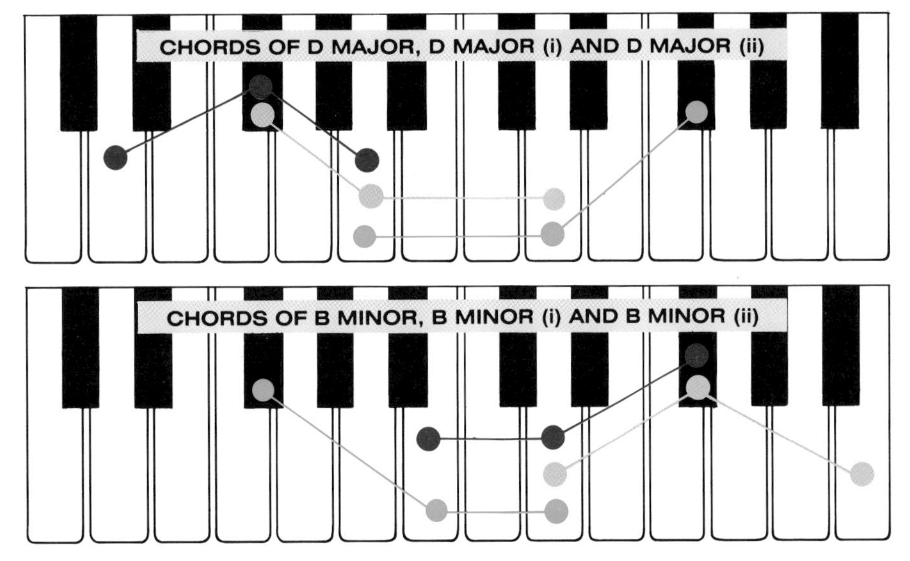

A SONG USING INVERSIONS

'OU'RE NOW ready to try a song that uses ›rimary triads in their basic form and in their ırst and second inversions.

The song we've chosen is 'Take My Breath Away' by Berlin—or at least the right-hand ›art. You'll be learning the very distinctive ›assline later, when we move onto left-hand ›laying, and after that we'll show you how to ›lay both right and left hand parts together.

And if you check out the words, shown here, 'ou can eventually sing along *and* play two-ıanded all at the same time!

SO HERE, for now, is the right-hand part of the verse and chorus. Berlin play the song in **A** major, but we've transposed it to the next major key down, **G** major, to make things easier.

As you can see, it really is quite simple. Each chord is exactly the same length—one bar—and each bar is four beats. And all the chord shapes used are ones you've already learnt: **C** major, **C** major **(i)**, **A** minor **(i)**, **G** major **(i)**, **E** minor **(i)**, **D** major **(i)**, **D** major **(ii)**, **B** minor and **B** minor **(ii)**. Refresh your memory by playing all these chords again before starting the song.

The running order shows you in which order to play the bars. We've arranged it so that the end flows back into the beginning, so you can keep going round and round until you've mastered it.

If you listen to the record, you'll hear that the chords are played very smoothly. You too should try to make the changes from one chord to the next as smooth as possible: give it a little of that *Top Gun* polish.

LYRICS, VOCAL MELODY AND RUNNING ORDER

VERSE 1

BAR 1 G G G G G D Watch-ing ev-ery mo-tion	BAR 2 F# F# F# F# F# D in my fool-ish lov-er's	BAR 3 E game;	BAR 4
BAR 1 G G G G G D On this end-less o-cean	BAR 2 F# F# F# F# F# D fi-n'lly lo-vers know no	BAR 3 E shame.	BAR 4
BAR 5 A A A A A E Turn-ing and re-turn-ing	BAR 6 G G G E G A to some sec-ret place in-	BAR 7 F# side;	BAR 8
BAR 1 G G G G G D Watch-ing in slow mo-tion	BAR 2 F# F# F# F# F# D as you turn a-round and	BAR 9 E say,	BAR 10 D E G A "Take my breath a-
BAR 1 G way."	BAR 2	BAR 9	BAR 10

VERSE 2

Watching, I keep waiting, still anticipating love,
Never hesitating to become the fated ones.
Turning and returning to some secret place to hide;
Watching in slow motion as you turn my way and say,
"Take my breath away."

VERSE 3

Watching every motion in this foolish lover's game;
Haunted by the notion somewhere's there's a love in flames.
Turning and returning to some secret place inside;
Watching in slow motion as you turn to me and say,
"Take my breath away."

'Take My Breath Away' was the key song in the hit movie *Top Gun*, which shot actor Tom Cruise (above) to stardom.

The song was written by veteran German disco music producer Giorgio Moroder with Tom Whitlock. Interestingly, it was Moroder who nurtured the talents of fellow German Harold Faltermeyer—the composer of 'Axel F'.

FULL PRIMARY CHORDS

A SLIGHT VARIATION of the primary triad is the full primary chord. It differs from the primary triad in that it has four notes instead of three.

These four notes are the three that make up the primary triad, plus the lowest note of the primary triad repeated one octave above.

For example, the basic primary triad **C** major has the notes **C, E, G**. So the basic full primary chord has **C, E, G** and **C**. The second **C** is one octave above the original **C**.

WE'VE MENTIONED that this is the *basic* full primary chord. Which means that, like primary triads, full primary chords can be played in first and second inversions.

So the first inversion of the full primary **C** major chord has the notes **E, G, C** and **E**. And the second inversion has the notes **G, C, E** and **G**.

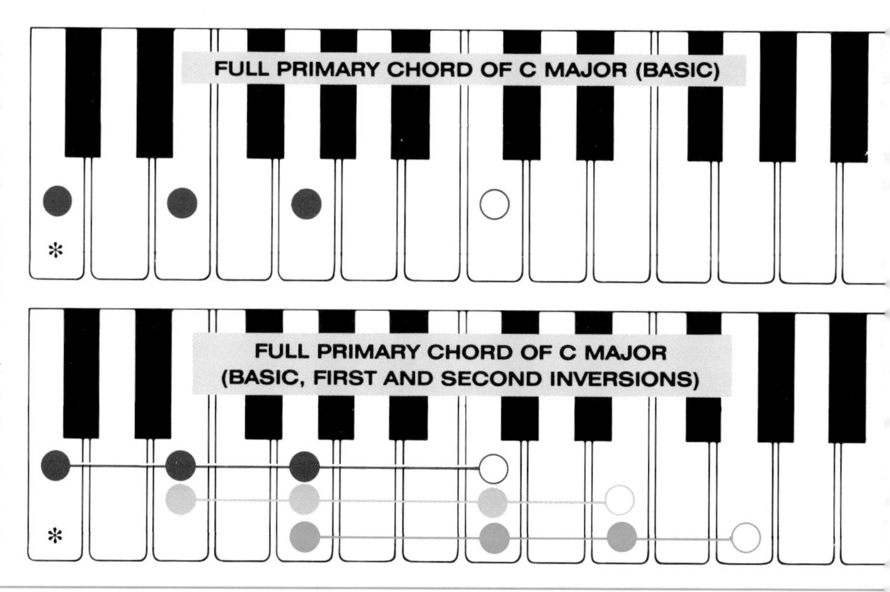

FULL PRIMARY CHORDS

YOU WILL find that full primary chords stretch your hands as you try to get your little finger across to the top note. If you've got small hands you may find them uncomfortable at first, but all you can do is persevere. Flexible hands are a crucial part of keyboard playing, so this will do them good.

Here's how we suggest you should finger a full primary chord:

Thumb (1) on the lowest note.

Second and third fingers (2 and 3) on the two middle notes.

Little finger (5) on the highest note.

IF THIS doesn't feel comfortable—and with some people's hands, on certain chords it will seem impossible—try this:

Thumb (1) on the lowest note.

Little finger (5) on the highest note.

Whatever feels right in between.

THE IMPORTANT thing is to get your thumb and little finger in the right place, especially when playing a series of chords, so that you shift smoothly from one chord to another.

You may find that in order to reach the top note with your little finger, you have to straighten it rather than arch it. Fine.

Enjoy the feeling of your hand spanning a ful octave. You'll really start to feel you're in control.

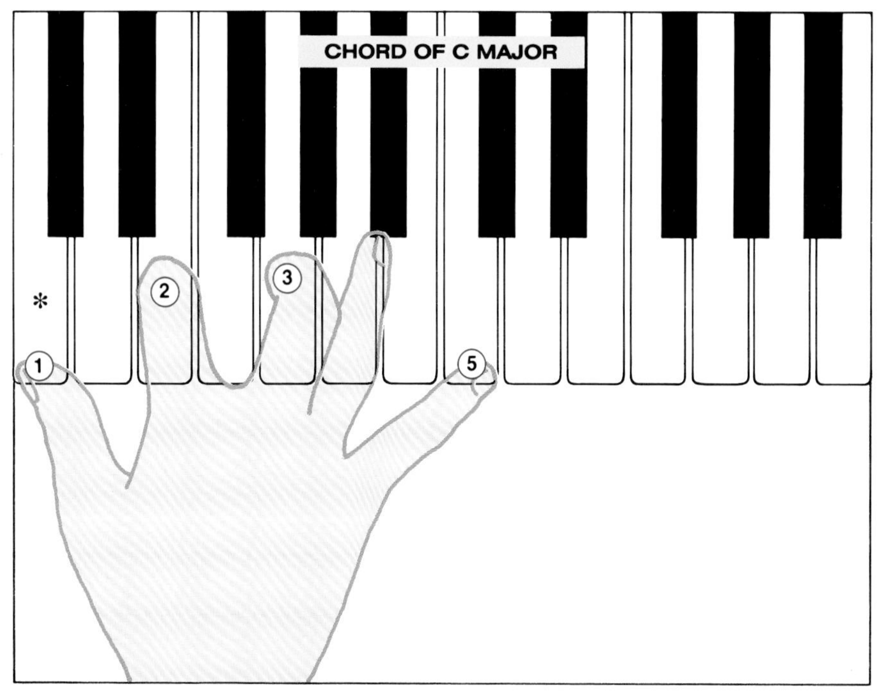

The six chords on these pages all work in the key of C major. Like their primary triads, all six full primary chords use white notes only.

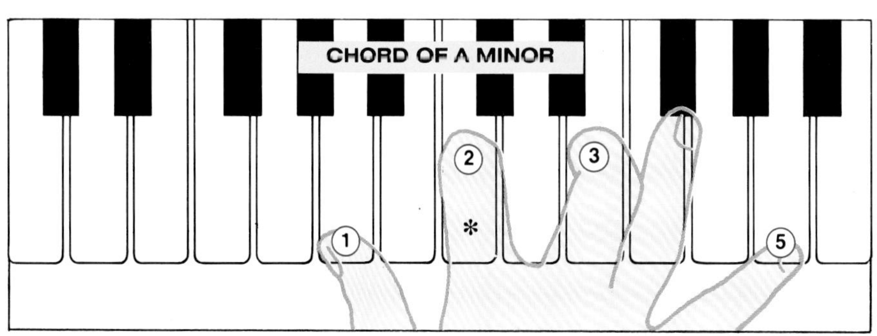

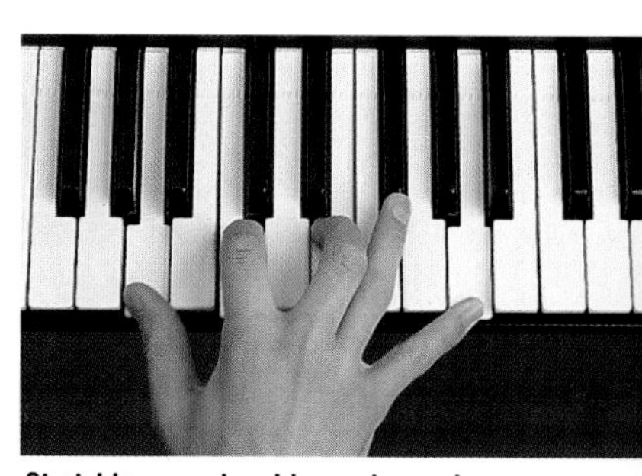

Stretching your hand is good exercise

ENERALLY, A FULL primary chord can
e used wherever a primary triad is used:
e only difference is the repeated note.
Just because there are four notes in a full
imary, it isn't necessarily a *better* chord.
s simply another option.
The overall sound of a full primary chord
fuller, so these chords may be more
ited to louder passages of music.
This shouldn't be taken as a hard and fast
le, however—it's really a question of
hat you prefer, and what the song needs.
ou can often combine both primary triads
d full primary chords in one section of
usic for a subtle variation.

S THEY are essentially the same chord,
e primary triad and full primary chord go
y the same name—**C** major, **A** minor or
hatever it may be.

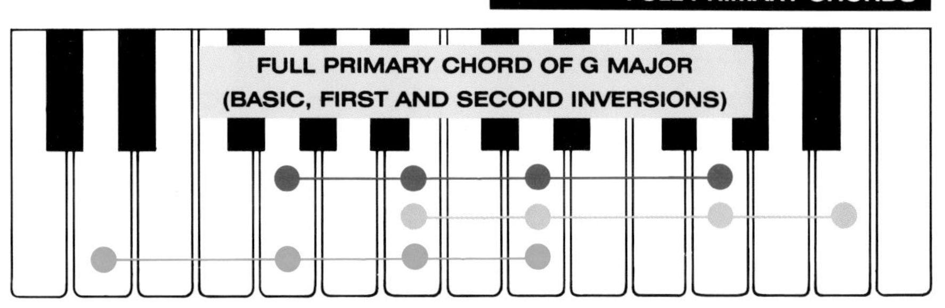

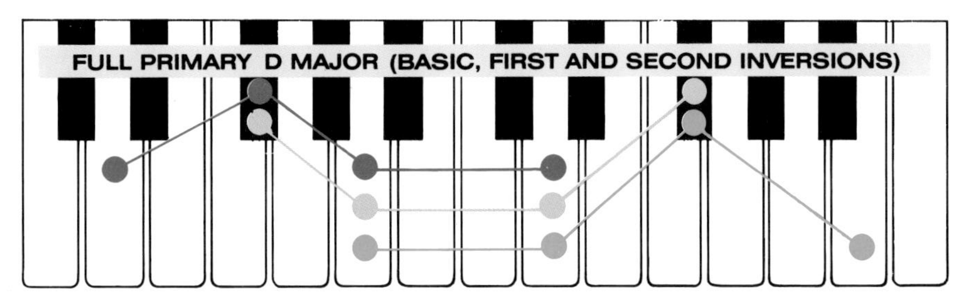

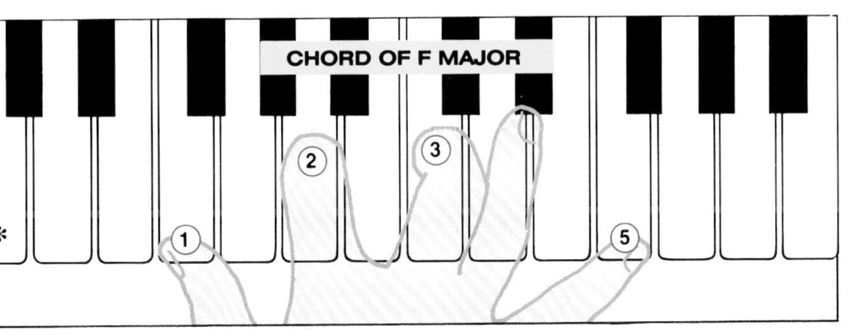

These chords sound good in various progressions.

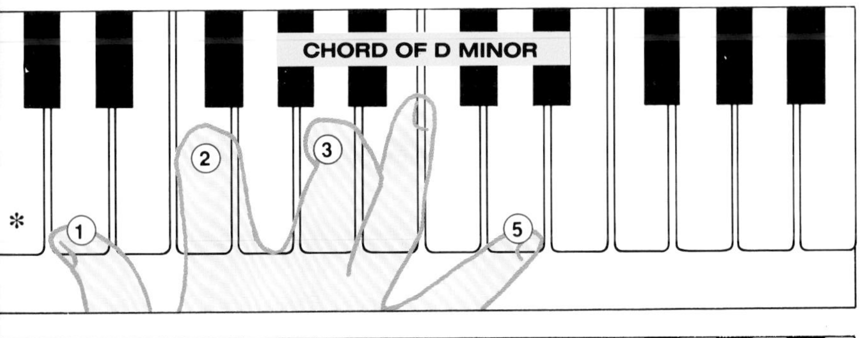

Try C then Am, F, G.

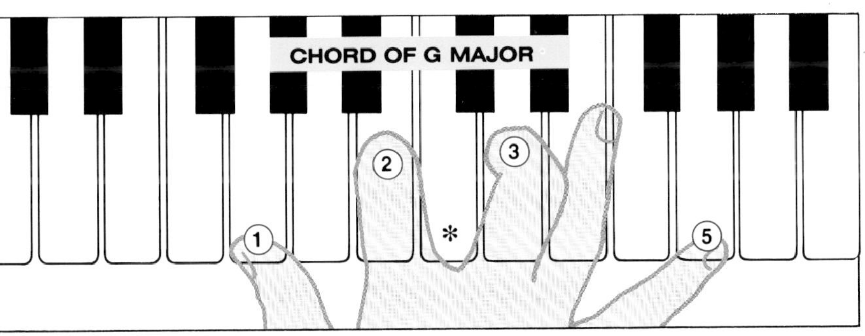

Try Am then C, Dm, Em.

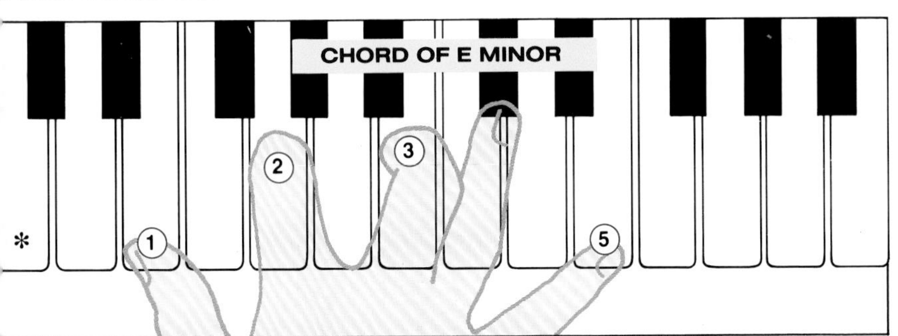

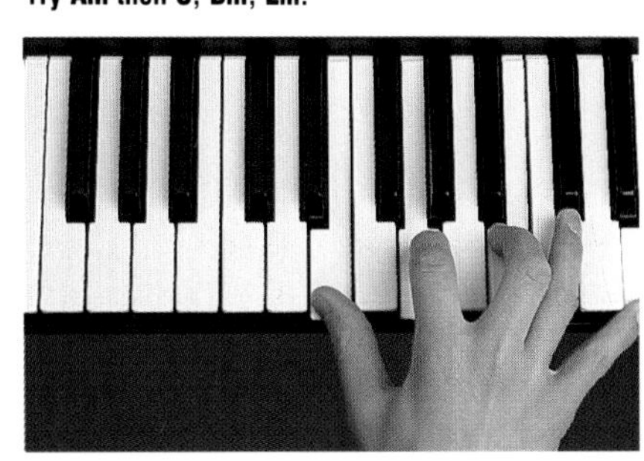
Try Am to Em in different rhythms.

ARPEGGIOS

IF YOU play the four notes of a full primary chord separately, one after the other—upwards and downwards in fairly quick succession—you'll be playing what's known as an 'arpeggio'.

In the key of **C**, for example, you should play **C** then move up to **E**, then **G**, then top **C** – and then back down to play **G**, **E** and **C** once more.

Arpeggios, like scales, are useful not only as exercises but as techniques which can be integrated into your playing style. Arpeggio and scale techniques can be used to fill the spaces between chords, or even as the basis for a solo. We'll be looking into this in greater detail later.

For the moment, try playing the full primary chords shown here as arpeggios. They're all based on scales you've already learnt.

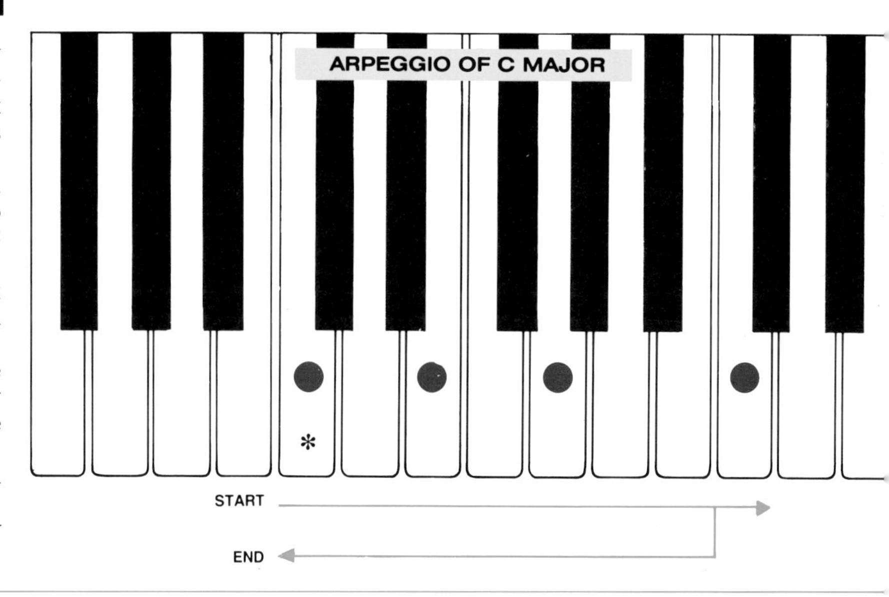

FULL PRIMARY CHORDS

NONE OF the full primary chords you've learnt so far contained black notes. Now they come into play.

This shouldn't cause too much of a problem, particularly as you're already familiar with the primary triads for all the chords shown here.

Try to stick to whatever fingering method you decided to use for the 'white note' full primary chords on the previous page.

Remember when playing the black notes to keep your finger dead centre on the key.

CHORD PROGRESSION USING FULL PRIMARY CHORDS

THE FULL primary chords on these pages are all those that work in **A** major and **F#** minor. Once you've mastered them individually, try this simple progression.

A MAJOR up to C# MINOR up to F# MINOR down to E MAJOR down to D MAJOR down to B MINOR down to A MAJOR and repeat A MAJOR

ONCE YOU feel happy with that, try playing each chord as an arpeggio.

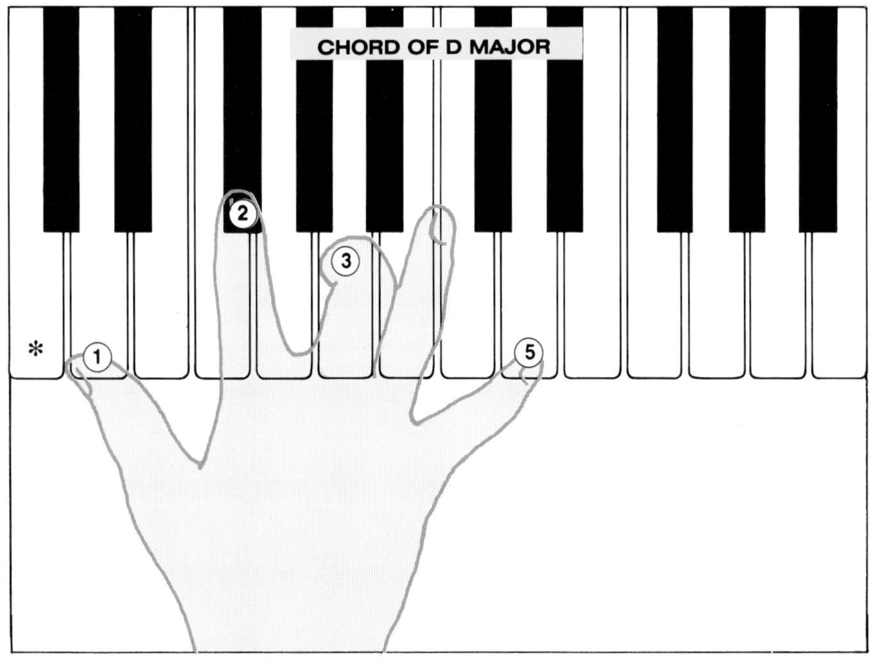

These are the six primary chords which work in the key of A major. Try playing them in different sequences.

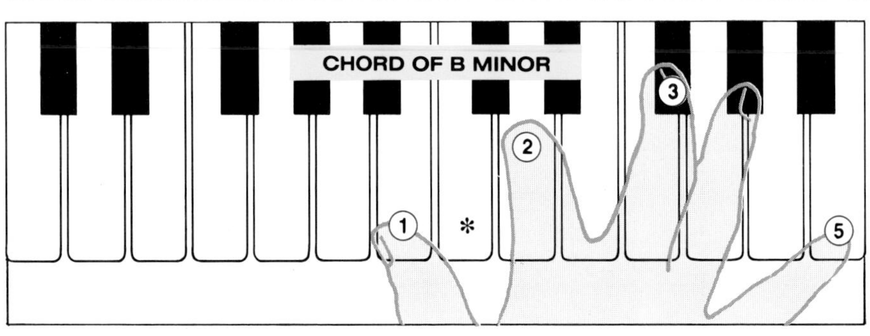

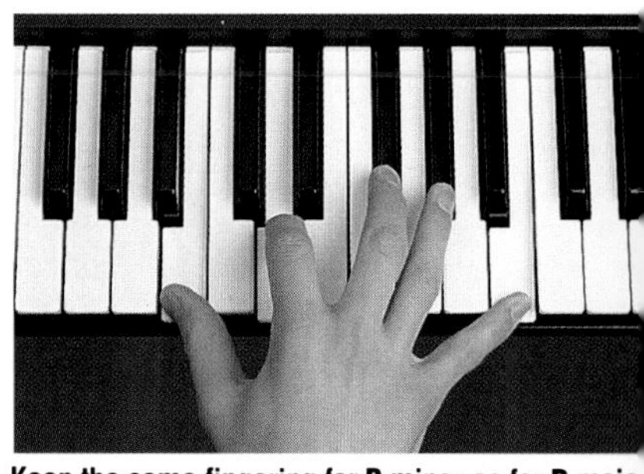

Keep the same fingering for B minor as for D major

PLAYING AN ARPEGGIO

/HEN PLAYING an arpeggio, try to nagine you're playing a scale, but missing e notes between the arpeggio notes. emember these points:

Release each key as you play the next ote in the arpeggio.

Play the top note only once so there is no lowing down' effect.

Give each note an equal length.

Play the whole arpeggio in one flowing otion, from bottom to top and back to the ot note again.

Every note except the top one is played vice: once on the way up, once on the ay down.

/HEN YOU'VE learnt this arpeggio of **C** ajor, try playing all the full primary ords in this section as arpeggios.

THE STORY SO FAR

LET'S RECAP on what we now have under our belts.

You should now be able to play 12 full primary chords. These are the same 12 chords which you already know in their primary triad form: **C**, **Am**, **F**, **Dm**, **G**, **Em**, **D**, **Bm**, **A**, **F#m**, **E** and **C#m**.

You now have enough full primary chords to operate in eight different keys: **C** major, **A** minor, **G** major, **E** minor, **D** major, **B** minor, **A** major and **F#** minor.

You've learnt the scales for all those keys, plus the 'flat' scales of **F** major, **D** minor, **B♭** major and **G** minor. And you know the primary triads used in those keys.

ON TOP of that, you know how to work out the scales in any key, major or minor.

You know how to work out any major or minor primary triad chord.

You know how to work out any major or minor full primary chord.

You know how to work out the basic, first and second inversions of any primary chord.

You know how to work out the chords that 'work' in any major or minor key.

You know how to transpose keys.

You know how to change keys.

You can play arpeggios.

IN SHORT, you're pretty much able to take care of yourself when it comes to using your right hand.

You're now ready for something completely different: how to play with your left hand.

FULL PRIMARY CHORDS

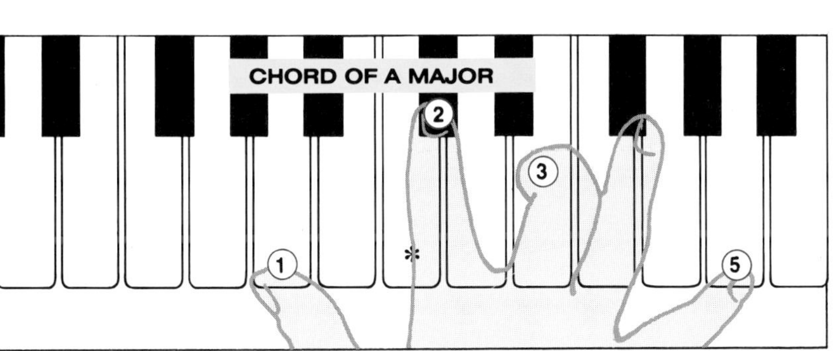

A full primary with one black note is tricky.

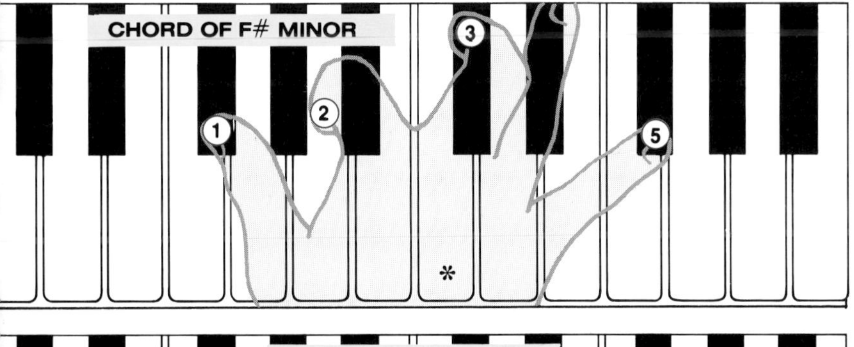

But two black notes is even trickier!

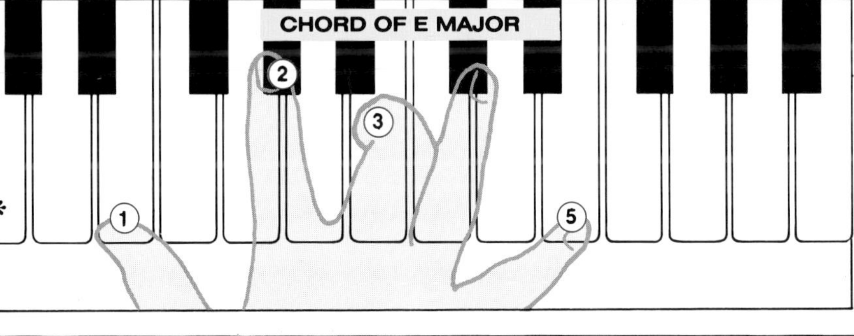

E major is the rock guitarist's favourite chord.

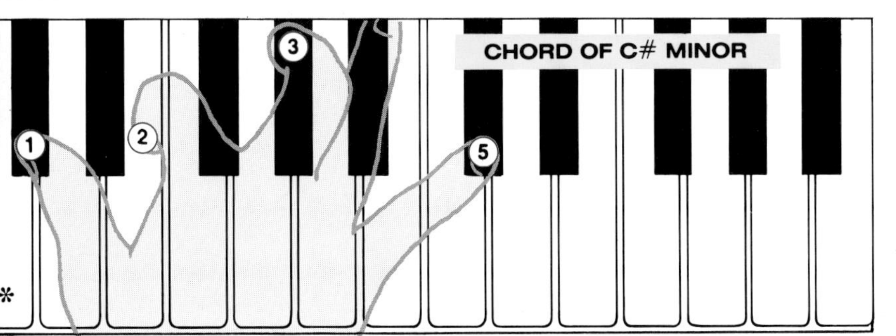

Three black notes—our toughest chord to date.

THE LEFT HAND

UP TO now everything you've learnt has involved your right hand only. In fact the left is almost as important, and it's time we got it working.

In general, there are two ways to play a keyboard using both hands:

1 The right hand plays chords in the middle to upper part of the keyboard, while the left hand plays a bassline in the lower part.

2 The left hand plays chords, usually in the middle of the keyboard, while the right hand plays either a lead 'solo' line or chords, sometimes on another keyboard.

Obviously, you may use both these techniques in the same song.

LET'S LOOK first at basslines. Basslines are important when playing on your own. They fill out the sound and give it movement.

In a band, however, it's not always a good idea to play basslines—that's the role of the bass guitar, and two basslines often clash.

Try to arrange songs so that you get the best of both instruments.

For instance you may want to double up on the bass guitar part to emphasize it—this can be very effective, but tricky. Or you may find that a synthesiser bassline sounds better than a bass guitar in a certain song or part of a song.

SO IT'S useful to be able to play basslines, if only for practice. To get your left hand used to playing, we'll try some scales first—the technique for playing basslines is quite similar to playing a scale.

Don't forget how we're numbering the left hand—in blue.

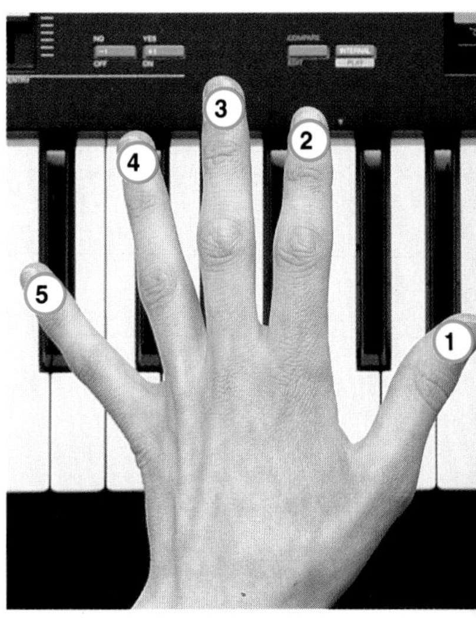

The left hand numbering system.

LEFT HAND SCALES

ALL THE rules about playing a scale with your right hand also apply to your left. Here's a reminder:

Release one note as you play the next.
Give each note equal weight and length.
Play the top note only once.
Play the scale in one continuous motion.
When playing a black key, make sure your finger is dead centre, in case it slips off.

NOTE THAT the starting notes of all our left hand scales are one octave below the starting notes of the corresponding right hand scales.

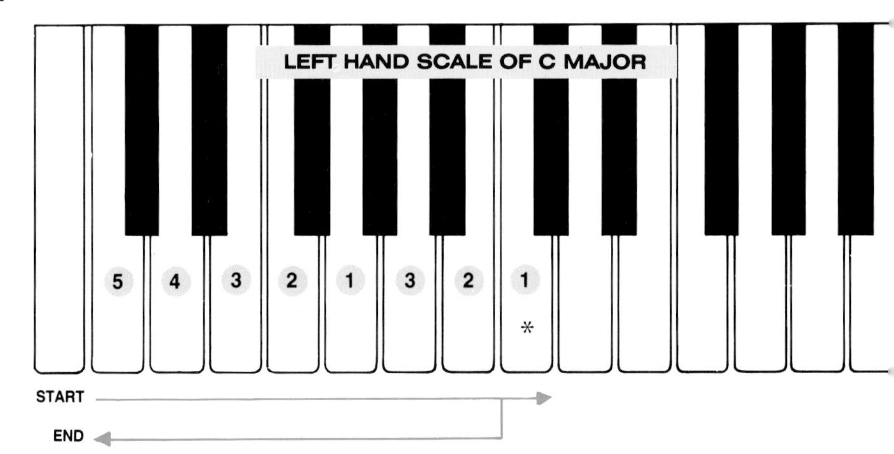

Note how the middle finger (3) crosses over the thumb (1) when moving from G to A on the way up the scale.

Note how the thumb (1) passes under the third finger (3) when moving from A to G on the way back down.

HE ORGAN has been with us for many ears in one form or another. Originally n instrument for cathedrals and concert alls, the organ began life as a large ructure of pipes, woodwork and mechanical parts.

It was only when portable electronic rgans came along in the late '50s that the rgan found its way onto pop records – nd a thin, artificial sound it was too, ompared to the real thing. Even so, one r two organs of this period had an ndearing and distinctive sound, for stance the Vox Continental, immortalised on the 1962 hit 'Telstar' by The ornadoes.

Perhaps the classic rock organ sound – nd the one most imitated on modern ynthesisers – was the Hammond organ, commonly used in the late '60s and early '70s by all types of rock band.

Keith Emerson of ELP finds a new way to play his Hammond organ: tipping it off the stage.

There are more recent organ-only instruments available. The best of the bunch are the Korg CX3 and BX3 which, although they rely more on circuit boards than mechanical parts, produce a very convincing Hammond-type sound.

These, however, are the exceptions. In general synthesisers have killed off the organ as an instrument in its own right. You might just as well buy a polyphonic synthesiser with a good organ sound – and much more besides. It'll be more reliable, more compact, lighter to carry and lighter on the pocket.

Leave the real Hammonds to those who can afford roadies and articulated trucks to carry them around!

LEFT HAND SCALE OF A MINOR

5 4 3 2 1 3 2 1 *

START

END

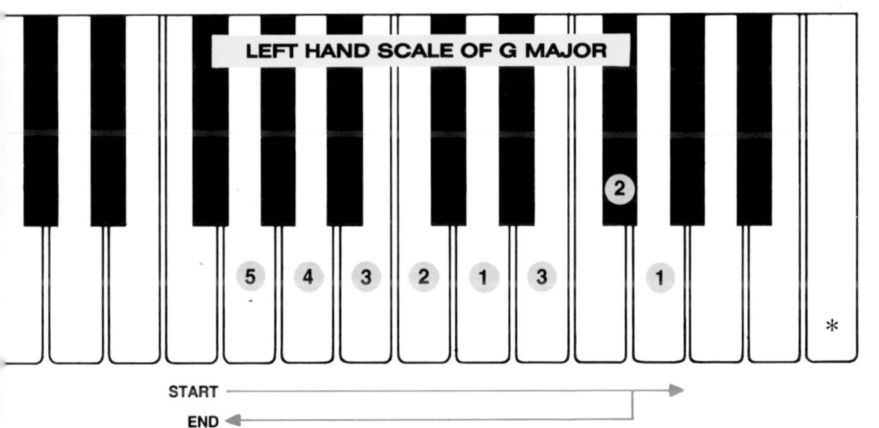

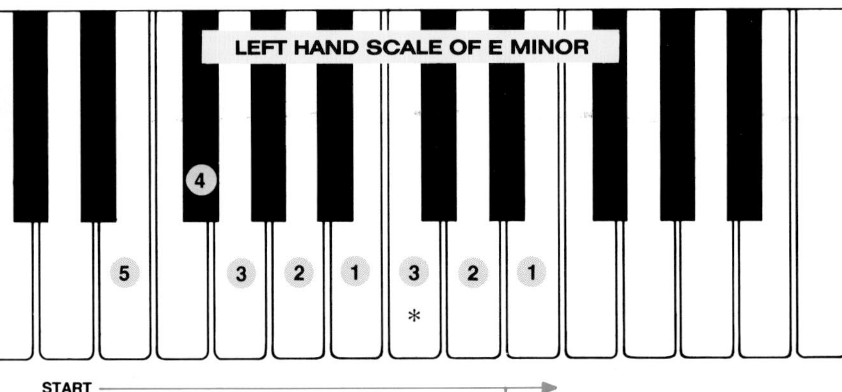

LEFT HAND SCALES

AS WITH your right hand, the more you practise with your left the better it will get.

If you are left-handed, you may find it easier, but if you're right-handed the chances are that your left hand will never acquire equal fluidity with your right. Don't worry too much, because the left hand tends to play set patterns, whereas the right often has a freer role.

Whatever you do, *don't* try to avoid using your left hand. It's true that plenty of keyboard players have managed to get away with being essentially one-handed, especially in recent years with so many programmable keyboards available. You can, too. But in the long run you'll only be selling yourself short.

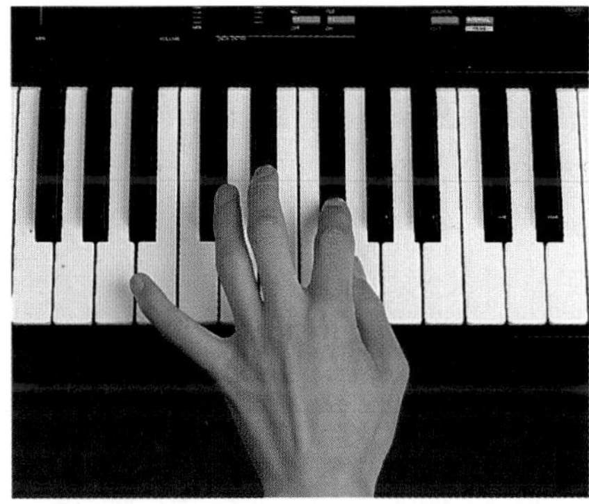

The second finger (2) playing the black note F# in the scale of G major.

The fourth finger (4) playing the black note F# in the scale of E minor. Take care to play black notes dead centre – and keep working on it.

DURING THE '70s electronic organs became increasingly home-orientated.

With the help of built-in gadgets like drum machines and automatic bass and chord accompaniment, absolute beginners could sound like a whole band.

What's more, since the sound was created electronically, why stop at an organ sound? In time a range of other sounds such as piano, flute and violin became available, and home organs became known simply as 'home keyboards'.

Rock musicians in general steered clear. Yet these keyboards are directly responsible for much that's happening in music technology today.

Take drum machines for example. Although quite basic at first, in time they became a separate unit from the keyboard, and they are used on 90 pe cent of pop records today.

And take the pre-set sounds. Until fair recently, all the sounds on a synth woul be created by the player. Now they don need to bother because almost eve new synthesiser has dozens of pre-s sounds stored in its memory.

Steve Naive of Elvis Costello's Attractions with Vox Continental organ on a Yamaha electric grand.

IT WAS in the late '70s that hom keyboards became popular on a wid scale. After the discordant thrash of pun guitar groups, a new kind of pop musi began to appear in Britain.

Inspired by the German band Kraftwer UK groups such as Depeche Mode turne their backs on the guitar in favour of a exciting sound produced entirely by elec tronic keyboards.

LEFT HAND BASSLINES

NOW THAT you've tried a few scales with your left hand, it's time to put it in a working context.

As we've said, one of the main uses for your left hand is playing basslines. Basslines can be as easy or as complicated as you want to make them. Many of the best and most common basslines are astonishingly simple, because the role of a bassline is very often to supply a basic rhythmic pulse and an underlying melodic guide. One note is often enough.

The key to these ultra-simple basslines is the rhythm. Here are three examples of rhythmic basslines which you may find useful.

THIS IS the first time you will have encountered the left hand version of our music grid. The only thing that's changed is the colour—for the right hand it was red, for the left hand it's blue.

Watch out for the fingering. Remind yourself of the left hand finger numbers by checking the picture on the previous page.

The starting point in each case is the **C** below middle **C**. As for tempo, it's probably best to try each bassline slowly at first, speeding up as you get used to it.

Our second bassline requires you to play two C notes one octave apart. It's quite a stretch. These two pictures show how it's done.

THE FIRST bassline style (below) is a very straightforward and regular rhythmic pattern using just one repeated note per bar (incidentally, in each of these examples there are four beats to the bar). The note in this case is C. In a song you would probably change bass notes as you changed chor playing the root note in each case. This solid styl is good for rocky songs such as Van Halen's 'Jump but it's also used as a kind of simple pulsebeat o slower songs such as U2's 'With Or Without You'.

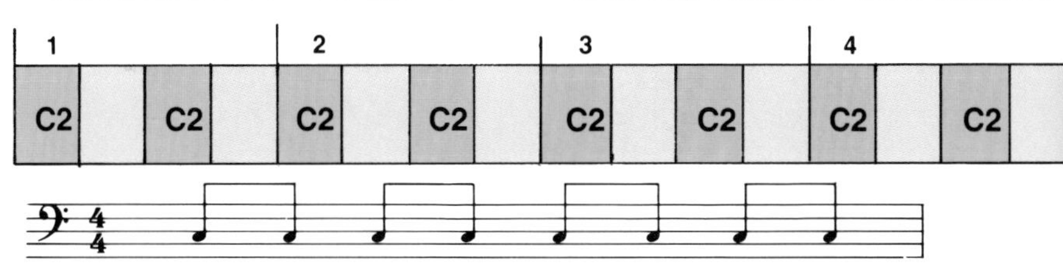

THE BASSLINE below is similar in rhythm to the first. The C notes however are now played in octaves one after the other: low C, high C, low C, high C, etc. This style has been used in many disc songs such as 'Blue Monday' by New Order, and Bronski Beat's 'Smalltown Boy'.

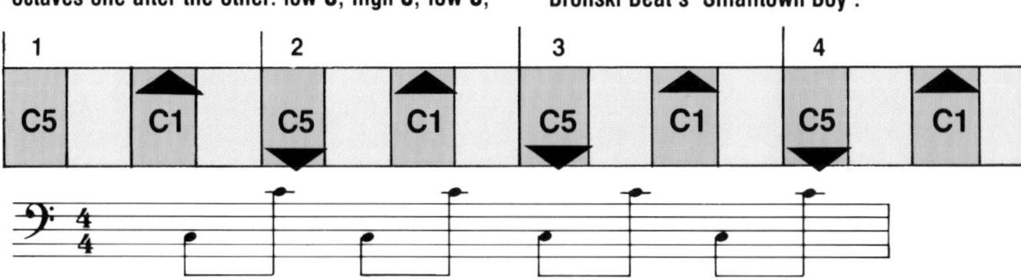

THIS THIRD bassline (below) follows a different rhythmic pattern to the other two. When played continuously on one note like this, it has a sort of dum-d-dum-d-dum-d-dum feel which is useful for all sorts of songs. You can hear this style in 'Everybody Wants To Rule The World' by Tears fo Fears, 'Fanfare For The Common Man' by ELP an 'Waterfront' by Simple Minds, among many other

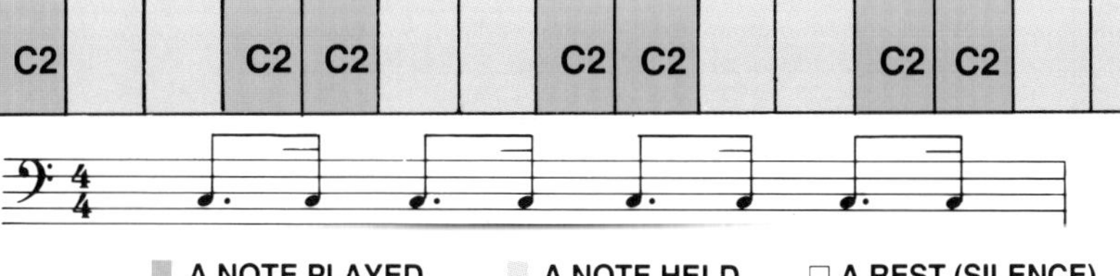

A NOTE PLAYED A NOTE HELD □ A REST (SILENCE)

ONCE YOU'VE played these three styles using just one repeated note per bar, try bringing different notes into play. Here are some sequences which can be applied to all three styles:

C1 down to **A3** down to **F5** up to **G4**.
C1 down to **G4** up to **A3** down to **F5**.
C5 up to **D4** up to **F2** up to **G1**.

Each note should be played continuously fo one bar, then move on to the next. The suggested fingering applies to the first and thi bassline styles—but in the 'octaves' bassline, you should always use your little finger and thumb.

In each case, when you get to the end of th sequence, simply start all over again.

The only problem in those early synth ays was the price – but help was at and. A Japanese company called Casio previously famous for its watches and alculators – started making keyboards. ne instruments they produced were neap, self-contained, portable, packed ith features, and above all fun to use – all anks to the silicon chip.

They soon became very popular, and ey still are. Other keyboard companies ich as Yamaha quickly followed suit.

This newer breed of home keyboards ave basically the same features as the d types, such as pre-set drums, ass, chords, and arpeggios (sometimes nown as an arpeggiator), a number of e-set sounds (mostly emulating known struments) and a built-in speaker.

Brian Eno—an early user of synthesisers with Roxy Music and, later, of Casio home keyboards.

The main advantage – apart from the price – is that they are portable and can usually be battery-powered.

Home keyboards are great instruments to learn on, but you'll have to turn those gadgets off (except the rhythm machine, which might be useful) if you want to learn to play properly.

The only problem is that the keys tend to be small. Also, some machines with an auto-chord feature have monophonic keyboards. Most however are polyphonic – choose one if you can.

If your home keyboard has an amplifier socket, you can even use it in a band—at least for a while. But in the long run, if you take keyboard playing seriously, you will almost certainly have to upgrade, probably to a polyphonic synthesiser.

LEFT HAND BASSLINES

OW TO try something a bit more interesting. s promised, here is the distinctive bassline of ake My Breath Away' by Berlin—the chords which you learned on page 42.

If you managed the three basslines opposite, this shouldn't prove too difficult. Use the grid exactly as before. Note that the music starts on the third beat of the first bar.

What you have here is the 'basic' bassline from the introduction—it doesn't take you right through the song. But it's enough to give the feel, and it makes sense played over and over.

TITLE	KEY	TEMPO	STARTING POINT
'TAKE MY BREATH AWAY' (INTRO BASSLINE)	G MAJOR	SLOW	D BELOW *

	1				2				3				4			
BAR 1									D 5		▲ E 4		▲ G 2		▲ A 1	
BAR 2	G 2 ▼														D 5 ▼	
BAR 3	▲ F# 3														B 5 ▼	
BAR 4	▲ E 4														D 5 ▼	
BAR 5	▲ F# 3								D 5 ▼		▲ E 4		▲ G 2		▲ A 1	

MUSICAL NOTATION FOR 'TAKE MY BREATH AWAY' (INTRO BASSLINE)

BASSLINES WITH CHORDS

WE MENTIONED earlier that there are two main ways of playing with two hands. One is to play chords with your right and a bassline with your left.

Below we show you the chords and bass notes for Berlin's 'Take My Breath Away'. After you've conquered that, however, you may want to try out ideas of your own. Perhaps you've come up with a chord sequence you really like, but you need a bassline to go with it. Here are some guidelines for how to work one out.

The main notes in your bassline are those played on the same beat as a chord. As a rule, none of these main notes should be unrelated to the key of the song. So if the song is in **C** major, you can safely play **C**, **D**, **E**, **F**, **G**, **A** or **B** as main notes in your bassline, because they are the notes in the scale of **C** major.

You can however sometimes use unrelated notes to 'connect' these main notes together. Let's take an example in **C** major. The chords are **C** major to **A** minor to **F** major to **G** major. The bass notes might be **C** (**C** major) to **B** to **A** (**A** minor) to **G** to **F** (**F** major) to **F#** to **G** (**G** major). The unrelated note **F#** connects the **F** and **G** notes.

When using unrelated notes in any situation, it's important not to dwell on them too long, or your music may become discordant.

YOU'LL notice in our example that there is a **C** note under a **C** chord, an **A** note under an **A** minor chord, and so on. This doubling up of the root note is a simple but effective way of plotting a bassline.

Just as the root note of a primary chord can be used as a bass note, so too can the other notes from the chord—namely the third or fifth.

When accompanied by a bass note taken from the chord, the inherent sound of the chord doesn't change, because that note is already present at a higher pitch. However, when you have a bass note that isn't present in the chord itself, the sound of the chord can change dramatically.

Technically, in fact, by adding a new note you are creating a new chord, and many musicians would argue that you should give it a new name. Unfortunately 'chords' like this can have confusingly complicated names.

In our opinion, it's clearer to say you're playing a **G** major chord over a **D** bass than a **D** major sixth suspended fourth chord—which is what some musicians would call it!

'TAKE MY BREATH AWAY'

THE MOMENT of truth has arrived—the first time you play your keyboard with both hands at once.

Our aim here is to play chords with the right hand, and an accompanying bassline with the left. This isn't as difficult as it may seem, especially when playing something as straightforward as 'Take My Breath Away'.

Before starting, remind yourself how to play the chords on their own (red) and then the bassline (blue).

Regarding the bassline, you'll notice that the second part of the grid (opposite) includes the second half of the verse and chorus, which you haven't learnt separately yet—so take time to do so before trying the song with both hands.

Once you've figured it out, and you get to the end of Bar 12, simply start back at Bar 2 again. You'll find the lyrics on page 43.

THE IMPORTANT thing to remember about playing with two hands is synchronisation: it's more important than ever to get the correct notes and chords on the correct beat.

TITLE	KEY	TEMPO	STARTING POINT
'TAKE MY BREATH AWAY' (VERSE AND CHORUS)	G MAJOR	SLOW	G(i) ABOVE * (RIGHT) D BELOW * (LEFT)

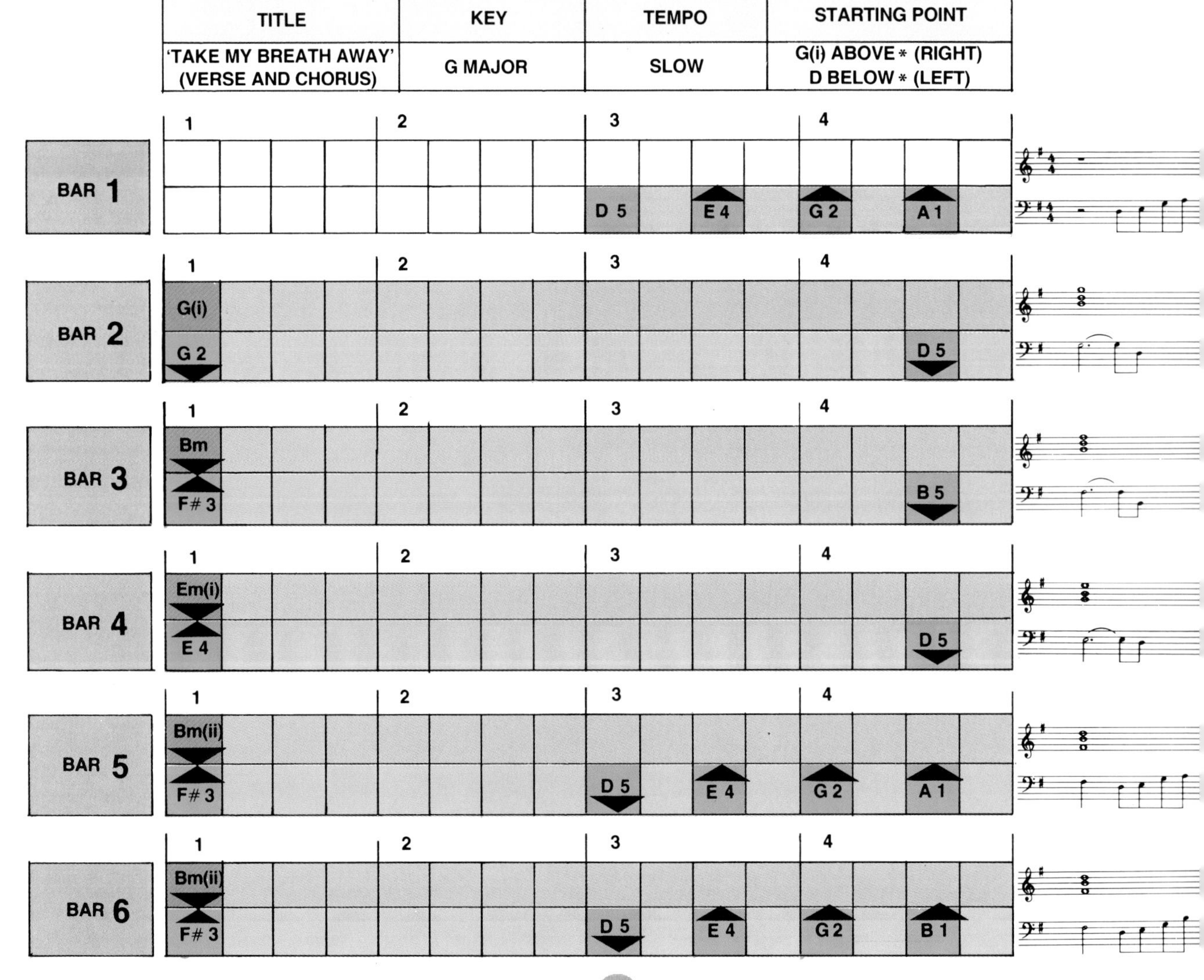

)BVIOUSLY, CERTAIN bass notes sound ›etter with certain chords. Here are a ›ouple of examples which sound good in ›e key of **C** major:

An **F** major chord over a **G** bass note (great when followed by a **G** major chord over a **G** bass).

A **C** major chord over an **A** bass note.

How you fill the gaps between your main bass notes is up to you. We've seen how they can be connected by other related or unrelated notes—that's one way. Another way might be to repeat the same single note, as in the basslines on page 50.

You may wish to change bass notes when the chord changes, but this is not always necessary or desirable. You could have the same bass note repeated in a set rhythmic pattern whilst changing the chords above it—this technique is used by Van Halen throughout the intro and verses of 'Jump'.

If the right hand chords are sustained for some time, you can try a more adventurous bassline—indeed, in 'Take My Breath Away' the left hand is more active than the right. On the other hand, a busy bassline might destroy a simple, subtle chord sequence—it all depends on the effect you're aiming to produce.

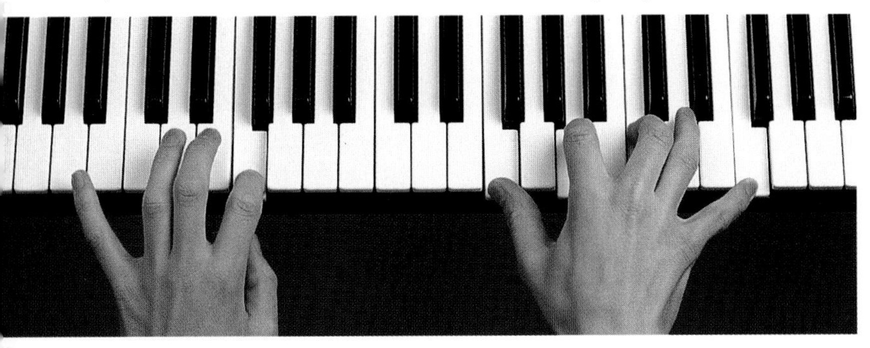

. typical bass note and chord combination: the left hand plays an F note while the right plays a full ›rimary chord of F major.

'TAKE MY BREATH AWAY'

This may be stating the obvious, but the red ›ight) and blue (left) parts of each bar should ›e read and played together. So for instance, ›n the first beat of Bar 2 you should play a **G(i)** ›hord and **G** bass note at exactly the same ›oment.

It will take time to get this right, so start ›owly and work from there.

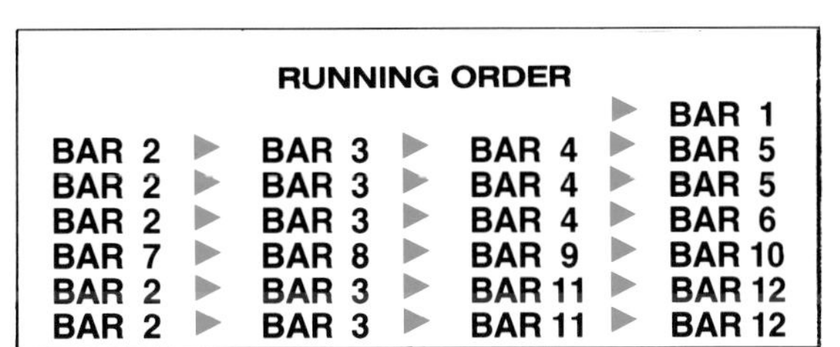

RUNNING ORDER

			▶ BAR 1
BAR 2 ▶	BAR 3 ▶	BAR 4 ▶	BAR 5
BAR 2 ▶	BAR 3 ▶	BAR 4 ▶	BAR 5
BAR 2 ▶	BAR 3 ▶	BAR 4 ▶	BAR 6
BAR 7 ▶	BAR 8 ▶	BAR 9 ▶	BAR 10
BAR 2 ▶	BAR 3 ▶	BAR 11 ▶	BAR 12
BAR 2 ▶	BAR 3 ▶	BAR 11 ▶	BAR 12

TITLE	KEY	TEMPO	STARTING POINT
'TAKE MY BREATH AWAY' (VERSE AND CHORUS)	G MAJOR	SLOW	(CONTINUED)

Bar	Hand	1				2				3				4			
BAR 7	Right	Am(i)															
	Left	A 2														E 5	
BAR 8	Right	C															
	Left	G 3														C 5	
BAR 9	Right	D(i)															
	Left	D 4														C 5	
BAR 10	Right	D(ii)															
	Left	D 4								D 5		E 4		G 2		A 1	
BAR 11	Right	C(i)															
	Left	C 4														A 5	
BAR 12	Right	D(i)															
	Left	D4								D 5		E 4		G 2		A 1	

RIFFS AND EMBELLISHMENTS

AS WE mentioned earlier, there's more than one way to use your left hand. Instead of playing basslines, it might play chords, leaving your right hand free to play a melody line or chords.

You shouldn't find it too difficult playing the chords you've learnt so far with your left hand. Obviously the fingering of each chord will have to change, but that's all.

Don't forget, left hand chords are usually played around the middle of the keyboard—not too far left, because they sound 'muddy' if played in too low a register, and not too far right, because it's very uncomfortable. Try it and you'll see.

SO WHILE the left hand plays chords, what is the right hand up to?

Well, it could be doubling up the left-hand chords, or playing 'stab' chords in the upper part of your keyboard, or on another.

Alternatively you could play a single-note set pattern. This is known as a riff.

Riffs play a major part in hard rock, usually blasted out by the guitarist—Eric Clapton's 'Layla' is a classic. But keyboard riffs are by no means unknown—as in Europe's 'The Final Countdown'.

A riff may be so prominent that without it there would be no song, or it could be almost subliminal, just ticking over in the background. It's the repetition that counts.

ANOTHER USE for your right hand would be to add embellishments: things which enhance the song, but without which it wouldn't actually fall apart.

You might for instance make one verse different from the last just by adding something. This is a way of sustaining interest and building a song's momentum.

Your embellishment could be as simple as a single note held over different chords. Or it could be a little more tricky—a rhythmic hammering on a note, a flurry of notes, an arpeggio maybe.

Another effective embellishment is a chord 'stab'—hitting a chord with a jolt in the gaps between the vocals.

Just be sure not to *over*-embellish. Keep it clean and keep it simple.

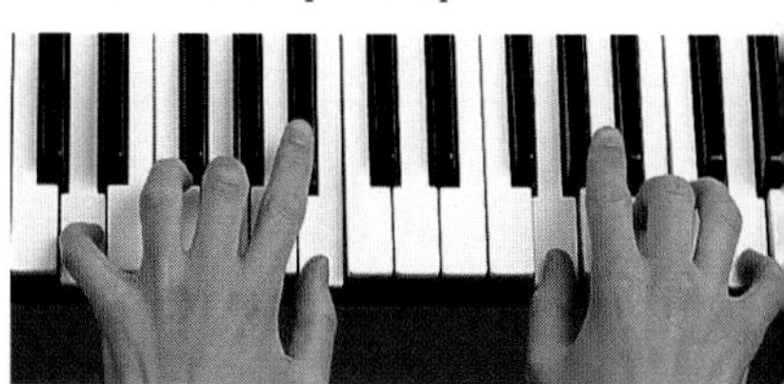

A right-hand stab chord of G over a left-hand G(ii).

LEFT HAND CHORDS

THESE ARE the left-hand versions of **C** major and **A** minor in their primary triad form.

You should find left-hand primary triads as straightforward to play as with the right hand. The fingering is exactly the same, except in reverse (for obvious reasons).

So instead of your right thumb on the lowest note of the chord, you have your little finger (5), and your left thumb (1) goes where your right little finger would go, on the highest note. The third finger plays the middle note, as it does with the right hand.

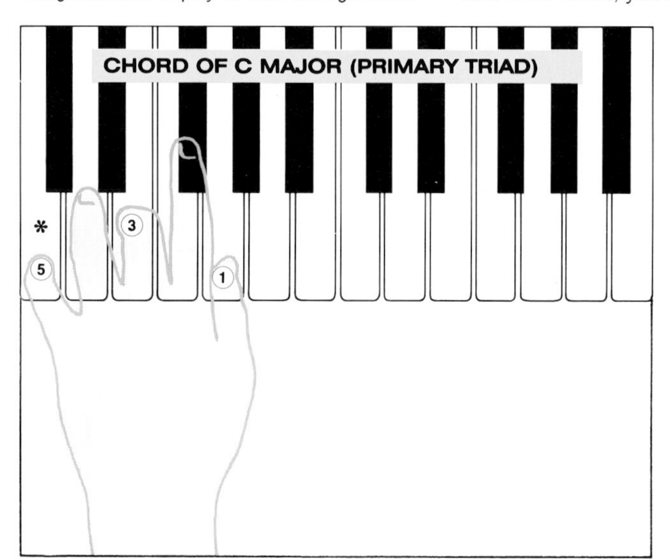

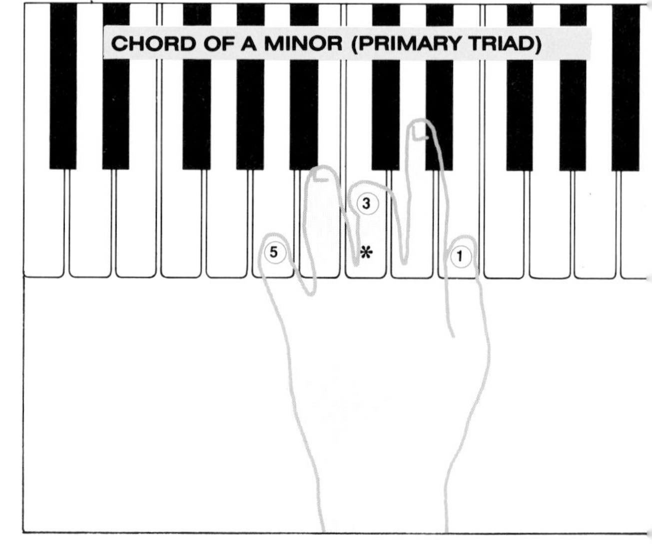

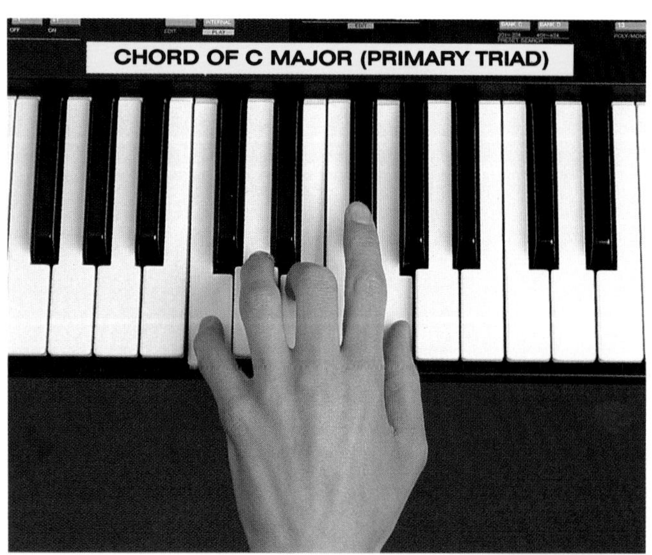

Don't forget to arch your fingers and keep your thumb straight, as you did with your right hand. Your forearm should be horizontal, to give maximum control over your movements.

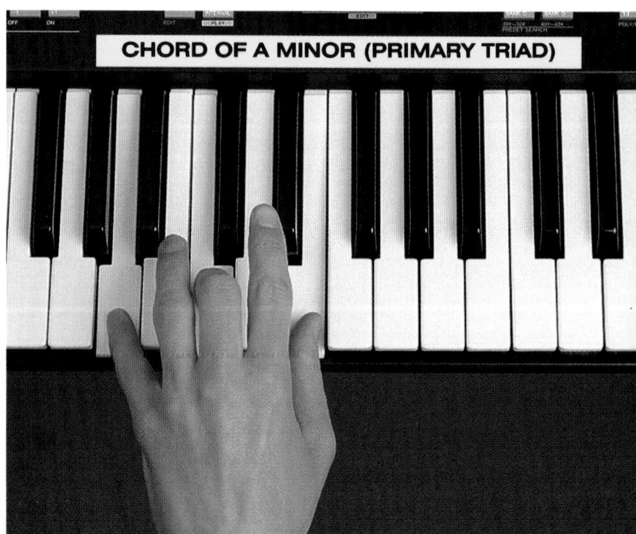

As with your right hand, you should find it easy to move from the C major primary triad to the A minor chord. Pair them together to give your left hand some exercise.

SOLO is where you take the spotlight: our chance to play something interesting nd generally show off a bit.

Most solos fall in the middle of a song, to ive the singer a break and change the nomentum.

When it comes to soloing, there's not a ot we can tell you—or should tell you eally. Original solos, whether improvised r rehearsed, are a personal statement.

Once you've learnt the essentials of eyboard playing, solos can be your aunchpad to your own expression— ssuming you're into solos anyway.

Some modern keyboard players say ney aren't interested in them, because ney break the rigid flow of a song.

But even a 'non-soloist' may want to fill a ap with something interesting, so here are few hints on the art of soloing . . .

● Solos are usually a series of single notes, perhaps with the odd chord thrown in for good measure. Therefore you need to practise different scales until playing a series of notes together becomes second nature—you can use chunks out of scales or arpeggios in a solo anyway.

● A simple solo might be the vocal melody played on the keyboard, in the manner of Phil Manzanera's guitar solo on Roxy Music's 'Jealous Guy'.

● Another method is simply to write a new catchy melody line, for instance Vince Clarke's synth solo in Yazoo's 'Only You'.

● If you're into hard rock or jazz funk, cynics might suggest that the main requirement is speed of fingerwork, as that's what impresses the fans.

If you really want to play faster, you'd better keep practising scales—though some people simply don't have the gift for fast playing anyway.

If you don't, don't worry. A few notes played with feeling can be just as effective as 100 notes a second.

● Don't worry too much what your left hand is doing. You don't *have* to have both hands on the keyboard at all times.

You may also need your left hand to operate various controls on your synth.

● When playing a solo, anything goes. Notes that are unrelated to the key can be added, as long as you don't dwell on them too long—this is particularly good for jazzy or bluesy solos.

Remember, too, that solos can be different rhythmically to the rest of the song—don't be afraid to experiment.

● Try to use different sounds for a solo—again, experiment.

LEFT HAND CHORDS

OU MAY find left-hand full primary chords a ttle trickier to play. As with the right hand, e've suggested what we think is the best ngering, but ultimately it's up to you.

As long as you keep your little finger (5) on the lowest note, and your thumb (1) on the top note of the chord, feel free to adopt the fingering with which you feel comfortable.

Many right-handed people find it harder to work their left hand accurately. All you can do is practise. If however you are left-handed, this is where it suddenly gets easier . . .

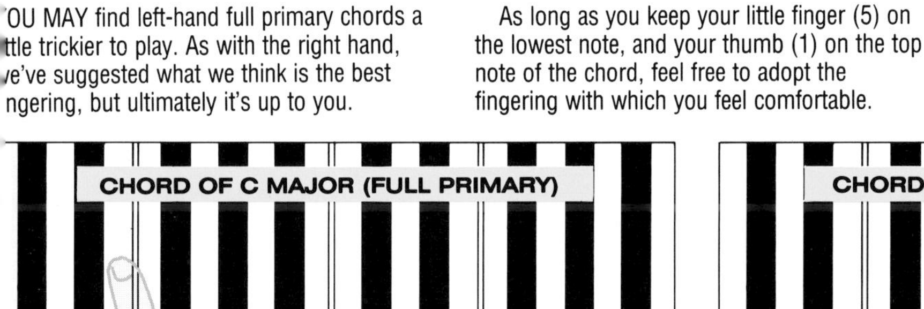

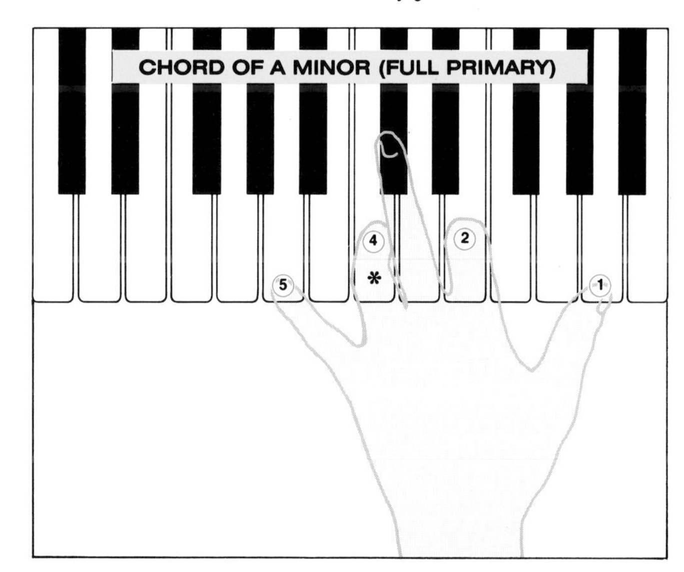

This is how we suggest you finger this chord. However, if you want to put different fingers on the middle keys, feel free—choose whichever is the most comfortable.

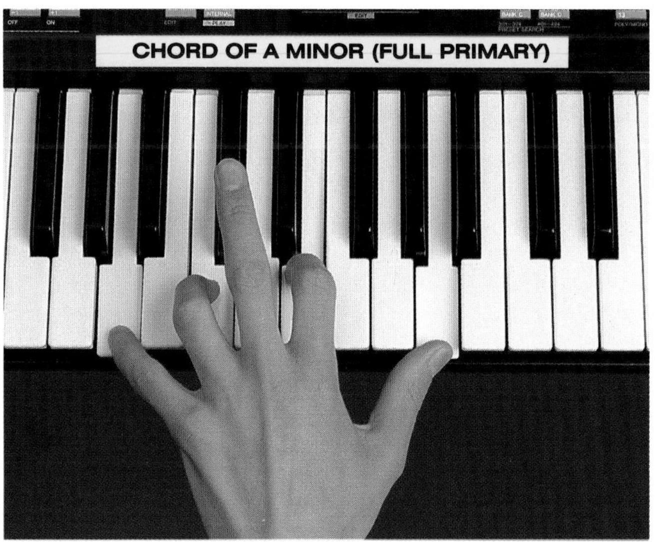

Whatever fingering you adopt for C major, stick to it for the A minor full primary chord—don't get into the bad habit of changing fingerings between chords of the same type.

LEFT HAND CHORD INVERSIONS

JUST AS right-hand primary chords can be played as inversions, so too can left-hand primary chords.

The only thing to bear in mind, as we mentioned before, is not to venture too high up the keyboard. A basic primary chord might be in the middle of the keyboard, which is fine, but if you move up the keyboard to play that same chord in its second inversion, you may find your left hand stretching too far to the right.

If that happens, don't forget that you don't have to move *up* the keyboard to play chords in their first and second inversions. You can move *down* to play the same chord shape an octave lower.

This is also true of right-hand chords, c course, but you're more likely to need with the left hand.

As a rule, the lowest note in a left-han chord shouldn't be higher than the **G** ju above middle **C**. So in the case of **G** majo your highest left-hand chord should be basic **G** major.

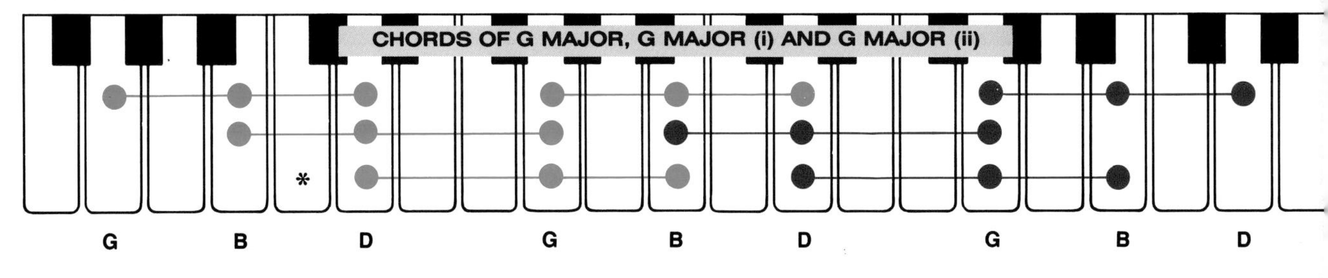

The inversions marked in blue are fine for both your left hand and your right hand, but the chords in red should only be played right-handed.

LEFT HAND INVERSIONS

THIS EXERCISE demonstrates the use of your left hand to play inversions. So here is the primary triad chord of **F** major in its basic version, first inversion (**i**), second inversion (**ii**) and basic version one octave higher.

You'll notice when you play left-hand inversions that, just like right-hand inversions, the fingering stays the same from one version to the next. So your little finger (5) plays the lowest note of the chord, your middle finger (3 plays the middle note of the chord, and your thumb (1) plays the highest note.

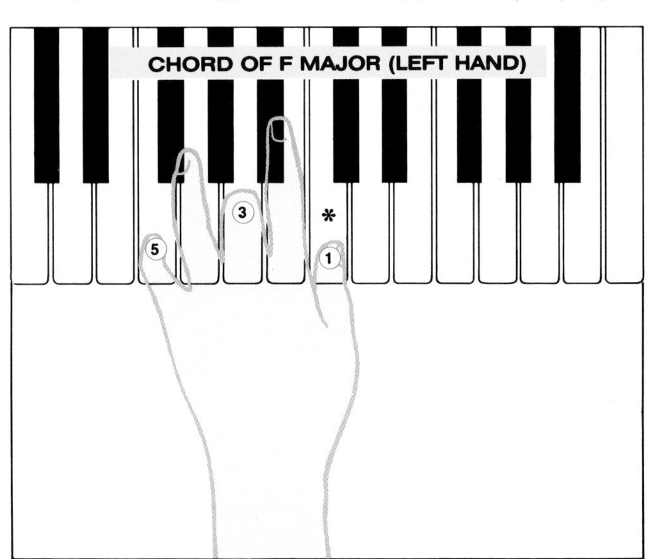

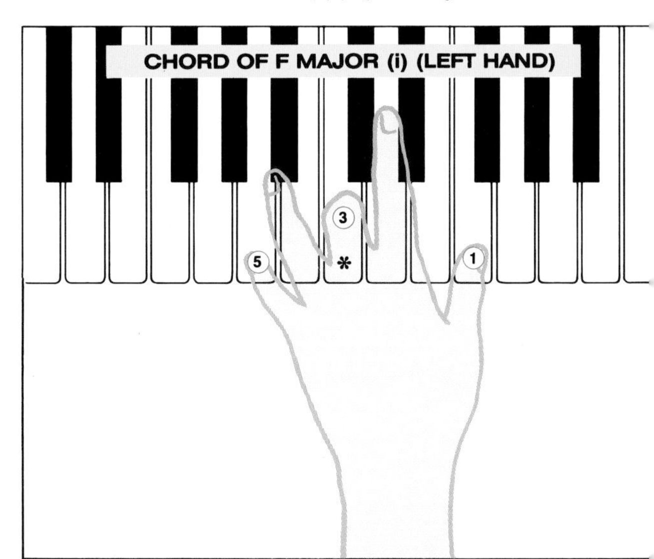

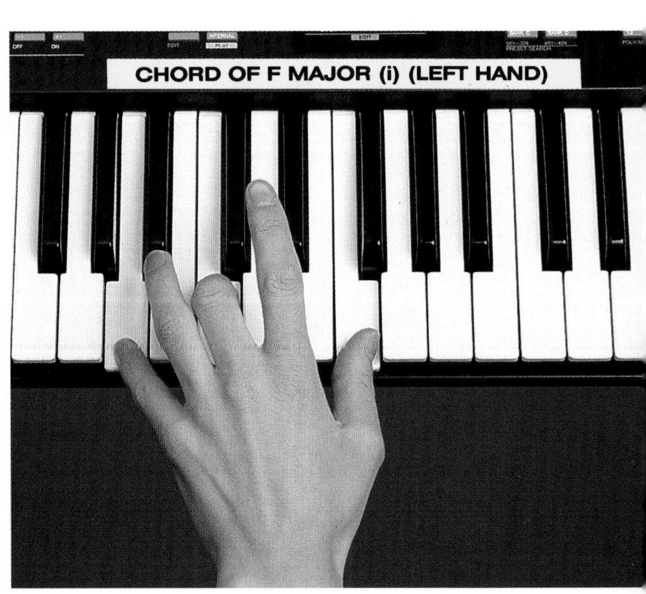

When playing left-hand inversions, aim for equal fluidity moving along the keyboard as you've achieved with your right hand.

'HEN WE talked about pianos and rgans, we recommended that you use a ynthesiser instead. Talking about home eyboards, we suggested that you will ant to upgrade to a synthesiser.

So you'll have gathered by now that the andard rock keyboard today is the ynthesiser – or to be precise, the olyphonic synthesiser.

What makes synthesisers so good? Vell, apart from being able to mimic ther keyboard instruments such as piano nd Hammond organ, thus making life a ot easier for the keyboard player, they an recreate the sounds of other nstruments too – cello, flute, violin, even e guitar.

But perhaps the most exciting thing bout synthesisers is that brand new sounds can be created and played as music, and stored in the synth's 'memory' for later use.

A good synth will also offer an amazing amount of control over sounds.

What's more, there are dramatic new developments in synthesiser technology almost every year. With all this going for it, it's easy to see why the synthesiser is the most in-demand instrument in music.

Peter Gabriel and the first polyphonic synth, the Polymoog.

ELECTRONIC SYNTHESIS began in the early '50s. RCA Records installed the first Music Synthesizer in a New York studio in 1955. The only problem was, it resembled a telephone exchange both in appearance and size!

Ten years later two Americans, Herb Deutsch and Robert Moog, succeeded in ►

LEFT HAND INVERSIONS

You shouldn't find these chords too difficult, s there are no black notes. If your left hand still eels rusty, try playing a few scales – they're all n the Chord Directory (pages 71–84).

Don't forget, whenever you play a chord – whether with your left or right hand – that you must play all the notes together or it will sound untidy. You should be able to handle this with your right hand by now, so work on your left until it reaches the same standard.

Don't worry if you don't get it right first time. The important thing is to keep practising.

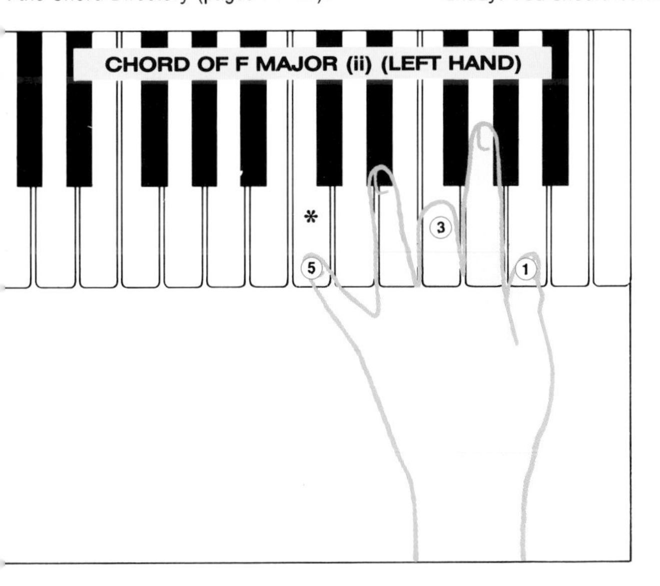

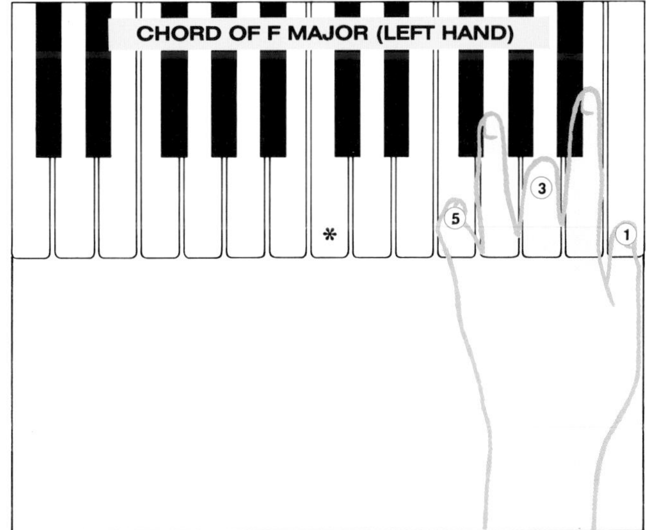

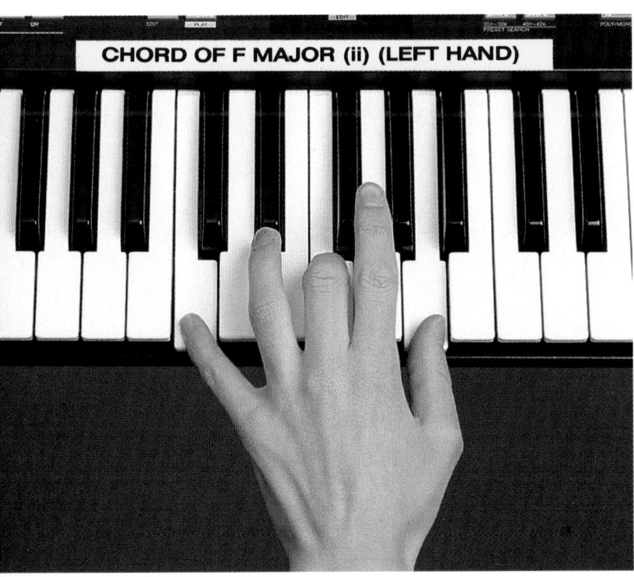

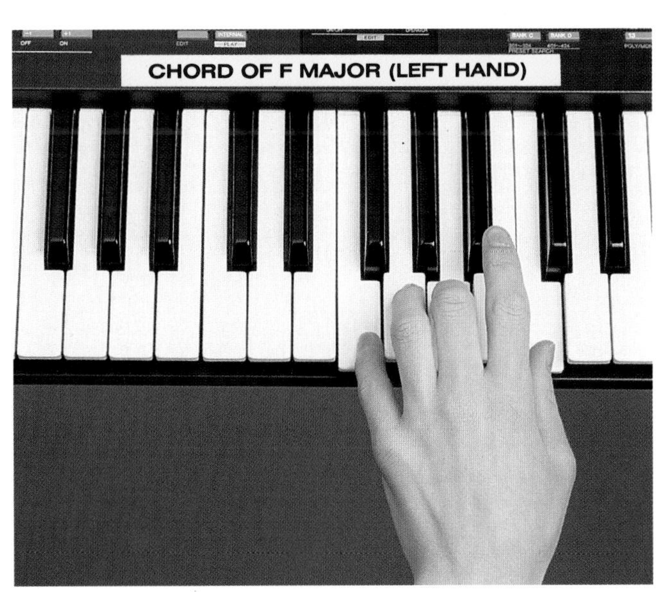

'he top basic chord of F major (right) will take your left hand about as far to the right as it's comfortable for it to go.

building a synth which offered many of the RCA system's facilities in a much more compact form. Known as the Moog Synthesizer, it was used in 1968 by Walter (now Wendy) Carlos to make a bizarre album called 'Switched On Bach'. The record was a surprise best-seller, and the synthesiser was finally on the map.

But it was the 1971 launch of the Minimoog – the first truly portable synth – that changed the face of music.

THE MINIMOOG was a small monophonic synth which was instantly seized upon for its strong 'fat' sounds. Although it could only play one note at a time, it was ideal for solos, bass lines and sound effects – explosions, hurricanes and so on.

The Minimoog was soon followed by rivals such as the ARP 2600, the AR Odyssey, and the British Putney VCS3.

Most monophonic synths had no 'mem ory', so you couldn't create a sound an then store it for later use. This meant th you had to create sounds on the sp using various knobs, switches and slider

This 'analog' system of sound creatic was positively primitive compared to th complex 'digital' technology of today synths. But some players prefer th simplicity of those early machines– especially the Minimoog, still used for i powerful bass and lead sounds.

POLYPHONIC SYNTHESISERS have on been around since 1978. Things got off a somewhat expensive start with the Pol moog, but it was rapidly followed by

David Ball of Soft Cell with Sequential Circuits' Prophet 5, and friend.

'AXEL F' WITH CHORDS

YOU'VE TRIED a song where you play chords with the right hand and a bassline with the left. Now to put the second method of two-handed playing into practice—chords with the left hand and something else with the right.

That something else could be any of the techniques we talked about on pages 54–5: riff, embellishment, melody line or solo. In this case it's a melody line you should know quite well by now—'Axel F'.

The chords we have suggested to accompany this tune are all chords you've already learnt with your left hand: **Am, G** and **F(i).** And of course, since we're in the key of **A** minor, they use white notes only.

You'll probably find it easier to play the right and left hand parts separately at first. When you feel you're ready, try both parts together—very slowly.

The important thing to remember is that any left-hand chord and right-hand note that appear on the same beat should be played exactly in sync. As with playing a bassline, synchronisation is most important.

TITLE	KEY	TEMPO	STARTING POINTS
'AXEL F' (MAIN THEME)	A MINOR	QUITE FAST	RIGHT: A ABOVE * LEFT: Am BELOW *

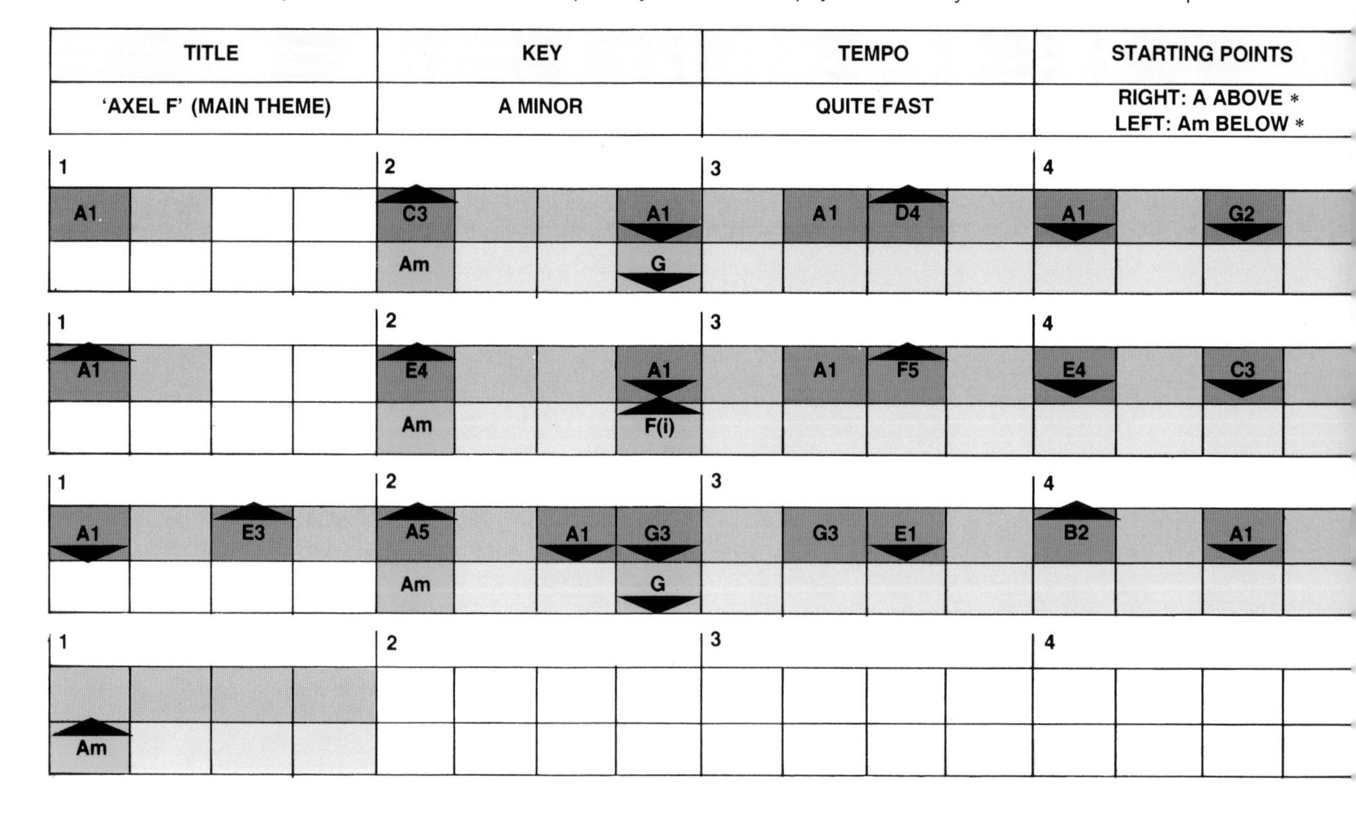

MUSICAL NOTATION FOR 'AXEL F' (CHORDS AND MELODY) IN THE KEY OF A MINOR

ariety of famous products: Oberheim's Voice and 8-Voice, Yamaha with their S-80, and Sequential Circuits with the gendary Prophet 5, used by most eyboard players at the time.

Japanese firms such as Roland and org followed Yamaha into the keyboard arket in the late '70s, and by the end of e decade there was a healthy number good synths to choose from.

At the same time, there was a major eakthrough in prices, thanks to an ultra-ieap British product called the EDP Wasp. It was quickly followed by a clutch cheap synths from Japan.

N THE early '80s the Japanese computer rm Casio launched its home keyboards ased on digital microchip technology.

Vince Clarke with the world's most successful synthesiser, the Yamaha DX7.

but another area of digital technology was about to produce a real quantum leap in sound production: digital synthesis.

The first digital synthesiser was Yamaha's DX7, launched in 1983. At last there was a portable polyphonic synthesiser at a price the average serious musician could afford.

After the simple knob and slider controls of the old analog synths, the DX7 was quite a shock to the system with its complex 'digital access control'. Although you played it like a traditional keyboard, when it came to creating and altering sounds it was more like a computer. But you only had to hear the DX7's superb sounds to know it was worth the effort.

Other manufacturers such as Korg and Roland moved in, and by the mid-'80s

'AXEL F' WITH CHORDS

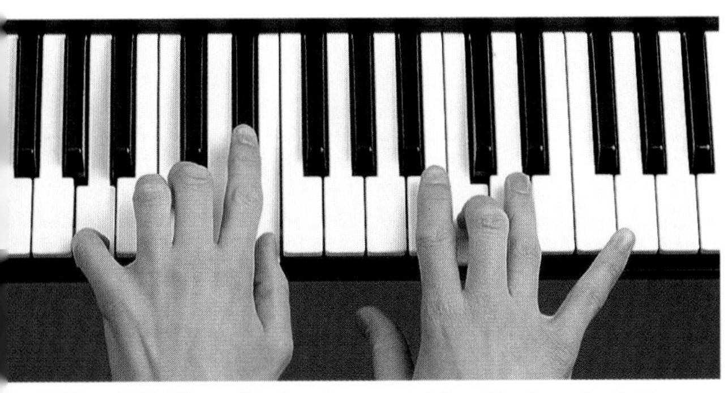

e right-hand third finger (3) plays C over a left-hand A minor chord. These e played exactly together on the second beat of Bar 1.

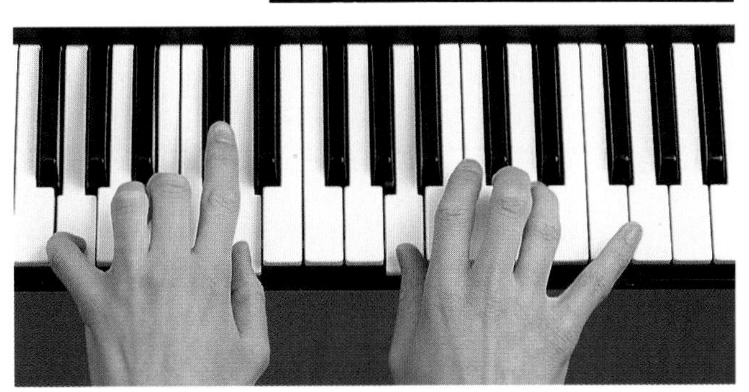

The right thumb (1) plays A over a left-hand G major chord in Bar 1. The G chord is held until the end of the bar, whilst the right hand is fairly busy.

e right-hand little finger (5) plays F over F major (i) in Bar 2. From Am to i) is a smooth chord change: the only new note is F instead of E.

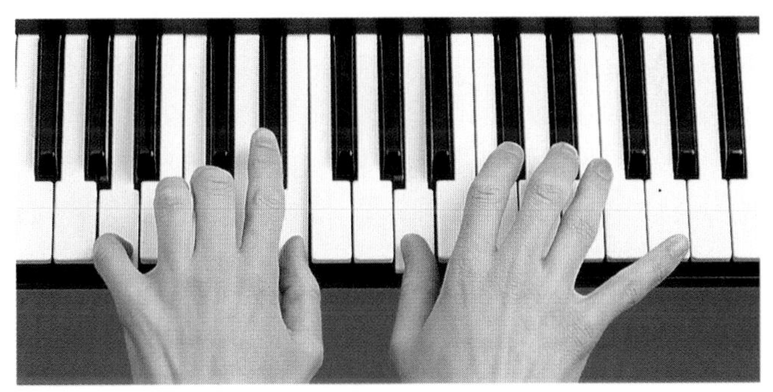

A left-hand chord of A minor played under a sustained right-hand A at the beginning of Bar 4. The A is held over from the previous bar.

DON'T FORGET, scales are just as important an exercise for your left hand as for your right. They are especially helpful for good bassline playing. Here are two more for you to practise—the scales of **F** major and its relative **D** minor. You should find them fairly straightforward, you just have to watch out for the black note **B♭**.

We won't be showing any more scales for either the left or right hands in the Instruction Manual section. This doesn't, however, mean that you shouldn't practise new ones.

You'll find the left and right hand fingering for every major and minor scale in the Chord Directory (pages 71–84). Try some of them *every* time you play, before you start, as a kind of loosener.

Also, when you feel you can play them fairly confidently, try playing both a left-hand and right-hand scale together—in the same key, of course!

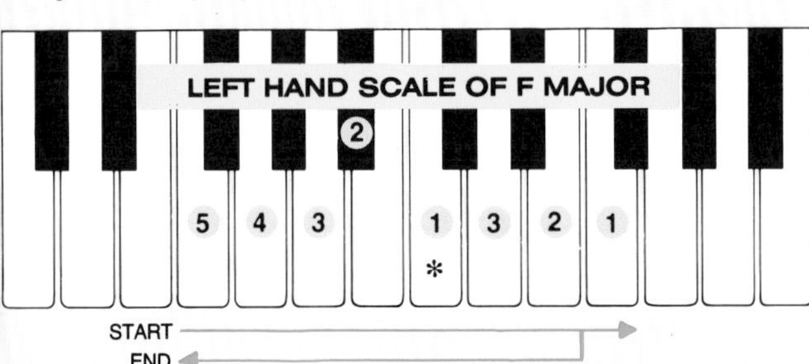

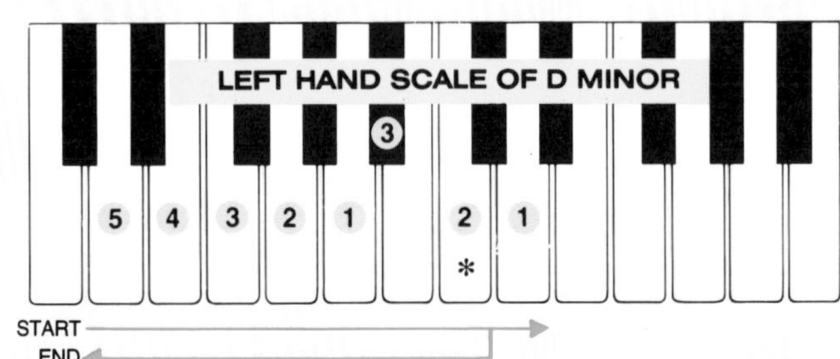

there was an array of excellent digital synthesisers on the market, with a vast range of devices, effects and sounds available. In 1985 Casio applied their cut-price home keyboards philosophy to the synthesiser, and it was a whole new ball-game yet again . . .

SO LET'S look at what a polyphonic synthesiser can actually do.

All modern synths are polyphonic, capable of playing more than one note at once. Some can play more than one sound at once, sometimes in different parts of the keyboard.

The keyboards are usually five octaves, with full-sized keys (although mini-synths usually have smaller keys and/or fewer octaves).

More sophisticated synthesisers may have velocity-sensitive keyboards, which play louder if you hit the keys harder. Some keyboards have 'after-touch', so that you can trigger various effects just by pressing harder as you play.

Most polyphonic synthesisers have programmable 'memories' in which sounds may be stored.

Most will also be supplied with 'pre-set' sounds, programmed in at the factory. You can usually 'edit' (alter) these pre-set sounds.

Most programming and editing is done by 'digital access control', using numbered buttons and a small screen of the type found on digital watches.

Effects available include chorus (which makes chords sound fuller), digital delay (echo or reverberation), pitch-bend (fo 'bending' notes in the way a guitarist doe when bending strings), and arpeggiatio (which turns a chord into an arpeggio).

IN OTHER words, there's a bewilderin range of things you can do with a goo synthesiser.

And on top of that, you can combin them with a whole range of other equip ment such as samplers and sequencers which we'll tell you about on pages 6 and 64.

It may sound a bit intimidating, bu don't let it put you off. Armed with th information in our Buyer's Guide (page 88–102), you should be able to enter th wonderful world of synthesisers wit confidence.

MAJOR SEVENTH CHORDS

NOW IT'S time to try playing a couple of seventh chords. From now on, we'll be showing all new chords in both left-hand and right-hand positions.

First we have a major seventh chord, namely **C** major **7**. You'll notice that the fingering doesn't differ from the fingering of full primary chords. And as with full primary chords, if you're more comfortable with a different fingering, use that – as long as your thumb an little finger play the two outside keys in the chord.

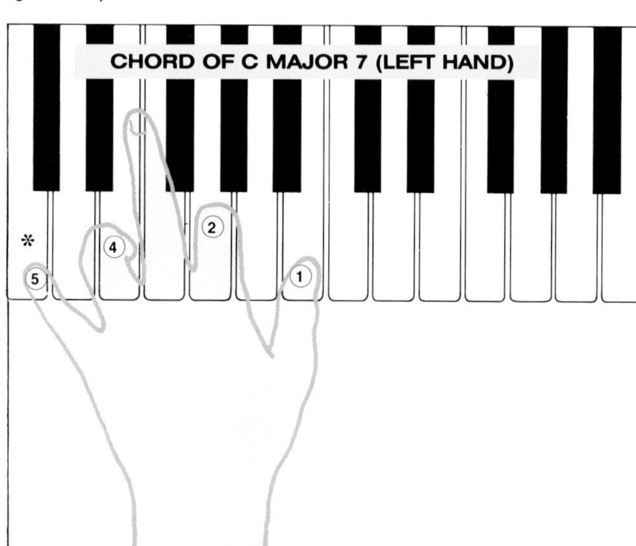

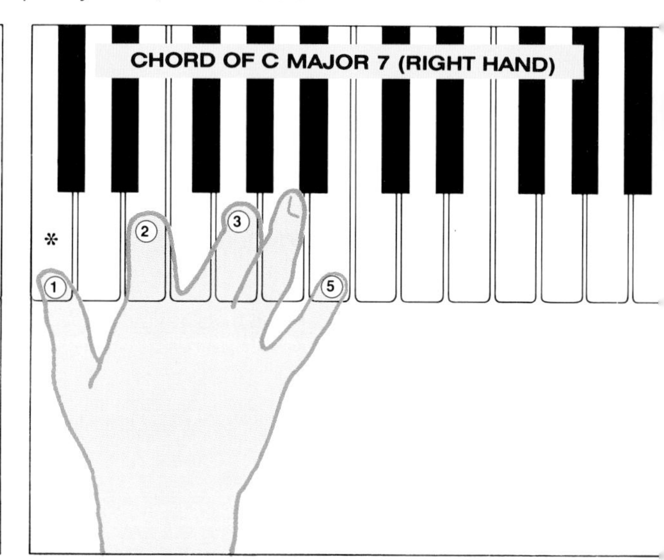

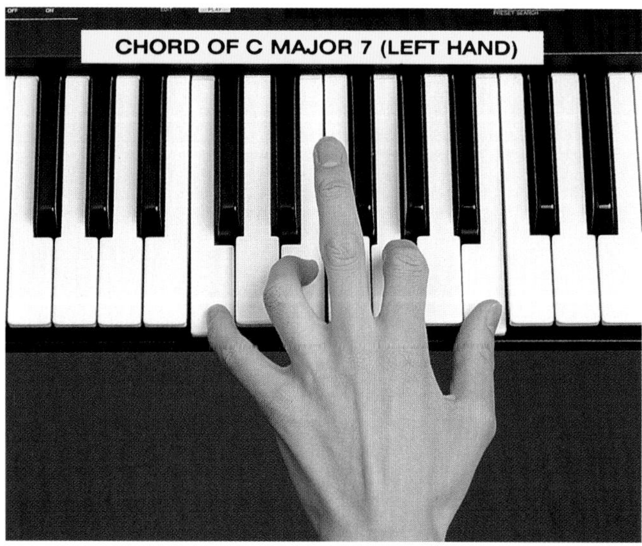

We've lined up the left-hand and right-hand pictures alongside one another, so you can see how the two hands' fingering compares. We suggest you finger seventh chords in the same way you play full primary chords.

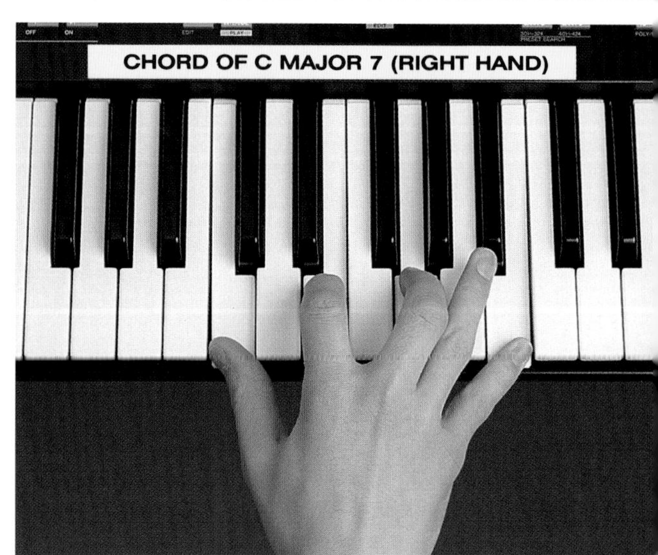

You might like to practise playing a chord with both hands at once – in differe parts of the keyboard, of course! It's great for hammering out loud or dramat chord progressions.

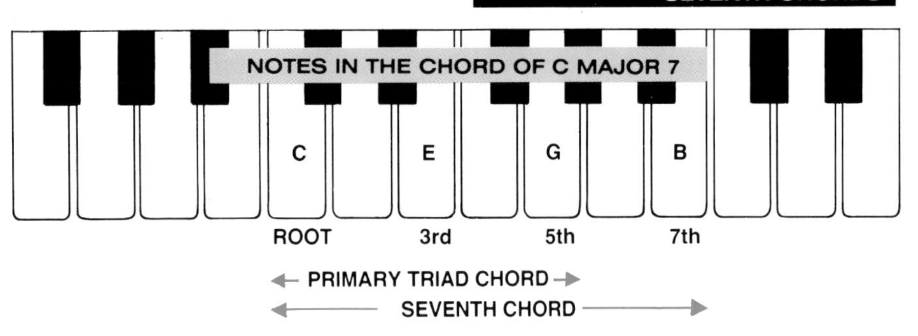

OW THAT you're used to playing prim-ry chords with either hand it's time to add nother chord type to your musical voca-ulary – seventh chords.

The name 'seventh', as you might have uessed, refers to the seventh note in a cale. For example, in the scale of **C** major e seventh note is **B**. In the scale of **A** inor, the seventh is **G**.

To construct a seventh chord, take the ree notes of any major or minor basic rimary triad – namely the root, third and fth notes in the scale – and simply add the eventh note in the scale.

Naturally, this means that all seventh hords are four-note chords.

ET'S LOOK at **C** major. The primary triad ontains the notes **C** (root), **E** (third) and **G** ifth). Add the seventh note, **B**, and that makes it **C** major **7** (or **C** major seventh).

Another example, using **A** minor: take the three notes of the primary triad (**A**, **C** and **E**) and add the seventh note in the scale, **G**. This gives you **A** minor **7**.

Technically, a seventh chord can be used in any chord progression instead of its primary chord – in other words, **C** major **7** can replace **C** major.

Let's say you have a chord progression of **C** major to **A** minor to **F** major (i) to **G** major (i). Replace **A** minor with **A** minor **7** for a subtle but effective variation.

Obviously if it's someone else's song, you can't do this. But if writing your own, it's worth bearing in mind.

MINOR SEVENTH CHORDS

ERE IS a minor seventh chord, namely **A** inor **7**. Notice that the fingering stays the ame as for the **C** major **7** chord. This goes for oth left and right hands.

Don't forget when you play a chord, to play all the notes simultaneously – this is harder with four-note chords, but you'll have to master it if you want to use seventh chords.

If your seventh note lags behind the rest of the chord you'll find yourself playing an ordinary primary triad followed by a single note, and you'll lose the effect of the chord.

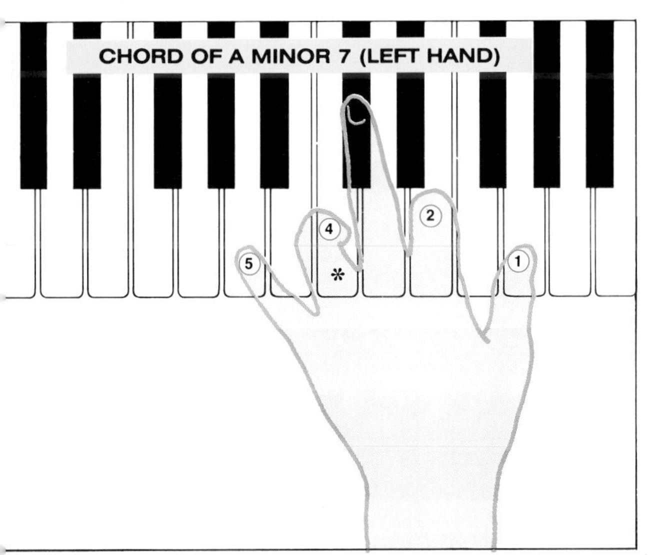

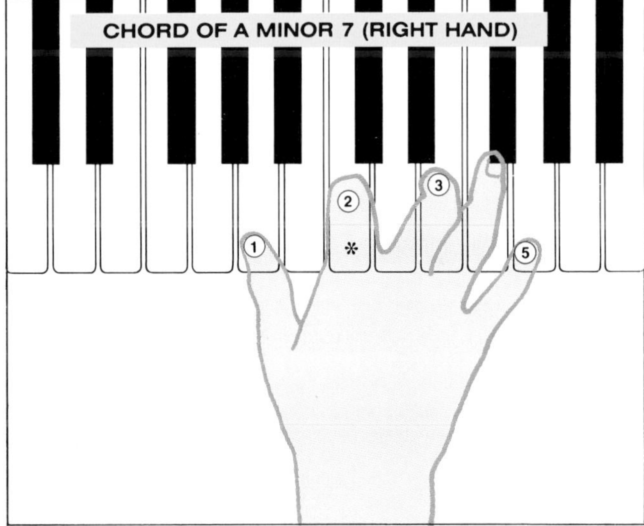

otice that the note you add to a minor chord to make a seventh – in this case, – is a note you can find in the related major chord (the notes in **C** major eing **C**, **E** and **G**).

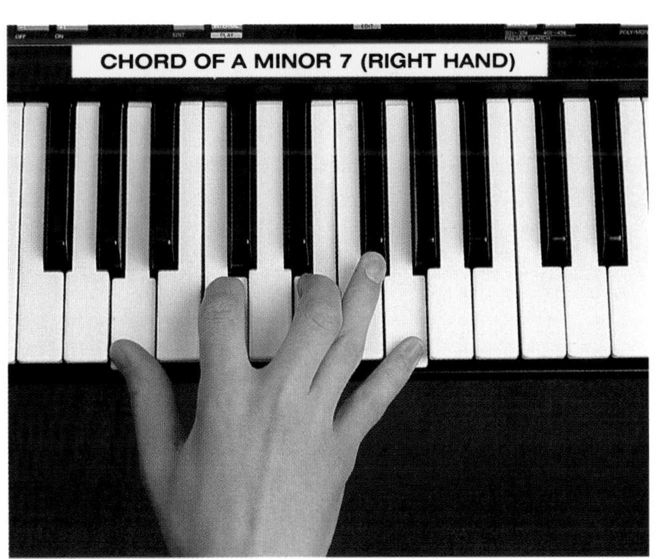

Because minor seventh chords are so closely related to major chords, they're used more often than you might expect, sometimes as a kind of subtle variation of their relative major.

SEVENTH CHORD INVERSIONS

LIKE PRIMARY chords, seventh chords can be played as inversions. But whereas there are just three versions of a primary triad chord (because there are just three notes), a seventh chord has four versions because it has four notes.

Let's take the case of **C** major **7**. The basic form, which we learned on the previous page, has the notes **C**, **E**, **G** and **B** in that order moving from left to right.

In its first inversion **(i)** we simply move one step to the right, giving **E** as the lowest note followed by **G**, **B** and **C** as the top note.

In its second inversion **(ii)** the notes are arranged **G**, **B**, **C**, **E**.

Finally, in its third inversion **(iii)** they are **B**, **C**, **E** and **G**.

WITH BASIC primary triads, full primary chords, and now seventh chords – plus all their inversions – you have quite a variety of chord types and shapes at your disposal.

Seventh chord inversions should be used for the same reasons as primary chord inversions: for smoother chord progressions and added musical interest.

Each inversion has its own character. If a chord somehow doesn't sound right in a song or progression, it may not be the chord that's wrong. It might just sound better in another inversion.

Major seventh chords have a jazzy feel, great in small doses, but don't give your listeners too much of a good thing!

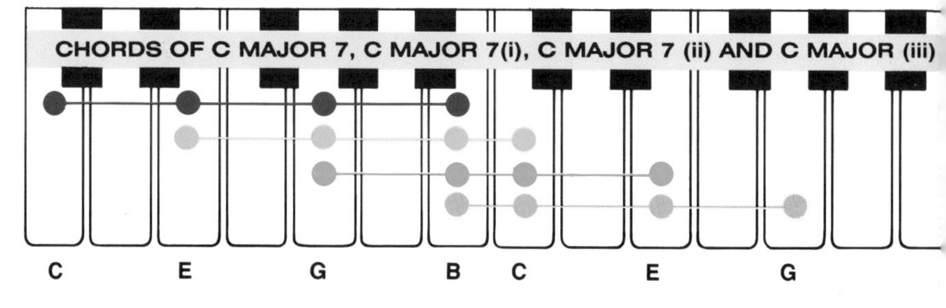

SEVENTH CHORD INVERSIONS

NOW LET'S try playing a major seventh chord and a minor seventh chord – **G** major **7** and its relative **E** minor **7** – in their basic forms and then in their first, second and third inversions (**i**, **ii** and **iii**). Do this using just your right hand for now.

The fingering of these chords shouldn't pose any great problems for you. The only note to watch out for is the black **F#** in **G** major **7**.

As long as your thumb (1) is on the lowest note of each chord, and your little finger (5) is on the highest note of the chord, feel free to

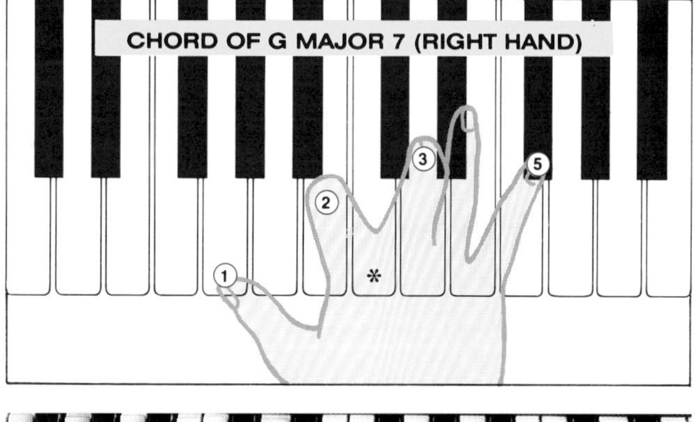

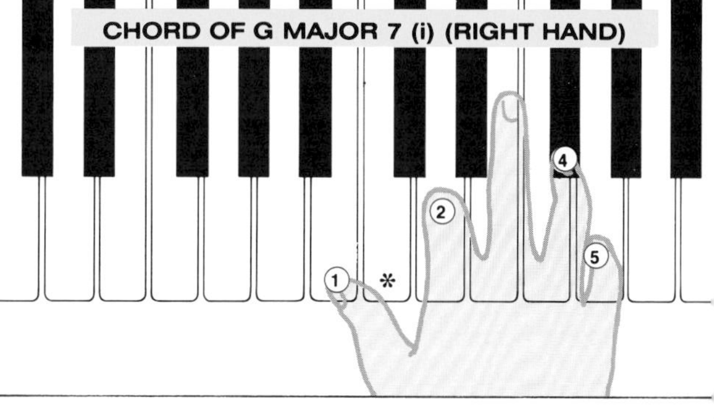

Playing seventh chord inversions is excellent exercise, because you're using four fingers in a series of different configurations.

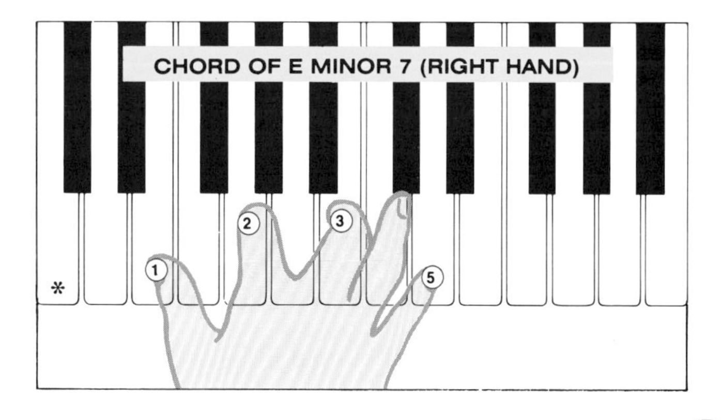

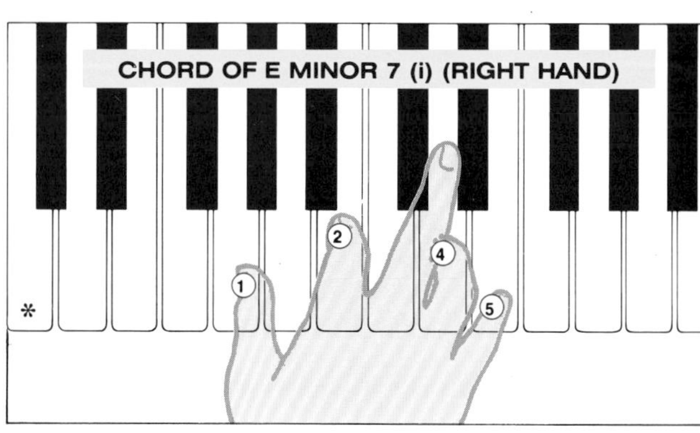

AUNCHED IN the early '80s, samplers :e machines for digitally recording ɔund and then playing it back on a eyboard. Any sound can be used. You an play it back at any pitch, and edit it in arious ways.

The first sampling 'systems', the Fair- ght CMI and the New England Digital ynclavier, were both expensive and ɔmplex. Their quality however reflected eir price.

E-mu Systems made things a little sim- ler and cheaper with the Emulator and mulator II samplers, and another Amer- :an company, Ensoniq, finally made amplers affordable with their Mirage in 985.

Inevitably Japanese companies like oland, Korg and Casio followed suit, with Casio producing the cheapest sampler ever—the million-selling SK-1.

Herbie Hancock samples the very best in digital technology—the Fairlight CMI sampling system.

SAMPLERS COME either as modules to be connected to another keyboard, or as full keyboards in their own right.

The sampling time available is usually very brief – a few seconds – but you only need to record long enough to get a decent 'sample' of a particular sound.

By connecting a microphone to your sampler, you can use any noise at all as a sound source. In practice many users stick to factory samples which come with the machine or on computer disks.

Some instruments described as samplers are actually sampling synthesisers which combine the two methods of creating sounds in one instrument.

ıange the fingering of the notes in between if it ıakes you feel more comfortable.

When playing these chords, try playing the ur different versions in quick succession. This is obviously good exercise, but it will also help you hear the different characters of the inversions, and perhaps spot them on records.

Don't forget, just as you can play a primary chord as an arpeggio, so you can 'arpeggiate' a seventh chord. The more you practise arpeggios, the easier it is to use them to embellish a song.

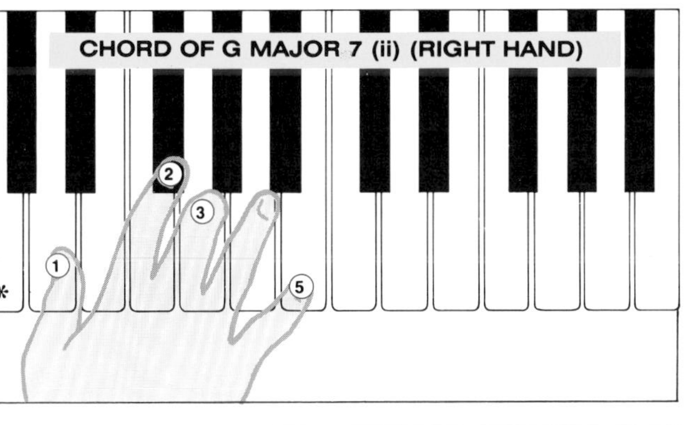

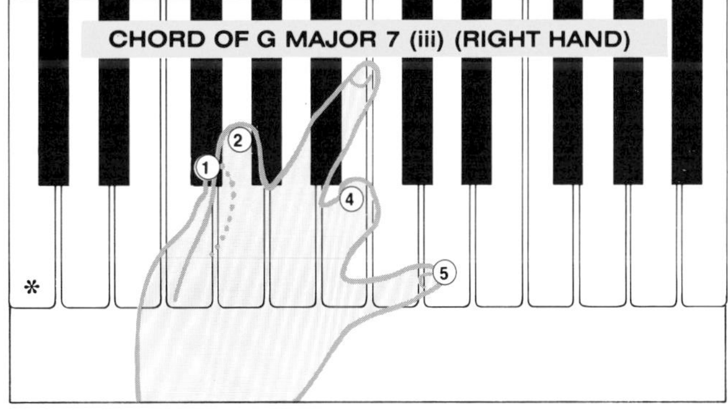

ote that the E minor 7 chord is closely related to G major – in fact it is G major with an E note added.

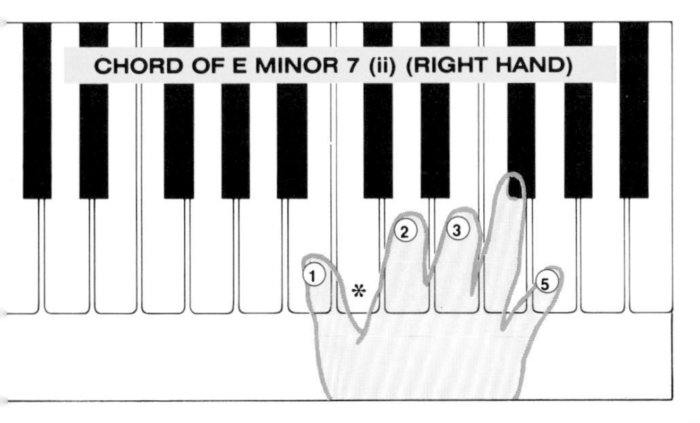

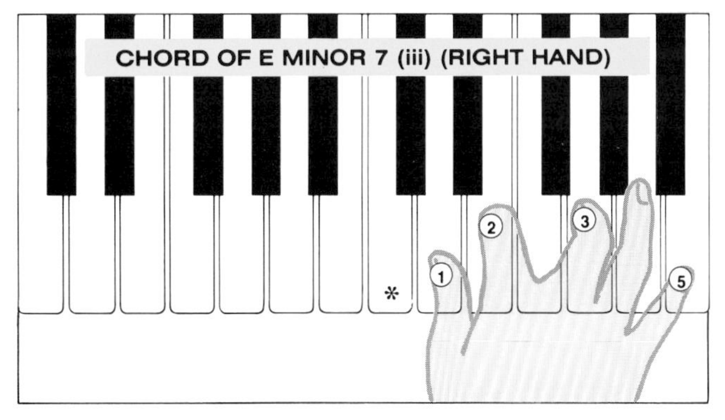

SEQUENCERS

SEQUENCERS ARE often known as keyboard recorders, because they are in effect tape recorders without tape.

A sequencer digitally records a sequence of notes or, if it is polyphonic, notes and chords, and stores this information in its memory.

When you want to hear what you've recorded, the information is sent to the keyboard which then plays itself. You can then experiment with different sounds, etc.

Sequencers are useful for many things. For example you can record a tricky keyboard part at snail's pace, then speed it up on playback.

When recording, you can record and perfect all your keyboard parts onto a sequencer, before finally committing them to tape.

This means you can save on studio time because you can record all keyboard data at home. It also means you won't have any annoying mistakes recorded on tape.

RECORDING INTO a sequencer can usually be done in one of two ways:

Real time. Recording in real time means you play your keyboard part 'live' into the machine, keeping time with a built-in metronome or a hooked-up drum machine. Once the data is recorded you can usually correct mistakes, move bits around, join bits up to make whole songs, speed it up, slow it down, and so on.

Step time. Recording in step time means that you enter one note or chord at a time – step by step. You can als specify lengths of notes and rests. An you can correct mistakes, etc, as with re time recording.

A good sequencer will also recor information about dynamics (if you keyboard is touch-sensitive).

The memory space varies. Wher memory is limited, you can usually 'dum information onto computer cassettes, ca tridges or floppy disks.

THESE INSTRUMENTS probably soun very exotic and technical – which the are! – but hopefully we've given you rough idea of what they can do. Th Buyer's Guide (pages 88–102) has a l more information about electron keyboards.

MAJOR 7 INVERSIONS (LEFT HAND)

NOW THAT we're acquainted with right-hand inversions of seventh chords, time to move onto the left. Although we're now showing all chords for both left and right hands, the right hand is always going to be more important for chords, which is why we showed that first.

Here's another major seventh chord with its relative minor – **F** major **7** and **D** minor **7**.

Don't forget, when playing left-hand chords not to stray too far to the right. So to play the second and third inversions of **D** minor **7** we move down the keyboard, not up.

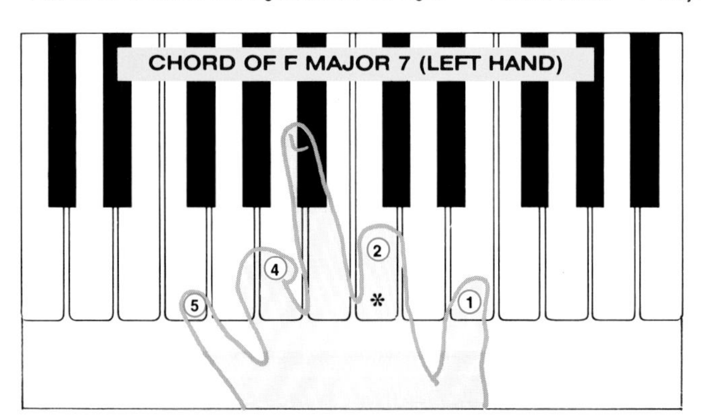

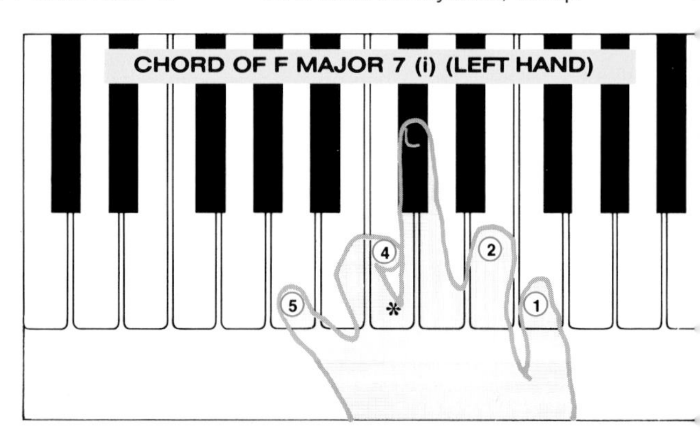

All the inversions of **F** major 7 and **D** minor 7 are played on the white keys, so you can use them in the key of **C**.

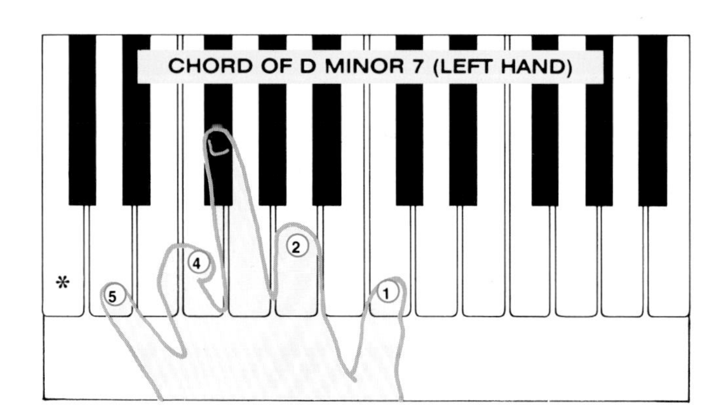

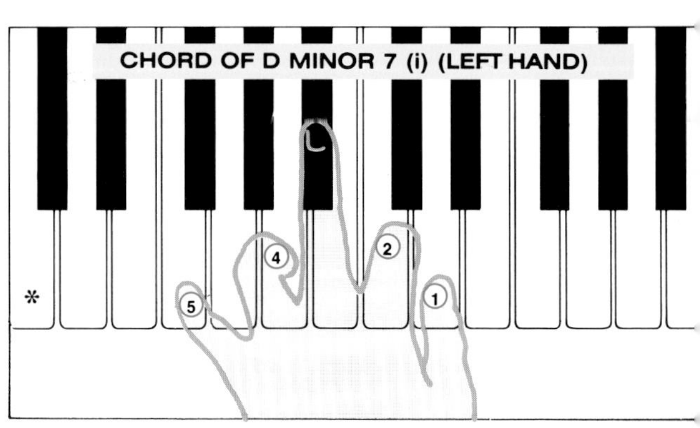

'HATEVER KEYBOARD you end up ing, the one thing you're going to need if u play live is amplification, so people can tually hear you. The same goes for when u play at home, unless you have an oustic piano or your keyboard has either ilt-in speakers or a headphone socket.

When playing an electronic keyboard e, it will usually be connected via a lead r two leads if your keyboard has a stereo tput) to one of the following:

An amplifier which in turn is connected a speaker; a 'combo', which is an ampli-r and speaker combined in one unit; or a A (public address) system.

The basic PA system consists of a power nplifier, two speakers (one for each side the stage), monitors (smaller speakers hich face the band so they can hear the sound going out through the main speakers), and a sound mixer (a box of knobs and/or sliders to which all microphones and some instruments are connected).

A mixer allows you to 'balance' the individual volumes of all the instruments and vocals, and to alter their tone. Effects units can also be connected.

The resulting 'mix' is then sent out to the power amplifier.

When playing live, the keyboards sound best going through a good PA system (which will usually be hired).

However, a good combo specifically designed for keyboard use will also suffice. Anything that has a power rating above 40 watts of volume, and at least two individual input sockets and individual volume and tone controls should be OK.

Thirty inches and 100 watts of power, the Roland CK100 is one of the best keyboard combos.

LEFT HAND ARPEGGIOS

'E MENTIONED that seventh chords can be ayed as arpeggios. What we haven't entioned is the fact that arpeggios can be ayed left-handed as well as right-handed.

Try these seventh chords as left-hand arpeggios, then try some major and minor full primary chords as arpeggios.

A left-hand arpeggio can even be used as a bassline, played under a right-hand version of the same chord, especially if it is a long, sustained chord. Just move your arpeggio an octave lower down the keyboard.

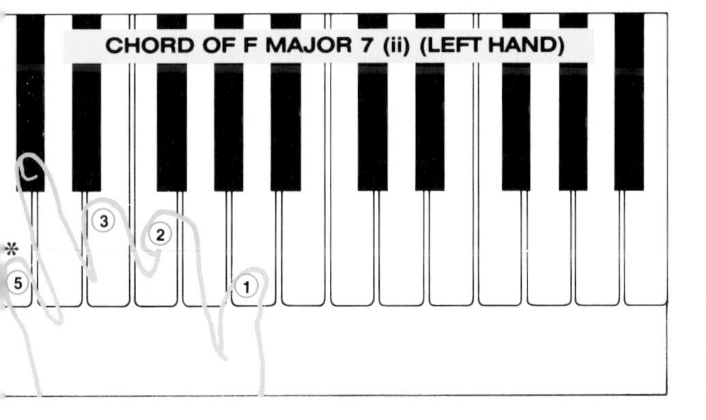

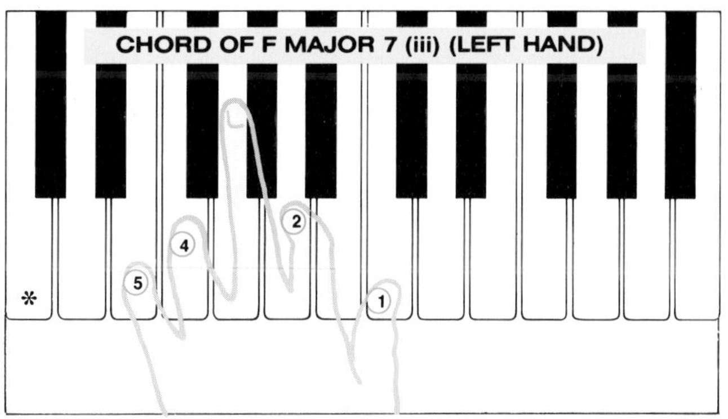

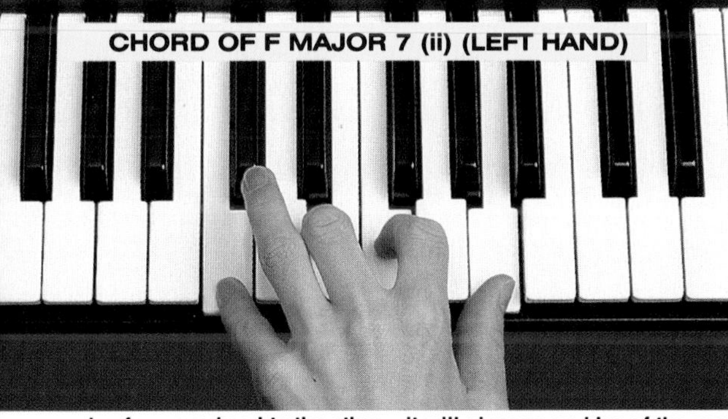

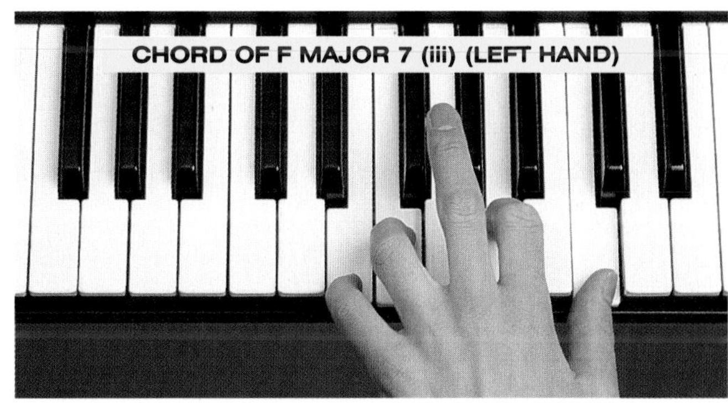

eep swapping from one hand to the other – it will give you an idea of the zones of the keyboard you prefer each hand to operate in.

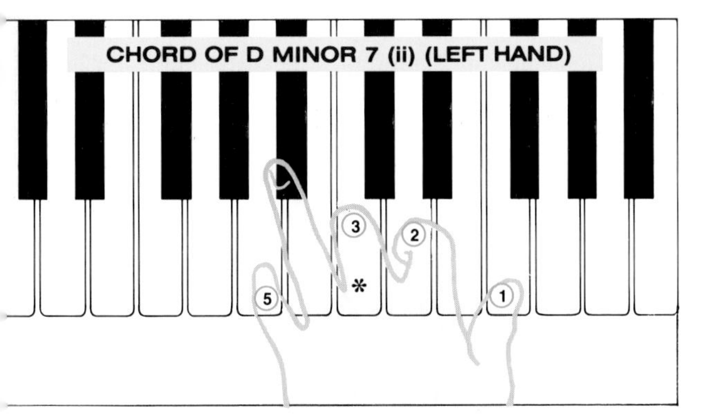

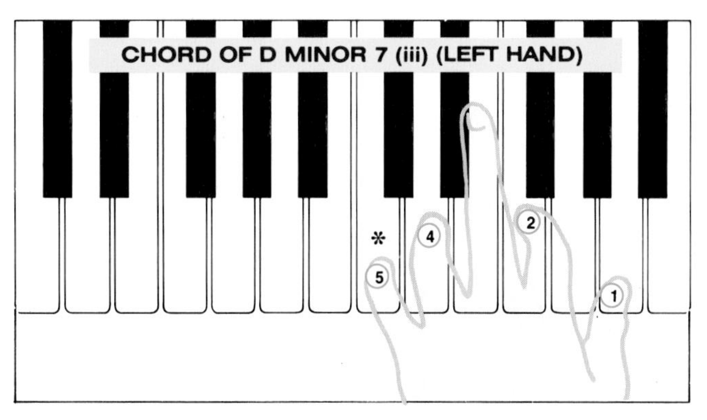

DOMINANT SEVENTH CHORDS

AS YOU KNOW, for every pair of major and minor keys, there are six primary chords which work in those keys – three major chords and three minors.

For example, in the keys of **C** major and its relative **A** minor we can use the chords of **C** major and **A** minor, **F** major and **D** minor, and **G** major and **E** minor.

Will the seventh versions of these chords work? The answer is yes – with one exception.

Let's look at the seventh chords for the keys of **C** major and **A** minor.

C major 7 has the notes **C**, **E**, **G**, **B**.
A minor 7 has the notes **A**, **C**, **E**, **G**.
F major 7 has the notes **F**, **A**, **C**, **E**.
D minor 7 has the notes **D**, **F**, **A**, **C**.
E minor 7 has the notes **E**, **G**, **B**, **D**.

All these notes are in the scales of **C** major and **A** minor, so the chords are OK.

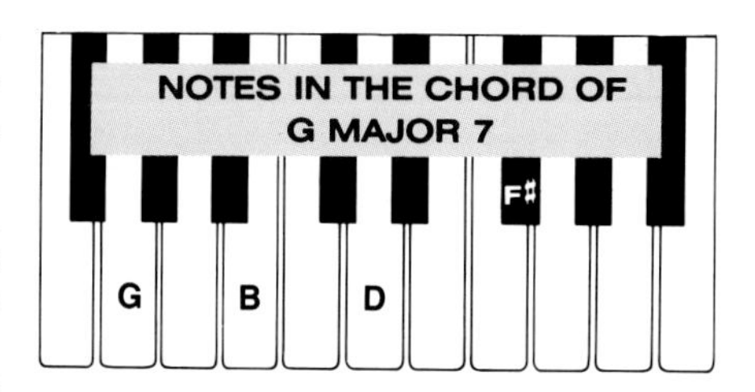

This chord won't work in the key of C major, because the F# note is not in the scale of C major.

Not so **G** major 7. It has the notes **G**, **B**, **D** and **F#** – and **F#**, of course, is not in the scales of **C** major and **A** minor.

As it stands, then, this chord can't be used in **C** major or **A** minor.

However there is a solution. The chord can be modified slightly so that it works –

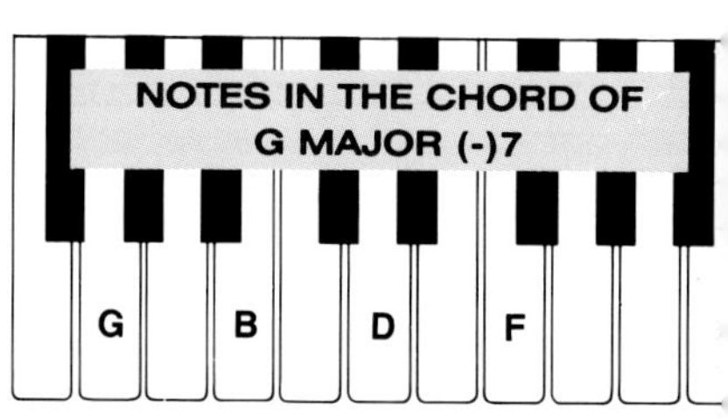

This chord *will* work in the key of C major, because we've replaced the F# with an F note, which is in the scale of C major.

and in so doing, it becomes known as th dominant seventh chord.

WE MODIFY a major seventh chord t make a dominant seventh by moving th seventh note down one semitone.

So in **G** major 7, for example, the sevent

DOMINANT SEVENTH INVERSIONS

AS WITH the other types of chord you've learnt, dominant seventh chords can be played as inversions. As there are four notes in the chord, three inversions are possible.

Below we have the four different versions of **G** major dominant seventh – or, to give them their strange looking abbreviated names: **G(-)7**, **G(-)7(i)**, **G(-)7(ii)** and **G(-)7(iii)**.

But don't worry about the names, just try playing them. You'll find them less offputting a soon as you wrap your fingers around them, and you'll soon find them indispensable.

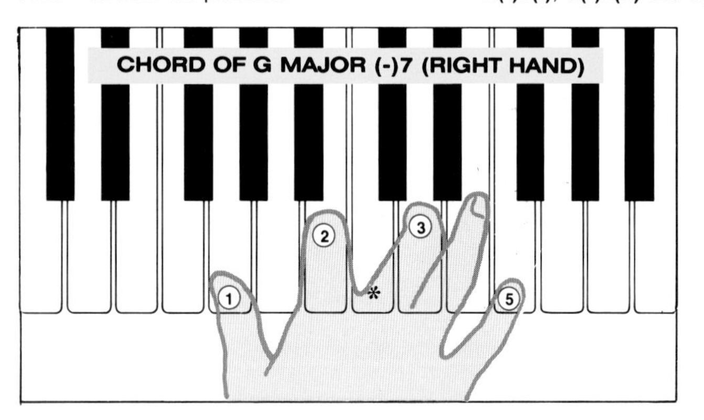

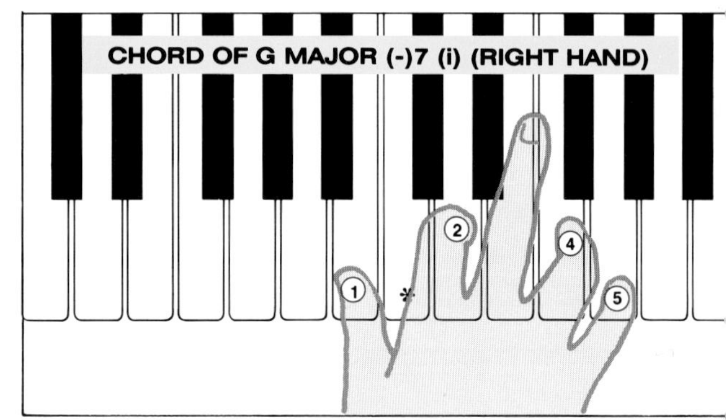

Notice that the fingering changes from one inversion to the next, according to how the keys are spaced.

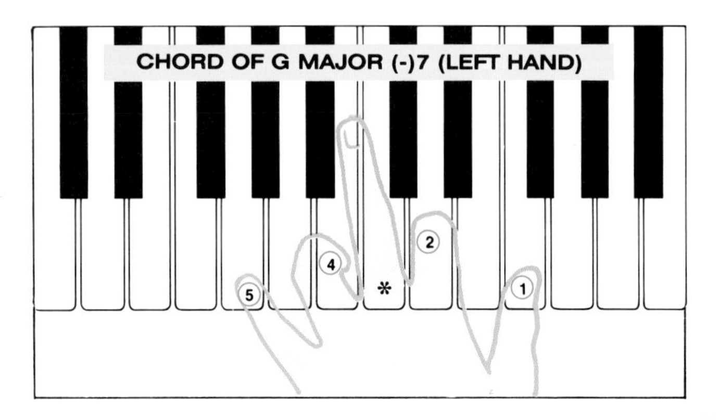

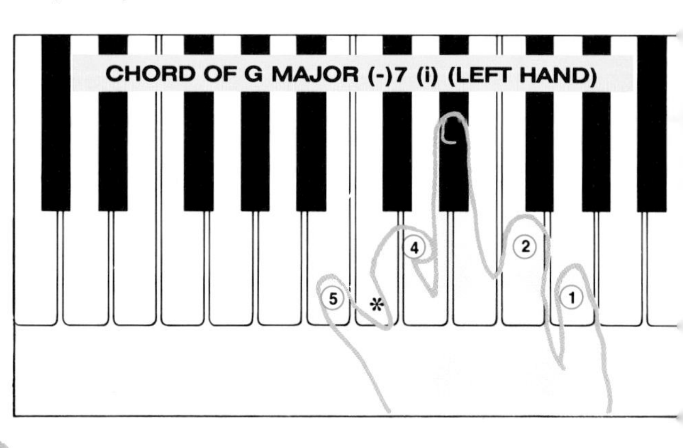

ote **F#** moves down one semitone to ecome **F**. And the **F** note, of course, *is* resent in the scales of **C** major and **A** inor, so this new chord can be used in iose keys.

The way we refer to the dominant eventh chord is like this: **G** major **(-)7**. The inus sign before the **7** indicates that it is ioved down one semitone.

THERE ARE a few things to bear in mind about the dominant seventh chord:

- It's rarely used in a minor key.
- The chord is always based on the fifth ote of the major scale. So in the key of **C** najor, the chord is **G** major **(-)7**, based on ne **G** note. In the key of **F** major, the elevant dominant seventh chord is **C** najor **(-)7**, because **C** is the fifth note in the cale of **F** major.
- For this reason, the chord will always be a major chord. You can't, for example, have **G** minor **(-)7** – and you don't need it, because the minor primary chords that work in a key will also work as straight seventh chords.
- There is only one chord of this kind in any major key, and the chord itself will only work in that one key.

WHEN WORKING on a song in a major key, experiment with the dominant seventh that works in that key.

A dominant seventh chord sounds particularly good when it's followed by the root chord of a key – for instance **G** major **(-)7** followed by a **C** major chord in the key of **C** major.

The dominant seventh chord can also be played in inversions, as you can see below.

WHY 'DOMINANT' SEVENTHS?

YOU MAY be wondering why this chord is called a 'dominant' seventh.

As you know, whenever we want to refer to the notes in a scale generally, we call them the root, second, third, fourth, fifth, sixth and seventh notes.

However, musicians with classical training often call them by these names: tonic (root), supertonic (2nd), mediant (3rd), subdominant (4th), dominant (5th), submediant (6th), and the leading note (7th).

You'll probably find these terms quite confusing, which is why we don't use them. Nevertheless, it's worth mentioning here.

The word we borrow, 'dominant', corresponds to our 'fifth'. If you remember, this new 'dominant' seventh chord is based on the fifth note in a major scale. To avoid calling it the 'fifth seventh', we call it by its traditional name: dominant seventh.

DOMINANT SEVENTH INVERSIONS

OU SHOULD know by now how inversions rogress up the keyboard:

The basic **G(-)7** has the notes **G**, **B**, **D**, **F**.
The first inversion **G(-)7(i)** has **B**, **D**, **F**, **G**.
The second inversion **G(-)7(ii)** has **D**, **F**, **G**, **B**.
The third inversion **G(-)7(iii)** has **F**, **G**, **B**, **D**.

Now that we're showing both left and right hand chord shapes together, put in some two-handed practice by playing different inversions with different hands – say, left **G(-)7** followed by right **G(-)7(iii)**. It's a good way to test how your left hand's coming along.

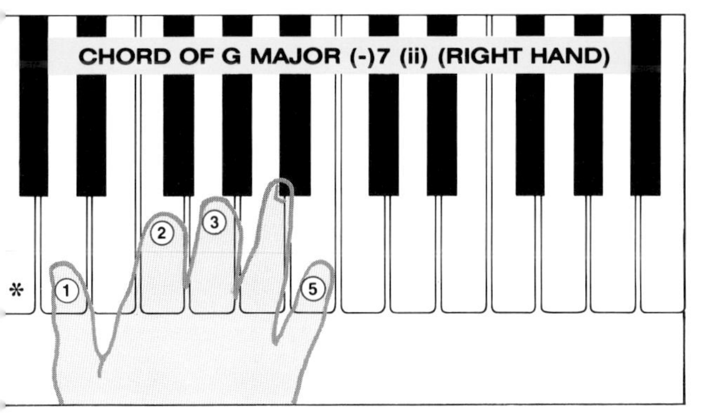

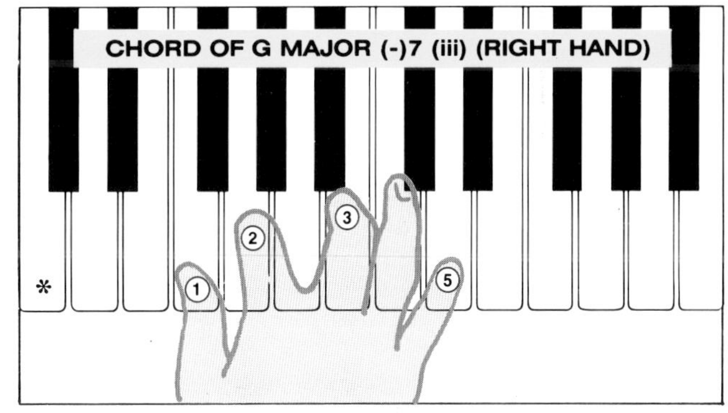

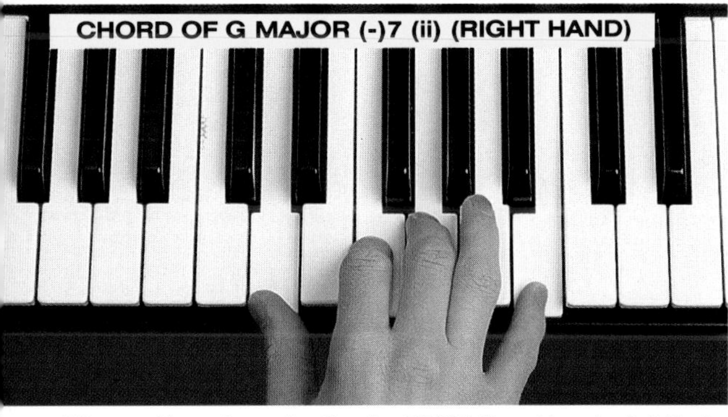

or a subtle use of inversions, play G major (-)7(ii) followed by a basic full primary C major – minimum effort, maximum effect.

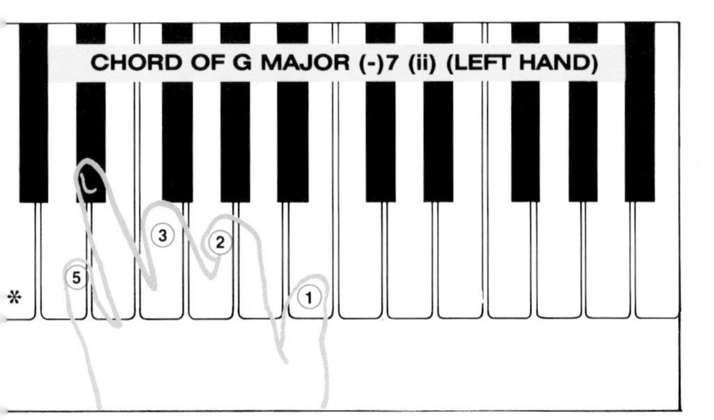

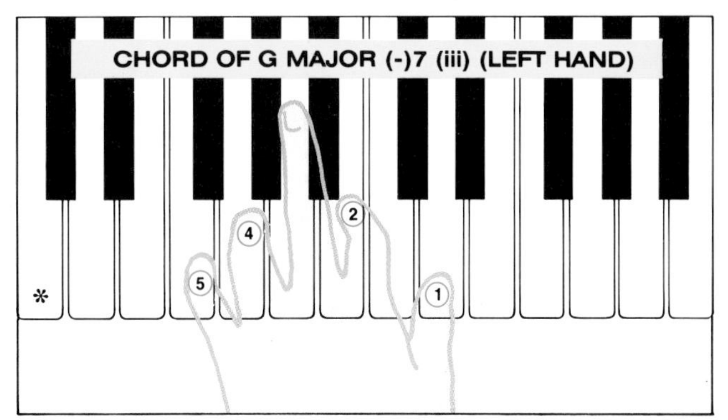

HOW TO READ MUSIC

HERE, AS promised, is our crash course in reading music the traditional way. Please note, these are only the basics—a detailed study would fill many more pages. There should be enough here, however, for you to begin to understand how all those little symbols relate to what you play and hear as music, if you're interested.

If you're not, that's OK. An ability to read music is useful, but by no means essential. Most rock musicians survive quite happily without it—and if all you want to do is write and play your own songs, it's unlikely that you'll need it either.

It's when you want to play other people's songs that it helps, because all sheet music uses traditional musical notation.

Chords are usually named on sheet music, but you will certainly need to read music if you want to play single notes.

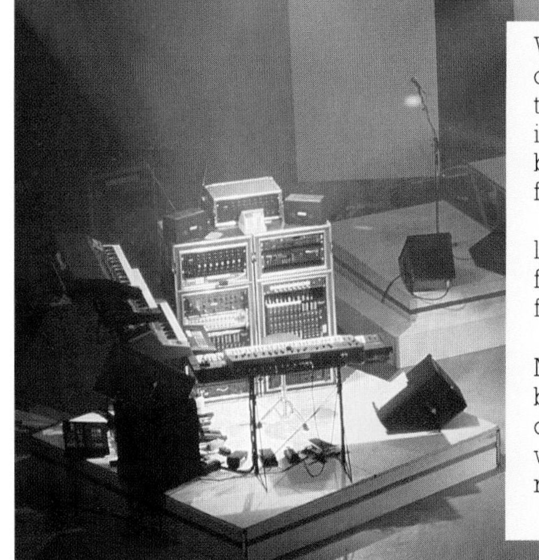

WE ARE now coming to the end of our Instruction Manual. The rest of the book is packed with valuable information for keyboard players, but as far as playing is concerned, from here on you're on your own.

Obviously, you've still got a lot to learn, but most of this will come from playing and finding out things for yourself.

Throughout the Instruction Manual we've tried to give you the basic information you need to develop a style of your own—it's what will make you a really good rock keyboard player.

The stage is all yours . . .

HOW TO READ MUSIC

NOTES

TREBLE CLEF

BASS CLEF

Here are two musical 'staves'. A stave consists of five horizontal lines, and is the traditional equivalent of our music grid. Just as we have separate grids for the right and left hands, so there are separate staves for each hand. Where our grids are marked red for right, blue for left, staves are marked with 'clefs'—treble clef for the right hand (top stave), bass clef for the left (bottom stave).

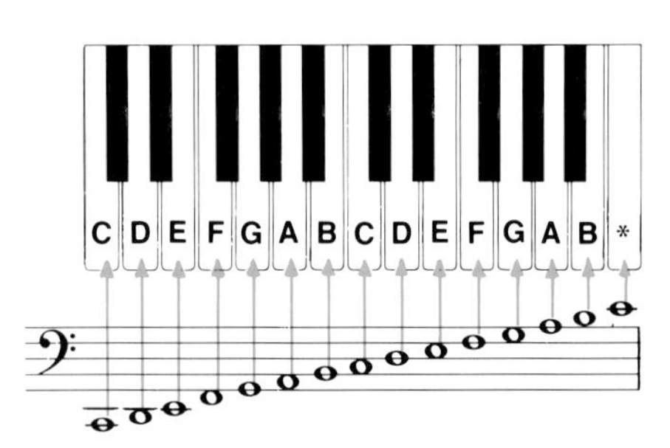

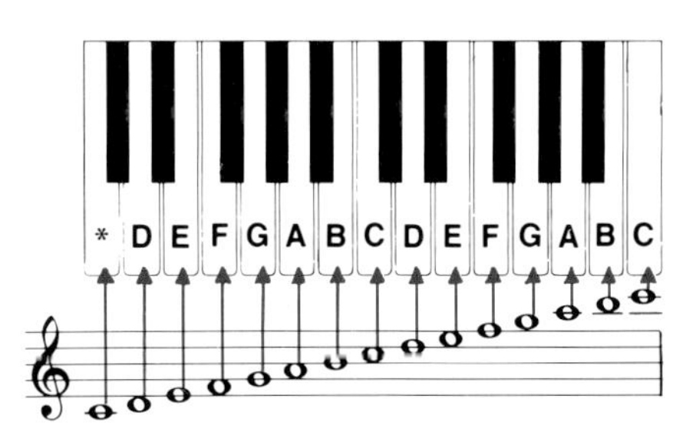

Musical notes are represented by circular symbols on or between the lines of a stave. Usually, notes below middle **C** are written on the bass stave, and notes above on the treble stave, with middle **C** common to both. You'll notice that some notes float above or below the staves, because there simply aren't enough lines on a stave for all the notes on a keyboard.

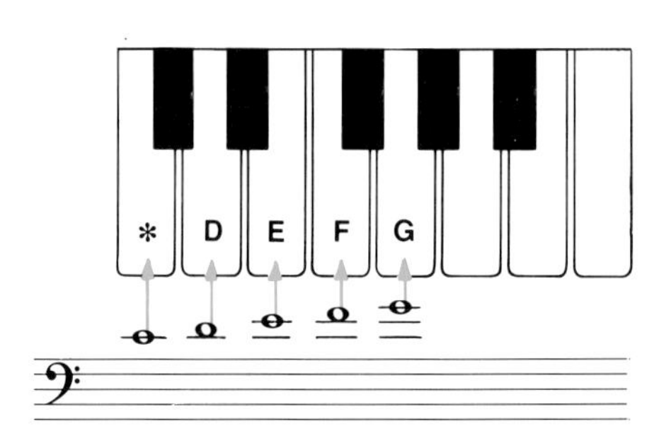

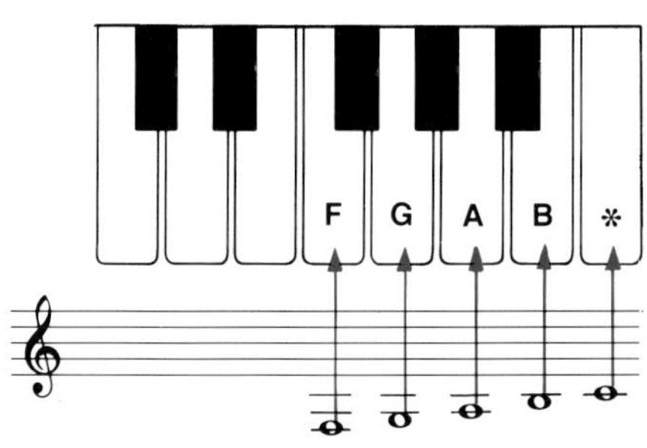

Often, as you know, the hands overlap; the left will play notes above middle **C**, and the right may play notes below. Here (above) is how these notes are represented.

At the beginning of each stave there's a 'key signature'. The notes on a blank stave correspond to the white notes only on a keyboard and you need the key signature to tell you which sharp or flat notes are present.

The key signature shown above has sharp symbols where the **F** and **C** notes fall; this means that all **F** and **C** notes are replaced by **F#** and **C#**. Therefore you are playing in the keys of **D** major or **B** minor, as they are the only sharp notes in those keys.

If there are no sharps or flats marked on a stave, the music must be in **C** major or **A** minor, as there are no sharp or flat notes in those keys. Here (above) are the key signatures for all the major and minor keys we've looked at in the Instruction Manual.

When a note unrelated to the key appears—for instance in a dominant seventh chord—that note is preceded by a sharp, flat or 'natural' sign, as above.

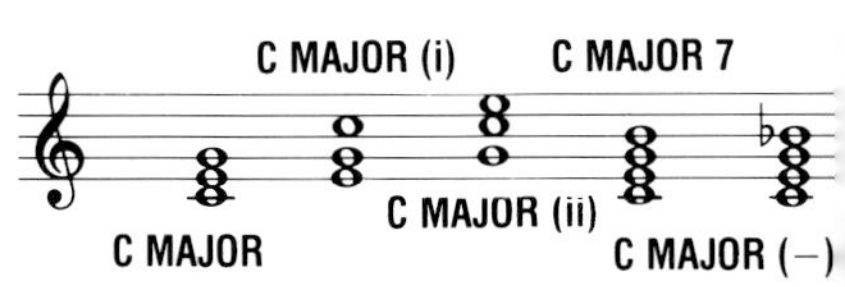

A chord is shown by stacking all the notes on top of each other, because they are played together.

)N THE following page, to close the ıstruction Manual, you'll find all the music rids you need to play The Human eague's 'Don't You Want Me' in its ntirety—playing chords with the right and and basslines with the left. Obviously, ıis is the most complicated exercise ou've attempted to date, so don't worry if it akes some time to get it right.

To make things a little easier, we've ivided the song into five sections: Intro, 'erse, Bridge 1, Bridge 2 and Chorus. Try ɔ master one section at a time, playing the ight and left hand parts separately at first, ıen together.

In each section there's a running order ɔr the bars in that section. The songwords re on page 29.

As we've mentioned before, 'Don't You Vant Me' actually swaps keys from **C** major to **A** minor. Don't let that put you off: it's actually quite straightforward, using mainly primary chords with plenty of inversions to keep you on your toes.

The tricky bits are the two Bridges. These include a major seventh chord, a minor seventh chord and a dominant seventh chord.

Also present momentarily are two primary chords unrelated to **C** major and **A** minor, namely **A** major and **E** major.

The main thing to watch out for, however, is a new chord you won't have seen before—**G(sus)4**.

We look at this chord, and others like it, at the end of the Chord Directory on page 84. But so that you can play it now, here is the chord shape and fingering required.

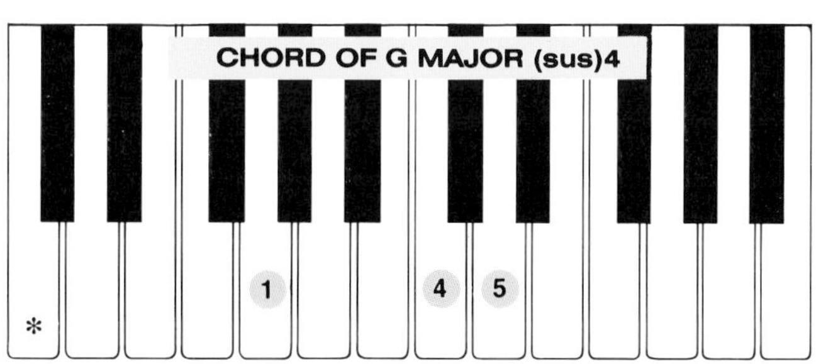

BEST OF luck with this song, which brings together just about everything you've learnt. If you can manage it, you can say without a doubt that you can now PLAY ROCK KEYBOARDS.

RHYTHM

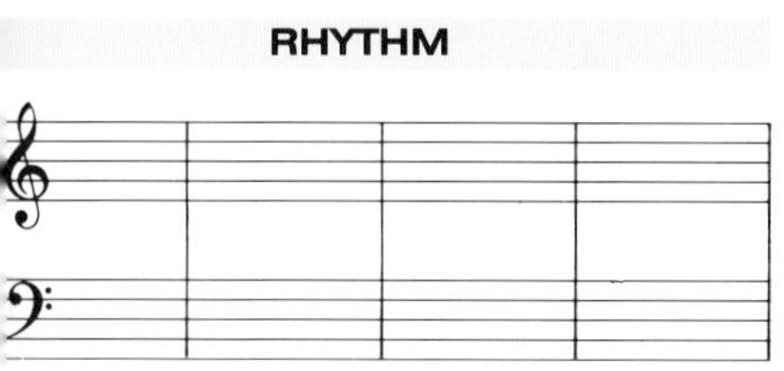

ˈlusic staves are divided into bars by regular ertical lines.

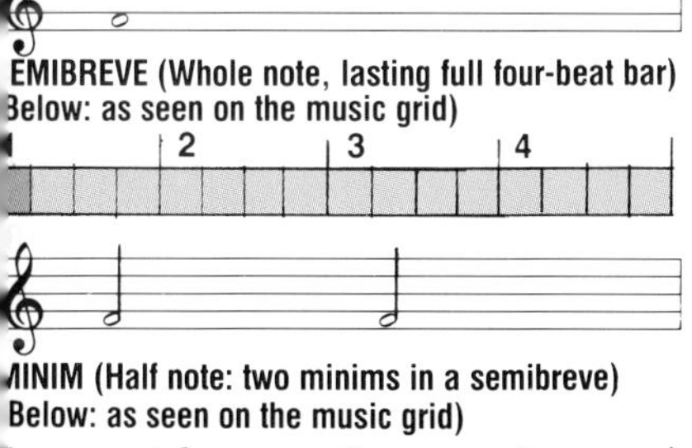

EMIBREVE (Whole note, lasting full four-beat bar)
3elow: as seen on the music grid)

ˈlINIM (Half note: two minims in a semibreve)
Below: as seen on the music grid)

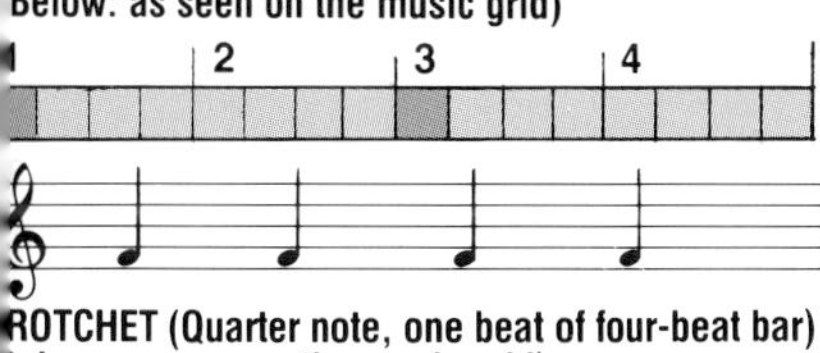

ROTCHET (Quarter note, one beat of four-beat bar)
elow: as seen on the music grid)

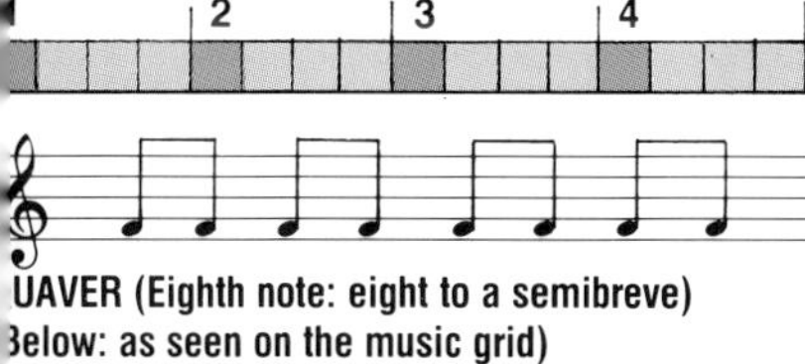

UAVER (Eighth note: eight to a semibreve)
3elow: as seen on the music grid)

EMIQUAVER (Sixteenth note, a quarter of a beat)
3elow: as seen on the music grid)

hese (above) are the different note lengths, in ɜlation to our music grid, and the names given ɔ them.

These are the three most common time signatures. The top number is beats per bar. The number below describes the beat—**4** means it's a 'quarter note' beat. Most rock songs are in **4/4**.

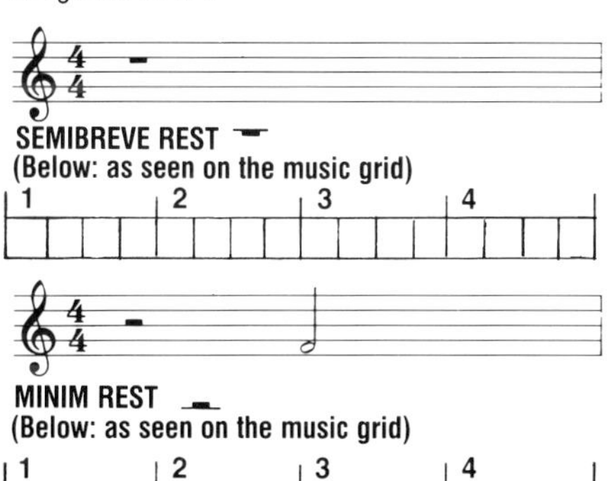

SEMIBREVE REST
(Below: as seen on the music grid)

MINIM REST
(Below: as seen on the music grid)

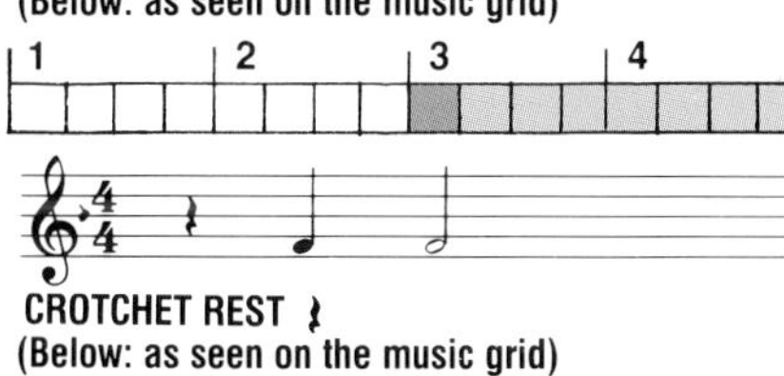

CROTCHET REST
(Below: as seen on the music grid)

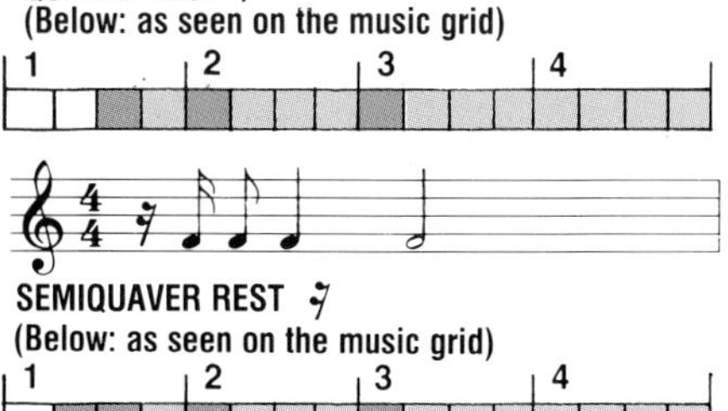

QUAVER REST
(Below: as seen on the music grid)

SEMIQUAVER REST
(Below: as seen on the music grid)

The symbols above represent 'rests' or silences. They also show how notes of different lengths can be used in one bar.

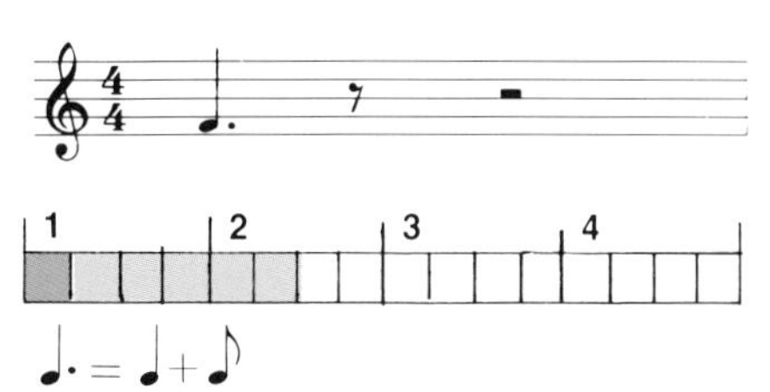

When a note is 'dotted', it lasts for its normal length plus half its length again.

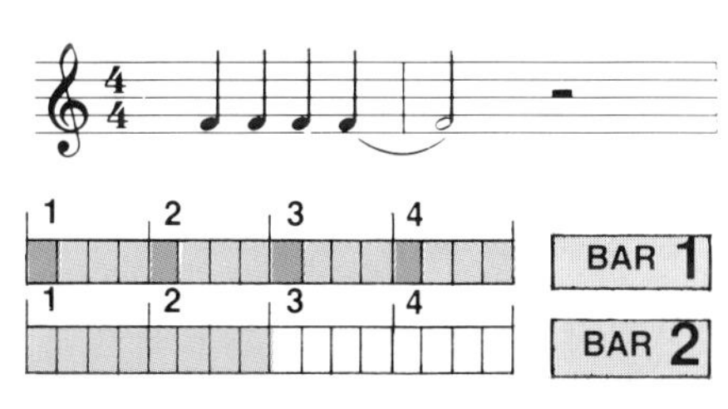

When two notes of the same pitch are 'tied' (linked by a curved line), the note is held for the total length of both notes. The note is not played twice, it is just sustained.

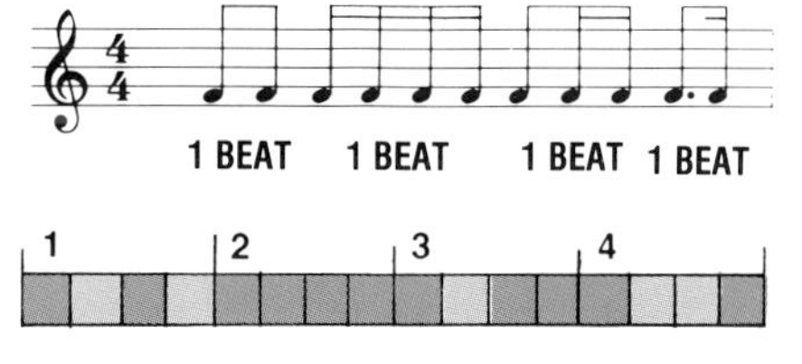

When more than one quaver or semiquaver occur on the same beat, unless there is a rest between them they are linked together. Unless they are 'tied' by a curved line, they are played separately.

Notes above the middle line of a stave usually have stems pointing downwards. Notes on the middle line can have either up or down stems.

'DON'T YOU WANT ME' COMPLETE

TITLE	KEY	TEMPO	STARTING POINT
'DON'T YOU WANT ME'	C MAJOR A MINOR	QUITE FAST	A BELOW * (LEFT HAND) Am ABOVE * (RIGHT HAND)

SONG RUNNING ORDER

INTRO/VERSE
BRIDGE 1/BRIDGE 2
CHORUS/VERSE
BRIDGE 1/BRIDGE 2
CHORUS/INTRO
CHORUS/CHORUS

Section	Bar	Line	1				2				3				4			
INTRO	BAR 1	Chord	Am															
		Bass	A3				A3			E5	G4		A3					
	BAR 2	Chord	F(i)															
		Bass	A3		E5		G4		C1									
	BAR 3	Chord	Em(i)															
		Bass	A3		C1		G4		A3									
	BAR 4	Chord	Em(i)												G		F	
		Bass	D2	E1	D2	C3	B4		A5									
VERSE	BAR 1	Chord	F														Am	
		Bass	F2		F2		C5	F2		C5	F2							
	BAR 2	Chord							G						G		F	
		Bass	G1		G1		D4	G1		D4	G1							
	BAR 3	Chord											C				G	
		Bass	F2		F2		C5	F2		C5	F2							
	BAR 4	Chord													G		F	
		Bass	G1		G1		D4	G1		D4	G1							
	BAR 5	Chord	G															
		Bass	G1		G1		D4	G1		D4	G1						E3	G2
BRIDGE 1	BAR 1	Chord	Am												Am		Em(i)	
		Bass	A1		A1		E4	A1		E4	A1							
	BAR 2	Chord													Em(ii)		F(i)	
		Bass	E2		E2		B5	E2		B5	E2							
	BAR 3	Chord													F		Dm(i)	
		Bass	F1		F1		C4	F1		C4	F1							
	BAR 4	Chord	Fma7				Dm7(i)				F		G					
		Bass	D2		D2		A5	D2		A5	G1						E3	G2
	BAR 5	Chord									Gsus4				G			
		Bass	D2		D2		A5	D2		A5	G1							
BRIDGE 2	BAR 1	Chord	A												A		G(–)7	
		Bass	A5		A5		A5		A5		A5		A5		A5		A5	
	BAR 2	Chord													G(–)7		C(ii)	
		Bass	B4		B4		B4		B4		B4		B4		B4		B4	
	BAR 3	Chord													C(ii)		E(i)	
		Bass	C3		C3		C3		C3		C3		C3		C3		C3	
	BAR 4	Chord																
		Bass	E1		E1		E1		E1		E1		E1		E1		E1	
CHORUS	BAR 1	Chord	F(i)								F(i)							
		Bass	F2		F2		C5	F2		C5	F2							
	BAR 2	Chord	G(i)								G(i)							
		Bass	G1		G1		D4	G1		D4	G1							

INTRO

1	2	1	3
1	2	1	4

VERSE

1	2	3	4
1	2	3	4
1	2	3	4
1	2	3	5

BRIDGE 1

1	2	3	4
1	2	3	5

BRIDGE 2

1	2	3	4

CHORUS

1	2	1	2
1	2	1	2

CHORD DIRECTORY

This 13-page Chord Directory shows you how to play most of the chords you are ever likely to need. It includes all the major and minor primary triads and full primary chords, all the major seventh, minor seventh and dominant seventh chords in every key, and their inversions. It also shows the scales for each key and suggested bass notes for each chord. And on page 84 we introduce you to eight new chords which you can use in any key.

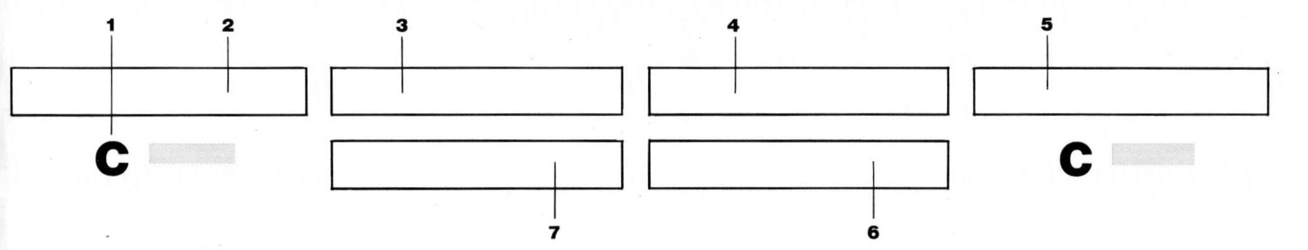

HOW TO USE THE CHORD DIRECTORY

Taking **C** major as our example, this is how each key is presented in the main part of the Chord Directory (pages 72–83):

1. Name of the key.
2. First chord diagram, showing a basic primary triad and full primary chord—plus, in each major key, the major seventh and dominant seventh chords; and in each minor key, the minor seventh chord.
3. The first inversions of all the chords in the first diagram.
4. The second inversions of those chords.
5. The third inversions of those chords.
6. Chord names and suitable bass notes for each chord. Notes listed in black appear in the scale for the key; red notes are 'unrelated'.
7. The scale for the key, and the correct fingering for playing the scale with either hand (red equals right, blue left).

SYMBOLS

● Notes to be played in the primary triad.
■ An optional note which may be added to the primary triad to make a full primary chord.
▲ A note which, when added to the primary triad, makes either a major seventh or minor seventh chord.
■ A note which, when added to the primary triad, gives a dominant seventh chord.

FINGERING

The Chord Directory contains no instructions on how to finger each chord. All the chord *types* have appeared elsewhere in the book with correct fingering, so you should be able to work them out without too much trouble. If in doubt, a general rule is that your thumb (1) and little finger (5) should play the two outside notes of the chord. Common sense should tell you where to put your other fingers.

CONTENTS

MAJOR PRIMARY & SEVENTH CHORDS

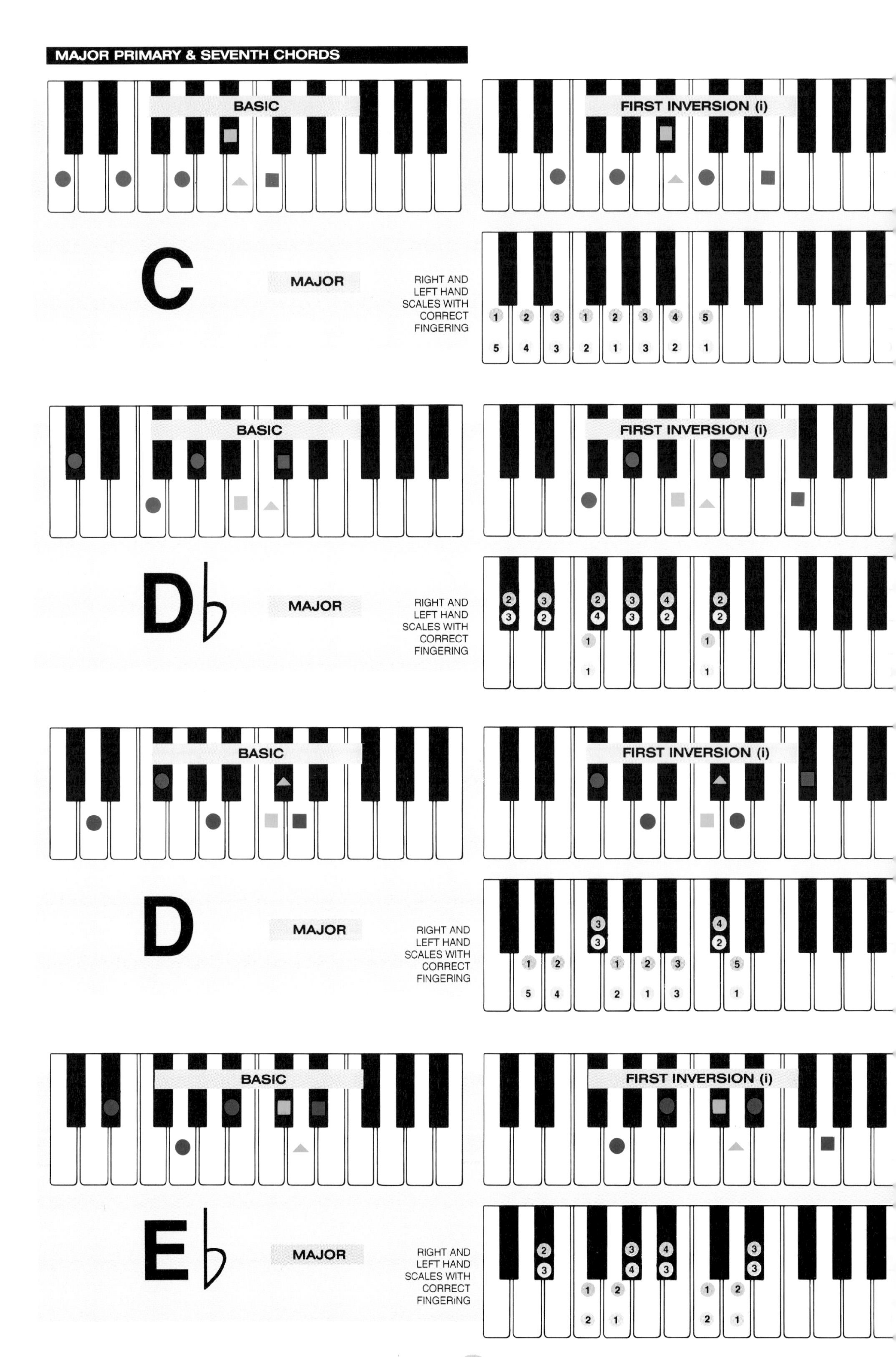

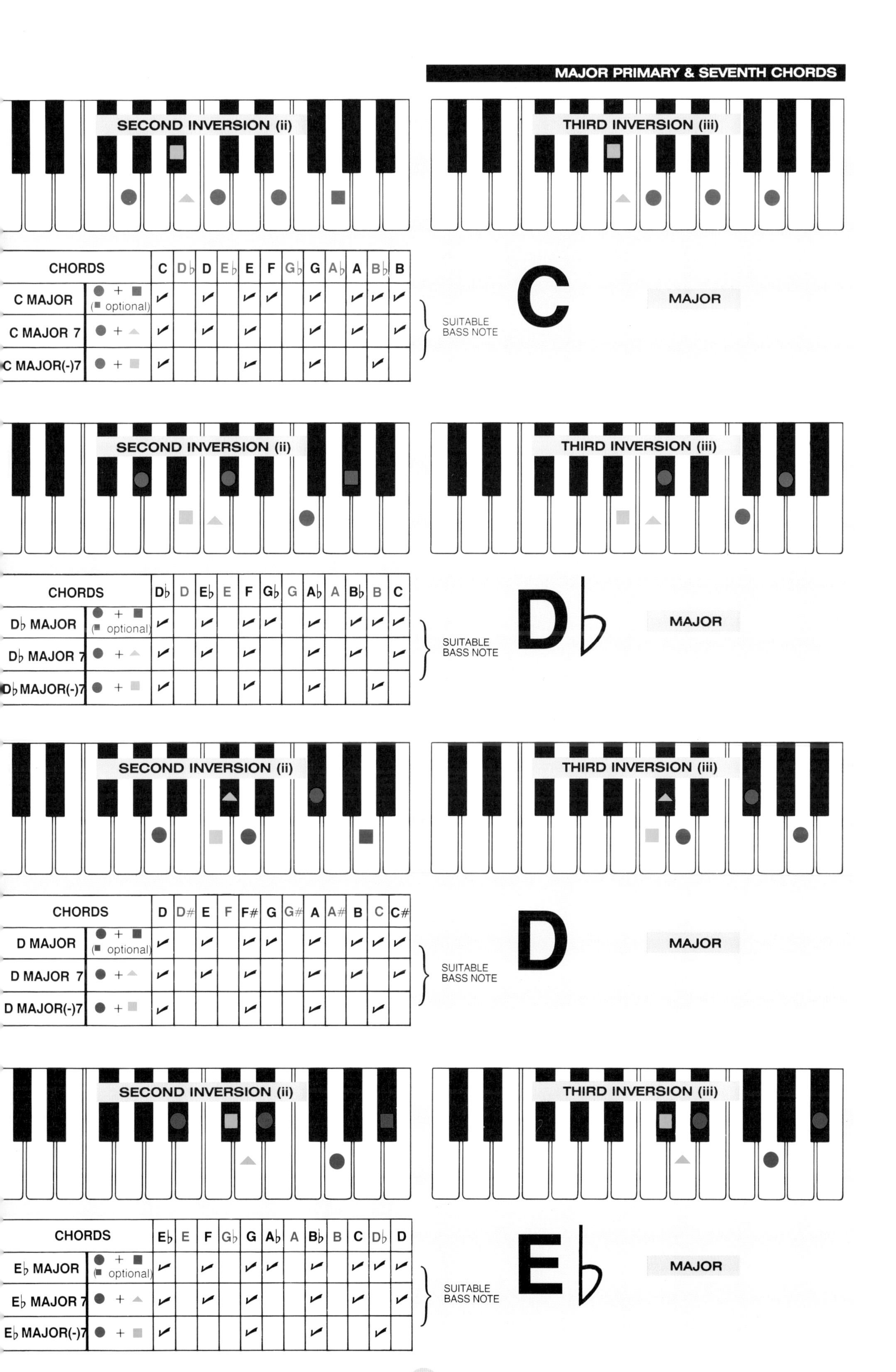

CHORDS		C	D♭	D	E♭	E	F	G♭	G	A♭	A	B♭	B
C MAJOR	● + ■ (■ optional)	✓		✓		✓	✓		✓		✓	✓	✓
C MAJOR 7	● + ▲	✓		✓		✓			✓		✓		✓
C MAJOR(-)7	● + ■	✓				✓			✓			✓	

SUITABLE BASS NOTE

C MAJOR

CHORDS		D♭	D	E♭	E	F	G♭	G	A♭	A	B♭	B	C
D♭ MAJOR	● + ■ (■ optional)	✓		✓		✓	✓		✓		✓	✓	✓
D♭ MAJOR 7	● + ▲	✓		✓		✓			✓		✓		✓
D♭ MAJOR(-)7	● + ■	✓				✓			✓			✓	

SUITABLE BASS NOTE

D♭ MAJOR

CHORDS		D	D#	E	F	F#	G	G#	A	A#	B	C	C#
D MAJOR	● + ■ (■ optional)	✓		✓		✓	✓		✓		✓	✓	✓
D MAJOR 7	● + ▲	✓		✓		✓			✓		✓		✓
D MAJOR(-)7	● + ■	✓				✓			✓			✓	

SUITABLE BASS NOTE

D MAJOR

CHORDS		E♭	E	F	G♭	G	A♭	A	B♭	B	C	D♭	D
E♭ MAJOR	● + ■ (■ optional)	✓		✓		✓	✓		✓		✓	✓	✓
E♭ MAJOR 7	● + ▲	✓		✓		✓			✓		✓		✓
E♭ MAJOR(-)7	● + ■	✓				✓			✓			✓	

SUITABLE BASS NOTE

E♭ MAJOR

MAJOR PRIMARY & SEVENTH CHORDS

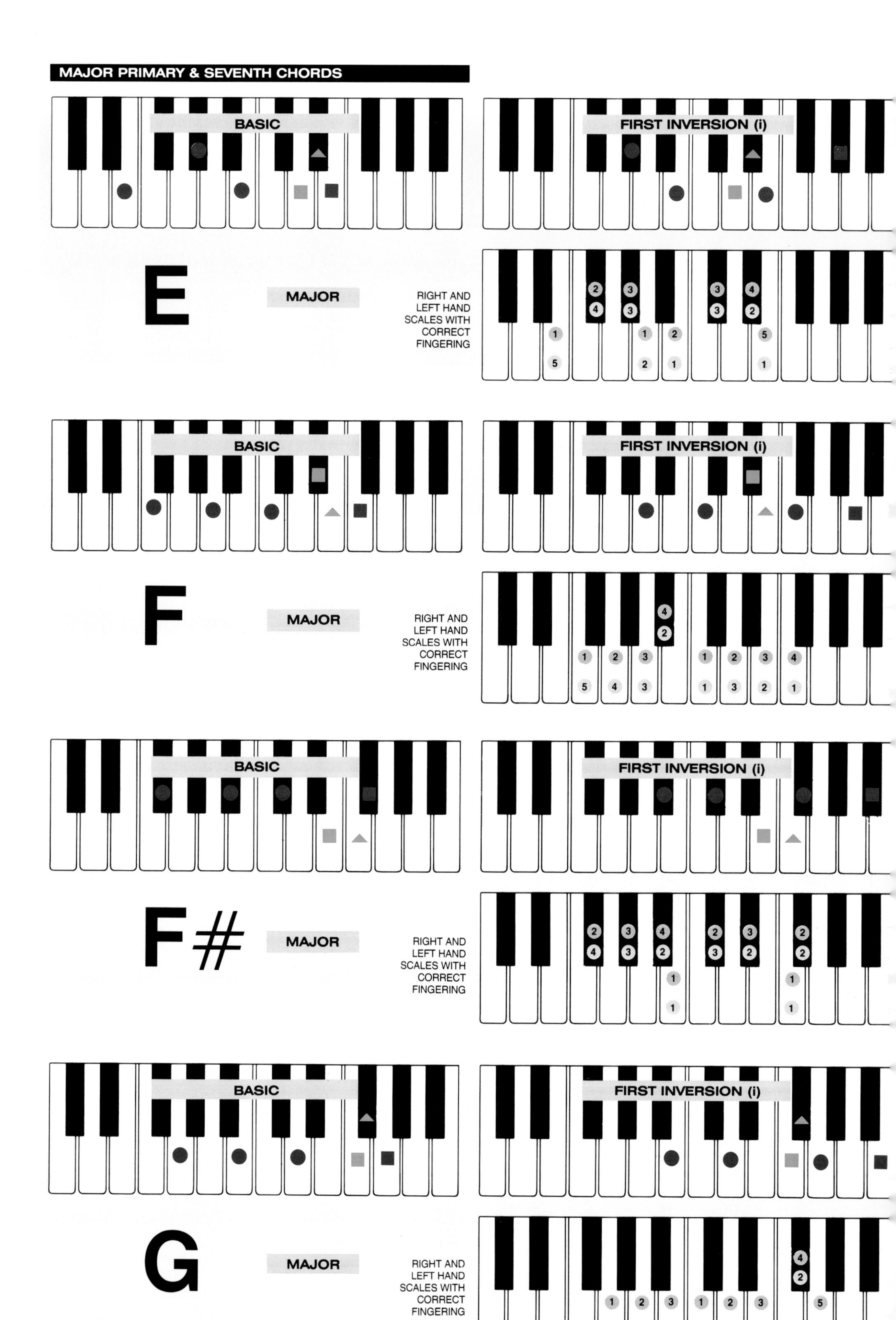

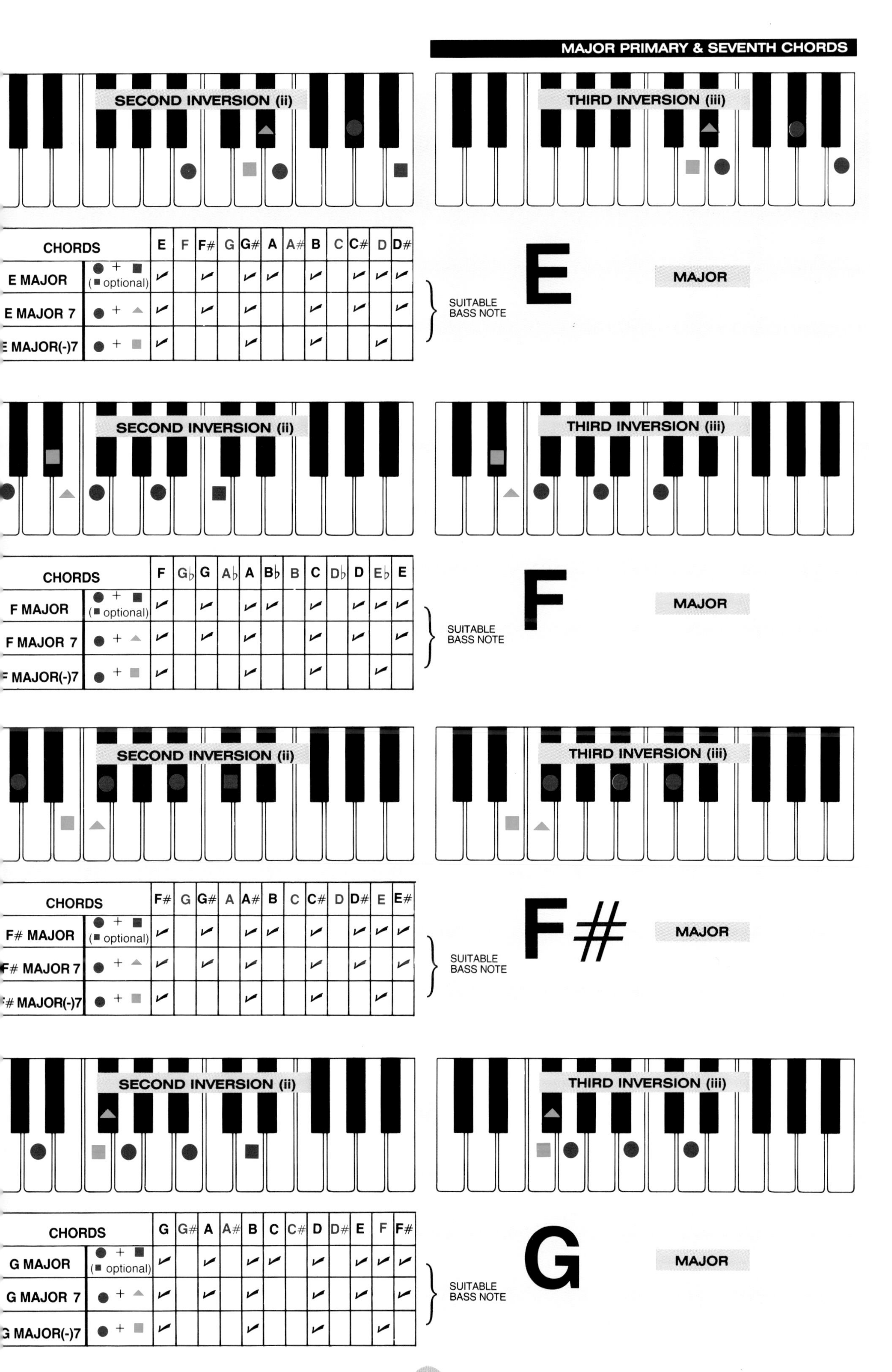

CHORDS		E	F	F#	G	G#	A	A#	B	C	C#	D	D#
E MAJOR	● + ■ (■ optional)	✓		✓		✓	✓		✓		✓	✓	✓
E MAJOR 7	● + ▲	✓		✓		✓			✓		✓		✓
E MAJOR(-)7	● + ■	✓				✓			✓			✓	

CHORDS		F	G♭	G	A♭	A	B♭	B	C	D♭	D	E♭	E
F MAJOR	● + ■ (■ optional)	✓		✓		✓	✓		✓		✓	✓	✓
F MAJOR 7	● + ▲	✓		✓		✓			✓		✓		✓
F MAJOR(-)7	● + ■	✓				✓			✓			✓	

CHORDS		F#	G	G#	A	A#	B	C	C#	D	D#	E	E#
F# MAJOR	● + ■ (■ optional)	✓		✓		✓	✓		✓		✓	✓	✓
F# MAJOR 7	● + ▲	✓		✓		✓			✓		✓		✓
F# MAJOR(-)7	● + ■	✓				✓			✓			✓	

CHORDS		G	G#	A	A#	B	C	C#	D	D#	E	F	F#
G MAJOR	● + ■ (■ optional)	✓		✓		✓	✓		✓		✓	✓	✓
G MAJOR 7	● + ▲	✓		✓		✓			✓		✓		✓
G MAJOR(-)7	● + ■	✓				✓			✓			✓	

MAJOR PRIMARY & SEVENTH CHORDS

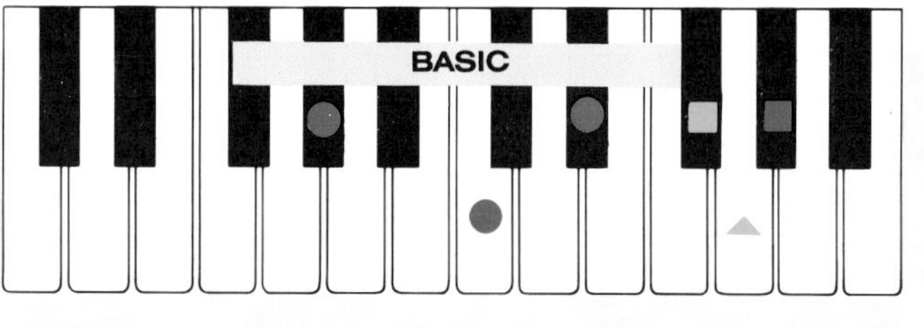

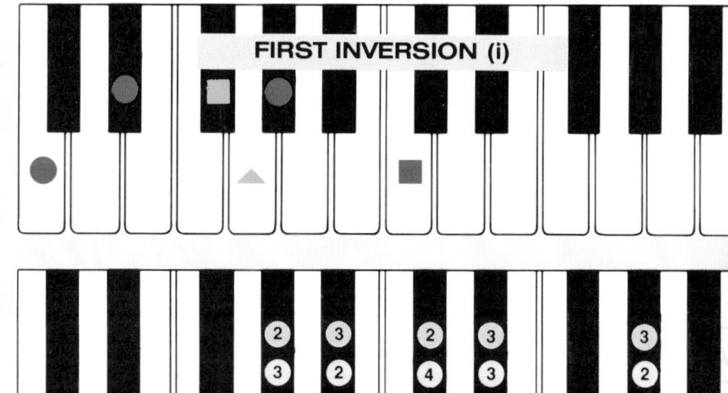

A♭

MAJOR

RIGHT AND LEFT HAND SCALES WITH CORRECT FINGERING

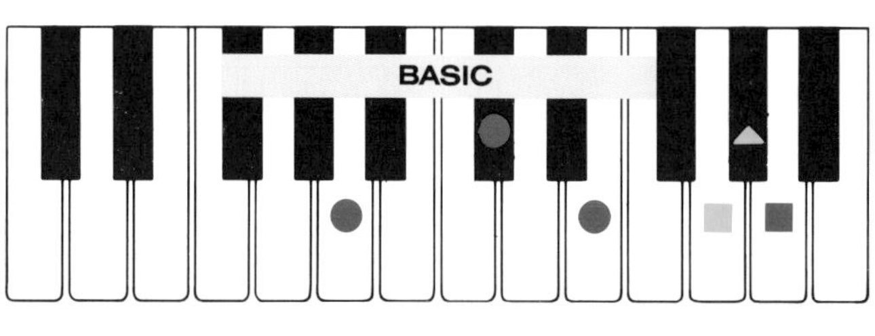

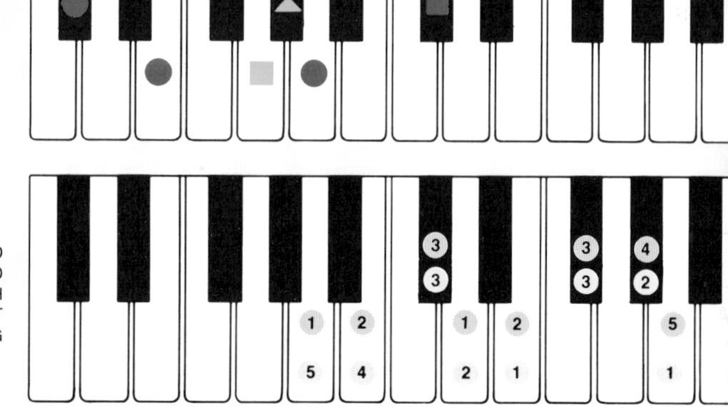

A

MAJOR

RIGHT AND LEFT HAND SCALES WITH CORRECT FINGERING

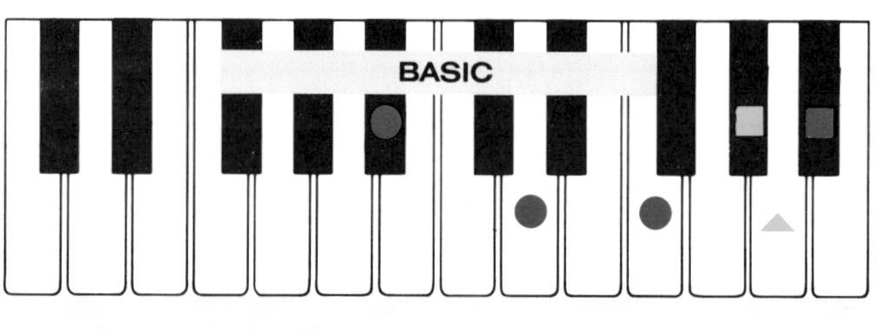

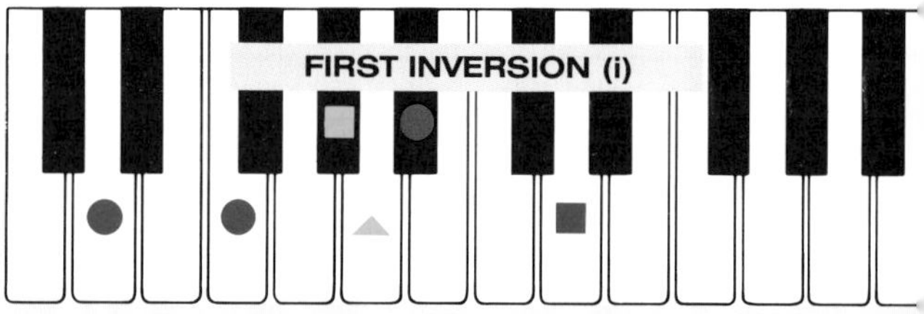

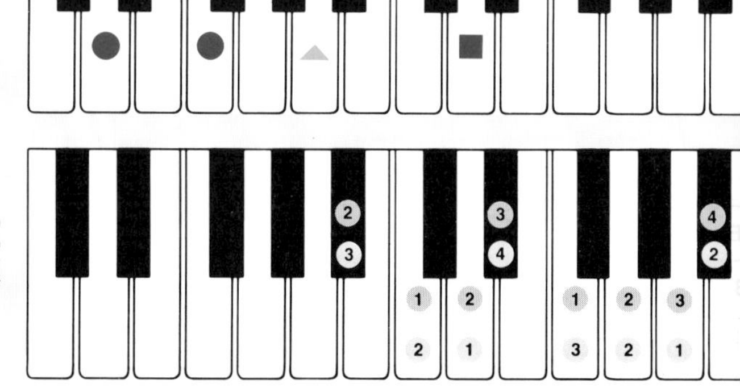

B♭

MAJOR

RIGHT AND LEFT HAND SCALES WITH CORRECT FINGERING

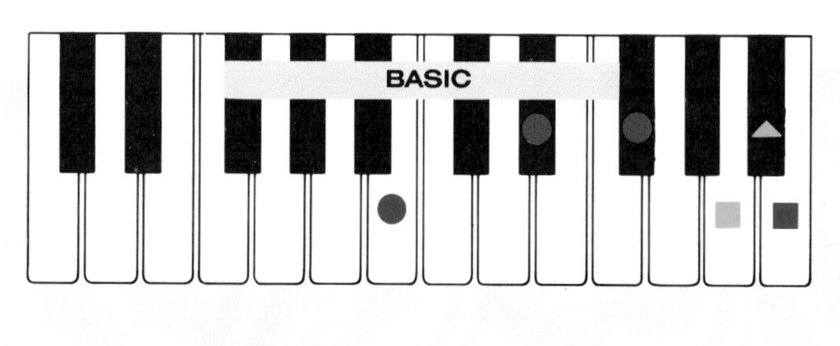

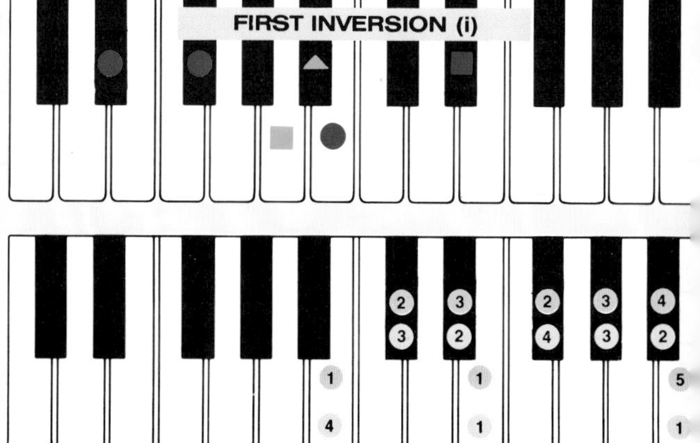

B

MAJOR

RIGHT AND LEFT HAND SCALES WITH CORRECT FINGERING

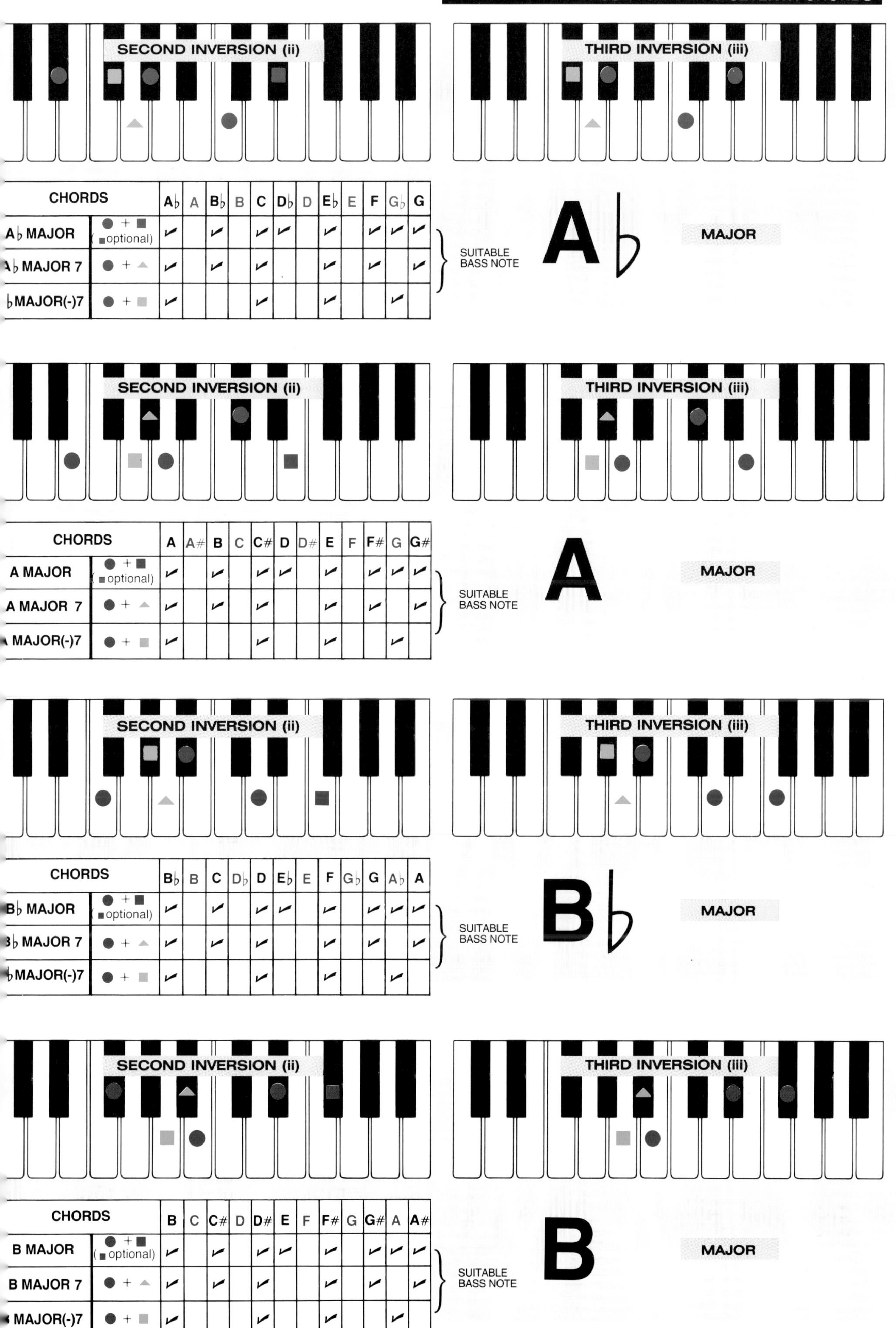

CHORDS		A♭	A	B♭	B	C	D♭	D	E♭	E	F	G♭	G
A♭ MAJOR	● + ■ (■ optional)	✓		✓		✓	✓		✓		✓	✓	✓
A♭ MAJOR 7	● + ▲	✓		✓		✓			✓		✓		✓
A♭ MAJOR(-)7	● + ■	✓				✓			✓			✓	

SUITABLE BASS NOTE

A♭

MAJOR

CHORDS		A	A#	B	C	C#	D	D#	E	F	F#	G	G#
A MAJOR	● + ■ (■ optional)	✓		✓		✓	✓		✓		✓	✓	✓
A MAJOR 7	● + ▲	✓		✓		✓			✓		✓		✓
A MAJOR(-)7	● + ■	✓				✓			✓			✓	

SUITABLE BASS NOTE

A

MAJOR

CHORDS		B♭	B	C	D♭	D	E♭	E	F	G♭	G	A♭	A
B♭ MAJOR	● + ■ (■ optional)	✓		✓		✓	✓		✓		✓	✓	✓
B♭ MAJOR 7	● + ▲	✓		✓		✓			✓		✓		✓
B♭ MAJOR(-)7	● + ■	✓				✓			✓			✓	

SUITABLE BASS NOTE

B♭

MAJOR

CHORDS		B	C	C#	D	D#	E	F	F#	G	G#	A	A#
B MAJOR	● + ■ (■ optional)	✓		✓		✓	✓		✓		✓	✓	✓
B MAJOR 7	● + ▲	✓		✓		✓			✓		✓		✓
B MAJOR(-)7	● + ■	✓				✓			✓			✓	

SUITABLE BASS NOTE

B

MAJOR

MINOR PRIMARY & SEVENTH CHORDS

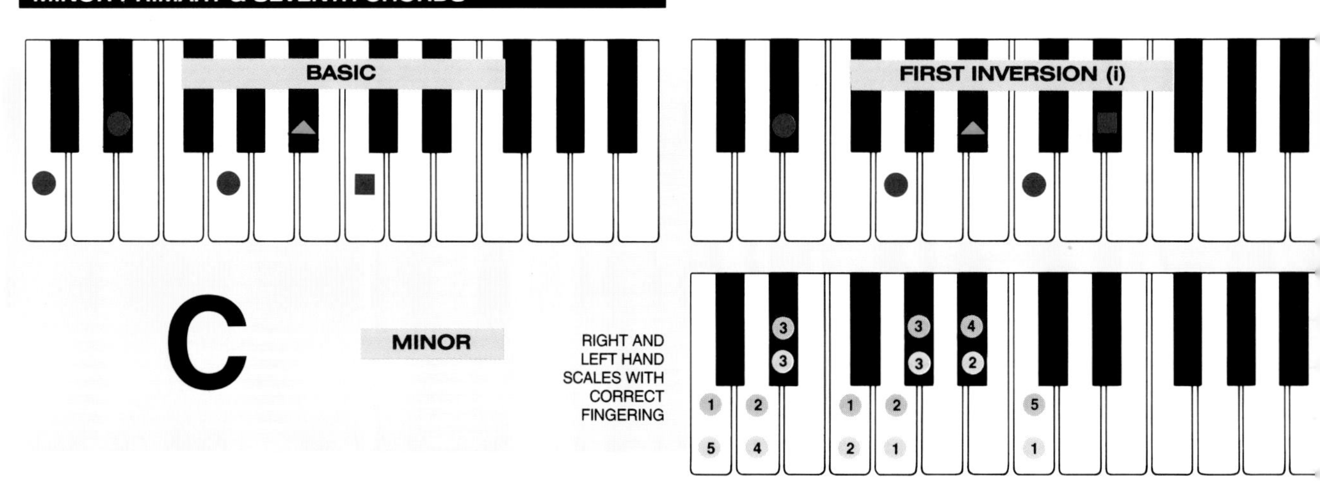
BASIC
FIRST INVERSION (i)
C
MINOR
RIGHT AND LEFT HAND SCALES WITH CORRECT FINGERING
3
3
3
3
4
2
1
2
1
2
5
5
4
2
1
1

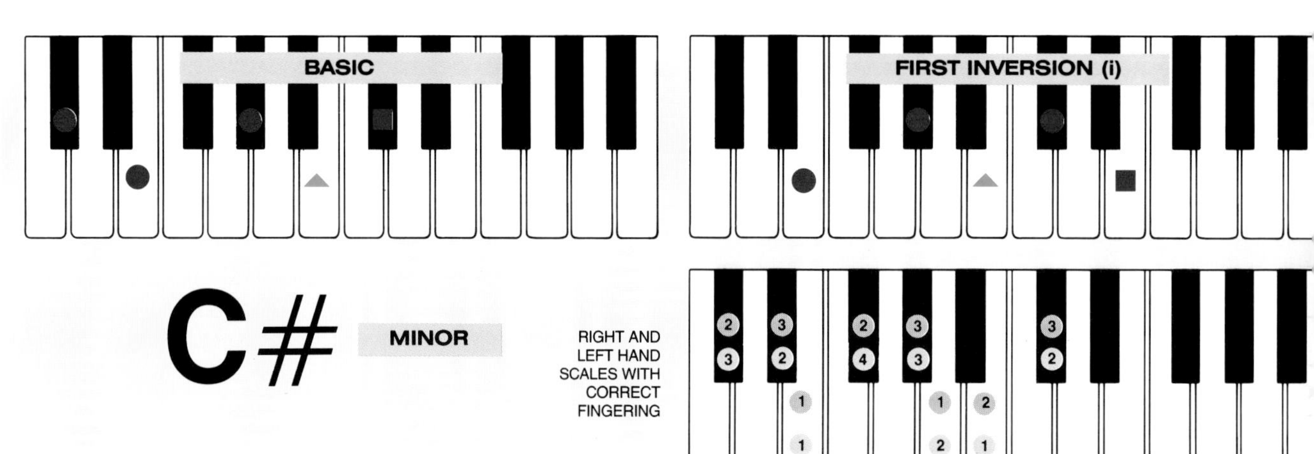
BASIC
FIRST INVERSION (i)
C#
MINOR
RIGHT AND LEFT HAND SCALES WITH CORRECT FINGERING
2
3
3
2
2
4
3
3
3
2
1
1
2
1
2
1

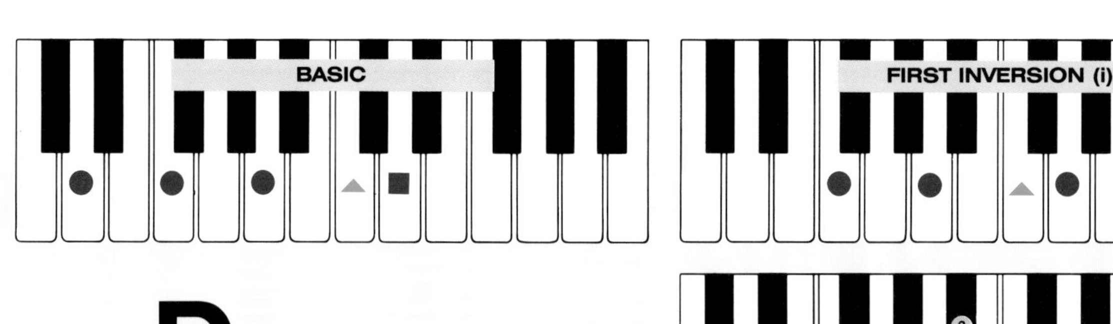
BASIC
FIRST INVERSION (i)
D
MINOR
RIGHT AND LEFT HAND SCALES WITH CORRECT FINGERING
3
3
1
2
3
1
2
4
5
5
4
3
2
1
2
1

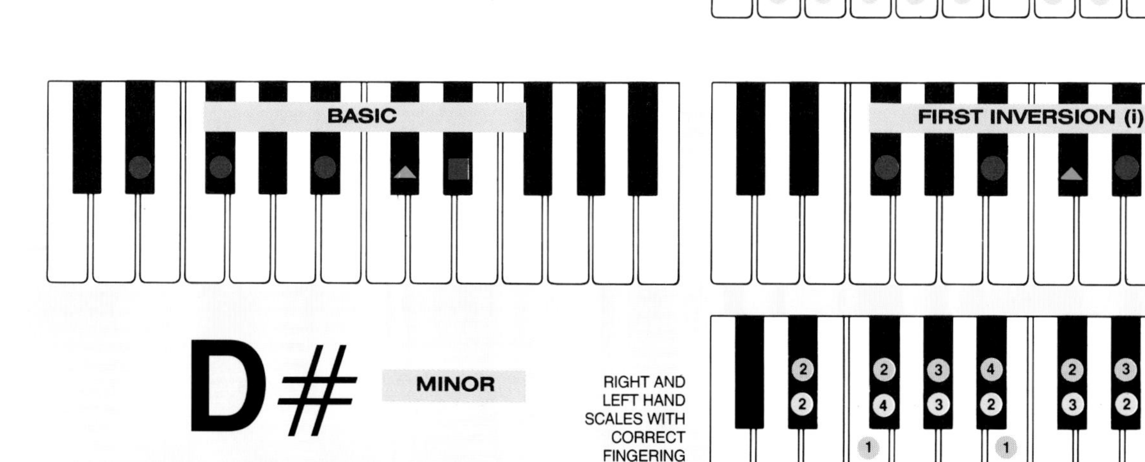
BASIC
FIRST INVERSION (i)
D#
MINOR
RIGHT AND LEFT HAND SCALES WITH CORRECT FINGERING
2
2
2
4
3
3
4
2
2
3
3
2
1
1
1
1

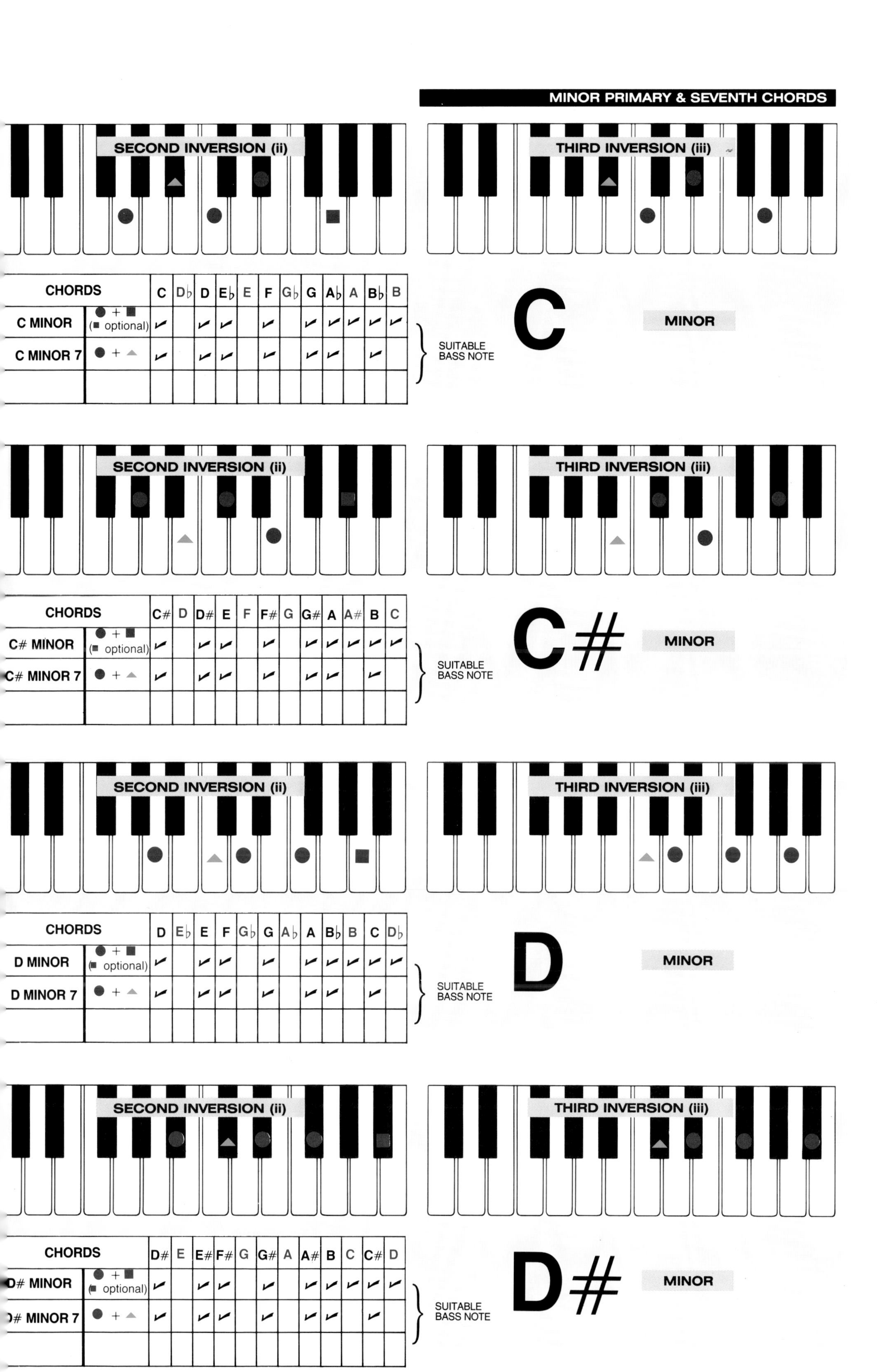

CHORDS		C	D♭	D	E♭	E	F	G♭	G	A♭	A	B♭	B
C MINOR	● + ■ (■ optional)	✓		✓	✓		✓		✓	✓	✓	✓	✓
C MINOR 7	● + ▲	✓		✓	✓		✓		✓	✓		✓	

CHORDS		C#	D	D#	E	F	F#	G	G#	A	A#	B	C
C# MINOR	● + ■ (■ optional)	✓		✓	✓		✓		✓	✓	✓	✓	✓
C# MINOR 7	● + ▲	✓		✓	✓		✓		✓	✓		✓	

CHORDS		D	E♭	E	F	G♭	G	A♭	A	B♭	B	C	D♭
D MINOR	● + ■ (■ optional)	✓		✓	✓		✓		✓	✓	✓	✓	✓
D MINOR 7	● + ▲	✓		✓	✓		✓		✓	✓		✓	

CHORDS		D#	E	E#	F#	G	G#	A	A#	B	C	C#	D
D# MINOR	● + ■ (■ optional)	✓		✓	✓		✓		✓	✓	✓	✓	✓
D# MINOR 7	● + ▲	✓		✓	✓		✓		✓	✓		✓	

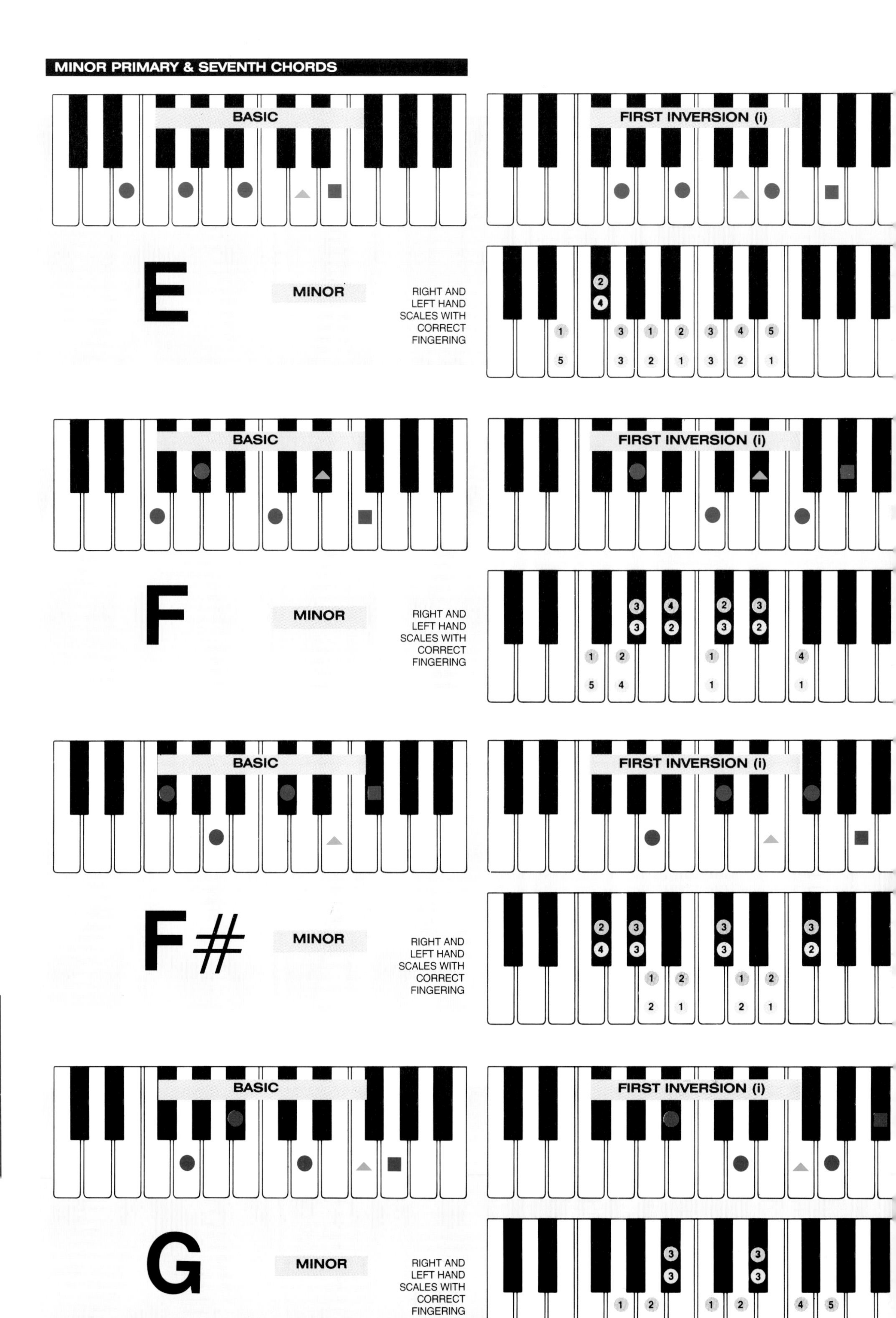
MINOR PRIMARY & SEVENTH CHORDS
BASIC
FIRST INVERSION (i)
E
MINOR
RIGHT AND LEFT HAND SCALES WITH CORRECT FINGERING
BASIC
FIRST INVERSION (i)
F
MINOR
RIGHT AND LEFT HAND SCALES WITH CORRECT FINGERING
BASIC
FIRST INVERSION (i)
F#
MINOR
RIGHT AND LEFT HAND SCALES WITH CORRECT FINGERING
BASIC
FIRST INVERSION (i)
G
MINOR
RIGHT AND LEFT HAND SCALES WITH CORRECT FINGERING

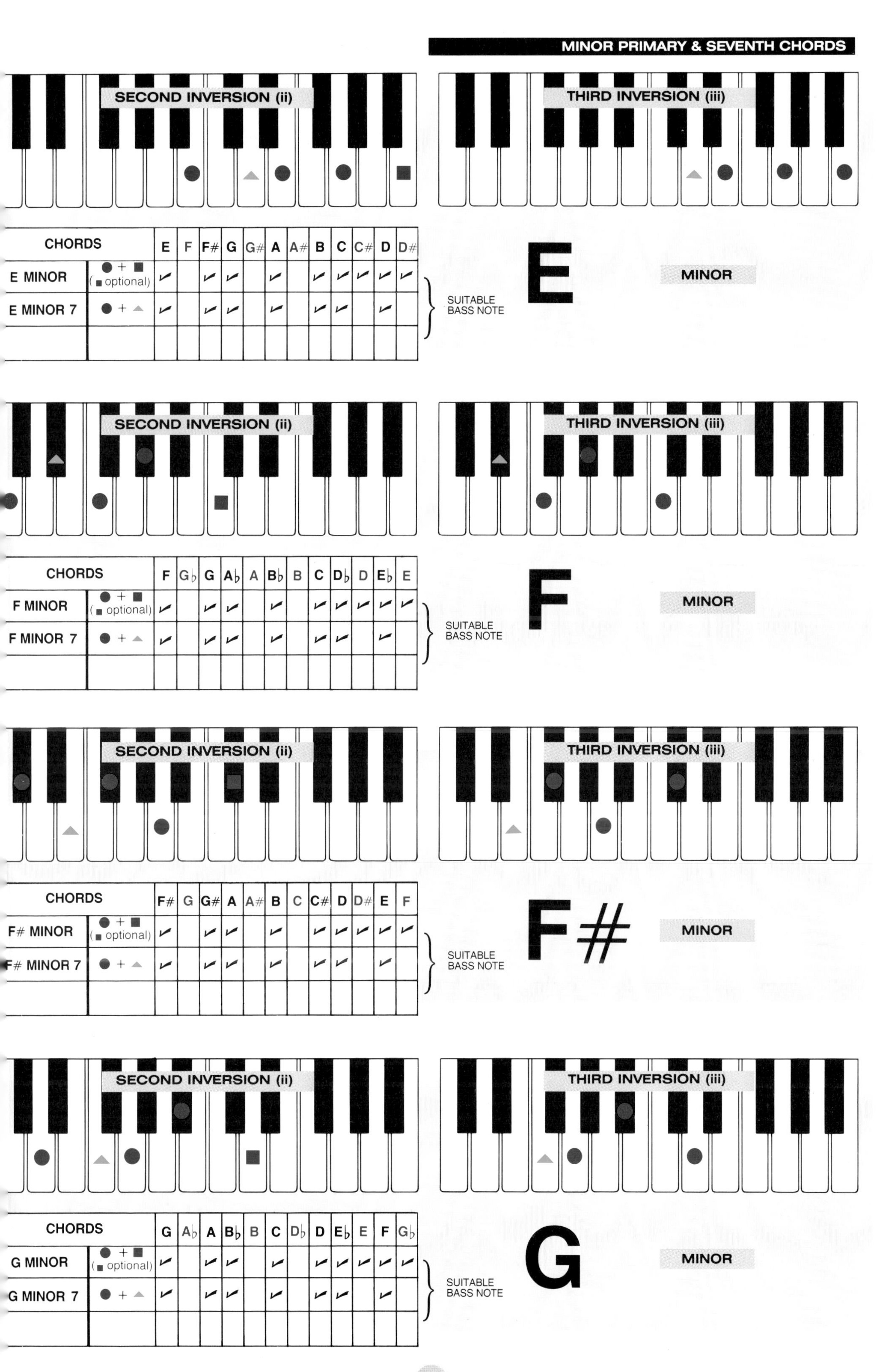

CHORDS		E	F	F#	G	G#	A	A#	B	C	C#	D	D#
E MINOR	● + ■ (■ optional)	✓		✓	✓		✓		✓	✓	✓	✓	✓
E MINOR 7	● + ▲	✓		✓	✓		✓		✓	✓		✓	

CHORDS		F	G♭	G	A♭	A	B♭	B	C	D♭	D	E♭	E
F MINOR	● + ■ (■ optional)	✓		✓	✓		✓		✓	✓	✓	✓	✓
F MINOR 7	● + ▲	✓		✓	✓		✓		✓	✓		✓	

CHORDS		F#	G	G#	A	A#	B	C	C#	D	D#	E	F
F# MINOR	● + ■ (■ optional)	✓		✓	✓		✓		✓	✓	✓	✓	✓
F# MINOR 7	● + ▲	✓		✓	✓		✓		✓	✓		✓	

CHORDS		G	A♭	A	B♭	B	C	D♭	D	E♭	E	F	G♭
G MINOR	● + ■ (■ optional)	✓		✓	✓		✓		✓	✓	✓	✓	✓
G MINOR 7	● + ▲	✓		✓	✓		✓		✓	✓		✓	

MINOR PRIMARY & SEVENTH CHORDS

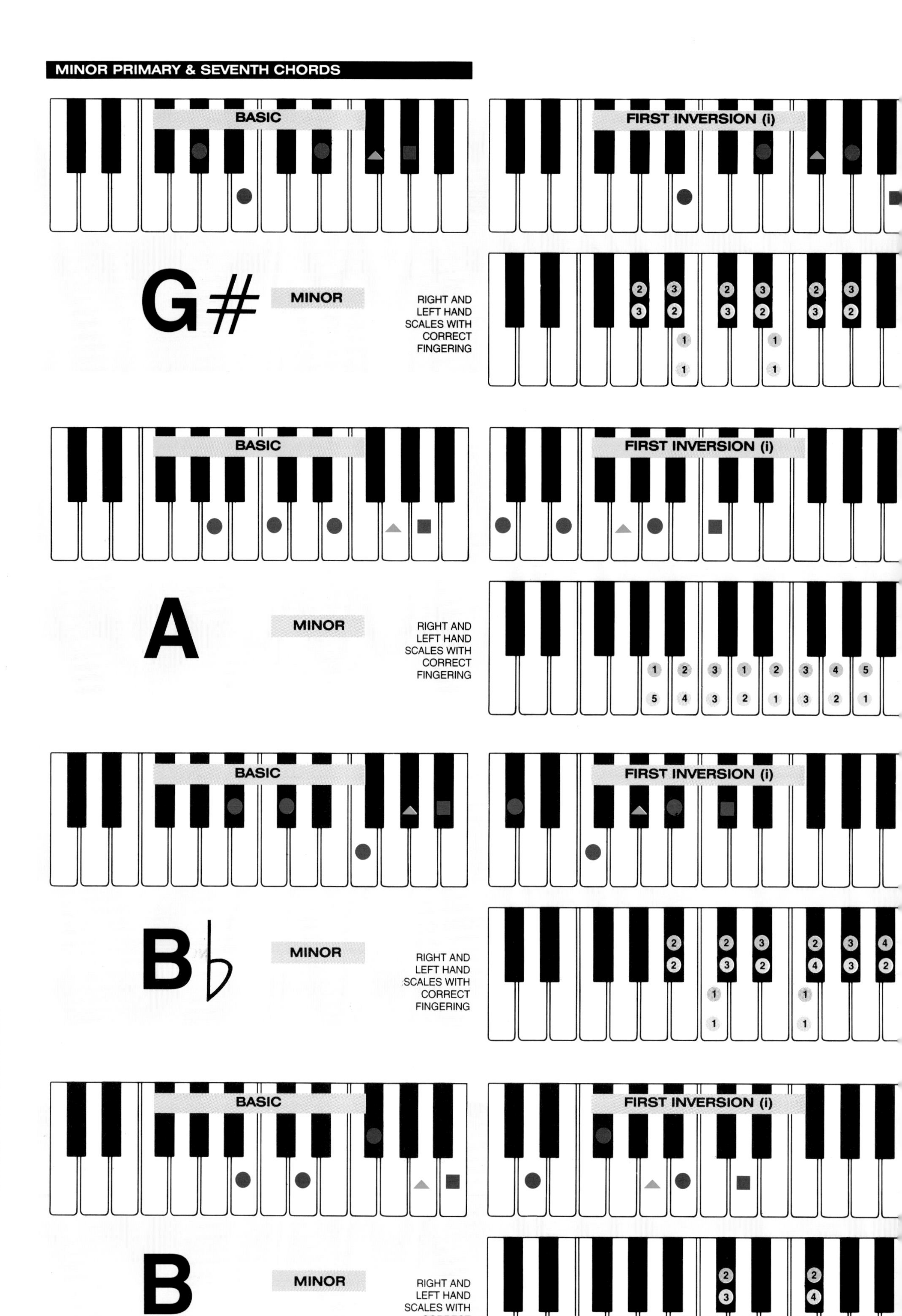

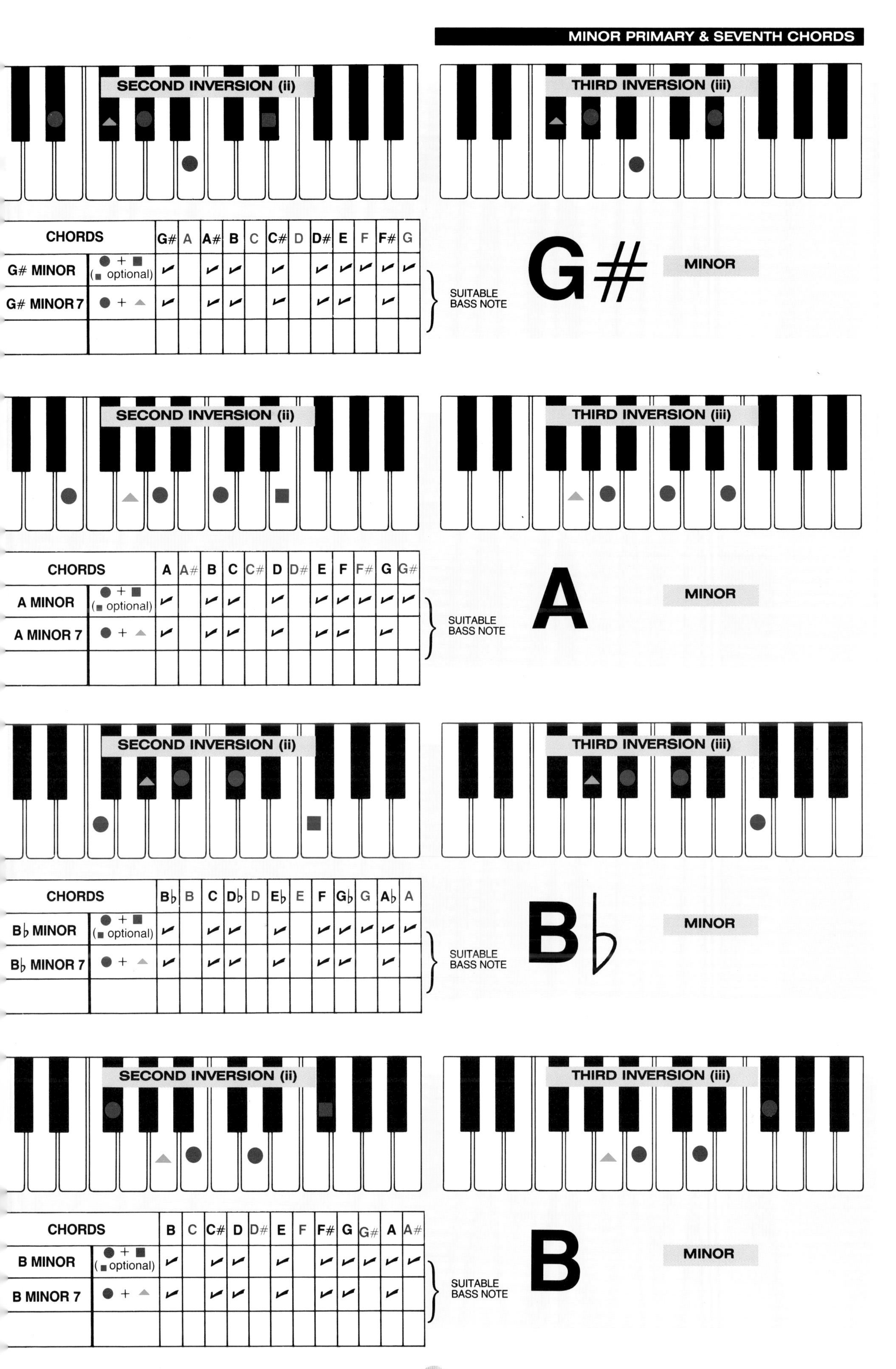

G# MINOR

CHORDS		G#	A	A#	B	C	C#	D	D#	E	F	F#	G
G# MINOR	● + ■ (■ optional)	✓		✓	✓		✓		✓	✓	✓	✓	✓
G# MINOR 7	● + ▲	✓		✓	✓		✓		✓	✓		✓	

SUITABLE BASS NOTE

A MINOR

CHORDS		A	A#	B	C	C#	D	D#	E	F	F#	G	G#
A MINOR	● + ■ (■ optional)	✓		✓	✓		✓		✓	✓	✓	✓	✓
A MINOR 7	● + ▲	✓		✓	✓		✓		✓	✓		✓	

SUITABLE BASS NOTE

B♭ MINOR

CHORDS		B♭	B	C	D♭	D	E♭	E	F	G♭	G	A♭	A
B♭ MINOR	● + ■ (■ optional)	✓		✓	✓		✓		✓	✓	✓	✓	✓
B♭ MINOR 7	● + ▲	✓		✓	✓		✓		✓	✓		✓	

SUITABLE BASS NOTE

B MINOR

CHORDS		B	C	C#	D	D#	E	F	F#	G	G#	A	A#
B MINOR	● + ■ (■ optional)	✓		✓	✓		✓		✓	✓	✓	✓	✓
B MINOR 7	● + ▲	✓		✓	✓		✓		✓	✓		✓	

SUITABLE BASS NOTE

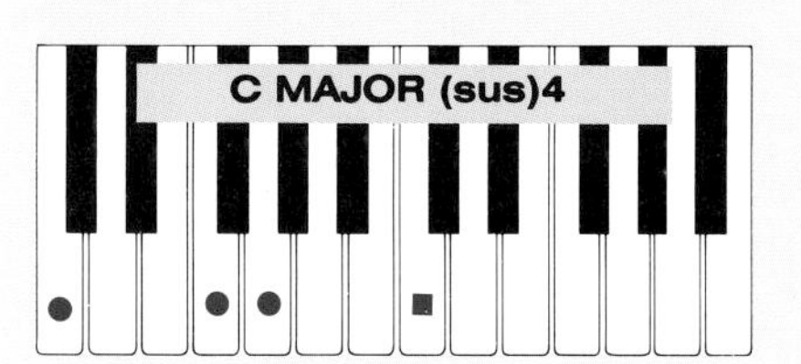

CHORD OF C MAJOR (sus)4
THIS CHORD is a slight variation of a major primary chord; the third note has been replaced by a 'suspended' fourth. This is simply the fourth note in the scale. So in **C** major, the **E** is replaced by **F**. A suspended fourth chord sounds particularly effective when followed or preceded by its primary chord – for instance from **C** major to **C** major **(sus)4**.

	C	D♭	D	E♭	E	F	G♭	G	A♭	A	B♭	B
BASS NOTES	✓	✓	✓	✓		✓		✓	✓	✓	✓	

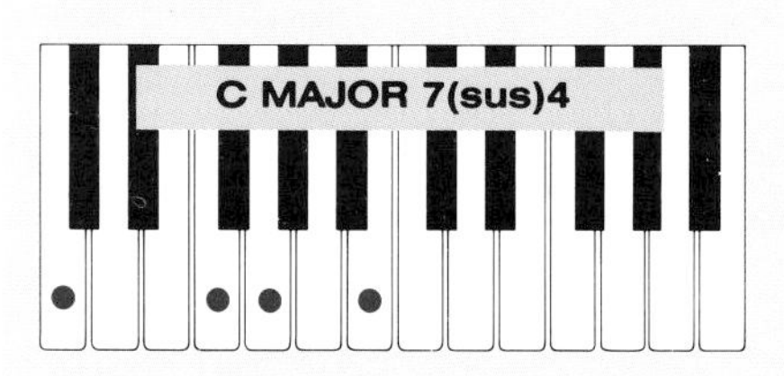

CHORD OF C MAJOR 7 (sus)4
THIS CHORD is a **C** major **(sus)4** with a seventh note added – or in other words, an ordinary **C** major **7** chord but with the third note replaced by a suspended fourth. The unrelated bass notes can make this chord sound a little harsh.

	C	D♭	D	E♭	E	F	G♭	G	A♭	A	B♭	B
BASS NOTES	✓		✓			✓		✓		✓		

C MAJOR (–)7(sus)4

CHORD OF C MAJOR (-)7 (sus)4
THIS CHORD is similar to a dominant seventh chord, but with the third note replaced by a suspended fourth. **C** major (-)**7** is the dominant seventh in the key of **F** major, and so sounds good followed by an **F** major chord. The same goes for **C** major (-)**7** **(sus)4.**

	C	D♭	D	E♭	E	F	G♭	G	A♭	A	B♭	B
BASS NOTES	✓		✓	✓		✓		✓	✓		✓	

IN EACH of these three suspended fourth chords, the third note in the scale has been replaced by a suspended fourth. You may remember that it is the third which differentiates a major from its equivalent (not relative) minor – the third note in C major is E, the third in C minor is E♭. On the other hand, the fourth note is the same in both the C major and C minor scales (it's F). This means that all three suspended fourth chords can be used in both major and minor keys.

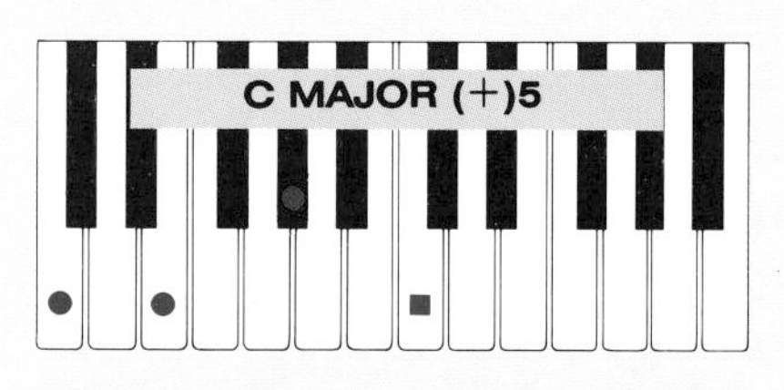

CHORD OF C MAJOR (+)5
THIS CHORD is more or less the same as a major primary chord, but with the fifth note 'augmented'. This means that it has been raised by one semitone – hence the (+)**5** symbol. So in **C** major, the **G** note becomes **G#**. This is a useful connecting chord between major and relative minor – for example, **C** major to **C** major (+)**5** to **A** minor **(i)**.

	C	C#	D	D#	E	F	F#	G	G#	A	A#	B
BASS NOTES	✓				✓				✓			

CHORD OF C MAJOR 7 (+)5
THIS CHORD is very much a 'one-off' chord which may be used only occasionally. It's a basic **C** major **7** chord, but with an augmented fifth. This chord can sound harsh if inverted.

	C	C#	D	D#	E	F	F#	G	G#	A	A#	B
BASS NOTES	✓		✓		✓		✓		✓	✓		✓

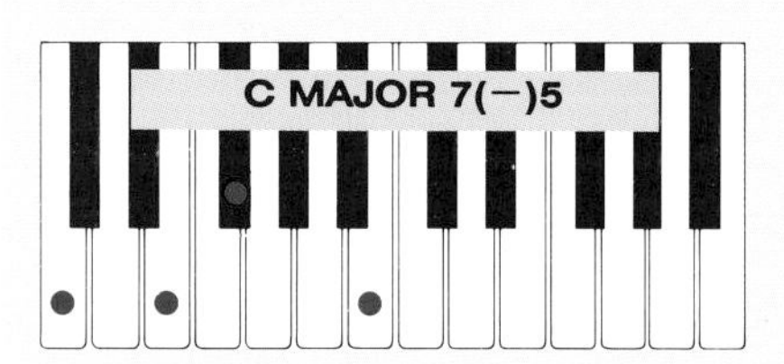

CHORD OF C MAJOR 7 (-)5
THIS CHORD is also similar to a basic **C** major **7** chord, but this time the fifth note is 'diminished'. This means it is lowered by one semitone – hence the symbol (-)**5**. In the case of **C** major, the **G** note becomes **G♭**. Sounds good when preceded by the basic major **7** chord – for instance **C** major **7** followed by **C** major **7** (-)**5**. Can sound harsh when inverted.

	C	D♭	D	E♭	E	F	G♭	G	A♭	A	B♭	B
BASS NOTES	✓		✓		✓		✓	✓	✓	✓		✓

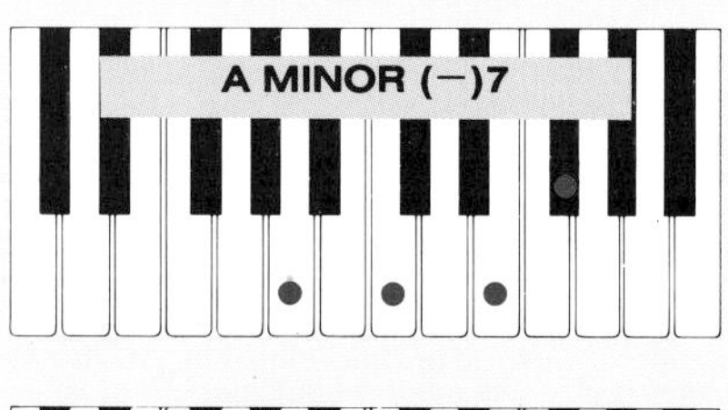

CHORD OF A MINOR (-)7
THIS CHORD is similar to **A** minor **7**, and is the same in principle to a major dominant seventh chord. That is, the seventh note is lowered by one semitone – so in this case, **G** becomes **G♭**. Sounds good when preceded by its minor seventh – in this case **A** minor **7**.

	A	B♭	B	C	D♭	D	E♭	E	F	G♭	G	A♭
BASS NOTES	✓		✓	✓		✓		✓		✓	✓	

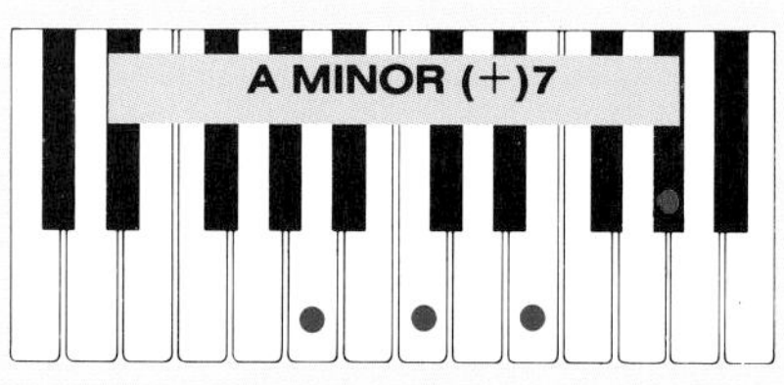

CHORD OF A MINOR (+)7
ANOTHER 'ONE-OFF' chord. It is a basic minor **7** with the seventh raised by one semitone (so **G** becomes **G#** in this case). Can sound harsh if inverted.

	A	A#	B	C	C#	D	D#	E	F	F#	G	G#
BASS NOTES	✓			✓		✓		✓		✓		✓

All the chords on this page are given in the keys of **C** major or **A** minor. They can of course be transposed into any key. Unless noted, they can all be inverted.

BUYER'S GUIDE

Faced with the staggering variety of electronic keyboards available today, you may well be wondering what on earth they all do, let alone which are the best.

That's where this Buyer's Guide comes in. Not only do we select the very best of the bunch, but we also give you a thorough rundown on how various instruments work. And to help still further, we translate into plain English all the technical jargon that surrounds electronic keyboards—and which often seems designed to confuse rather than clarify.

So step this way for the keyboard buyer's guided tour . . .

The Buyer's Guide is divided into three sections, which run alongside one another for a full 17 pages.

The top section of each page is an overview and explanation of electronic keyboards and related subjects: synthesisers, sound, samplers and MIDI.

Beneath that, in the left-hand column you'll find a comprehensive A–Z of electronic technical terms.

And taking the main space on each page there's a detailed review section. We concentrate on polyphonic synthesisers, but there are also numerous home keyboards and other instruments such as electric pianos and samplers.

In terms of price, we've set a maximum figure of £2000 ($3000). Anyone setting out to learn rock keyboards is unlikely to spend more than this, and the vast majority of keyboards fall within this range anyway.

If you haven't yet bought a keyboard, this guide should help you to pick a first instrument that will suit you in terms of budget, type of sounds and overall sophistication.

If you've already invested in an instrument but realise as your playing progresses that you need something different, the guide should help you to upgrade, for example from a low-cost home keyboard to a mid-priced professional synth. For this reason, we have also included a couple of the best synth modules (keyboardless MIDI synthesisers and samplers which are controllable from any MIDI keyboard).

Because budget is undoubtedly your major consideration, we've listed instruments according to price. The price banding is as follows:

Low price: up to £300 ($450)
Low-mid price: £301–500 ($451–750)
Mid-price: £501–1000 ($751–1500)
High-mid price: £1001–1500 ($1501–2250)
Top price: £1501–2000 ($2251–3000)

CONTENTS

INTRODUCTION

IF YOU don't have a keyboard of your own yet, or if you do but you want to upgrade – from a home keyboard to a synthesiser for instance – then this Buyer's Guide is for you.

You'll notice that home keyboards, polyphonic synthesisers and samplers take the lion's share of our coverage. They are the instruments we feel you're most likely to be interested in.

The functions of a home keyboard should be fairly easy to understand, once you've ploughed through its instruction manual. Synthesisers and samplers, on the other hand, are by nature far more complex – though they don't have to be.

SYNTHS CAN BE SIMPLE

ALTHOUGH MOST synthesisers and samplers offer enormous scope for creating your own sounds, they also offer a great many ready-made sounds for anyone who doesn't want to get too technical and would rather just make music.

Most synthesisers come supplied with a healthy array of 'pre-set' sounds, with more available on plug-in cartridges, cassettes or disks.

And most samplers come with a number of floppy disks containing ready-to-use sounds. You just load the disk and you're away.

Despite what some people say, there's nothing wrong with pre-set sounds; for beginners and professionals alike, they can be a godsend.

To take one example – the Yamaha DX7, which is probably the best-selling synthesiser of all time, offers more scope than most for complex sound programming. Yet it's a well-known fact that the vast majority of its users don't know hov to program it at all: they simply use it as 'pre-set replay' machine, because it built-in sounds are so good. With 32 pre sets, plus two cartridges containing 6 sounds each, you've got 160 sounds t choose from before you begin!

However, we aren't about to neglec anyone who would like to delve a b deeper into synthesis and sampling Right here in the Buyer's Guide we take fairly in-depth look at the various func tions of both instruments, and how the determine a finished sound.

Please don't be put off by the technica jargon you will inevitably come across i the next few pages – you can take it o leave it. And if you're not sure abou certain terms you can always check i our Electronic A-Z.

A PROFESSIONAL SET-UP

TO KICK off our equipment section, here's a typical professional keyboard set-up—this one belongs to Mike Lindup of Level 42. There's an analog synthesiser (Sequential Circuits' Prophet 5), a digital synth (Yamaha DX7), a sampler (Emulator II), a sampler/synthesiser (PPG Wave) and a master keyboard (Yamaha KX88). Mike also has a Yamaha QX1 sequencer and, behind him, a bank of MIDI expanders, effects units and mixers (not pictured).

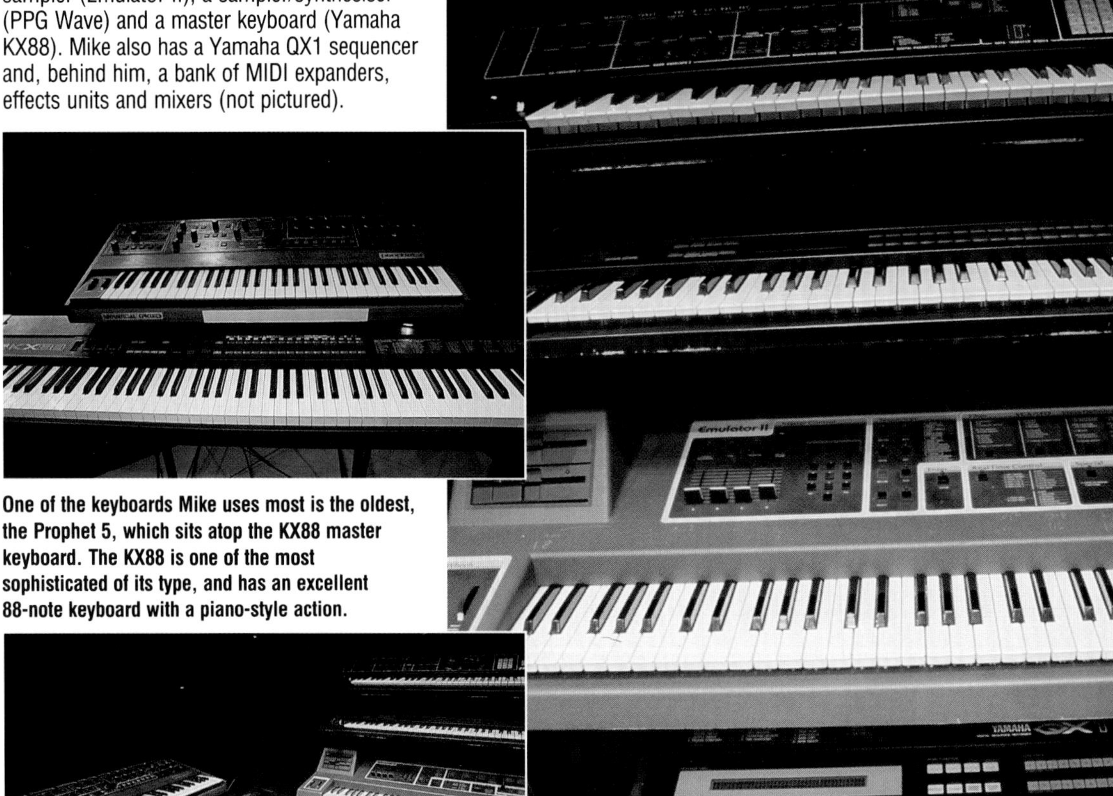

One of the keyboards Mike uses most is the oldest, the Prophet 5, which sits atop the KX88 master keyboard. The KX88 is one of the most sophisticated of its type, and has an excellent 88-note keyboard with a piano-style action.

Above: Level 42's keyboards onstage, with the Prophet 5 and KX88 facing the audience. One of Mike's most useful instruments is the QX1 sequencer—a complex machine which handles most of the routine keyboard parts, leaving Mike free to jump around stage from time to time.

From top: PPG Wave, DX7, Emulator II and QX1.

et Shop Boys use Yamaha's popular DX7 synth.

ONE THING to look out for in our reviews is whether an instrument has MIDI.

MIDI – Musical Instrument Digital Interface – is a communication system enabling you to transfer information from one MIDI instrument to another, whether they're made by the same manufacturer or not.

If you only own one keyboard, even if it has MIDI you can't use the MIDI system because it needs another MIDI instrument or piece of equipment to communicate with.

If you do buy another MIDI item, however, here's a brief rundown of some of the things MIDI can do for you.

USING MIDI

LET'S SAY you already own a synthesiser and now fancy buying either another synth or a sampler. By connecting the two instruments via MIDI (using a simple cable), you play both off one keyboard.

If you want to get a fuller sound, or a synthesised sound and a sampled sound mixed together, you can have exactly the same notes coming out of both instruments at once.

Depending on what information each instrument can transmit or receive via MIDI, it may be possible to pitch-bend or modulate the sound of both instruments using just one control, to sustain the sound of both instruments using just one foot pedal, to change from one sound to another on both instruments using just one button, and so on.

MODULES

AN ALTERNATIVE to buying another complete keyboard would be to buy it as a 'module' (or 'expander'), which is a ▶

ASIO HOME KEYBOARDS

HANCES ARE that if you're looking for a heap, polyphonic, starter keyboard, you'll be rawn to the name Casio. This company has uch a proliferation of products in the low and ow-mid price range that it's impossible to over them all individually.

Take comfort, therefore, from the fact that ou can hardly go wrong with a cheap Casio: hat you can get for the money will almost ertainly beat what other manufacturers (with he possible exception of Yamaha) can offer.

Key to the bewildering range of Casios you nay encounter in a store is the prefix system. s regards home keyboards, PT models are nini-keyed; MTs are polyphonic and nonophonic but with mini keys still; CTs are olyphonic with full-size keys. The more recent Z range are professional polysynths, with ither full-size or mini keys. SK is the new ange of affordable digital samplers, again in nini or full size versions, while HT denotes a ew range of 'home synthesisers'.

Casio home keyboards almost without xception feature Casio Chord, which is a ystem whereby you can programme in any najor, minor or seventh chord without actually aving to play it. There will also be auto unctions such as auto bass, which generates a ass line to accompany the chord you're laying, auto rhythms, where percussion atterns can be selected, and auto-arpeggio, hich 'arpeggiates' the chord.

These features help you to sound good and uild up your confidence when you're only at he one finger stage, but some of them still ome in extremely useful when you're quite ccomplished! Just make sure they don't stop ou learning to play properly.

There are over 20 home/fun Casio keyboards orth looking at in the lowest price bracket, so e've divided them into eight groups on this age and the next.

CASIO CT-360. Latest of the lower-priced CT keyboards, the eight-note-polyphonic 360 features Casio's PCM auto rhythms, 12 pre-set keyboard sounds, real time memory for song recording and 49 keys.

CASIO CT-630. With 60 pre-set sounds, the eight-note-polyphonic 630 has sounds created by phase distortion (as used on Casio's professional CZ synthesisers). It has auto rhythms, a memory for two songs, keyboard split and auto-harmony.

CASIO MT-70/85/110/800/CT-501/810. Educational instruments with light-pen bar-code readers and melody lights to teach you the rudiments of music as you enjoy yourself. The MT-800 is particularly good value: it reads songs off computer cartridges, has detachable stereo speakers and facilities for mixing in an external signal.

Watch out, too, for the new MT-110 (above) with real time memory that can record your best efforts.

CASIO MT-40/41/45/35/36/46. Portable keyboards with built-in speakers, numerous auto functions and battery power. Fun rather than seriously usable sounds.

ADSR Attack, decay, sustain and release.

AFTER-TOUCH A keyboard with after-touch will respond to further pressure on the keys after they've been played. Effects such as vibrato and pitch-bending can be introduced just by pressing harder on the keys.

ALGORITHM The term coined by Yamaha to describe the configuration (arrangement) of operators (digital sine waves) which creates each sound in an FM synthesiser.

ANALOG Analog and digital are the two types of polyphonic synthesiser. Analog sounds are produced by altering the control voltages of a synthesiser's three main circuits – the VCO, VCF and VCA. These circuits correspond to the three main elements of sound: pitch, timbre and volume respectively. Analog synths are good at producing full, warm sounds.

ARPEGGIATOR A device which produces an arpeggio based on one chord held down on the keyboard.

ATTACK The first stage in the ADSR sound envelope, which describes how a sound varies with time. Attack is the start of the sound.

AUTO BASS A computerised feature of many home keyboards which generates an automatic bass accompaniment from chords or single notes played with either hand, and whose speed is set by a speed or tempo control.

AUTO CHORDS Another home keyboard computerised feature which creates complex chords automatically when you hold down just one or two keys.

AUTO RHYTHM A further feature of most home keyboards, auto rhythm brings into play a built-in drum machine which usually offers a selection of pre-set rhythms (various rock, disco and latin styles generally dominate) plus the facility for intros (before you start the tune) and fills (fancy little link pieces between different sections of the tune). The speed or tempo of the rhythm is determined by a speed control. When this feature is used simultaneously with auto bass and auto chords, the whole lot is referred to as auto accompaniment, because it allows you to play your melody line over the top of a complete 'band'.

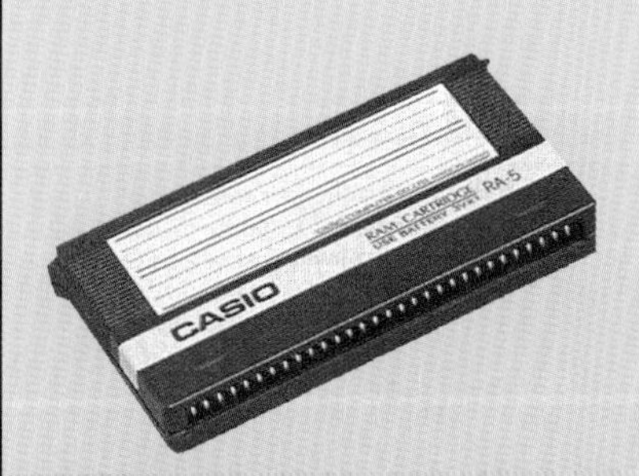

This Casio RAM cartridge can store 64 sounds.

CARTRIDGE A solid state digital recording device somewhat smaller than a conventional tape cassette which slots into some keyboards and associated equipment to provide extra memory capacity for storing more sounds. There are two types – RAM cartridges and ROM cartridges. See also separate entries for RAM and ROM.

synth or sampler with everything the keyboard version's got except the keyboard.

This module can then be controlled by your existing synth or sampler via MIDI, and you can do all the things that you can do with two connected keyboards.

If you just want to hear the module and not the 'master' keyboard, you turn the keyboard's volume down. If you just want to hear the keyboard, you change the MIDI channel on either the keyboard or the module.

There are 16 MIDI channels. For one instrument to communicate with another via MIDI they must both be set to the same channel – let's say channel 12. If one is set to channel 12 and the other is set to channel 13, they're completely independent of each other.

MIDI master keyboards may seem expensive, considering they can't make a sound on their own, but they're popular with professionals. The Roland MKB-200 is one of the more affordable.

CASIO MT-68/CT-405. The MT-68 moves into synthesiser territory with its 20 pre-set sounds, alterable by changing their envelope shapes. It has 768 auto-accompaniment variations and 12 auto rhythms. CT-405 is its large-keyed equivalent.

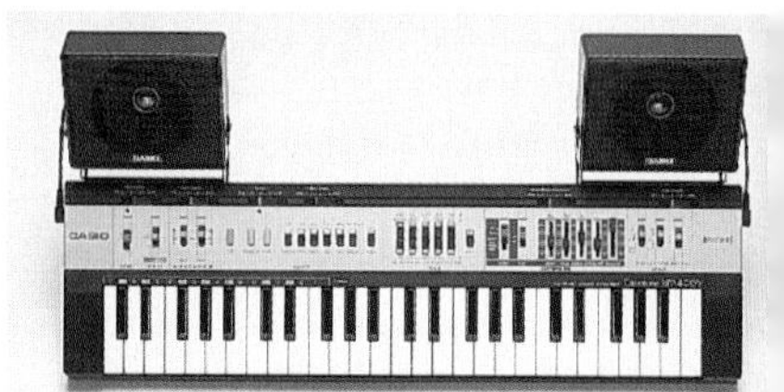

CASIO MT-400V/CT-410V. Another home keyboard pair with synth features. The 20 pre-set sounds can be edited as can the drum sounds. Sound quality is definitely of a more 'pro' character.

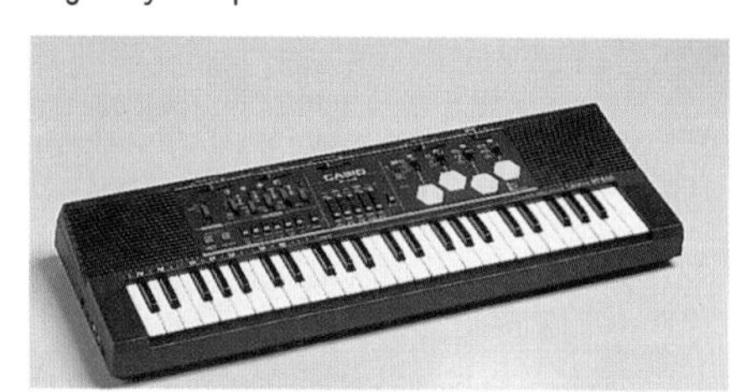

CASIO MT-500. One of the newest Casios, featuring built-in electronic drum pads in addition to the popular 20 pre-set sounds. The pads access PCM drum sounds, and there is back-up from the usual auto-rhythm section and Casio Chord. An even newer version, the MT-520, has now been released.

CASIO PT-50/80/30/20. Monophonic keyboards all, but with sophisticated auto-chord accompaniments to flesh out the limited sounds and rhythms available. Look out too for the PT-87, with Melody Guide to rate your performance by playing a fanfare appropriate to your level of skill!

YAMAHA PSR-21
Home keyboard/released 1986/16 FM sounds/49 keys/auto rhythm/auto bass-chord

ONE OF a new breed of home FM keyboards, the PSR-21 has 16 sounds which you can edit as you play, but can't store – it has no computer memory. It's a compact keyboard with a fairly standard auto bass and chord system, and it has good enough sounds and is sufficiently straightforward to encourage a beginner to persevere.

It has a bigger, low-mid-priced brother, the PSR-31, which lacks the editing system but offers high quality drum sounds and a larger (61-note) keyboard – better to play.

The 21, with its scope for playing around with the basic sounds, offers more creativity.

YAMAHA PSS-460
Home keyboard/released 1986/21 FM sounds/49 keys/programmable drums/auto bass-chord

NOT ONLY does the PSS-460 boast FM sounds, but you can also edit them in analog style, which makes this otherwise typical home machine a very easy introduction to the world of synthesisers.

You edit your sounds using six sliders. Unfortunately, your edits are not programmable – you can't save them in a computer memory – but one can be retained in the edited position when you switch off, and you can always note the slider positions you prefer.

Standard features like auto bass/chord and programmable drums round off one of the best-sounding home keyboards around.

MASTER KEYBOARDS

SINCE MIDI means that one instrument can control many others, the most important instrument is the one that's in control. Rather than using a synthesiser or sampler for this function, why not use a special MIDI instrument?

That is the reasoning behind the master keyboards now on the market.

The master keyboard has no sounds of its own – it simply has a keyboard and various MIDI controls which can trigger other instruments or modules. The more sophisticated the master keyboard, the more flexible the controls.

Another application of the master keyboard principle is in portable MIDI remote controllers which you can 'sling on' like a guitar, giving you a guitarist's freedom onstage. Most of the big synth manufacturers now have a remote control model in their ranges.

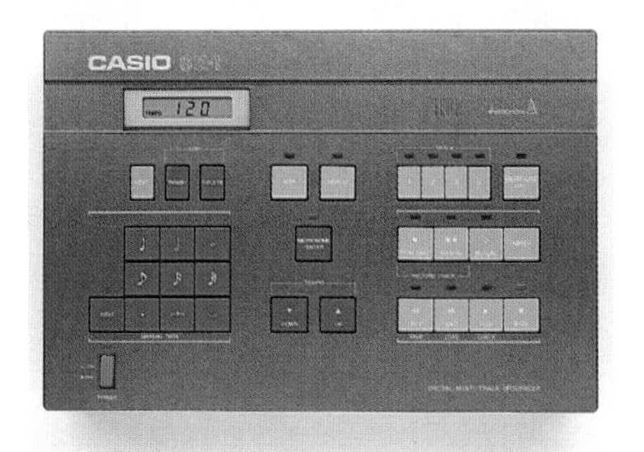

The Casio SZ-1 is one of the simplest MIDI sequencers you can buy, because its main controls are similar to those on a conventional tape recorder: fast forward, rewind, etc. But better still, the SZ-1 is also one of the cheapest sequencers.

At some point, you may also wish to buy a sequencer (a keyboard recorder, see page 65). Most sequencers have MIDI. You use MIDI to record your playing data onto the sequencer, and the information is sent back to the keyboard via MIDI.

MIDI can be relatively simple – two instruments playing together. Or it can be extremely complex – as you'll discover if you ever find yourself with half a dozen keyboards, MIDI drum machines and MIDI effects units to contend with, as many professional players do.

If your keyboard has MIDI, don't feel you're missing out if you don't use it. But when you're ready for it, MIDI can be a keyboard player's best friend.

CASIO SK-1
Home digital sampling keyboard/released 1986/8-bit mode/9.3kHz frequency/1.4 seconds maximum/32 keys

OF COURSE Casio had to be the company to bring sampling into the lowest price range. The spec's not professional, but the SK-1 samples quickly and easily (there's a built-in microphone) and the samples can be played four-note polyphonically. There's automatic triggering and looping.

Only one sample can be stored in memory. But there's also a synthesiser section, including eight sounds and custom creations, plus 11 drum patterns, auto-chords and a three-channel programmer to store 400 steps of polyphonic playing, a sequence of 99 chords and a 198-step solo. Since the SK-1's launch, it's been joined by a whole family: the SK-8, SK-100, SK-200 and SK-2100.

YAMAHA PSS-560
Home keyboard/released 1986/21 FM sounds/49 keys/custom drums/auto bass/sequencer

THIS INSTRUMENT shares the PSS-460's 21 sounds but also enables you to vary bass sounds and to program drum patterns and orchestral sounds. It offers a large variety of drum and percussions sounds, and the facility for linking these to your own bass sound and auto-chords gives you much more scope for creativity than the average home keyboard.

Other plus points are its sequencer, stereo speakers, battery power option, sustain, vibrato and auto-harmony.

CASIO CZ-101
Polyphonic synthesiser/released 1985/8 DCOs/49 keys/16 pre-set sounds/16 programmable memories

CASIO'S FIRST 'professional' synth to employ their phase distortion sound creation method was the mini-keyed CZ-101, which you can see pictured below. Apart from its small keys and some minor changes in the layout of the controls, the CZ-101 sounds and plays exactly like the CZ-1000, which is reviewed in the 'low-mid' section.

Crazy band Devo onstage, using the 'sling-on' SH-101 (far right in picture). Released in 1982, it was Roland's last monophonic synthesiser, and it's still a good buy if you want a mono synth.

ELECTRONIC A-Z

CHORUS Not just the catchy bit in a song, but also an effects device which makes a sound fatter by detuning it slightly and sending out both sounds at once. So in effect, it doubles up the sound. Chorus is also known as 'ensemble'.

CV/GATE This is the pre-MIDI method of controlling one piece of equipment from another. CV - control voltage - is the means by which the pitch of the note is conveyed, and the standard adopted by most manufacturers was one volt per octave. Gate simply means an on/off switch, so gate information tells the receiving instrument that a key has been held down (on) or released (off). Synthesisers with a CV/Gate input have a standard ¼-inch jack socket labelled CV/Gate on the rear panel, and can be controlled by another synthesiser or by an analog sequencer with a CV/Gate output socket.

DCA Digitally controlled amplifier - the digital equivalent of the analog synthesiser's VCA (voltage controlled amplifier) which controls the volume of the sound.

DCO Digitally controlled oscillator - the digital equivalent of the analog synthesiser's VCO (voltage controlled oscillator). It is the basic sound source of the synthesiser, and digital control makes it more reliable, solving problems of tuning drift (going out of tune) which were common to earlier analog synths.

DCW Digitally controlled wave - the digital equivalent of the VCF (voltage controlled filter) on Casio CZ synthesisers. It performs soundshaping and filtering duties.

DECAY The second stage in the standard ADSR soundshaping envelope which describes the way a sound behaves with time. Decay describes the behaviour of the sound immediately after the initial striking of the key.

DELAY/DIGITAL DELAY Delay is an echo effect which can be programmed to give you anything from a subtle repeat to thicken up a sound, to a cavernous echo-echo-echo. Digital delay offers far better sound quality, as each echo is identical to the original sound, and doesn't fade away unless you set it to.

DETUNING In synthesisers with two oscillators per note, it is often possible to tune one oscillator sharp or flat in respect to the other. This may be a slight detuning, to produce a fattening of the sound and effects such as phasing, or it may be in full note intervals (such as third, fourth or fifth) to produce a harmony effect from holding down a single key—a kind of two-note chord.

DIGITAL Digital technology has now largely replaced the older analog style of producing and controlling sound in synthesisers. It is much more sophisticated and reliable, though it was prone to being too clean and clinical (lacking the 'warmth' of analog sounds) in some of its early incarnations. Digital technology is at the heart of computer design, and it is the application of computer technology to music which has brought about recent advances such as sampling and MIDI. Digital synths may feature DCOs, or other digital sound sources such as the algorithms of FM synths, or sampled and resynthesised natural sounds, which are then shaped and modulated by filtering sections, envelope generators, LFOs, etc.

THE SYNTHESISER and the sampler are the two most widely used keyboard instruments in rock and pop today.

The information about them and other keyboards in the Instruction Manual was very general, to give you an idea of what each instrument is capable of.

Whilst this is fine for pianos, organs and home keyboards, the synthesiser and the sampler are worth a closer look, if only to explain some of the technical jargon associated with these highly complex instruments.

RECAP

LET'S START with a brief recap. With a synthesiser, be it polyphonic or monophonic, you can create totally original sounds to play as music. A synthesiser can also mimic known musical instrument sounds such as the piano, organ, trumpet or violin, and can be used for special effects sounds like the wind, trains or explosions.

Polyphonic synthesisers can be divided into two groups – analog (the old school) and digital (the new breed). All monophonic synthesisers fall into the analog category.

With a sampling keyboard, or a 'sampler' as it's known, you can digitally record or 'sample' any everyday sound – a dog barking, a glass smashing, someone shouting – and replay that sound at any pitch on the keyboard. This basic sound can be modified in many ways to suit your needs.

Before going into more detail about either instrument, it's important first to have some understanding of sound itself. We'll try to keep it simple!

Aretha Franklin and Keith Richards after recording Aretha's 'Jumpin' Jack Flash', with the Yamaha DX100 synth. It's similar to the DX27 reviewed on page 93, but has smaller keys and fewer octaves.

WHEN A MICROPHONE picks up a sound, this sound is converted into electrical signals which can then be amplified or recorded.

If a microphone is connected to a machine called an oscilloscope, these electrical signals can be represented visually on a screen. When a sound is picked up, what you see on the oscilloscope screen is basically a single wavery line. This line can be regular or haphazard, depending on the sound. The line is called a waveform.

Sound can basically be described as vibrations of the air around us. The greater the number of vibrations, the higher the pitch a sound will be. This results in a very 'wavery' waveform.

The fewer vibrations there are, the lower in pitch a sound is. This makes the waveform less wavery on the oscilloscope screen.

FREQUENCIES

THE NUMBER of vibrations per second is called a 'frequency' (in other words, how frequent the vibrations are).

A frequency is measured in Hertz (Hz for short). For example, 100Hz indicates that there are 100 sound vibrations per second; 400Hz indicates that there are 400 sound vibrations per second. So the higher the Hertz number, the higher in pitch the sound is.

Every musical note has its own frequency number. For instance, **A** above middle **C** is around 440Hz.

Doubling a frequency number makes the note an octave higher. Halving it makes it an octave lower. So **A** below middle **C** is around 220Hz.

HARMONICS

AS YOU know, no two sounds are absolutely identical. Musical sounds can, however, share the same frequency. When you play a **C** on a piano and the equivalent **C** on a guitar, they are both playing at the same pitch, hence the same frequency. And yet the timbre (quality of sound) is different.

What makes them sound different is 'harmonics'.

Harmonics can loosely be described as 'secondary frequencies'. As we have already said, **A** above middle **C** is around 440Hz. The **A** note one octave above is double that frequency: 880Hz. So, between these two notes there are in effect 440 different frequencies.

And yet there are only 12 distinct notes. This means that each note spans a broad ▶

LOW-MID PRICE

CASIO CZ-230S
Home keyboard/99 sounds/4-note polyphonic/49 keys/programmable PCM drums/step time sequencer/MIDI

THE MINI-KEYED CZ-230S is wolf in sheep's clothing: it's really a PD (phase distortion) synthesiser but earns its 'home' label by virtue of its small keys, built-in auto features, pre-set sounds and integral speakers.

The polyphony is rather limiting as you can only play four notes at a time. But there are pitch wheel and key transposer (though sadly no vibrato). And the sounds, though uneditable, are excellent.

Ten memory channels are provided for storing your own rhythm patterns. The keyboard is used for sequencer step-time programming.

CASIO CZ-1000
Polyphonic synthesiser/released 1985/ 8 DCOs/49 keys/16 pre-sets sounds/ 16 program memories/MIDI

PERHAPS THE classic model in Casio's first generation of phase distortion synthesisers, the CZ-1000 was launched as the standard-size-key version of the sling-on CZ-101, and was later joined by the CZ-3000 and CZ-5000, a mid-priced synth that is exceptional value.

The phase distortion method generates hard-edged and funky sounds, and you can do a lot with them. There's also double mode, which enables you to combine two different sounds.

OSC Oscar Mk7
Programmable monophonic-duophonic synthesiser/released 1983/2 DCOs/37 keys/ 36 memories/sequencer/arpeggiator/MIDI

THE BRITISH Oscar is remarkable for fat, juicy, analog Minimoog-type sounds stabilised by digital control, and you can store 36 sounds at a time.

Novelties of the design include the use of the keys themselves to recall sounds from the memory, and they're also used to operate the sequencer.

The sequencer can store 22 sequences totalling 1500 notes plus sound changes. You can use any sequences as a backing track to accompany your own 'live' performance on the keyboard.

'Ordinary' features, such as a wide variety of basic waveforms, key transposition, portamento, pitch and mod wheels abound, and it's no wonder that, even before the addition of MIDI with the Mk7 variant, the Oscar was called the king of monophonics.

YAMAHA CE-20
Multi-instrument keyboard/released 1982/ 14 mono-poly FM sounds/49 keys/touch sensitive

LAUNCHED BETWEEN Yamaha's GS-1 and DX7 synths, the CE-20 used FM for pre-set sounds, and it may still be worth buying secondhand.

It's a small neat instrument whose most outstanding pre-set sounds include flute and trombone.

Other pre-sets, not quite as classy but still good, are brass, horn, organ, electric piano, harpsichord and strings. it has a wide-ranging effects section.

DIGITAL ACCESS CONTROL (DAC) Most modern synthesisers, whether digital or analog, feature digital access control. The basis of DAC is the small LCD panel on which the sounds in the synth's memory can be displayed, one at a time, and edited, by calling up each parameter or element of the sound one at a time and increasing or decreasing its value as desired. It is a more laborious, less instantaneous form of control than the analog control (knobs, switches and sliders) common to earler analog synths. But it is cheaper and takes up less space, since apart from the small screen, all that is needed is a set of buttons for the memory banks (these usually double as parameter buttons), and a knob or up/down buttons for changing the values.

DRUM PADS Currently unique to a couple of Casio home keyboards are a set of pressure-sensitive hexagonal pads on the control panel connected to the instrument's built-in rhythm unit which can be 'played' with fingers or sticks as if playing actual drums.

EDIT The most common way of creating the sounds you want to hear is by selecting a sound already programmed into the instrument's memory and editing it. Editing is achieved by taking any element or parameter of the sound to which the instrument gives you access and changing its value. With most polyphonic synthesisers and samplers, once you have edited the original sound until you hear exactly what you want, you must 'write' your edit into the memory, either in addition to or in place of the original sound, or the new sound will be lost when the synth is switched off. With many home keyboards and a few synths, however, there is no facility for programming the edit permanently and you can retain the edited sound only as long as the synth is switched on.

EFFECTS UNITS Also known as signal processors, these are devices which apply some treatment to the sounds coming out of your instrument, such as reverb or echo. Professional signal processors are usually built to a 19-inch width and standard range of depths for bolting into a standard rack. Cheaper versions come in the form of floor 'pedals' designed primarily for guitarists. Some synths now have built-in digital delay lines to create a variety of effects, but most keyboards have some kind of effect built in – chorus is very popular on synths and chorus or tremolo on pianos.

ENVELOPE GENERATOR/STAGES The envelope generator is the element of the synthesiser's circuitry which controls the way the sound behaves with the progression of time. The most common type of envelope generator is four-stage, consisting of the parameters Attack, Decay, Sustain and Release (see separate entries). Some recent digital synths have introduced more sophisticated six- or even eight-stage envelopes, which simply means that the duration of the sound is chopped up into even more segments over which you can exert control. Envelopes are commonly applied to the volume and tone (filtering) elements of the sound.

EQ (EQUALISATION) EQ is the 'professional' term for tone control. In synthesisers (the Roland D-50 excepted), there is no EQ section as such, since the filters perform all tone control tasks. But in pianos it is common to have treble, bass and even middle controls. These may be passive (which means that all they do is cut higher frequencies out of the frequency band they affect), or active, which means they can both cut and boost the frequencies in the relevant bands.

range of frequencies. However, not all the harmonics in that frequency range will be present. And it is the combination of harmonics that distinguishes one sound from another.

A sound that has no harmonics at all, that is just a single constant frequency, is called a pure tone. There are no sounds in nature like this – it can only be created electronically. When viewed on an oscilloscope, a pure tone gives a snake-like curved line.

This is known as a sine waveform. The electronically generated sine waveform is the most basic sound source of a synthesiser.

When sine waves of different frequencies are mixed together, a new waveform is created, and this is the starting point of most synth sounds.

WHEN SINE waves of different frequer cies are mixed together, new waveform are created.

In an analog synthesiser, the soun waveforms are generated by an electr cal circuit called a Voltage Controlle Oscillator (VCO). This circuit also dete

SINE WAVE

SAWTOOTH WAVE

SQUARE WAVE

The most common basic sound waveforms used in synthesiser sounds are the sawtooth wave, with bright, sharp characteristics, and the square wave, with a hollow, nasal quality.

The Technics SX-PX5 electric piano: high quality sounds for a reasonable price.

TECHNICS SX-PX5

Piano/5 sounds/76 keys/velocity sensitive/ chorus/tremolo/real-time sequencer

THIS IS the baby of the new Technics family of SX-PX pianos; there's also the high-mid price SX-PX7 and top price (within our price range) SX-PX9 with which it shares many features. The PX7 and PX9 are identical, in fact, save for cosmetic styling, while the PX5 makes economies in its MIDI spec, keyboard and effects.

The high quality sounds are based on PCM samples of 'natural' keyboard sounds and five are on offer in all three instruments, ranging from acoustic through electric to clavi. It has a two-track sequencer which lets you record up to 2700 notes.

The more expensive SX-PX9 electric piano has everything the PX5 has, plus a better MIDI spec an an effects section.

ines at what pitch the sound will be: iore voltage = more vibrations = higher ound.

At this point, the waveform is just one onstant tone, the aural equivalent of a mp of stone. In short, the sound has to e sculpted.

This is done by the various parameters synthesiser has to offer. Parameters are le controls that can alter a sound.

The most important parameter on a ynthesiser is probably the Voltage Con-olled Filter (VCF). This circuit deter-nines the timbre of the finished sound (its uality – harsh, soft, mellow, etc).

Analog synthesis is sometimes known s 'subtractive synthesis'. You start off vith a waveform full of different harmon-:s. To create a new timbre, you filter ome of these harmonics out, subtracting them using the VCF. Think of it in the same way as a sculptor chiselling away at his stone.

The next most important parameter on a synthesiser is the Voltage Controlled Amplifier (VCA). This circuit determines the overall volume of a sound.

THE ENVELOPE

TO EACH of these parameters (the VCF and VCA) what is known as an 'envelope' can be applied (courtesy of the synth's envelope generator).

An envelope enables you to specify how the sound will change in volume and timbre, from the moment it's first heard to when it stops. A basic envelope has four 'stages' – Attack, Decay, Sustain and Release (ADSR for short).

Let's look at what can be achieved when an envelope is applied to the VCA (which, as you remember, controls volume).

On an analog synthesiser, the Attack, Decay, Sustain and Release parameters will each have their own knob or slider.

Attack controls the first part of a sound. If a slow attack is set, the sound fades in gradually. If a fast attack is set, the sound reaches a specified volume peak quickly.

The Decay control lets you specify what happens to the sound after it reaches its initial peak. If a fast decay is set, the sound will die away very quickly. This is effective for percussive effects. If a slower decay is set, the sound will fade gradually.

Now the Sustain parameter takes over. It keeps the sound at a constant volume level until you take your hands off the keyboard.

The Release parameter enables you to ▶

LOW-MID PRICE

AMAHA DX27

olyphonic synthesiser/released 1986/ operators/49 keys/192 memories/touch ensitivity (internal)/MIDI

AMAHA'S EIGHT-VOICE-POLYPHONIC DX27 just one rung up from the lowest-priced rofessional' keyboard in their FM range – the X100, which is essentially identical, though naller, with mini keys and fewer octaves.

As you'd imagine, these cheap keyboards fer a considerably pared-down version of the M found in the DX7. But with the same umber and type of algorithms (the basic wave ombinations which make up FM sounds) as und in the DX21 and CX5M Music Computer, e're clearly not talking Toytown.

The DX27 and DX100 have no less than 192 e-set sounds, which can be edited – and you n store your sounds alongside the pre-sets.

The character of the sounds is undoubtedly the DX21 arena, which means they have the arity and punch that make FM so remarkable. nd there are new sounds not previously found the FM armoury. But at the same time you n't always get the rich sound that the more pensive models offer, and you can't mix unds or split the keyboard.

You select, edit and programme your sounds using the now standard digital access ntrol method, where sounds are called up on e small LCD screen. There are green oblong sh-buttons to change the tones, and these uble as function selectors.

As with the DX21, the five-octave keyboard the DX27 is not itself touch sensitive, but its unds can become touch sensitive when you gger them via MIDI from another keyboard hich does have touch sensitivity.

And there are a lot of useful performance atures, such as a programmable key-change cility – you can play in, say, **C** major, and ve the sound come out in any key you want. also has pitch wheel and portamento.

The DX100 has been styled to work as a live ng-on synth, with strap attachments and tional battery power.

Not surprisingly, this economical pair are garded by Yamaha as "perfect entry yboards" into FM. A good first buy.

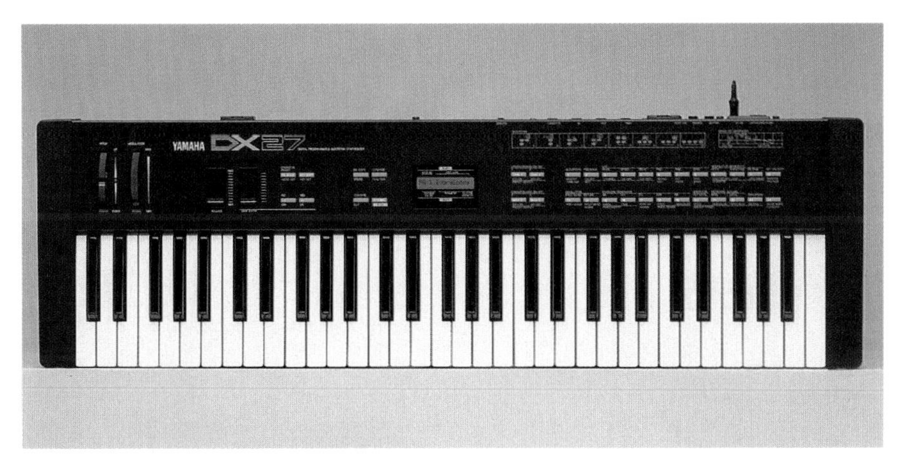

An ideal first keyboard, the Yamaha DX27 is packed with features and has 192 different pre-set sounds.

The keyboards collective (from left): Herbie Hancock, Tom Dolby, Stevie Wonder, Howard Jones and a vast array of keyboard equipment onstage at the US Grammy Awards in 1985.

Roland MKS-20 expander, a piano in a box!

EXPANDER This is a keyboardless version of a synthesiser or sampler, sometimes absolutely identical internally, but sometimes with extra features. It connects to your existing synth (or master keyboard) via MIDI and is a much cheaper way of giving yourself a bigger and more versatile sound than by buying a second synthesiser. Expanders are also referred to as modules, and are usually designed to fit in a standard 19-inch wide rack or simply sit on top of your existing synth. Because of MIDI, you are not restricted to using an expander of the same make as your keyboard.

FILTER The basic tone control device in a synth or sampler, the filter works by filtering out certain harmonics from the sound generated by the sound source (the VCO, DCO, etc), and allowing the rest to get through. The common VCF (voltage controlled filter) may be 'low pass', which means only harmonics below a specified cut-off point get through; 'high pass', which dispenses with low harmonics; or 'band pass', which allows only mid-range harmonics to be heard.

FLOPPY DISK A medium for storing digital information originally developed for computers. Most samplers rely on floppy disks for storing samples, which then have to be 'loaded' into the machine before it can be used. Similarly, sounds or sequences can be 'dumped' or 'saved' to disk. A few synthesisers, such as the Yamaha DX7IIFD, have built-in floppy disk drive.

FM A type of digital sound creation invented in America by Professor John Chowning which revolutionised synthesisers when it was used in the Yamaha DX7, and is based on frequency modulation, like FM radio. It is remarkable for the naturalness or 'humanity' of the sounds it can create; also for clarity, percussiveness and cutting edge.

GLISSANDO A fast run of notes. When this feature is available on a keyboard, it means that the synthesiser can automatically play such a run in semitones between the first and second keys you press.

LAYERING If a keyboard has a layering facility, you can mix two sounds together. Doing this, however, will usually halve the polyphony of your keyboard, say from eight-note to four-note.

LCD Liquid Crystal Display: information displayed on a small illuminated screen, of the type found on a digital watch. Look out for backlit LCD screens, because they can be seen in the dark—a very necessary facility for any gigging keyboards player, but one which many manufacturers mysteriously overlooked until quite recently! Some synths have LED (Light Emitting Diode) screens, which use illuminated figures.

LOOPING A facility offered by most samplers in order to artificially lengthen the time of the sampled note, by repeating it continuously. The reverse of this is known as truncating.

specify what happens to the sound when you 'release' the keys.
If a quick release is set, the sound will stop dead. With a slow release the sound will fade out, quickly or slowly depending on the setting.

If an envelope is applied in the same way to the VCF, you can change the timbre of the sound over a period of time.

Many newer synthesisers enable you to create far more complex envelopes – with some having as many as eight stages (as opposed to the four-stage envelope we have looked at).

OTHER PARAMETERS

THOSE ARE the main parameters that determine a sound. Here are just three among many others:

A **Low Frequency Oscillator** (LFO) is a separate oscillator which generates a very low frequency with a small numbe of vibrations per second and a pitc inaudible to the human ear. The vibra tions 'modulate' the main sound, whic means that they regularly alter the pitc ever so slightly to create a 'vibrato' c warbling effect.

A **Ring Modulator** adds certain harmo nics for 'ringing' sounds, like bells.

The **Noise** parameter is made up of number of random frequencies whic result in a harsh sound (like when there a break in transmission on television This is good for special effects sound like wind, waves and explosions. Mixin noise in with an ordinary musical soun can also be effective.

OSCILLATORS

PERHAPS THE most noticeable diffe ence, soundwise, from one synthesiser t

Stevie Wonder and part of his onstage keyboards set-up. Stevie is playing the classic Fender Rhodes electric piano reviewed below—*his* Fender classic is 'Sunshine Of My Life'.

ENSONIQ ESQ-1

Polyphonic synthesiser/released 1986/ 24 oscillators/61 keys/40 memories/ 80 cartridge memories/touch sensitive/ sequencer/MIDI

ENSONIQ'S FIRST – and mighty impressive – venture into the synth market is an eight-note-polyphonic synth with strong basic sounds and a wide range of possibilities. You can layer and split the keyboard, and there's a built in chorus.

DAC programming is aided by a large fluorescent display showing 10 sound programs simultaneously. The sequencer is eight-track with 2400 (expandable to 10,000) note capacity. The keyboard can play eight different sounds and/or melodies simultaneously, thanks to MIDI Mode 4.

In all, the ESQ-1 offers far more than you get for the same money elsewhere.

FENDER RHODES Stage 73 MkV

Electric piano/released 1984/touch sensitive/73 keys/active EQ

THE FENDER RHODES is probably the best-known stage piano in the world, with a pedigre that goes back well over two decades. Its warm, bell-like sounds, produced by hammers hitting aluminum tines, have been heard in several variations on the basic theme – such a the 1965 Suitcase 88 model, a 'compact' 54-key variant and even a MIDI version.

The MkV incorporates the Suitcase's pre-amp to provide active equalisation, plus hard Neoprene hammer tips thoughout, to increase overall brightness and compensate for the somewhat murky bass end, making it undoubtedly the best version to date.

Sadly, production has recently been discontinued, but the odd new model may still be knocking around.

e next is in the number of Voltage ontrolled Oscillators per note. Some ynthesisers have one VCO per note, the ajority have two, and a few have as any as three or four.

So if a synthesiser is eight-note olyphonic (meaning it can play up to ight different notes at a time) and has 16 COs, there will be two VCOs for each ote. In other words, each note can be ade up of two basic sounds. This gives ou a lot of options.

Each VCO could have a different aveform, and maybe different VCF and CA settings, to give a complex sound.

On the other hand, each VCO could ave the same waveform and the same ettings for a fatter, powerful sound. One CO could be detuned slightly to eighten this effect.

So, the more oscillators a synthesiser has per note, the more powerful the overall sound will be.

ANALOG PROGRAMMING

PROGRAMMING AN analog synth was a relatively straightforward process of fiddling about with the various parameter knobs, sliders and switches on the control panel until you found a combination that sounded good.

In most cases, this sound could then be stored in a memory space, leaving the knobs free to create another new sound.

Nowadays, however, manufacturers make their instruments much cheaper by getting rid of all those external moving parts and simply offering digital control over the sounds – music by numbers. Which brings us to something called Digital Access Control (DAC) – but not, however, to fully digital synthesisers.

DIGITAL CONTROL

EACH MANUFACTURER has its own system of Digital Access Control – some are more complicated than others. Let's look at Korg's DW8000 as an example.

On this instrument, all the different parameters are given a number; for example the Decay parameter in the VCF envelope is number 42.

A 'menu' (a list) of what number each parameter is, is printed on the control panel.

Let's say you want to alter parameter number 42 (VCF Decay). First, you press the parameter button in the centre of the panel. Using a key pad (eight numbered buttons), you type in the number 42.

This number will light up on the LED screen (like that on a digital watch).

MID PRICE

OLAND Alpha Juno-2
olyphonic synthesiser/released 1986/ DCOs/128 memories/61 keys/touch ensitive/MIDI

LONG WITH the Alpha Juno-1, this six-note- olyphonic synth is a direct descendant of the med Juno-60, taking the same gutsy analog ounds and editing parameters but endowing em with total digital control – the old knobs nd sliders have been replaced by an LCD creen, push buttons and the Alpha Dial arameter wheel.

Advantages over the Juno-1 which make the Juno-2 more attractive include a five (as opposed to four) octave keyboard with both velocity and after-touch sensitivity, and the facility for 64 extra sounds to be stored on cartridge.

It comes with 64 pre-set sounds and 64 programmable sounds. Each sound can have only one oscillator per note, which means they can sometimes sound a bit thin, but the result is still an appealing, if slightly pricey, non-digital package.

ROLAND Juno-106
Polyphonic synthesiser/released 1984/ 6 DCOs/128 memories/61 keys/MIDI

Released between the totally analog Juno-60 and the digitally controlled Alpha Junos, the Juno-106 was a successful MIDI upgrade of the 60 with a bigger program memory. Definite improvements included a firmer keyboard action, portamento and chorus. Features which disappeared included separate LFO button and arpeggiator.

Full MIDI spec completed an update which still has a lot going for it. Worth looking out for secondhand.

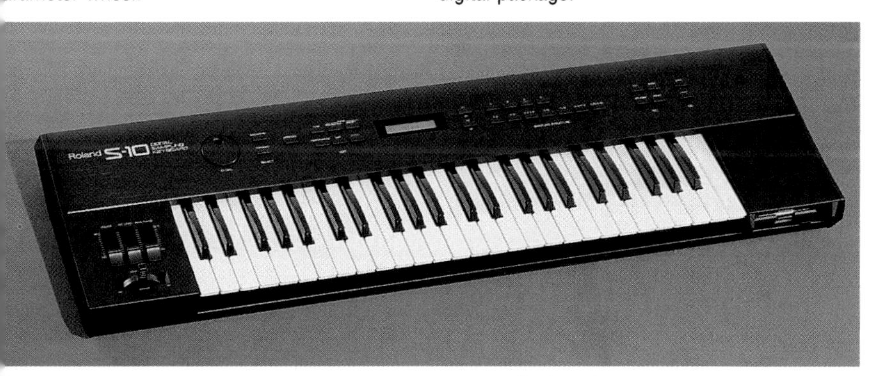

OLAND S-10
ampling keyboard/released 1986/12-bit node/30kHz frequency/4.4 second aximum/49 keys/MIDI

/ITH A SHORT, velocity-sensitive keyboard nd eight-note-polyphony, the S-10 is one of e best priced keyboard samplers of more or ss professional standard.

You can store samples on computer disk. /hen using them you can assign them to three separate keyboard zones.

The keyboard length may be a limitation, and you can't change your sounds much once they've been sampled. But for the basic purpose of acquiring usable samples of decent duration at an acceptable sampling rate, the S-10 comes in at the right level. Ideal for players who don't see why a sampler should cost ten times or even twice what they'd spend on a synth.

Vince Clarke of Erasure playing the versatile Casio CZ-1 synthesiser in his Notting Hill, London, home studio. Erasure vocalist Andy Bell looks on. We review the CZ-1 next page.

MEMORIES The means by which sounds are stored in synthesisers and other keyboards. Some memories may be purely pre-set, others programmable, which is to say you can store sounds you've created yourself. Groups of memories are usually called banks; individual ones may be called channels.

MIDI Musical Instrument Digital Interface: a universal standard system introduced in the early '80s which enables instruments made by one manufacturer to transmit or receive data to or from another instrument made by the same or another manufacturer. This is done via a simple lead or leads from one instrument to the other.

MINI-KEYED With small keys.

MOD/MODULATION This enables a player to bring in a programmable vibrato effect (which makes the sound waver), using a wheel, joystick or after-touch.

MODULE A keyboardless MIDI instrument (see expander) which can be controlled by any MIDI keyboard. In a completely modular system, you would use a MIDI master keyboard to drive as many synth/piano/sampler modules as you required.

MONOPHONIC Capable of playing only one note at a time.

OPERATORS A term used by Yamaha to describe the digital sine waves which make up the sounds in FM synthesisers by distorting each other. As in FM radio, operators may be either carrier waves or modulating waves, depending on their position in the overall configuration (see algorithm). Operators replace the DCOs or VCOs of non-FM synths.

OSCILLATOR The basic sound source of most synthesisers is an electronic device which oscillates (vibrates) and whose oscillation rate or frequency can be varied to produce notes of different pitch.

PARAMETER A particular element of a synthesiser sound that can be altered separately (using a knob, button, slider, etc).

PATCH Strictly speaking, a patch is simply a connection between two electronic devices, and early synthesisers often featured patchboards or patchbays which enabled you to connect the different elements of the synth in various different combinations using jack leads. Today, however, patch is generally an all-embracing term meaning a specific sound, plus any routings and control functions you may have assigned to it before programming it into one of your instrument's memories.

PCM Pulse Code Modulation is a method of digitally encoding (recording) natural sounds and storing them in such a way that they can be edited like synthesised sounds. Initially used to create more realistic percussion sounds in drum machines, PCM is now occurring more frequently as a sound source in digital synths.

PD Phase Distortion is a type of digital sound generation involving distortion of sine waves. It was developed by Casio for its professional CZ range of synthesisers, and is similar in some respects to Yamaha's FM. The system uses three components – DCO sound source, DCW filter and DCA amplifier, each of which can be shaped by an eight-stage envelope generator.

Another LED screen will show you the current value of the parameter – meaning the point it's at in its particular range. In the case of parameter 42 the range is 0 to 31 (this information is printed next to the parameter's name and number on the menu).

A knob or slider on an older analog synthesiser might only offer you a range from 1 to 10, simply because a knob car only be turned around so far. With digita technology you have more choice withir the same range.

So let's say the current value of Parameter 42 is 16. If you want to make it 21 how do you do this?

You can either use buttons or a slider The buttons will increase or decrease the

The popular Korg DW-8000, like most modern synths, has Digital Access Control—explained above.

KORG DW-8000
Polyphonic synthesiser/released 1985/touch sensitive/16 oscillators/64 memories/MIDI
THE SOUNDS in this synthesiser are based on 16 digitally encoded versions of 'real' instruments which can be edited with relative ease, and their hybrid digital-analog nature offers great originality. Also included in the package is a digital delay effect which can be separately programmed for each of the 64 memories.

The cheaper keyboardless version of this synth, the EX-8000, is a rackmount expander. It not only performs all DW-8000 tasks (except arpeggiation) but also lets you zone, split or layer sounds, even from a keyboard on which these are supposedly not possible.

There's also an MEX-8000 memory expander which you can buy to store four sets of 64 sounds.

KORG Poly-800II
Polyphonic synthesiser/released 1986/8 DCOs/49 keys/64 memories/sequencer/MIDI
BASED ON the incredibly popular Poly-800 of the mid-'80s, the Poly-800II has many of its predecessor's economies and idiosyncrasies – four-octave keyboard, joystick – while adding numerous extras that help you get even more out of the fat, full sounds, not to mention a set of much-improved factory pre-set sounds.

Extras include digital delay, full MIDI spec, tone controls, and noise. The sequencer is polyphonic, with 256-note capacity and flexible step-time programming.

CASIO CZ-1
Polyphonic synthesiser/released 1986/16 DCOs/touch sensitive/61 keys/128 internal memories/64 cartridge memories/MIDI
THE LATEST addition to Casio's Cosmo Synthesiser range of professional phase distortion synths, the CZ-1 is 16- or eight-note-polyphonic, depending on the sound you are using. The CZ-1 features the classic PD combination of DCO, DCW and DCA to create sounds. There are many pre-set sounds and up to 64 sets of panel settings can be held in the memory, so that parameters and on/off setting can be switched immediately to any stored combination. Another welcome feature is parameter copy, which saves time when you're copying envelope patterns.

With MIDI, it is possible to output up to eigh monophonic sounds simultaneously. A real feature-packed instrument.

BIT 99
Polyphonic synthesiser/released 1985/ 12 DCOs/61 keys/99 memories/touch sensitive/MIDI
MADE BY Crumar in Italy, the Bit 99 is the superior (and cheaper) descendant of the Bit 1 synthesiser, remarkable for the quality of its sounds.

The control panel features stencilled flow charts which tell you what part of the synth each control will affect. There's a useful edit/compare feature by which you compare your edited sound with the original unedited sound, and an even more useful 'park' feature where you can dump sounds temporarily while you find a home in the computer memory. Up to 3 sounds can be chained, so that you can go from one to the next more easily, and there's a full MIDI spec.

When you split the keyboard it becomes jus three-note polyphonic, which is very limiting, but if you want great sounds, easy editing and easy programming, the Bit 99 is a dream – as i its keyboardless expander version, Bit 01.

SEQUENTIAL PROPHET 5
Polyphonic synthesiser/released 1978/ 10 VCOs/61 keys/120 memories
Now available only secondhand, the Prophet 5 was a revelation when it was released in 1978. Its rich brassy sounds, lush strings and unlimited bell/gong type effects can still hold their own against digital technology today – even though its five-note polyphony is now on below the generally accepted minimum.

alue one number at a time. The slider vill quickly rush through the numbers which is useful if you want to change a alue from 10 to 99, for example).

Once you're happy with the alteration ɔ your sound, you write it into the nemory. Press the 'program' button in he centre of the panel and you're back in ormal play mode.

In this mode, the key pad is used to elect different sounds, which are also umbered (according to the memory pace each sound occupies).

ANALOG/DIGITAL

ƆTHER SYNTHESISERS have a separate button for each parameter. However, once you've selected a parameter, you vill still be given a number on a screen or display, which you alter in the same way, using up/down buttons or a slider.

Players either love or loathe Digital Access Control. If you're new to synthesisers, you'll probably get used to it quickly.

The advantages are that it gives you far more control over the sound, it makes synthesisers cheaper and less likely to go wrong (too many knobs can spell trouble).

The disadvantages are that it takes a lot longer to program, and the DAC systems don't really lend themselves to 'real-time' alteration of parameters: which means if you're playing live you can't change settings in an instant, as you can with a 'knobs and sliders' synthesiser.

It's worth mentioning that for most of their DAC synthesisers, Roland offer a plug-in 'knobs and sliders' box as an optional extra for those players who have a bit more money and can't get used to the new system.

DIGITAL SOUNDS

THE FACT that an ordinary analog synthesiser has digital control doesn't in fact mean that the sounds themselves are of digital origin. They are still produced in the time-honoured analog way.

A digital synthesiser produces, controls and stores its sounds digitally.

Sampling keyboards also use digital technology. As we shall be looking at samplers later, we'll explain it then.

All you need to know for now is that digital synthesisers are capable of a complexity and richness of sound that few analog instruments can achieve. Their biggest problem, however, is that they can be very difficult to program, because the sounds are so complex.

MID PRICE

ҮAHAMA DX-21
Polyphonic synthesiser/released 1985/
4 FM operators/61 keys/128 pre-set sounds/
ouch sensitive (internal only)/MIDI

THE DX21 is Yamaha's comparatively simple answer to the complexities of FM programming. Its excellent DX-7 type sounds, playable eight-note-polyphonically, are available 32 at a time.

You can program performance functions like portamento individually for each sound. You can layer, split and detune, assign pitch bending to the highest or lowest note in a chord if you wish, and store MIDI information in the memories. Editing is essentially DX-7 style, but simplified by reducing the range of various parameters.

The DX21's keyboard isn't touch-sensitive, but the synth itself is when played via a velocity-sensitive MIDI keyboard.

YAHAMA PF-80
Digital piano/released 1986/10 FM sounds/
88 keys/chorus/EQ/tremolo/split/MIDI

ALTHOUGH THE PF-80 and the cheaper 76-key PF-70 were developed in response to demand for MIDI versions of the PF-10 and 15, they are well removed from their predecessors.

The ten FM sounds on offer (acoustic and electric pianos, harpsi, vibes and clavi) have less hissing 'FM noise'.

On top of that, you get the pleasure of playing a weighted, dynamic, full-span keyboard.

As for MIDI, there are enough facilities to qualify for master keyboard status, while, at the other end of the spectrum, practice and home playing are catered for by mutable internal speakers.

YAHAMA PSR-70
Home keyboard/released 1985/
32 monophonic and polyphonic FM sounds/
61 keys/auto PCM drums/auto bass-chord/
music programmer/MIDI

THE PSR-70 has a wide choice of pre-set FM sounds and customisable PCM drum section, auto bass and chords. All of these can be recorded onto the music programmer, which holds up to three songs. It all adds up to outstanding value for money.

While 'slimmed down' from the PS-6100 in price and size, the PSR-70 is bristling with features and its polyphonic sounds actually seem superior to the PS-6100's. There are DX-7 quality monophonic sounds and you can use the keys to add various latin percussion instruments to the PCM drumkit, which is clever enough to take care of intros, fills and endings.

If you can't stretch to a PSR-70, the 60 and 50 (the latter without monophonic section) are also well worth looking at.

Andy McCluskey of OMD with (front) the classic Prophet 5 synth (reviewed opposite). The big white thing behind it is a Mellotron, used by '60s bands such as The Moody Blues.

PERFORMANCE ORIENTATED An indication that an instrument has been designed with live work in mind, which is to say with its performance controls (those which you use for expression as you're playing the keyboard – mod wheel, pitch wheel, etc) conveniently sized and placed, and its programming and memory-recall facilities optimised for quick edits and changes.

PITCH The frequency of a note. Treble is high-pitched, bass is low-pitched.

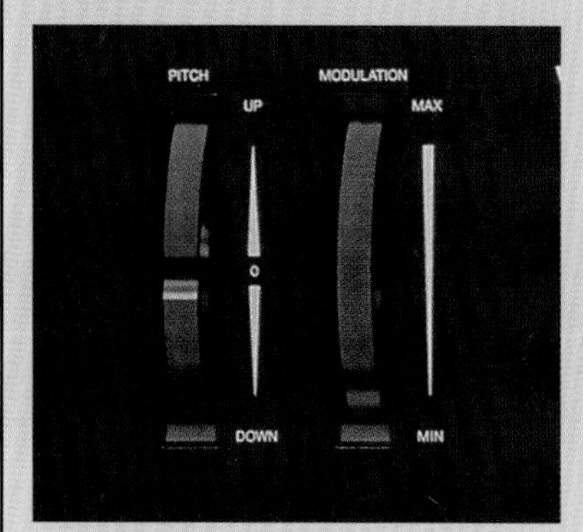

Pitch bend and modulation wheels.

PITCH-BEND Controlled by either a wheel, a joystick or after-touch on the keys, pitch-bend enables you to 'bend' a note to give the same effect as a guitarist bending his/her strings. The 'bend range' can usually be programmed from about one semitone to a whole octave.

POLYPHONIC Capable of playing more than one note at once. If a polyphonic synth is described as eight-note polyphonic, it can play eight notes at once, and so on.

POLYSYNTH Polyphonic synthesiser.

PORTAMENTO Technical term for glide, when the note you play swoops smoothly up or down to the next note. Available on many synthesisers.

PRE-SET A pre-set sound, which comes built-in to your keyboard's memory. Some pre-sets are editable, others you can only use as they are supplied.

PRO Professional.

RACKMOUNT A rackmount unit or module is one built to a width of 19 inches for bolting into a standard equipment rack. Keyboardless synthesisers, modules, expanders and some samplers are built to this design, as well as most studio-type effects units.

RAM If your sounds are stored in RAM – Random Access Memory – you can recall them, edit them and store them in a permanently edited form at will. The programmable memory section of a synthesiser is RAM, and a RAM cartridge is an extra memory cartridge which plugs into the instrument and allows the same facility, like a blank tape that you can record over as many times as you want.

REAL TIME A recording made in 'real time' is recorded 'live', as if you were using an old-fashioned tape recorder (as opposed to the 'unreal' time of step time recording). Real time recording mistakes can usually be tidied up afterwards.

Also, to make matters even more confusing, different manufacturers have different methods of digital sound creation. For example, Yamaha have FM synthesis (Frequency Modulation), Casio have PD synthesis (Phase Distortion), Sequential Circuits have VS (Vector Synthesis) and now even Roland, famous previously for analog-only instruments, have LA synthesis (Linear Arithmetic).

It would be impossible to go into each system in any great detail here. If you buy a synthesiser using one of the above systems, its instruction manual will tell you all you need to know.

What you know about analog synthesisers should help you understand digital synths: the technology is different but the principle's the same. The next section, on samplers, describes digital technology.

Nick Rhodes of Duran with the Roland Jupiter 8, a typical analog synth packed with sliders.

AKAI S900
Rackmount digital sampler/released 1986/ 12-bit mode/40kHz frequency (variable)/ 48 seconds maximum sample/MIDI
THE AKAI S900's economical rackmount format, combined with its performance quality, has established it as an industry standard.

The 900 gives you multi-sampling (32 splits across your MIDI keyboard), velocity cross-fading (so that you can fade from one sound to another simply by pressing harder on the keys), eight-note polyphony and a built-in disk drive for storing your sounds on floppy disk. All of this assigns it indisputably to professional territory.

At maximum sample rate, the S900 offers 12 seconds of sampling time, and it also offers familiar analog-type editing facilities – LFO, envelope generators, filters – with which to treat the samples.

The overall outlay on an S900 and a decent MIDI keyboard undoubtedly buys you a better class of sampling than established keyboarded samplers at the equivalent price.

Mick Talbot of The Style Council playing the Yamaha DX7. Although the DX7 can imitate Hammond organ and Fender Rhodes electric piano, Mick generally prefers the real things.

CASIO FZ-1
Polyphonic sampling keyboard/released 1987/16-bit mode/36kHz frequency/116.5 sec max/64 memories/61 keys/touch sensitive/ MIDI
WITH FULL 16-bit sampling, the Casio FZ-1 looks set to wipe the board with most other sampling keyboards anywhere near the same price.

Its very respectable 36kHz sampling frequency gives a 14.5 seconds maximum sample time, increasing to 58.2 seconds at 9kHz, and by adding the optional RAM cartridge these figures are expanded to 29.1 seconds and 116.5 seconds respectively.

Sixty-four basic waveforms created through sampling can be stored and edited via eight-stage envelope, LFO, and looping, and eight banks of settings (split, etc) can also be stored.

Data can be stored via a built-in floppy disk drive, and displayed on a wide LCD screen which allows monitoring of waveforms and simple real-time editing.

ROLAND D-50
Polyphonic synthesiser/released 1987/ 32 Partials/7 Structures/61 keys memories/ 64+ 64 memories/reverb/MIDI
ROLAND'S FIRST digital synthesiser creates its sounds by the firm's new Linear Arithmetic Synthesis method, whose ease of use and FM-like character make it a very attractive proposition.

Sounds are constructed, for each of the eight voices, by up to four 'partial' waveforms which combine in pairs to produce 'upper' and 'lower' tones, which in turn combine to create complete sound patches, according to your choice of one of seven tone parameters called structures.

Sixty-four sounds, with associated patching and control data (including EQ, chorus and reverb, and a choice of keyboad modes) can be stored in onboard memories, and 64 more sounds can be stored on the optional memory card.

A PG-1000 programmer is available for the faint-hearted—it's a separate unit with simpler, analog-style controls.

A SAMPLING keyboard can digitally ecord any sound, which can be played back at any pitch on the keyboard.

You can also modify your sound – edit t – using many of the same controls that ou find on a synthesiser.

Most samplers come with a full five-octave keyboard. Usually they'll have pitch-bend and modulation. Often they'll have chorus. They may also have touch-sensitive keyboards. And of course hey'll have MIDI.

So what makes a sampler different rom a synthesiser? Not a lot – except that whereas a synth generates its own sounds, a sampler uses sampled 'natural' sounds.

Almost all samplers have a range of eady made' sounds available on computer floppy disk.

Add to that the obvious fact that your sampler can sample any sound direct from a synth, and you may start to believe that samplers are the better bet.

You could be right. The main thing standing in the way of samplers right now is price. But that's dropping rapidly, and in the unpredictable world of electronic instrument technology, it's distinctly possible that samplers will ease synths out of pole position.

The only other slight drawback is sound quality. Because a synth generates its own sounds, you don't have any annoying extraneous noises messing up a synth sound, in the way you can do when sampling via a microphone.

BIT WORDS

SO LET'S take a look at how samplers work. We've said that samplers record digitally – what does that mean? And, with reference to digital synthesisers, what is digitally produced sound?

When information is fed into a computer, it is converted into 'bit words' for storage. A 'bit' is a Binary digIT (hence 'digital'). There are only two binary digits, or binary numbers if you like. These are 0 and 1.

A bit word is a combination of any number of these binary digits. 01 is a 2-bit word, 10010010 is an 8-bit word.

To a computer, each bit word represents a different piece of information. If the longest word it can handle is a 2-bit word, only four permutations are possible: 00, 11, 01 and 10. Therefore this computer will be able to handle very little information.

Computers with 8-bit or 16-bit capacity ▶

MID-HIGH PRICE

ROLAND MKS-80 Super Jupiter
Polyphonic synthesiser module/released 1984/16 oscillators/touch sensitive/64 sound memories/64 sound pairs/MIDI

EIGHT-VOICE POLYPHONIC, the MkS-80 has many innovatory features.

It boasts eight VCFs, eight VCAs and 16 envelope generators, while the 128 internal memories may be supplemented by a further 256 on cartridge.

Programming by DAC is somewhat laborious but an analog style programmer, the MPG-80, is available as an extra purchase – it's a panel of knobs and sliders which plugs in.

A wide range of pitches and waveforms is on hand, together with numerous routing, filtering and polarity options.

There's a wide variety of waveforms, and it has a good MIDI spec.

YAHAMA DX7
Polyphonic synthesiser/released 1983/ 6 FM operators/touch sensitive/61 keys/ 32 memories/ROM & RAM cartridges/MIDI

THE DX7 changed the sound of music. It also revealed the difficulties of programming FM. Result: the majority of users have contented themselves with just its pre-set sounds, which are stunning. With 32 pre-sets and literally hundreds of different ROM cartridges available with 64 or more sounds on each—most made by independent firms rather than Yamaha—the choice is almost endless.

Familiar features include LFO, portamento, glissando, pitch bend and modulation. The keyboard responds to velocity and after-touch and adequate, though hardly all-embracing, MIDI is provided.

The sounds are bright, dynamic, right at the cutting edge, making the DX7 an industry standard unsurpassable except by the brand new DX7IID.

RELEASE The fourth stage in the common ADSR envelope or behaviour pattern of a sound. It describes what happens to the sound after the key has been released.

ROM If your sounds are stored in ROM – Read Only Memory – then they remain unchanged in that memory, whatever treatments you might apply to them while the instrument is switched on. ROM sounds are factory presets which are sometimes supplied in the synth memory but may come in extra ROM cartridges which plug into the instrument. With many synths, it is possible to unload sounds from internal ROM or ROM cartridge into the synthesiser's RAM, where they can be edited in the usual way.

SAMPLING FREQUENCY Digital samplers record their samples by high speed 'sweeping' across the frequencies picked up by the microphone. They analyse the sound by breaking it down into thousands of portions every second, like thousands of points on a graph. The higher the sampling frequency or sample rate, the closer together are the points on the graph, and so the more accurately is the sound recorded. The 'mode' indicates the complexity of information which the sampling computer can process; 8-bit mode is considered low by today's standards, 12-bit is good and 16-bit is state-of-the-art. The maximum sampling time, measured in seconds, is simply the maximum length of sample which the machine can record. With most samplers, the sampling frequency range goes down as the sampling time goes up. So the highest quality samples will be the shortest, and a long sample will be lower in quality. 40–50kHz is considered a professional sampling range, and at this sample rate you'd be looking for a sampling time of ten seconds or more.

SEQUENCER A sequencer is a recording device, but it records note information rather than actual sounds, in the same way as a piece of sheet music does. When built into a synthesiser, or plugged into a synth or drum machine, the sequencer 'plays' the instrument according to whatever has been programmed into it. Programming may be real time, when the device records note information exactly as it is performed on the keyboard, or step time, where notes and rests are 'tapped in' just as you would write them in on a music manuscript. Early sequencers were analog devices, but modern ones are all digital, and may be called microcomposers or digital recorders.

SIGNAL PROCESSOR See effects units.

SLING-ON A term applied to keyboards (especially remote keyboards) which are lightweight, often battery-powered, and fitted with guitar-type strap buttons to enable them to be slung on the shoulder and played like a guitar.

SPEC Abbreviation for specification, which means a list of technical features.

SINE WAVE The mathematical description of the simplest basic waveform or oscillation, which when represented graphically is like a repeating S-shape.

SPLIT A split facility enables you to split the keyboard, either at a set point or a point designated by you. You can then play one sound on one side of the split and a different sound on the other – for instance, a bass sound below and a string sound above.

can obviously handle a lot more detailed information.

Nowadays, by some miracle of technology, sound can also be converted into bit words for storage. A compact disc, for example, is basically a disc full of binary digits which are converted into music when 'read' by a laser beam.

In the same way, a digital synthesiser stores its basic waveforms or operators, and its finished sounds, as bit words. And when a sampler 'digitally' records a sound, it is converted into bit words for storage.

Most of the affordable samplers available at the moment are 12-bit. More professional and more expensive samplers like the Fairlight CMI and the New England Digital Synclavier are 16-bit, and as such are capable of storing far more detailed information about a sound than a 12-bit sampler – which means the quality of the sound will be better.

Nevertheless, 12-bit is good enough for most people's needs. Incidentally, the Emulator II, which is something of an industry standard, is only 8-bit, so the 'more bits the better' philosophy doesn't always hold true.

SAMPLING RATE

A GOOD sampler will offer you at least ten seconds of sampling time (that is, you can record a sound lasting up to ten seconds) at its highest sampling rate.

The sampling rate or frequency is how many times per second the in-coming sound is analysed. Like sound frequencies, this is measured in Hertz (Hz).

So if a sample rate is 20,000Hz (20kHz), this means that the sound is analysed

Tony Banks of Genesis with a keyboard set-up that includes the original Yamaha DX7 (reviewed on the previous page) and the much-acclaimed Roland JX-10 synthesiser (reviewed opposite).

ENSONIQ Mirage

Digital keyboard sampler/released 1985/ 61 keys/touch sensitive/8-bit mode/ 38kHz frequency/8 second max/sequencer/MIDI

THE FIRST sampler available at a sensible price, the Mirage crammed an impressive spec into its sleek, clean design. Up to 16 different sounds can be sampled across the keyboard and playing can be eight-note polyphonic. You can also play up to eight monophonic sounds at once.

Familiar synthesiser features such as VCOs, envelope generators, VCOs, detuning to thicken the sound, layering, mod and pitch wheels give you scope for extensive treatment of the basic samples, which are stored on floppy disks.

The sequence capacity is small but can be expanded by cartridge, and eight sequences can be saved to disk. There's full 16-channel MIDI, and a keyboardless version at almost half the price.

KAWAI EP-705M

Electric piano/released 1985/3 sounds/ 75 keys/touch sensitive/chorus/MIDI

DESIGNED, LIKE the Yamaha CP-70/80, for stage use, the Kawai is a portable piano, strung upright with conventional, hard and honky-tonk piano sounds.

These can be chorused, or used separately, or together in any combination.

The action is fast but well weighted for dynamic playing, and the results, especially in stereo, are rich and cutting but natural.

It has a very good basic MIDI spec, which means that it should make a good master keyboard.

The piano is set into a console which can be moved around on casters.

There is also a grand piano version, the EP-308M, with features which are identical except for its larger, 88-note keyboard and increased MIDI memories.

20,000 times per second.

The higher the sampling rate, the better the quality of the sample. The optimum rate is anything above 40,000Hz.

Most samplers offer you a choice of sample times. However, the longer you want your sample to be, the lower the sampling rate becomes, which means that the quality deteriorates. A higher sampling rate will also handle higher frequency sounds better.

So an ideal sampler will be 12-bit, and offer you 12 to 14 seconds of sample time at a sampling rate of around 40kHz.

LOOPING

ONCE YOU'VE got a sample you're happy with, what can you do with it? Well, you can leave it as it is – but the chances are that you'll want to modify it.

The Truncate function (also known as Start point/End point) enables you to chop off any unwanted bits at the beginning or end of the sample (say you were sampling a drum sound off a tape and someone was singing just before it).

You may then want to 'loop' the sample, to make it longer. As you know, you've only managed to sample a few seconds of the sound; this may be fine for short, percussive sounds or sounds that fade out within a few seconds (the piano for example), but if you've sampled a constant sound such as an organ, you will have to loop it to get it to last as long as you require.

This means finding a fairly constant part in the waveform of the sound, and making it into a continuous loop.

Manual looping, where the player finds a loop point by DAC, can be very hit and miss. It can be made slightly easier if you connect your sampler to a home computer (if the software is available): the waveform will be represented graphically on the screen for you to edit. (The Roland S-50 sampler can actually be plugged directly into a TV, and the Casio FZ-1 has a built-in screen.)

Unless you are very lucky, however, you will always have some annoying click or 'glitch' at the loop point. Thankfully, most samplers now have some sort of 'auto-loop' function which takes most of the headache out of looping.

MULTI-SAMPLING

AS WE have said, a sampler lets you play back any sound at any pitch on your keyboard.

Unfortunately, if you play the sound at a pitch some distance away from the pitch ▶

ROLAND JX-10
Polyphonic synthesiser/released 1986/
24 DCOs/76 keys/touch sensitive/
164 memories/sequencer/MIDI

JUSTIFIABLY CALLED a megasynth, the JX-10 has been built up to a quality rather than down to a price, with beautiful, clean finish and well-weighted keyboard.

It has two DCOs and two ADSRs per note. With its many programming possibilities, the JX-10 not only matches, but often surpasses current digital synthesisers – and does so with a simplicity of control which invites you to experiment.

There are 50 pre-set sounds, 50 programmable memories, and 64 memory spaces for sound combinations (of two sounds and up to 40 parameters).

There's a rather basic polyphonic sequencer and a fun feature called Chase Play for delay effects.

The sounds themselves have been described as a cross between a DX7, PPG and Jupiter 8, which says it all: they're excellent.

YAHAMA DX7IID
Polyphonic synthesiser/released 1987/
6 FM operators/61 keys/touch sensitive/
64 memories/64 ROM or RAM cartridge memories/MIDI

THE LONG-AWAITED DX7 mark 2 is no disappointment. It's unmistakably DX7 in character, yet improved in vital areas. 'FM noise' has been virtually eradicated, and it has increased memory power both internally and using a new-style 64-sound cartridge (and, on the DX7IIFD, a built-in disk drive too).

The control panel now includes several assignable controls and a bigger, backlit LCD screen displaying far more data at one time (making programming easier). There's also a better MIDI spec. Additions include the facility to split or layer sounds and store eight-note-polyphonic combinations.

It also offers a micro tuning facility, so that you can tune notes individually to a pitch slightly above or below normal – should you want your synth to sound out of tune! (Or, more seriously, to investigate alternative tunings.)

And at its heart, again, are a batch of irresistibly classy FM pre-set sounds.

STEP TIME Enables you to program a sequencer or recorder one note or chord at a time – step by step – and to specify how long that note/chord should be, and where there are rests. This can then be played back at the correct speed. A step is one stage in the sequence, whether a note, chord or rest.

SUSTAIN Third stage in the four-stage ADSR envelope which describes the way a synthesised sound behaves with time. It relates to the way the sound behaves while the key remains pressed down.

TIMBRE The tone of a sound.

TOUCH-SENSITIVE If a keyboard is touch-responsive it responds to how hard you play it, either giving more volume (in which case it's velocity-sensitive) or an effect (via after-touch). Velocity sensitivity normally affects volume but can often be used to affect timbre or to bring in a second sound.

TRANSPOSER A device within an instrument which allows you to change the pitch of the keyboard. A transposer is usually used to transpose a piece of music which is set in a difficult key so that it can be played in an easier one but will sound the same. So you can play in **C** major but the sounds can come out in **F#** major if you want!

TREMOLO A device built into some pianos to produce a modulation effect. The modulation is of volume rather than pitch, although the term is commonly misused by guitarists to describe vibrato.

TRIGGERING Activation of a sound source, as from the keyboard of a synthesiser. One device, for example a sequencer, may trigger (play) another, such as a synthesiser; or a master keyboard may remotely trigger a sound module via MIDI. Before MIDI, such triggering was achieved via trigger inputs/outputs (see also CV/Gate).

VCA Voltage Controlled Amplifier – the circuit in a synthesiser which controls the volume of the sound (sometimes replaced in digital synths by a DCA).

VCF Voltage Controlled Filter – the circuit in a synthesiser which controls the tone or timbre of the sound.

VCO Voltage Controlled Oscillator – the basic sound source of all analog synthesisers, whose pitch changes according to the size of the control voltage from the keyboard. Replaced in later analog synths and most digital synths by the DCO.

VELOCITY-SENSITIVE If a keyboard is velocity-sensitive, it responds to how hard you play it. The harder you play, the louder the sound. Velocity sensitivity can affect tone of a sound, or bring in another sound.

VIBRATO Modulation of the pitch of a note above and below the true pitch to produce a pleasant wavering effect, normally achieved on keyboards by applying an LFO – Low Frequency Oscillator – to the note.

VOICE Note or sound created by individual oscillator or oscillator group. The total number of oscillators determines the total number of voices, and thus how many notes can be played simultaneously.

at which it was sampled, it can end up sounding totally different – which is a pain if you're sampling something with a sound you want to remain recognisable, such as a piano.

To overcome this problem, most samplers now offer a 'multi-sampling' option which means you can split the keyboard, say into octaves, and sample a sound at different pitches for a truer representation. Indeed some samplers let you split the keyboard as many as 60 times, so you can sample each note individually.

EDITING

ONCE YOU'VE truncated and looped your sound, maybe even multi-sampled it, you can play it as it is or, if your sampler has an analog processing section, treat it as though it was a basic waveform – as on a synthesiser.

Many samplers have recognisable parameters such as VCF/DCFs, VCA DCAs, LFOs and ADSR to shape your basic sound into something totally unrecognisable from the original.

As if to get their own back, many synthesisers now use sampled waveforms as well as electronically generated ones for their sound sources (for instance the Ensoniq ESQ-1).

Of course, samplers are still a relatively young breed. They are improving all the time – so who knows what exciting developments there will be in this area of music over the next few years?

So there it is—what can only be described as a crash course in electronic keyboards. But hopefully, having read this, you'll be able to approach a synthesiser or sampler with some confidence.

British synth wizard Paul Hardcastle (left) and French synth wizard Jean-Michel Jarre, both playing the sling-on Yamaha KX5. This is probably the most popular of all the portable MIDI keyboard controllers (explained on page 88). It makes no sounds of its own, but controls other keyboards by remote control via a MIDI lead. If the two keyboards look different, that's because Jean-Michel has painted his a delicate shade of pink to match his jacket!

SEQUENTIAL Prophet VS
Polyphonic synthesiser/released 1986/ 32 oscillators/61 keys/touch sensitive/ 200 memories/arpeggiator/MIDI

THE VS is Sequential's first digital synthesiser with a sound different from other Prophets and other digitals, based on 128 pre-set digital waveforms with 32 more you can create yourself by Vector Synthesis (hence VS) using a joystick.

Digital precision combines with analog 'humanity' here. The programming parameters will please analog fans – comprehensive filters five-stage envelope generators – but imaginative 'digital' features like looping, repeat and real-time stereo panning are also most welcome.

The arpeggiator is nifty and polyphonic to boot. It's possible to have eight monophonic sounds playing at once if connected to a sequencer via MIDI.

A highly original and rewarding instrument.

WHO'S WHO

From rock rabblerousers like Jerry Lee Lewis to sophisticated songwriters such as Randy Newman, from electronic pioneers like Kraftwerk to the digital pop of Scritti Politti, these are the players who've helped make keyboards the most influential instruments in rock.

Listening is an important part of learning any instrument. Take note of the work of any of the artists in this section: there's a lot that you can pick up, as long as you don't copy them too closely. Listen, learn, then do your own thing.

CONTENTS

Art Of Noise arranger Anne Dudley finds light and shade with her Fairlight CMI sampler.

ART OF NOISE (ANNE DUDLEY)

AFTER FALLING out with producer Trevor Horn's ZTT organisation over the credit for the 1984 hit 'Close To The Edit', which was a state-of-the-art sampling masterpiece, Art Of Noise emerged as a separate human entity on the China label and Anne Dudley emerged as the 'musical' part of the team.

Classically trained, she played keyboards on a host of Horn hits (some of which she co-wrote), and her distinctive attack can be heard on songs such as Frankie Goes To Hollywood's 'Two Tribes', Wham's 'Bad Boys' and George Michael's 'Careless Whisper'. Her flair for arranging is equally in demand.

The formation of Art Of Noise with Fairlight boffin JJ Jeczalik and producer/engineer Gary Langan yielded the LP 'In Visible Silence' and classic cuts: 'Beatbox', 'Moments In Love'.

Kate Bush: singer, songwriter, producer, keyboard player.

KATE BUSH

ONE OF few female singer-songwriters to be highly regarded for her keyboard work, Kate Bush was an early exponent of the Fairlight CMI. Its capability for manipulation of natural sounds and the human voice has undoubtedly played a part in her distinctive approach to recording.

Hailing from South East London, she was originally inspired by Elton John. "I thought he was fantastic," she says. "At that time pop was mainly guitar—I didn't know anyone else playing piano and writing songs."

Kate signed to EMI at the age of 16 and released her first album 'The Kick Inside' in 1978. Her first single 'Wuthering Heights' topped the UK charts early that year, signifying the start of a phenomenal career, based on an unusual combination of writing, singing and playing talent, topped with an inescapable sensuality expressed through lyrics, dance, mime and video.

Between 1978 and 1982 she released three more albums – 'Lionheart', 'Never For Ever' and 'The Dreaming' – which not only yielded a string of hit singles (including 'Breathing', 'Babooshka' and 'Army Dreamers') but also provided the means for her to design, build and equip her own recording studio.

Its completion was followed by six months of songwriting and nearly a year of recording, resulting in 1985 in the 'Hounds Of Love' album, which re-established her as a major innovative force. She'd always been dedicated to experimental songwriting and searching for new sounds. With a whole studio at her disposal, the results were staggering.

With a highly developed production sensibility which she applied to her own singing and playing and to the contributions of other musicians such as synthesist Kevin McAlea, Bush managed to endow 'Hounds Of Love' with a haunting, melodic quality, exuding olde worlde warmth yet slotting right into the leading edge of contemporary digital pop thinking.

In 1986 her singles career was gathered together in a compilation, 'The Whole Story', which included a remix of 'Wuthering Heights' featuring powerful new vocals.

Classic cuts: 'Wuthering Heights', 'Running Up That Hill', 'Cloudbusting'.

Booker T (bottom right), with Steve Cropper (top left), Duck Dunn (top right) and Al Jackson.

BOOKER T

FORMED IN 1960 as the house rhythm section for Stax Records, Booker T And The MGs played on dozens of soul classics by the likes of Otis Redding and Wilson Pickett. With Booker T Jones on keyboards, Steve Cropper guitar, Donald 'Duck' Dunn bass and Al Jackson drums, they also cut some classic instrumental tracks in their own right – typified by the lean, spare funk of their 1962 US hit 'Green Onions' which went on to become a standard.

Booker T's bluesy organ and Cropper's gritty guitar set the pattern which culminated, in 1968, in their biggest international hit 'Time Is Tight', from the soundtrack of the film *Uptight*.

The band split up in 1972 but left a legacy of tightness and sense of the 'groove' which is instructive to anyone with instrumental ambitions. Classic cuts: 'Green Onions', 'Red Beans And Rice'.

Dave Gahan, Alan Wilder, Martin Gore and Andy Fletcher tune into MTV to see if they can catch Erasure.

DEPECHE MODE
A SEMINAL one-finger synthi-pop band of the early '80s, Basildon boys Depeche Mode were one of the first groups to consist of just synth players (Vince Clarke, Martin Gore and Andy Fletcher) and a singer (Dave Gahan).

Their early material, written by Clarke and typified by the catchy disco-floss singles 'Dreaming Of Me' and 'Just Can't Get Enough', had a naive charm which developed into a more musicianly maturity when Gore took the creative reigns on Clarke's departure to form Yazoo. He was replaced by another synthesiser player, Alan Wilder.

By the mid-'80s, with four album releases ('Speak And Spell', 'A Broken Frame', 'Construction Time Again' and 'Some Great Reward') and a consistent record of UK hit singles, Gore had helped replace their simplicity with techno-sophistication, imagination, and a judicious dash of Germanic metal machine music.

Depeche Mode now occupy an enviable niche: sensitive, serious *and* successful.

They are also the only British synth group of their generation who haven't augmented or ditched their synthesisers, or split up. Classic cuts: 'Everything Counts', 'People Are People'.

DEVO
WEIRD BOYS from Akron, Ohio, Devo rode to cult status on the New Wave of the late '70s with their artfully conceived anti-music. Brash, edgy and almost terminally strange, it drew pastiche and genuine aggressive originality from a melee of jerky rhythms, squeaky synths and hissing guitars.

Frontman Mark Mothersbaugh was the first to use the little EDP Wasp synth on stage (at a London show), and co-writer/conceptualist Jerry Casale experimented with every new piece of hardware that became available, as their sound developed through LPs 'Q: Are We Not Men? A: We Are Devo', 'Duty Now And For The Future' and 'Freedom Of Choice' to 1981's 'New Traditionalists', reckoned to be their peak with its strong musicality and thoroughly electronic production. Classic cuts: 'Whip It', 'Through Being Cool'.

Mark Mothersbaugh with six synths, Roland CSQ100 sequencer, Moog Vocoder, baby mask and specs.

ABBA (BENNY ANDERSSON) Andersson's jaunty synth and piano was the dominant instrumental sound on Swedish quartet Abba's staggering run of Europop hits in the '70s. His trademark was dramatic full piano chords, epitomising Abba's skilful blend of art and tack. Classic cuts: 'Knowing Me, Knowing You', 'Dancing Queen'.

A-HA (MAGS FURUHOLMEN) Perhaps the archetypal global pop band of the '80s, Norway's A-Ha back their marketable image with a deceptively high standard of musicianship and composition. The crucial musical elements are the chattering synths of Magne Furuholmen, the angelic vocals of Morten Harket, and the sweeping songs by Mags and guitarist Pal Waaktaar. Classic cuts: 'Take On Me', 'The Sun Always Shines On TV'.

ASIA (GEOFF DOWNES) Virtuoso Downes is the keyboard wiz with muso superstar quartet Asia. First emerged in Buggles with Trevor Horn, with whom he briefly joined Yes. Classic cuts: 'Video Killed The Radio Star' (Buggles), 'Heat Of The Moment' (Asia).

ATTRACTIONS (STEVE NAIVE) With Elvis Costello's brilliant Attractions, Naive added the quirks and spice to their 'new wave' no-nonsense attack, and has followed Costello through innumerable stylistic twists, from maudlin country to gritty soul. Naive now has his own group Perils Of Plastic as 'sideline'. Classic cuts: 'Oliver's Army', '(I Don't Want To Go To) Chelsea'.

THE BAND (GARTH HUDSON & RICHARD MANUEL) Hudson's organ and Manuel's piano were major intertwining components in The Band's melee of American musics. Band found fame as Dylan's mid-'60s backing band and then forged own career, culminating in 1976 farewell concert, filmed by Martin Scorsese as *The Last Waltz*. Classic cuts: 'The Weight', 'The Night They Drove Old Dixie Down'.

PAUL CARRACK Veteran of UK rock scene, tending to stick firmly in R&B vein through associations with Ace, Squeeze (where he replaced the excellent boogie pianist and TV compere Jools Holland – who later replaced Carrack's replacement Don Snow), Nick Lowe's Cowboy Outfit, Mike And The Mechanics, and many others. Classic cuts: 'How Long' (Ace), 'Tempted' (Squeeze), 'Silent Running' (Mike And The Mechanics) (all of which he sang).

Ray Charles at the grand, Fender Rhodes behind.

RAY CHARLES Early soul/R&B superstar who crossed over to massive pop success with ballads like 'I Can't Stop Loving You' (1962) and 'Hit The Road Jack' (1961), Charles defined the art of blues singer/pianist and was a huge influence on Stevies Wonder and Winwood. Classic cuts: 'Georgia On My Mind', 'What'd I Say'.

COMMUNARDS (RICHARD COLES) Formed in 1985 by ex-Bronski Beat singer Jimmy Somerville and keyboardist/saxist Coles, The Communards use both traditional and modern instruments and sounds in an adventurous mix ranging from synth-pop to bluesy piano-backed ballads. Classic cuts: 'Don't Leave Me This Way', 'So Cold The Night'.

The Yamaha DX7 (centre), posing alongside Vince Clarke (front).

VINCE CLARKE

VINCE CLARKE is the antithesis of the traditional keyboard player. His approach stems directly out of '80s technology, and the scope it offers to a non-proficient keyboard user.

With Andy Fletcher, Martin Gore and Dave Gahan, he founded Depeche Mode in their hometown of Basildon, Essex at the turn of the '80s. Together they decided to trade in their guitars for monophonic synthesisers, a drum machine and backing tapes.

This odd group played legendary 'futurist' nights organised at an East London 'pub' venue by the equally legendary Some Bizzare Records supremo Stevo, and got themselves a track on the resulting 'Some Bizzare' compilation album in 1981.

The early style of Depeche Mode was very much a product of Clarke's songwriting skills and basic 'one-finger' keyboard approach which earned the band its classic 'synthipop' status.

Depeche were taken under the wing of experimental electronics buff Daniel Miller of Mute Records. They released three singles, 'Dreaming Of Me', 'New Life' and 'Just Can't Get Enough', plus a debut album, 'Speak And Spell', before Vince left the band, to resurface in 1982 with Alison 'Alf' Moyet as Yazoo.

The unlikely combination of Vince's plinkety-plonk, squeaky-clean, sequencer programmed pop songs and Alf's gutsy blues vocals proved irresistible. Their first single 'Only You' reached number two in the UK, the follow-up 'Don't Go' number three and their first album 'Upstairs At Eric's' number two.

Minor American success followed under the name Yaz, adopted because Yazoo was registered to another US band, and the duo notched up two further UK hit singles – 'The Other Side Of Love' and 'Nobody's Diary' – and a second album, 'You And Me Both', before parting company.

During his time as half of Yazoo, Clarke had continued with his idiosyncratic style of writing, programming and playing.

The major difference was that he was now doing it on a Fairlight CMI instead of a Roland monosynth.

After a one-off venture with Feargal Sharkey called Assembly – who had a top five UK hit titled 'Never Never' – he resurfaced with current group Erasure, a pure pop outfit with Alison Moyet soundalike Andy Bell on vocals but a slightly less 'synthesised' feel to the instrumentation. Vince was soon back in the British top ten with his fourth successful liaison.

Classic cuts: 'Just Can't Get Enough' (Depeche Mode), 'Only You' (Yazoo), 'Sometimes' (Erasure).

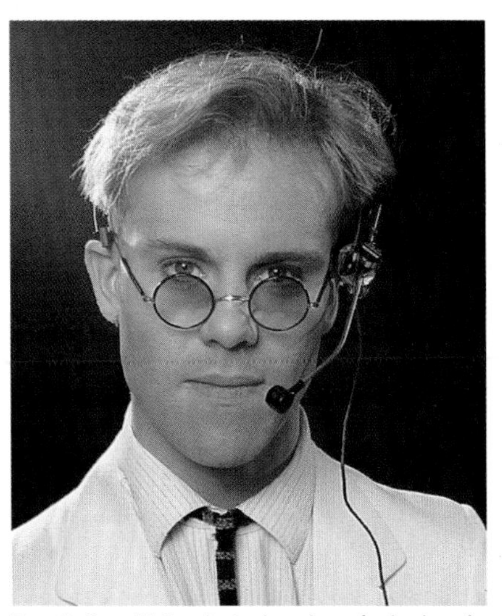

Tom Dolby with headset microphone for keyboard players who can't remain in one place to sing.

THOMAS DOLBY

A MUSICIAN'S musician, Thomas Dolby brings fearsome imagination and technical prowess to modern pop music.

His first solo album for his own Venice In Peril label 'The Golden Age Of Wireless', released in 1982, was remarkable for Dolby's use of a PPG Wave computer to record most of his keyboard and drum sounds. This was not the more familiar Wave 2,2 keyboard system, but actually an adapted lighting computer which had once been used to control Tangerine Dream's lightshow. For the time it was an advanced, if oddball, set-up.

But it was with a non-LP track, 'She Blinded Me With Science', whose video cleverly promoted his image as an English eccentric, that he scored his first singles chart success.

Dolby's 1984 LP 'The Flat Earth' turned out to be an antidote to the 'nutty professor' image, capitalising on natural sounds (captured via a Fairlight CMI) and returning to his favourite instrument, the piano – notably on a version of Dan Hicks' 'I Scare Myself'. But it was 'Hyperactive' which gave him the album's big hit single – again accompanied by a technically advanced promo video, to match its wacky techno-pop.

Since then, Dolby has worked on numerous one-off projects such as Dolby's Cube, recording with George Clinton and Ryuichi Sakamoto, providing the backing band for David Bowie's Live Aid appearance and producing Joni Mitchell's 'Dog Eat Dog' album. In March 1987 his first soundtrack album was released; taken from the Ken Russell film *Gothic*, it was a suitably Wagnerian pseudo-classical opus played entirely on the Fairlight CMI sampler.

Classic cuts: 'She Blinded Me With Science', 'Hyperactive'.

Duran Duran onstage with Nick Rhodes (right) playing Roland Jupiter 8 synth.

DURAN DURAN (NICK RHODES)
UNDOUBTEDLY THE most successful act spawned by the so-called 'New Romantic' phase of British pop in the early '80s, Duran Duran were able to back their glam image with a high degree of musicianship. The keyboards and production ideas of Nick Rhodes helped steer them between the extremes of 'dressed-up rock' and pure synth pop to an ideal commercial compromise.

Exploiting the advantages of state-of-the-art technology to the full, they notched up over a dozen consecutive hits singles and five equally well-received albums, from 'Duran Duran' (1981) to 'Notorious' (1986).

Nick describes his musical role as "fine-tuning bits of melody to construct a tight locking song. Duran songs always have high melodic content with lots of interlocking parts and it's important to fit them all together. When we're recording, I have so many keyboard parts to do that I'll still be tinkering around when the others are out on the town!"

Two satellite groups – Power Station (with Robert Palmer) and Arcadia, featuring Rhodes, Simon Le Bon and Roger Taylor, also had success. Classic cuts: 'The Reflex' (Duran Duran), 'Election Day' (Arcadia).

Keith Emerson live at 1976 Montreal Winter Olympics, playing the Yamaha GX1 mega-synth.

KEITH EMERSON
ONE OF the grand old men of rock keyboards, Keith Emerson first enjoyed public notoriety with progressive rock act The Nice in the late '60s, exploiting his phenomenal classical technique while subjecting his Hammond to unspeakable abuse in wild stage shows.

When The Nice broke up in 1969, Emerson cast around for a suitable substitute, recruiting bassist Greg Lake from King Crimson and drummer Carl Palmer from The Crazy World Of Arthur Brown and debuting Emerson, Lake and Palmer at the 1970 Isle Of Wight Festival.

Emerson's taste for showmanship meant that everything new had to be tried, and he continued to be associated with keyboard development throughout his long stint in ELP, and into his subsequent solo career, with at least 16 albums to his credit. Classic cuts: 'America' (The Nice), 'Fanfare For The Common Man' (ELP).

Brian Eno got mad with Roxy Music, stern with Bowie, and moody with U2.

BRIAN ENO
A CONFIRMED 'non-musician', Eno has been a vital if quiet influence as player and producer of electronic music for a decade.

Chief poseur and weird soundmaker in the original Roxy Music, he left in 1973 to pursue a solo career which included partnerships with Robert Fripp and John Cale.

In the mid-'70s, his interest turned to ambient music and he recorded several 'environmental' LPs including 'Music For Airports', as well as the more accessible 'Before And After Science'.

Eno's artistic credibility and 'bankability' were confirmed when he co-produced Bowie's 'Low' and 'Heroes' albums. He has since produced U2's 'The Unforgettable Fire' and 'The Joshua Tree' and three Talking Heads LPs, as well as partnering David Byrne on 'My Life In The Bush Of Ghosts', with its pre-sampling 'found music' style. Classic cuts: 'Discreet Music', 'Heroes'.

CRUSADERS (JOE SAMPLE) Consummate jazz stylists The Crusaders have travelled a long way since their '60s billing as The Jazz Crusaders, via jazz-funk and pop hits with singer Randy Crawford to worldwide fame, with Sample's distinctive electric piano a major part of their appeal. He has recorded five solo albums, most recent being 'Oasis' (1985). Classic cuts: 'Street Life' (featuring Randy Crawford), 'Rhapsody In Blue'.

DEEP PURPLE (JON LORD) The classic rock organist, Lord formed Purple in the '60s with guitarist Ritchie Blackmore, moving from pop ('Hush', 1968) to formulate the earliest heavy metal ('Black Night', 1970). Lord experimented with rock/orchestral fusion ('Concerto For Group And Orchestra', 1970), but his work with Purple and, later, Whitesnake has been characterised by the force, flash and pomp of mainstream metal. Now back with Purple. Classic cuts: 'Black Night', 'Smoke On The Water'.

DIRE STRAITS (ALAN CLARK & GUY FLETCHER) Although dominated by Mark Knopfler's presence as singer/writer/guitarist extraordinaire, the Dire Straits sound garners much of its CD gloss from the incisive and flexible keyboards work. Classic cuts: 'Walk Of Life', 'Tunnel Of Love'.

FATS DOMINO Roly poly rock and roll pioneer with rolling New Orleans piano style featuring laconic 'walking' bass parts to match lugubrious vocals. Classic cuts: 'Blueberry Hill', 'Ain't That A Shame'.

Doors Robby Krieger, Ray Manzarek, Jim Morrison and John Densmore.

THE DOORS (RAY MANZAREK) Despite the overwhelming presence of singer/icon Jim Morrison, it was Manzarek whose unmistakable, flowing organ style was The Doors' musical hallmark. He also supplied all the band's bass parts, on organ foot pedals, whilst his brooding electric piano dominated their moodier tracks. Classic cuts: 'Light My Fire', 'Riders On The Storm'.

DR JOHN Alias Mac Rebennack, from New Orleans, Dr John started out as the psychedelic voodoo 'Night Tripper' (1968) but reverted to his Louisiana piano-man roots for later R&B hits. Classic cuts: 'Walk On Gilded Splinters', 'Right Place, Wrong Time'.

EURYTHMICS (DAVID A. STEWART) Now seen mainly as a guitarist and producer, it was Stewart's use of brusque synth sounds combined with Annie Lennox's glacial vocals that first brought Eurythmics international success. Classic cuts: 'Sweet Dreams (Are Made Of This)', 'Who's That Girl?'.

BRYAN FERRY Better known as singer/songwriter with Roxy Music, Ferry's use of the piano as compositional tool and prop has been as important in Roxy's influential style as his use of it as an instrument, where it slots into their dense musical mix with characteristic ease. Classic cuts: 'Virginia Plain', 'Jealous Guy'.

Aretha Franklin in the '60s: a great singer and superb pianist on her own material.

ARETHA FRANKLIN

THE FIRST lady of soul, raised on gospel, recorded for Columbia for six years before moving to Atlantic and winning her first real success.

Although her singing and songwriting were the talents highlighted by massive hits like 1967's 'Do Right Woman – Do Right Man' and 1968's 'Think' and 'I Say A Little Prayer', her brilliant gospel piano style was the backbone of much of this early material. The astonishing range of Franklin's vocal style was mirrored in her playing from the gentle shimmy of 'I Say A Little Prayer' through the gospel passion of '(You Make Me Feel Like) A Natural Woman' to the pounding stacatto of 'Think'.

For a decade Aretha reigned supreme, the world's top black artist by some distance. The mid-'70s seemed to bring a cooling of the fire, but the '80s and another change of label saw an upturn in her career. Her covers of soul standards won her new acclaim, and in the mid-'80s she made a major comeback via her duets with Eurythmics' Annie Lennox ('Sisters Are Doing It For Themselves') and George Michael ('I Knew You Were Waiting') along with solo hits such as 'Who's Zoomin' Who' and 'Get It Right'. Classic cuts: 'I Never Loved A Man (The Way I Love You)', 'Respect'.

GENESIS (TONY BANKS)

THE SUCCESS of the current line-up of Genesis – Tony Banks, Phil Collins and Mike Rutherford – spans the '70s and '80s, with some nine albums released since the departure of Peter Gabriel in 1975.

The original band was formed at Charterhouse private school in the '60s, and despite some false starts, which included a debut album produced by Jonathan King, they persisted through personnel changes to establish their art-rock style with albums like 'Trespass' and 'Nursery Cryme', recorded in the early '70s.

Tony Banks, a quintessential part of the band since the beginning, was instrumental in shaping the particularly 'British' keyboard-based sound of the group on such milestones in their career as 'Foxtrot', 'The Lamb Lies Down On Broadway', 'Trick Of The Tail' (the first post-Gabriel album), and 'And Then There Were Three' (which marked the departure of guitarist Steve Hackett).

But Banks was also interested in solo projects and he released 'A Curious Feeling' in 1979. He later followed this with two more solo albums, 'The Fugitive' (1982) and 'The Wicked Lady' (1983).

In the same period he'd worked on Genesis' increasingly commercial 'Duke', 'Abacab', 'Three Sides Live' and 'Genesis', since which, with the exception of 1986's 'Invisible Touch', the three members have been engaged almost exclusively in solo projects interspersed with live appearances.

Classic cuts: 'I Know What I Like', 'Follow You, Follow Me'.

PAUL HARDCASTLE

PAUL HARDCASTLE was a UK funk producer and remix expert until he won public acclaim in 1985 with '19', a song which, from a production point of view, was a perfect promotional vehicle for digital sampling and 'scratch' mixing effects.

'19' was inspired by a TV documentary called *Vietnam Requiem*, which pointed out that the average age of the American soldiers fighting in the war was just 19. The documentary's director also directed the remarkable 'scratch effect' video for the single, which helped get it to No.1 in a dozen countries.

Genesis men Collins, Rutherford and Banks.

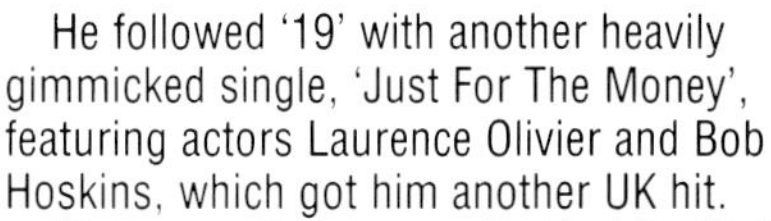

He followed '19' with another heavily gimmicked single, 'Just For The Money', featuring actors Laurence Olivier and Bob Hoskins, which got him another UK hit.

More recently he scored a big hit with 'The Wizard', his theme tune for top British pop TV show *Top Of The Pops*. With its clever, catchy blend of hi-tech, hip-hop, jazz-funk and pop, it's the archetypal Hardcastle record.

Paul Hardcastle: a keyboard player who revels in digital technology.

HERBIE HANCOCK

HERBIE HANCOCK is one of those seminal keyboard players who have had a major influence not just on the development of keyboard music but also on the instruments used to create it. And while his roots are in jazz, he has proved himself a mighty contender in the far more commercial areas of funk and mainstream chart music too.

He notched up his first hit songwriting credit when Mongo Santamaria covered 'Watermelon Man' which Hancock had written for his debut album 'Takin' Off'. But it was the five years he spent working with Miles Davis in the mid-'60s which established his importance, playing on great albums such as 'The Sorcerer' and 'In A Silent Way'.

He formed the Herbie Hancock Sextet in 1968, and his experiments with electronic keyboards and funk sounds led to his major crossover album 'Headhunters', one of the key early jazz-funk records. Hancock became a leader of the new movement, and despite a brief return to 'real' jazz in the late '70s has consolidated that position.

He has even had hit singles applying his skill on the vocoder (a synth in which the envelope of the sounds is controlled by speaking into a microphone) to 'I Thought It Was You' and 'You Bet Your Love', which charted in the UK in 1978 and '79 respectively. Their 'talking synth' sounds were widely imitated particularly by the New York electro-funk bands which sprang up around the

Original Human League, from left: Adrian Wright, Martyn Ware, Ian Craig Marsh, Phil Oakey.

HUMAN LEAGUE
FORMED IN 1977, The Human League soon established themselves as innovative exponents of electronic music. They released their first album 'Reproduction' in 1979, a year before the departure of their two 'musicians' forced singer Phil Oakey and lights operator Adrian Wright to re-group.

They hurriedly learned to play synths and recruited synth/bassist Ian Burden, guitarist Jo Callis, and novice dancer/singers Susanne Sulley and Joanne Catherall. It was an inspired gamble. The new League came with an 'electronic Abba' sound which caught the public mood and propelled both the 'Dare' LP and single 'Don't You Want Me' to the top of the UK charts in 1981 – a double first for totally electronic pop which was to signal the start of a new 'British invasion' of America.

Subsequent albums 'Hysteria' (1985) and 'Crash' (1986) were patchy in comparison, though yielding characteristically deadpan, melodic disco hit singles. Classic cuts: 'Don't You Want Me', 'Human'.

turn of the decade.

In 1983 Hancock took a giant step into the modern rock world with 'Rockit', a huge hit both sides of the Atlantic featuring a blend of hip-hop 'scratch' effects and jazz-funk which has been immensely influential on other artists such as Paul Hardcastle and Mantronix.

He switched directions again in 1986 to compose an Oscar-winning soundtrack for *Round Midnight*, a tribute to 25 years of jazz with Hancock back on the piano. Classic cuts: 'Round Midnight', 'Rockit'.

Herbie Hancock: a jazz-funk player with a rock star's sense of attack.

Christine McVie: a hot pianist.

FLEETWOOD MAC (CHRISTINE McVIE) A '60s British blues pianist with Chicken Shack, Christine Perfect joined Fleetwood Mac in 1970 and with them rose to world stardom with their mega-platinum soft-rock album 'Rumours', staying faithful to piano most of the time. In the Mac saga, she married bassist John McVie, but has since split though both remain in the band. Has released two solo albums – 'Christine Perfect' (1970), 'Christine McVie' (1984). We wonder what the next will be called . . . Classic cuts: 'I'd Rather Go Blind' (Chicken Shack), 'Rhiannon'.

PETER GABRIEL Leader of the '80s breed of digitally aware singer-songwriters, along with his sometime singing partner Kate Bush. Former Genesis singer Gabriel enlists the full range of sampling and sythesiser techniques – plus state-of-the-art videos – to supplement his very personal writing style. Classic cuts: 'Sledgehammer', 'Games Without Frontiers (Jeux Sans Frontieres)'.

DARYL HALL Previously a Philadelphia session pianist on Stylistics records, Hall's brilliant pop songwriting and soulful singing dominated Hall & Oates' massively successful career, with his keyboards an integral part. Classic cuts: 'She's Gone', 'Private Eyes'.

HEAVEN 17 Synth-playing founder members of pioneering UK electronic group Human League, Martyn Ware and Ian Craig Marsh quit the League in 1980 to form Heaven 17 with singer Glenn Gregory. The combination of synthesiser sounds with black dance rhythms has been explored on a series of varied albums—'Penthouse And Pavement' (one side R&B, one electronic), 'The Luxury Gap', 'How Men Are' (dominated by the Fairlight CMI), and 'Pleasure One'. Classic cuts: 'Temptation', 'Crushed By The Wheels Of Industry'.

BRUCE HORNSBY Virginian leader of Bruce Hornsby & The Range, country-tinged light rock group revolving around Hornsby's flowing piano. Classic cuts: 'The Way It Is', 'Down The Road Tonight'.

ISLEY BROTHERS (CHRIS JASPER) Cousin to the five Isleys, Jasper's electronic keyboards and Ernie Isley's Hendrix-style guitar propelled band from '60s Motown cult to '70s world superstars. Now in Isley Jasper Isley. Classic cuts: 'Fight The Power' (Isleys), 'Caravan Of Love' (IJI).

JAPAN (RICHARD BARBIERI) Starting out as British glam-rock New York Dolls copyists, Japan metamorphosed into highly successful art-rock stylists. With influence from Riuichi Sakamoto they absorbed oriental sounds into a gentle electronic keyboard mix, with Bryan Ferry soundalike David Sylvian's vocals projecting a sensitivity which brought them a huge UK teen audience. They split in 1982 at the height of their fame; Barbieri and drummer/synth player Steve Jansen still work together. Classic cuts: 'Quiet Life', 'Ghosts'.

IAN KEWLAY Leader of Paul Young's group The Royal Family, Kewley is the major influence on Young's blend of traditional soul with hi-tech rock. Classic cuts: 'I'm Gonna Tear Your Playhouse Down', 'Wherever I Lay My Hat'.

Jean-Michel Jarre lights up his bizarre custom keyboard.

JEAN-MICHEL JARRE

DEVELOPING IN Paris along a parallel path to Japanese and American contemporaries Isao Tomita and Walter (now Wendy) Carlos, Jean-Michel Jarre brought electronic music to opera in 1971, to such acclaim that he was able to build a successful career in films and the like.

But it was his 'Oxygene' LP in 1977 which brought him international success with the kind of melodic, 'electronic orchestral' material which is today called new age music by its followers and muzak by its detractors.

'Oxygene' was followed in 1979 by the equally successful 'Equinoxe', and with a talent for showmanship on a gigantic scale which he still exhibits, Jarre performed music from the two albums in the open air in Paris to an audience of an estimated one million live spectators and 100 million global TV viewers.

For his next, 'Magnetic Fields' (1981), he went one better by becoming the first Western 'pop' artist to perform in China since the Cultural Revolution.

1986 saw Jarre reaching even more outrageous heights of spectacle with a multimedia event staged in Houston, Texas, in which he lit up and 'played' the entire city. He repeated the feat when the Pope visited Jarre's hometown of Lyon, France, also in 1986. Classic cuts: 'Oxygene Part IV', 'Fourth Rendezvous'.

Two great singer-songwriter-pianists together: Billy Joel (left) and Randy Newman.

BILLY JOEL

'PIANO MAN' was an early Joel hit, and it's a well-earned title. Throughout his long, successful career the piano has been at the forefront – both electric ('Just The Way You Are') and acoustic ('An Innocent Man').

As a performer his range is great, from the acapella sidewalk harmonies of 'The Longest Time', through heartfelt ballads to hard rock, always with a heavy dose of traditional rock and roll.

Joel is very much a traditionalist: he started his working life in the New York music factory studios, then chanced his arm playing solo piano in bars before his rock career took off. He assembled a fierce live band, and polished his writing, playing and singing skills to a chart gloss, yet he still 'keeps the faith' both with rock and with his social roots.

Classic cuts: 'Just The Way You Are', 'Uptown Girl'.

Karl Bartos and Wolfgang Flur of Kraftwerk, with some of their custom-built electronic percussion.

KRAFTWERK

SEMINAL GERMAN synthesiser band Kraftwerk was formed in 1970 by Ralf Hutter and Florian Schneider. Working with legendary producer Conny Plank, they had set out to "simulate not only the instrumentation of rock, jazz and pop but of European classical forms as well" but soon became inextricably identified with a robotic disco style.

This was taken to exaggerated extremes by their laboratory technician stage clothes, their computer generated publicity photos, and their absurdist devotion to technology (to the extent of having a melody line played on an electronic calculator!).

Kraftwerk's obsession with technology was also evidenced on a more serious level in some brilliantly innovative records, starting with the 1974 LP and single 'Autobahn'. 1977 saw the classically bleak 'Trans Europe Express', followed by 'The Man Machine', but it was the next album 'Computer World' in 1981 which gave them an unexpected UK chart-topper with 'The Model'/'Computer Love'.

After 1983's 'Tour De France' single—a big hip-hop hit—they took a break from recording, to emerge in 1987 with 'Electric Cafe'. Classic cuts: 'Autobahn', 'The Model'.

Goodness gracious, great balls of fire—it's Jerry Lee Lewis in his '50s finery.

Awopbopaloobopalopbamboom—it's Prince . . . sorry, Little Richard.

JERRY LEE LEWIS & LITTLE RICHARD

TWO ROCK 'N' ROLL greats who both performed and composed on the piano, Jerry Lee Lewis and Little Richard were born the same year – 1935 – and got their first big hits within a year of each other – in 1957 and '56 respectively.

Their musical backgrounds – country for Lewis, gospel/blues for Richard – were the two ingredients which, when brought into

Elton John: along with Stevie Wonder, rock's most successful keyboards player.

ELTON JOHN

A GIANT in pop whose ability to write classic commercial songs shows no signs of diminishing after 20 years in the music business, Elton John still retains the strong association with the piano which characterised his earliest work.

His relaxed but accomplished playing style – the result of school piano lessons and early experience on the London R&B circuit – has been the perfect partner to dozens of memorable songs, mostly written in partnership with Bernie Taupin. And though on record and in live performance, synthesisers play their part, the grand piano (or its electrified equivalent) remains his first love.

Success first came in 1970 with the classic hit 'Your Song', taken from his second album 'Elton John'. It remains the quintessential Elton John song, with its easy melodic flair and rippling piano lines.

Over the next five years Elton went from great success, to greater, to greater still, at one point becoming arguably the top rock artist in the world. His hard-rocking shows, catchy songs and absurd costumes made him the ideal American stadium act.

Albums over this period included 'Goodbye Yellow Brick Road', 'Caribou', 'Captain Fantastic And The Brown Dirt Cowboy' and 'Rock Of The Westies'. His endless list of hit singles included 'Crocodile Rock', 'Daniel', 'Bennie And The Jets' and 'Don't Let The Sun Go Down On Me'.

1978 saw the departure of lyricist Taupin, to be replaced by Gary Osborne, and signified a lower profile for Elton. For a while, there were more greatest hits LPs being released than new material.

His renaissance came in 1982 when Bernie Taupin rejoined him, and hit singles began rolling off the production line again: 'I Guess That's Why They Call It The Blues', 'I'm Still Standing', 'Wrap Her Up', and more.

Even the most abbreviated list of classic cuts would have to include 'Your Song', 'Rocket Man', 'Crocodile Rock', 'Goodbye Yellow Brick Road', 'I Guess That's Why They Call It The Blues', 'I'm Still Standing'.

ontact, exploded into rock 'n' roll. And these wo were the most explosive rock 'n' rollers f the lot, hammering their pianos with their eet and joyfully belting out their "*awopbopaloobopalopbamboom*s" and "*goodness gracious great balls of fire*".

Yet it's interesting to note that, after giving ock some of its all-time classic songs – Lewis' compositions include 'Whole Lotta Shakin' Goin' On' and 'Great Balls Of Fire', while Richard wrote 'Long Tall Sally', 'Lucille' and 'Good Golly Miss Molly' – and inspiring generations to follow in their footsteps, both returned to their pre-rock roots in later life. Classic cuts: 'Great Balls Of Fire' (Lewis); 'Tutti Frutti' (Richard).

AL KOOPER Hotshot '60s American keyboardist, played organ with Dylan during his revolutionary early electric period then starred in series of best-selling 'supersession' albums with guitarist Mike Bloomfield. Also played on Hendrix's 'Electric Ladyland' and Stones' 'Let It Bleed'. Classic cuts: 'Like A Rolling Stone' (Dylan), 'Voodoo Chile' (Hendrix).

MADNESS (MIKE BARSON) The original 'nutty boy', skinhead Barson was a major part of UK hit machine Madness, and their musical guiding light. His piano and organ steered them through a strange blend of ska and spoof, towards mainstream pop; when he quit at the end of '83 they lost their way. Classic cuts: 'My Girl', 'Our House'.

JOHN MAYALL Massively influential British blues pianist/organist. Graduates from his Bluesbreakers include Eric Clapton, Peter Green, John McVie, Mick Taylor, Jack Bruce, Aynsley Dunbar, Mick Fleetwood, Jon Hiseman. Classic cuts: 'Double Crossing Time', 'My Time After A While'.

MANFRED MANN The old 'Mann' of British rock keyboards, had hits in '60s with jazzy pop combo Manfred Mann and in '70s with progressive rockers Earth Band. Classic cuts: 'Do Wah Diddy Diddy', 'Blinded By The Light'.

RANDY NEWMAN Brilliant tongue-in-cheek songwriter and pianist whose songs have been covered by many others. Classic cuts: 'Sail Away', 'Short People'.

GARY NUMAN Inspired by Bowie, Numan played on the robotic imagery of synth music to win huge UK pop audience in late '70s. Retired from live work in 1981 to concentrate on flying; has since become increasingly unfashionable, though he still retains his fascination for die-hard Numanoids. Classic cuts: 'Are Friends Electric?', 'Cars'.

OMD (PAUL HUMPHRIES) Founded in Liverpool in 1978 with singer/keyboardist/bassist Andy McCluskey and backing tracks courtesy of a tape recorder called Winston, Orchestral Manoeuvres In The Dark started life as UK synth-pop duo. Have since signed up full band, but continue to score melodic pop hits based on Humphries' keyboards. Classic cuts: 'Enola Gay', 'Forever Live And Die'.

Billy Preston with ARP Odyssey monosynth, the Minimoog's early rival.

BILLY PRESTON Teenage virtuoso Preston announced his presence with series of early '60s Hammond organ showcase sets titled 'The Most Exciting Organ Ever', etc. Later became sideman for both Beatles and Stones, launched solo career with late-'60s peace anthem 'That's The Way (God Planned It)', then forged successful career as solo artist with huge hits in USA including organ instrumentals 'Outta Space' and 'Space Race'. Classic cuts: 'Billy's Bag', 'Outta Space'.

ALAN PRICE Newcastle singer-songwriter whose organ shot Animals' 'House Of The Rising Sun' to world hit status in 1964. His blues style brought solo success with 'I Put A Spell On You'. Later turned to trenchant protest with 'The Jarrow Song' (1974) and wrote score for *O Lucky Man*. Classic cuts: 'House Of The Rising Sun' (Animals), 'Simon Smith'.

Howard Jones gets a helping hand on his sling-on Moog Prodigy monophonic synthesiser.

HOWARD JONES

HOWARD JONES could justifiably be called 'Mr MIDI', because he was the first keyboard player to exploit MIDI to the full by doing solo shows where his back-up band was nought but a stack of MIDI-ed up equipment.

His debut single 'New Song' catapulted this 'unknown' into the UK top three in 1983, and was followed in the next three years by nine consecutive UK top twenty hits, two hit albums – 'Human's Lib' and 'Dream Into Action' – along with a well-received collection of remixes, 'The 12" Album'.

His third 'proper' album 'One To One' broke new ground with a more sophisticated collection of songs.

Despite the fact that he now works live with a full band line-up, the lure of MIDI remains strong in the studio. The recording of 'One To One' involved the SRC Friendchip, a sophisticated time controller, to correct fractional timing mismatches on the MIDI-triggered music.

Most of the album was sequenced on a Linn 9000, with his new Fairlight Series III providing most of the drum, bass and percussion sounds which in turn triggered a variety of keyboards including DX7, Super Jupiter and Juno 60, plus Emulator-sampled guitar sounds. The DX7, Linn 9000 and Emulator are Howard's 'basic group' which, along with a clutch of effects, travel with him everywhere.

Jones has a reputation as an equipment hoarder, believing that every instrument has its own strenghts.

He still has great affection for his Moog Prodigy "because of the oscillator sync sounds it has", and used that old standby, a Minimoog, for bass sounds on 'One To One'. The Fairlight – an instrument he swore he'd never use – was also employed to sample noises around the house, and to record a tap-dancing sequence which appears on 'Step Into These Shoes'.

It's a far cry from the early days, when he used a Sequential Pro-One on stage with a Juno-60 arpeggiating over the top! Classic cuts: 'What Is Love', 'New Song'.

MIKE LINDUP

LEVEL 42 began life as a cult jazz-funk outfit. Their initial fame was based on the phenomenal bass-playing talents of Mark King. But as the other members have come to the fore, Level 42 have crossed over to burgeoning pop success based on the complementary vocals of King and Mike Lindup, the tight playing of the Gould brothers (drummer Phil and guitarist Boon), and Lindup's finely meshed keyboard skills.

Level 42's Mark King, Boon Gould, Mike Lindup and Phil Gould at Montreux.

Level 42 began recording in 1981, but the breakthrough was their 1985 LP 'World Machine', produced by the band with assistance from West African musician Wally Badarou.

'World Machine' sold over 2.5 million copies worldwide, giving them a US top ten hit with 'Something About You' and seven number one placings for the follow-up 'Lessons In Love'. 'Running In The Family', from the 1987 LP of the same name, was another major singles success.

Level 42 are set to reach even greater success. They can groove as hard as any jazz funk act, and yet they write superb commercial pop. Lindup himself is equally adept with delicate piano cascades ('Leaving Me Now') or beefy stabs of synthesised 'horns' ('Running In The Family).

Mike may occasionally be seen playing without his colleagues; he has recently followed Mark King down the instrument demo road, doing solo shows for Yamaha featuring their FM speciality keyboards.

Classic cuts: 'Leaving Me Now', 'Something About You', 'Lessons In Love'.

lichael McDonald: one of the best composers, ingers and keyboard players in modern rock music.

ICHAEL McDONALD

IRST COMING to notice for his work on teely Dan's 1975 'Katy Lied' album, singer/ eyboard player Mike McDonald joined The)oobie Brothers in 1976. With his soulful inging and blue-eyed funk electric piano tyle, he effected a change of direction for the)oobies toward R&B rhythms, which pawned 1979's classic 'Minute By Minute' lbum with its award-winning title track and Vhat A Fool Believes' singles.

McDonald's first solo project 'If That's Vhat It Takes' was hailed as a masterpiece on elease in 1982, and 1985's 'No Lookin' ack' scaled even greater heights.

But it wasn't until 1986 that he became a ousehold name, when his duet with Patti abelle 'On My Own' – the epitome of adult op – became a worldwide best-seller. He cored another hit that year with 'Sweet reedom', the title track for a digitally emastered compilation of great moments rom his Doobies and solo careers. Classic uts: 'What A Fool Believes' (Doobie rothers), 'Ya Mo Be There' (James Ingram vith Michael McDonald).

eil Tennant watches Chris Lowe play the PPG Vaveterm synth sampler.

ET SHOP BOYS (CHRIS LOWE)

OP JOURNALIST Neil Tennant and rchitectural student Chris Lowe met in a usic shop, so the story goes, and it was their mutual obsession with synthesisers that brought them together as The Pet Shop Boys.

Their five-year partnership came to fruition in 1986 with the stunning worldwide hit 'West End Girls' – a meeting of Lowe's clipped, ethereal synth sounds and Tennant's lisping, knowing vocals.

Their debut LP 'Please' was full of dance and pop songs fuelled by clever lyrics and superb synth sounds and rhythms. With some justice, Tennant described himself and Lowe as "the last of the great synth duos".

The Pet Shop Boys' interest in hi-NRG and Italian disco resurfaced in the 'Disco' collection of 12-inch remixes in late 1986. Classic cuts: 'West End Girls', 'Suburbia'.

Yellow Magic Orchestra with Sakamoto (top left) amid their highly complex stage set-up.

RYUICHI SAKAMOTO

A FOUNDER member of Yellow Magic Orchestra with Haruomi Hosono and Yukihiro Takahashi, Ryuichi Sakamoto has had a major influence on the way synthesisers have been used in rock and pop music in the '80s.

YMO were initially perceived as an Oriental version of Kraftwerk, by whom they were obviously influenced. But their pioneering work with music computers (they were the first to use a Roland MC-4 on stage) and their blending of traditional Japanese themes into an expression of life in ultra-modern Tokyo ('the technopolis') quickly established a unique identity for their music – a blend of ancient and very modern Oriental sounds –for which they coined the name 'technopop'.

Their progressive style influenced not only the electro-duos who formed the backbone of Britain's New Romantic movement in the early '80s, but also the electro-funk/rap outfits such as Afrika Bambaataa who've since emerged from the streets of New York, and their advanced ideas are still surfacing today in the work of British bands like Depeche Mode.

Now a solo artist, Sakamoto supplied the soundtrack for the film *Merry Christmas Mr Lawrence* in which he starred with David Bowie (it brought Sakamoto a UK hit single in the form of 'Forbidden Colours' featuring ex-Japan singer David Sylvian). He also played keyboards on Public Image Limited's 'Album'. Classic cuts: 'Tong Poo', 'Technopolis'.

SIMPLE MINDS (MICK MacNEIL) A founder member, MacNeil shared the Minds' ideal of combining the energy of punk with the vision of British art-rock (Bowie, Roxy Music). Commercial success came with 1982's 'New Gold Dream' album, which heralded a more mature sound in which the spiky fills and luxuriant backwashes of MacNeil's keyboards were a key factor. Subsequent albums 'Sparkle In The Rain' and 'Once Upon A Time' have shown the Minds achieving a stadium sound with power and subtlety. Classic cuts: 'Promised You A Miracle', '(Don't You) Forget About Me'.

JIMMY SMITH The man who put the Hammond on the jazz and R&B maps, the king of '50s keyboards and huge influence on '60s jazz/blues players, cut over 80 albums. Classic cuts: 'Walk On The Wild Side', 'The Cat'.

SOFT CELL (DAVE BALL) Ball was the keyboard-playing half of archetypal '80s electro-duo Soft Cell. To match Marc Almond's highly-charged vocals, Ball developed a rich and gutsy Prophet 5 style notable for its melodic and emotive content, featured on a string of brilliant singles. Their most famous single 'Tainted Love' was a brilliant electronic reworking of '60s soul. Later records ranged from the melodramatic torch song 'Say Hello Wave Goodbye' to the manic paranoia of 'The Art Of Falling Apart', with Ball's synths serenely melodic on the former, brutally discordant on the latter. Cell split in '85, and remain one of pop's most-missed groups; Ball has recorded one solo set, 'In Strict Tempo'. Classic cuts: 'Tainted Love', 'Say Hello Wave Goodbye'.

SPECIAL AKA (JERRY DAMMERS) Dammers was the leading light of UK's late '70s ska revival, heading own Midlands label Two Tone which launched Specials, Beat, Selecter. A man of integrity and a keyboard player/composer of great vision, Dammers piloted The Specials through first hard-hitting ska, then experiments with MOR, then into highly politicised anti-sexist, anti-racist stance. Classic cuts: 'Ghost Town', 'Nelson Mandela'.

Stranglers Dave Greenfield, Jean Jacques Burnel, Jet Black and Hugh Cornwell.

STRANGLERS (DAVE GREENFIELD) Some would accuse Greenfield of learning Doors' 'Light My Fire' by heart and retailing it at any opportunity, but his racing keyboard style helped set Stranglers apart from rest of UK's '76 punks, and his hard-edged tones have helped sustain their attack into the '80s. Classic cuts: 'Golden Brown', 'No More Heroes'.

SUICIDE (MARTIN REV) Late '70s New York duo – Rev's minimalistic synth pulsebeats underpinning Alan Vega's manic vocals – who came and went with punk but had influence on early UK synth duos such as Soft Cell. Classic cuts: 'Dream Baby Dream', 'Rocket Rocket USA'.

STYLE COUNCIL (MICK TALBOT) A past jazz-blues organ specialist, Talbot formed Style Council with ex-Jam star Paul Weller in 1983. Weller ditched Jam's aggressive guitar style for Isleys-influenced soft soul, instrumentally led by Talbot's Hammond organ and Fender-Rhodes electric piano sounds, sometimes achieved on Yamaha DX7. Classic cuts: 'You're The Best Thing', 'Long Hot Summer'.

Green with an E-mu Drumulator drum machine (top left) and Roland MSQ-700 sequencer (top right).

Steve Porcaro: one of Los Angeles' top session players, along with his drummer brother Jeff.

SCRITTI POLITTI

SCRITTI POLITTI produced the most digitally FM-eral pop album to date, in the immaculate, complex yet highly accessible 'Cupid & Psyche '85'.

The sound of that LP and immediately preceding singles 'Wood Beez' and 'Absolute' (the latter a US number one) could hardly have been predicted from Welsh singer Green Gartside's avowedly amateur efforts with early Scritti incarnations for Britain's original indie label Rough Trade.

But though the roots of a new pop sensibility can be traced back to the memorable single 'The Sweetest Girl' in 1981, it was Green's subsequent link-up with New York musicians David Gamson and Fred Maher plus producer Arif Mardin which lent the second LP its classic blend of soulful songwriting and hi-tech execution.

The breathtaking Scritti sound has since appeared on their production of Chaka Khan's 'Love Of A Lifetime'. Classic cuts: 'Wood Beez', 'Absolute', 'Hypnotize'.

TOTO (STEVE PORCARO)

TOTO WERE drawn from the Los Angeles session pool which supplied the likes of Steely Dan, Earth Wind & Fire and Barbra Streisand with the best in studio musos.

Their debut album 'Toto' (1978) spawned three US hit singles and one in the UK, and spent almost 12 months in the US album charts.

Their most notable success came in 1982 with 'Toto IV', producing three US and two UK hit singles and sweeping the board in the 1983 Grammy Awards.

Vocalist Bobby Kimball left shortly afterwards, but the instrumental line-up of the band recorded the soundtrack to *Dune* in 1984.

Keyboard player Steve Porcaro, like his brother, drummer Jeff, has been closely involved with equipment manufacturers over the past nine years, amassing a studioful of products for personal evaluation. Classic cuts: 'Rosanna', 'Africa'.

PRINCE

PRINCE'S ONSTAGE persona of singer-guitarist-extreme poseur tends to disguise his importance as a keyboard player and keyboard sound creator. His distinctive approach to synthesisers, even from his first album, released in 1980, redefined the way keyboards could be applied to what was initially seen as technofunk.

He undoubtedly absorbed numerous influences along the way – such as the electronic backwashes for which Yellow Magic Orchestra were particularly noted.

His fourth album '1999' found him presiding over a unique regime of synthesised sounds that ranged from those oriental, dreamlike, ambient effects to clipped brass stabs and sparse percussive treatments.

"Presiding over" is the key, because exactly who plays what on Prince records has always been shrouded in a certain mystery.

It's almost certain that he played all the instruments on his first three albums, 'Prince', 'Dirty Mind' and 'Controversy' – apparently favouring Oberheim synthesisers – although by the time of 1983's '1999' it seemed that regular keyboards player Matt 'Doctor' Fink and guitarist Dez Dickerson were making a contribution.

Calling himself the Starr Company and Jamie Starr, Prince was also spreading his influence outside his own performances, putting together and largely defining the sound of both The Time (a pastiche funk band fronted by Morris Day) and Vanity 6, who had metamorphosed into Apollonia 6 by the time his 'Purple Rain' album and film were released in 1984.

By now Prince's stage band The Revolution included the excellent Lisa Coleman on keyboards alongside guitarist Wendy Melvoin. With the break-up of the band in 1986/87, they decided to team up together.

Prince also brought Sheila E to prominence with 'The Glamorous Life', gave Sheena Easton a controversial hit with 'Sugar Walls' – all with the inimitable Prince sound – and donated key hit songs to The Bangles ('Manic Monday') and Chaka Khan ('I Feel For You').

'Purple Rain' was very much his guitar hero album, but subsequent LPs 'Around The World In A Day', 'Parade', and 1987's 'Sign 'O' The Times' have seen a return to both electronic and acoustic keyboard sounds, combined with a sparse, funky guitar style.

The distinctive Prince approach – now often just called the Minneapolis sound – can also be heard in the work of Jimmy Jam and Terry Lewis, who left The Time to concentrate on a production career which has been phenomenally successful, both for themselves and for artists such as Janet Jackson, Force MD's, The Human League and Alexander O'Neal.

Prince has broken dozens of records in his meteoric career. 'Purple Rain' sold nine million in the US alone, giving him two No.1 singles ('When Doves Cry' and 'Let's Go Crazy'), and staying at the top of the album charts for 24 weeks in a row. Twice in 1984 he had two US top ten singles at once, and his third No.1 single 'Kiss' kept his own composition 'Manic Monday' by The Bangles off the top spot in April 1986!

Classic cuts: '1999', 'Little Red Corvette', 'When Doves Cry', 'Pop Life'.

oger Powell in Utopia's smart-suit 'mod' period—efore they became hi-tech hippies.

Vangelis, the movie soundtrack specialist, with the Minimoog monophonic synthesiser.

UTOPIA (ROGER POWELL)

N 1974, the already legendary singer/uitarist/writer/producer Todd Rundgren ormed Utopia, with Roger Powell on eyboards plus Kasim Sulton and Willie Wilcox.

Powell soon became recognised as pearheading a new style of rock keyboard laying which was sufficiently sharp and ggressive to compete head on with undgren's highly proficient lead guitar.

He became involved in product evelopment, launching the Powell Probe, a ling-on remote keyboard that predated the enre (and MIDI) by more than five years.

Like the rest of Utopia, he wrote and sang a hare of the classic material that appeared on uch albums as 'Oops! Wrong Planet' 1977), 'Adventures In Utopia' (1980) and Swing To The Right' (1982) but his solo ecording career has unfortunately shown ather less flair. Classic cuts: 'Trapped!', Love In Action'.

VANGELIS

A GREEK composer and keyboard player who has specialised in film soundtracks, Vangelis Papathanassiou's crowning achievement was his Oscar-winning soundtrack for *Chariots Of Fire,* whose main theme was the best selling synth instrumental ever.

Its universal appeal was summed up by Vangelis himself as "contemporary and yet in keeping with the movie's very Victorian concept. So it's music of today, influenced by the spirit of another era."

Vangelis is the archetype of an electronic musician applying technology to traditional musical virtues. "I try to be as flexible as possible, and not repeat myself."

Certainly this goes for his film soundtracks: after *Chariots'* naturalistic sounds he supplied the eerie electronic score for *Bladerunner* (1982). Has recorded with Jon Anderson of Yes, and soundtracked *Missing.* Classic cuts: 'Chariots Of Fire', 'State Of Independence' (Jon & Vangelis).

rince in rare keyboards-playing pose, with the Yamaha electric grand piano.

SUPERTRAMP (RICHARD DAVIES & ROGER HODGSON) Mid-'70s English pop-progressive group whose long but catchy songs relied heavily on atmospheric synth sounds and melodic Wurlitzer electric piano. Classic cuts: 'Dreamer', 'The Logical Song'.

TANGERINE DREAM Experimental German synthesiser group formed in '67 by Edgar Froese and Christophe Franke who created dreamlike soundscapes using unconventional instruments in early days of electronic keyboards. Tangerine Dream now specialise in film soundtracks. Classic cuts: 'Phaedra', 'Ricochet'.

ULTRAVOX (BILLY CURRIE) Keyboards player and violinist Currie has been a major part of Ultravox, from their early robo-punk days, through their pomp-rock New Romantic phase (including the synth-orchestrated epic 'Vienna'), to their latterday rock-pop accessibility, dominated by thick synth sounds. Has also played with Visage. Classic cuts: 'Vienna', 'Dancing With Tears In My Eyes'.

PETER VETTESE One of Britain's most in-demand session players, Vettese has played with Go West, Frankie Goes To Hollywood, Paul McCartney and others. His advice to beginners: try to get a synth with touch-responsive keyboard that's fairly easy to edit, gives a blend of warm sounds and digital edge, and has some sequencing power. The Ensoniq ESQ1 fits the bill, but if it's out of your price range, he recommends Yamaha's PSRs. "Whatever you buy, make sure it's something that allows you to play with other people, not just alone at home." Classic cuts: 'Rage Hard' (Frankie), 'I Just Died In Your Arms Tonight' (Cutting Crew), 'Step Right Up' (Jaki Graham).

TOM WAITS Eccentric gruff-voiced singer-songwriter and jazz pianist who has brought sleazy tales of US barroom lowlife into the CD age. Much admired by other singers (Paul Young covered 'Soldier's Things' from Waits' acclaimed 'Swordfish Trombones' album). Classic cuts: 'Frank's Wild Years', 'The Piano Has Been Drinking'.

STEVE WINWOOD Gifted multi-instrumentalist who found fame with Spencer Davis Group in '60s; his soulful piano, organ and vocals powered hits like 'Keep On Running' and 'I'm A Man'. Later formed more whimsical Traffic who had hits such as 'Paper Sun' and 'Hole In My Shoe', then supergroup Blind Faith with Eric Clapton, then re-formed Traffic, maintaining flow of acclaimed, highly musical material. Solo since '75, continues to create fine work such as 1980's 'Arc Of A Diver', with experimental use of synths and other keyboards, and 1986's 'Back In The Highlife', mainstream rock/funk with consummate class. Classic cuts: 'Gimme Some Lovin'' (Spencer Davis), 'Higher Love'.

Dieter Meier of Yello comes up for air.

YELLO Probably the first musicians to base an entire album on sampling ('Solid Pleasure', 1980), Swiss duo Boris Blank and Dieter Meier cut their classic to date in 1983 – the Fairlight-dominated 'You Gotta Say Yes To Another Excess'. Its powerful, doom-laden but danceable tracks brimmed with found sound; an influential work. Classic cuts: 'I Love You', 'Lost Again'.

Wakeman's well-worn set-up includes Minimoogs, Fender Rhodes, Hammond, grand and Mellotron.

RICK WAKEMAN

THE MAN who took pomp-rock and keyboards virtuosity to its limits, Wakeman is best known for sprawling orchestral works like 'The Myths And Legends Of King Arthur And The Knights Of The Round Table' (1975, recorded with a 45-piece orchestra and 48-singer choir, and staged on ice!), and his work with Yes, which varied from some of their more accessible material ('Fragile') to the heights of pomposity ('Tales From Topographic Oceans').

Wakeman's earlier sessions included Bowie's landmark album 'Hunky Dory', and he has produced a massive body of music – to much critical scorn – ranging from the soundtrack of Ken Russell's bizarre 1975 movie *Lisztomania,* to his 1981 LP with Tim Rice, '1984'. Classic cuts: 'Space Oddity' (David Bowie), 'Going For The One' (Yes).

Saxist/keyboard player Edgar Winter manages to play both at once and still stay centre-stage.

EDGAR WINTER

BROTHER OF hard rock/blues guitarist Johnny, Edgar had a taste for jazz which led to his choice of piano, organ and saxophone as first instruments. His self-produced 1970 debut album 'Entrance' was an astonishing declaration of pop-jazz versatility.

Surprisingly, Winter then changed direction completely, for the R&B showmanship of his White Trash band. This in turn was replaced by the classic Edgar Winter Group line-up including Dan Hartman and guitarist Ronnie Montrose, whose blending of everything from melodic pop to heavy funk gave them commercial success with the instrumental track 'Frankenstein' off 'They Only Come Out At Night' (1972).

Rick Derringer replaced Montrose for two albums, after which they all concentrated on solo careers – low key in Winter's case. Classic cuts: 'Frankenstein', 'Free Ride'.

Stevie Wonder: a keyboard player whose work runs the full emotional span.

STEVIE WONDER

ALTHOUGH STEVIE Wonder is rightly admired as one of the most important and consistent of contemporary singer-songwriters, his contribution to keyboard playing shouldn't be underestimated.

Proficient on the piano at age eight, he scored his first hit single five years later with 'Fingertips Part 2' – a number one in the USA. This and subsequent '60s singles for Tamla Motown like 'I Was Made To Love Her', 'For Once In My Life', 'My Cherie Amour' and 'Yester-Me, Yester-You, Yesterday', were more notable for his vocal prowess and harmonica skills than for keyboards. But by 1970, with the release of 'Signed, Sealed, Delivered' –incredibly, his 18th album – his music exhibited a new experimental direction, followed three albums later in 1972 by a real quantum leap in the form of 'Music Of My Mind'.

This was a solo tour-de-force employing numerous electronic keyboards, including Moog and ARP synthesisers. It alienated many of the old soul fans but won him a major new white rock audience, who were then primed for its 1973 sequel 'Talking Book', the classic Wonder album, stuffed full of standards such as 'You Are The Sunshine Of My Life' and 'Living For The City'. Among them was 'Superstition', featuring the Hohner Clavinet which, in Wonder's hands, established the standard funk keyboard sound for practically the next decade.

Wonder's next album 'Innervisions' featured a brilliant range of songs, from the upbeat 'Higher Ground' to the downbeat 'All In Love Is Fair' and Stevie snatched five 1974 Grammy awards – a feat repeated the next year with 'Fulfillingness' First Finale'.

The double 'Songs In The Key Of Life', released in 1976, was regarded by many as one of the albums of the decade. Stevie appeared to lose his way a little with the sprawling 'Secret Life Of Plants' (1979), but the '80s began with 'Hotter Than July' – a superb album with the ecstatic classics 'Masterblaster' and 'Happy Birthday'. Subsequent albums such as 1985's 'In Square Circle' showed no signs of his talent or his influence waning after a quarter of a century of recording.

From his later, more keyboard-orientated career, classic cuts must include 'Superstition', 'You Are The Sunshine Of My Life', 'Masterblaster', 'I Just Called To Say I Love You'.

BUSINESS SECTION

So far, so good. You've read the Instruction Manual, Chord Directory, Buyer's Guide and Who's Who—how to play, what to play, what to buy and who to look out for. You're ready to join the music business.
Now how do you get your foot in the door?

That's where our Business Section comes in. In it you'll find a rundown of the various ways you might develop your talent, either as a professional or part-time musician.

And to finish the book off, there's a detailed chart of how the music industry operates, showing the relationships between all the different people who work in it, and the stages an artist's work goes through on its way to the public.

The music business is often referred to as a jungle. We can't tell you how to be king, but we can help you cut your way through to your goal.

CONTENTS

IF YOU'VE followed every stage of this book and put in plenty of practice time, you should now have a good grasp of the basic elements of rock keyboards playing. You're ready to take things a stage further – so where do you go from here?

If you decide to put a band together, you'll find there's a lot of practical matters that have to be sorted out.

The first thing to consider is – who's in the band? You're going to end up spending a lot of time together, so compatibility is vitally important. Also, it makes sense if you're all at roughly the same level of musical ability. Carrying someone who's not really competent slows down rehearsals and recording, puts live performances at risk, and generally ends in tears.

IN REHEARSAL

HAVING SET your line-up, you're going to need somewhere to rehearse – a stumbling-block for many young bands. Ideally of course you need a place where you can leave your gear permanently, that's soundproof and entirely free of charge. The reality usually falls well short of this ideal, but a number of options are available, depending on the kind of area you live in. Church and meeting halls are often available for a reasonable fee, some clubs are open during the day for rehearsals, and in many towns there are purpose-built rehearsal rooms – though obviously these charge commercial rates for their accommodation.

If you can get hold of somewhere private but are worried by the noise factor, consider soundproofing the premises yourself. Ideally you need acoustic tiles of the type used in recording studios, but heavy material draped around the walls can make a surprising difference.

Then there's the question of transport. A gigging band needs a truck or van, and this is one area where it's best to spend as much as you can afford. Unreliable transport is really worse than none at all. Don't forget that you can always hire transport, and in the early days when times are tight this can make a lot of sense.

MONEY MATTERS

WHICH BRINGS us to the question which most often bedevils starting-out bands: money. At the beginning everything – equipment, transport, rehearsal rooms – is going to *cost* you money. You're going to have to make some early decisions on just how you're going to handle these expenses.

Does one member of the band act as treasurer, extracting contributions from the others and handling the bills as they come in? Should you open a bank account in the band's name? Do you all make the same contributions, whether you have day jobs or not?

If you have money coming in from gigs you'll have some floating capital, so proper administration becomes even more vital. How much money goes into each member's pocket, how much into a band fund? Do you all get equal shares?

The point is, you have to deal with the money angle up front, so that everyone knows exactly what's going on. Make sure that detailed records are kept and you'll reduce the chances of 'misunderstandings' at a later date.

PLAYING IN HARMONY

HOWEVER, RUNNING a band isn't all administration – there's also the question of music! The first thing is to agree amongst yourselves about the type of music you want to play. If three of you are committed punk revivalists and the fourth is a secret admirer of Barbra Streisand, you're not going to get very far.

You're bound to have musical tastes that differ to some extent, but as a band you need to make sure everyone is pulling in roughly the same direction.

"People think of me as a soul fan, but you should have heard my first group—we sounded like Siouxsie And The Banshees. I definitely prefer being in a group: there's less pressure and you can call on other people's opinions. It can be really boring on your own." **ALISON MOYET**

ALL YOUR OWN WORK

WHATEVER KIND of music you want to play, at some point you're going to have to think about original material. When you first start playing together you'll probably fall back on the rock standards and twelve-bar blues you all know.

This may get you local gigs, but if you've got your eyes set on greater things, sooner or later you're going to have to start writing.

In the next chapter we'll be giving you some more detailed advice on how to go about it.

THE FIRST GIG

SO THERE you are. Four or five of you have got together. You've begged, borrowed or even bought most of the equipment you need and you've got somewhere to rehearse. No problems with 'musical direction' – you've already put together an hour's worth of material. How do you get it heard?

Well, don't forget that you've got access to a ready-made public that is disposed to think well of you – a public that consists of your friends and relatives. The chances are that sooner or later your band will be asked to play at a wedding, party or some other private function, and you'll have the perfect opportunity to try out your skills in front of a live audience (assuming you play 'party' music). One booking can lead to another, and if you're lucky you'll soon find you've got some money coming in and the beginnings of a reputation.

THE IMAGE IS THE MESSAGE

LOCAL PARTIES and functions are only the first step on the road to professional employment – nevertheless, you should start as you mean to go on and have a few thoughts about the kind of visual image you want to project.

It doesn't matter that much at this stage, as you'll develop your own visual style as you go along, but it is always worth thinking in terms of impact and originality. What is it that's going to distinguish you from the next band?

PRACTICE MAKES PERFECT

YOUR FIRST gig is bound to be a little 'untidy'. The audience might have enjoyed it, but there *was* that embarrassing moment when half the band thought the number had finished while the other half carried on regardless. . . You have to admit your performance did leave a little bit to be desired. So what do you do?

You go back to your rehearsal room and work your way through the whole set again. Then you do it again. . . and again, until you get absolutely everything right, from the introduction of the first number right the way through to the encore.

Don't waste time when you're rehearsing. Get down to business as soon as possible. How you rehearse depends to a great extent on what kind of band you are. You might have a leader/songwriter who demos his or her song and then tells all the other members of the band exactly how to play them – or every member of the band might make their own contribution to every arrangement.

However you handle it, try and get every song note-perfect – a good test is whether each member of the band can play his or her part all the way through without accompaniment. Go on until you get it right – but if you really can't seem to get it together, leave it for another day. There's nothing worse than hammering away at a song you're beginning to get heartily sick of.

OFF THE RECORD

ONE FURTHER thought. If you're reading this book, the chances are you're the sort of person who listens to a lot of records. From now on, try and listen analytically. Keep asking yourself questions. . .

Why is this a hit song? Why is this keyboard solo a classic? Why is this band exciting, that one boring?

In rock, as in all art and entertainment, half the trick is knowing what's good. You can have all the talent in the world, but if you don't know how to edit yourself – how to cut out the overblown, the pretentious and the simply boring – your abilities may well pass unnoticed.

IF YOU want to get ahead in the music business you've got to write your own material. There are artists who make it with other people's songs, but they're few and far between.

The pop industry runs on hit songs, and your writing can influence a manager or record company A&R man just as much as your performing skills.

It's also worth remembering that generally speaking, writers end up richer. Your name in small letters under the title of a song means a whole lot of extra money in royalties.

GETTING STARTED

SO, HOW do you start? Well, the chances are that you've already fiddled around with a few snatches of lyric and some simple chords – and you've been disappointed because your efforts somehow didn't sound like chartbusters.

Well, don't worry about it – practically everyone who starts writing songs produces a lot of rubbish to begin with. There's only one way to get better – and that's to keep on doing it. There's no substitute for experience, and if you're prepared to be ruthless with yourself and accept constructive criticism from others, the chances are that your writing will gradually improve.

There is no set method of writing songs. For one thing, there is no set goal. Some people just want to write top 50 hits; others have something to say, whether lyrically or musically, and hang the commercial potential.

Even when two writers do share a goal – say, to get a number one single – they very rarely go about it in the same way.

Having said that, if your aim is to get a recording contract, the best thing you can have in your portfolio is a clutch of potential chart songs.

GETTING A HIT

WE CAN'T TELL you how to write a hit song, but we *can* get you in the ballpark.

First, your song has to make musical sense. Think about the relationship between notes and chords you've already learnt – for instance, the way **C**, **Dm**, **Em**, **F**, **G** and **Am** work together in the key of **C**.

If you're a songwriter, music is your language. The better you know it, the more you can do with it. If you want to break the rules, go ahead. But it will help if you know them first – and discordant songs are unlikely to get you signed to CBS.

Secondly, keep it simple. Most hit songs revolve around a limited number of chords, riffs and rhythms. Today's top songwriters such as George Michael and Bruce Springsteen frequently revisit the same musical ground trodden by Smokey Robinson or Bob Dylan in the '60s, and they wouldn't pretend otherwise.

It's even more important for you, as a new songwriter, to keep your material direct and immediate. You only have a limited time to win over your audience, whether that audience is in a dancehall or behind a record company desk. They need to be able to make sense of it in a hurry.

WORKING METHODS

GOOD SONGS rarely write themselves. Mostly it's hard work. So set aside time for songwriting. If you simply wait for inspiration to strike, you'll end up with a very thin repertoire.

How you actually go about songwriting is of course very largely up to you. Some writers go for a melody and then fit lyrics around it. Some take the reverse approach. Many match snatches of words to melody as they go along, redrafting them into coherent lyrics later. Sometimes a good title can set off a whole song.

Consider right at the start what your strengths and weaknesses are. If you've got a good ear for a melody but fumble over the lyrics, or vice versa, the solution may be to find a partner.

"We argue a lot—it's the only way to get something really good. Both of us have to be satisfied with a song: the secret is in editing our own work. If things don't sound good, wedon't labour over them, we just reject them. There are plenty of half-finished songs around." ANNIE LENNOX, EURYTHMICS

Working in a partnership certainly has advantages. You get built-in criticism, and there's always someone there to help you along when your enthusiasm flags.

SONG STRUCTURE

WITHIN MAINSTREAM pop or rock, songs still tend to follow the traditional song structures: intro/verse/chorus/verse/chorus/solo/verse/chorus, etc.

If in doubt, use these devices: they give the song pacing, and ensure that it doesn't just drone on and on.

Make sure you know what you want to achieve. The structure can reinforce the mood through repetition, climax, sudden changes of direction...

Think about who is to perform it. If you're in a band, some of your songs may not suit the group. Don't let that stop you finishing them: it's all good practice and you may be able to use the song later. But if you're writing with the group in mind, imagine them performing it as you write, and try to build in elements that will flatter their talents.

Above all, give it some shape: a beginning, middle and end if you like.

Once you've got a song on the way, make sure you write down all the elements on paper – chords, melody line, and any ideas you might have for riffs, basslines or solos – using either musical notation or some other system such as our musical grids. There's nothing more frustrating than 'losing' a song.

It's also a good idea to record each song onto tape, even if it's just a portable cassette recorder – for a start, you can hear it more objectively – but don't make this your only record.

SELF-PROTECTION

OK, LET'S say you've come up with a clutch of respectable songs. How do you stop your precious works from being ripped off?

In the first place there's no need to worry unduly. As a general rule, people in the music business don't want to steal your songs. If you have the ability to write saleable songs, they'd rather sign you to a publishing and/or recording contract so that they make money out of you in the future as well as now.

As soon as you write something and record it, on paper or on tape, you own the copyright. The problem is to prove it. One cheap, simple way to do this is to seal it in a package and send it to yourself by registered post. Don't open the package: the postmark proves when it was sealed and posted. In most cases this should be sufficient, but it doesn't guarantee complete legal protection.

Another method is to deposit your tape or manuscript with a bank or solicitor, and get a statement from them saying when it was deposited, and that the person depositing it claimed to be the author.

If you really want to be certain – particularly if you are moving into a position where people in the business are beginning to hear your songs – the best thing to do is consult a lawyer, preferably one with music business experience.

If your songs prove to be commercially viable, the chances are that at some stage you will sign to a publisher. The publisher's job is to try to get your songs used, and to collect royalty payments on your behalf whenever your song is played, recorded or printed.

Once your songs are being performed live, on radio or TV or on record, you will be eligible to join the organisations which exist to collect royalties for composers and songwriters. In the US these include BMI (Broadcast Music Inc.), ASCAP (American Society of Composers, Authors and Publishers) and the Harry Fox Agency; in Britain the PRS (Performing Right Society) and the MCPS (Mechanical Copyright Protection Society).

In the meantime, however... just keep on writing. Remember, huge hits have been written in ten minutes – and after all, you've got to have *something* to put on the demo tape...

MAKING A DEMO

THE DEMO tape is the calling card of the music business. Every morning, all over the world, thousands of cassettes drop onto the doormats of managers, agents, promoters, DJs and record companies. Whether they're good, bad or indifferent, they carry the hopes of countless young people who think they've got what it takes to make a living in music, and maybe become the next big thing.

So what happens to all these musical missives? If you make a demo and send it off to take its chances amongst the armada of tapes floating around, will it even get listened to?

Perhaps surprisingly, yes it probably will. Every band tells stories of demos despatched into the blue never to be heard of again, but in general if you send someone a tape they'll get to hear it – eventually. You may have to wait months to hear from them, you may never hear from them at all – but you can be pretty sure that at some point your tape will have been given a whirl.

It'll get heard because – although the opposite often seems to be the case – the music industry is always desperate for new talent. Very few managers or record companies can afford totally to ignore the tapes that turn up on their doorsteps.

On the other hand, listening to unsolicited tapes is not a priority. Music business professionals are generally going to deal first with acts recommended by people already known to them (one of the reasons why any contact is better than none). Your tape will most likely be heard first by a secretary or junior staff member of the organisation you sent it to. It will only reach the boss by a process of elimination.

Don't forget, if the executive *is* impressed by your tape, he or she probably still has to convene meetings, canvass other people's opinions, and go through the whole corporate decision-making process before getting back to you – so when it comes to submitting demos, patience is a virtue.

WHAT THEY WANT TO HEAR

SO WHAT can you do to make sure that your demo overcomes all the hurdles and makes the best possible impression? What do people in the music business *want* to hear?

As ever, it doesn't do any harm to have some great songs. The ideal demo tape is one which contains one or more obvious major hits, preferably requiring little or no alteration or re-arrangement. If it is of master tape quality, yielding records that can be released without re-recording – so much the better!

Apart from hits, the professionals look for signs of originality – 'newness' if you like – but you don't have to be eccentric or peculiar. At the time of writing, the record business is not going overboard on art-rock, and that situation looks likely to remain the same for some time.

They also want to hear strong, distinctive vocals, at least competent instrumental skills, and signs of genuine talent. Don't forget that ultimately they're looking for something they can sell, something that is going to give people so much pleasure that they are actually prepared to pay for it.

Some of the things they don't want to hear are: lengthy instrumental workouts (unless the band in question is working in an essentially non-vocal field like jazz-rock – and then the instrumental skills should be exceptional); cover versions, unless they're done in such a way as to have new and saleable qualities; and solo voice-and-acoustic-guitar performances. The latter were of course staple fare a few years ago, but nowadays the average music business executive tends to reach for the stop button at the first sign of a tinny acoustic chord.

"We came to London in 1983 and toured all the record companies without success. But we kept making demo tapes, and eventually the manager of the demo studio offered to manage us. The first company he approached signed us up." MORTEN HARKET, A-HA

The question is, how can you make your demo stand out from the crowd of hopefuls and also-rans?

PRESENTATION

THE ANSWER can be summed up in one word: presentation. A great many bands let themselves down by a lack of basic professionalism when it comes to demo tapes. Often even the appearance of the demo – scruffy packaging, smudged hand-written titles – is enough to put off potential listeners. When it comes to the music, poor sound quality, badly thought-out arrangements and even fluffed notes often push interesting ideas and genuine talent into the background.

So adopt a professional attitude right from the start. Consider first how much you can afford to spend – bearing in mind that, as in most other fields, you tend to get what you pay for.

Even if you are operating on a tight budget, you should dismiss the thought of making a demo at home. (Unless you're broke *and* you've got a really brilliant song – most music business professionals pride themselves on their ability to spot an outstanding song however poor the quality of the recording.) Your best bet by far is to book yourself into a professional demo studio.

By doing so you'll not only gain the benefits of professional recording equipment and facilities, you'll also be able to draw on the skill and experience of a professional recording engineer. With a professional behind the mixing desk, you can concentrate on your performance, on making your demo what it should be – a 'demonstration' of your band's ability when playing at the top of its form.

CHOOSING A STUDIO

THE QUESTION then arises – which studio should you pick? The choice is endless, ranging from converted rooms in private houses (these can sometimes be surprisingly good, usually due to the enthusiasm of their owner/operators), through purpose-built professional demo studies all the way up to the major studio complexes where the hits are made.

Costs can also vary enormously, depending on the number of tracks available, the size of the studio, the facilities, the studio's reputation and other factors. But one thing worth bearing in mind is that the hourly rate tends to drop the further you get from the city. Sometimes a lengthy trip can yield surprising dividends in terms of affordable studio time.

The best thing is to ask other musicians. The good (or bad) word about a studio soon gets around, and musicians who have actually used the facilities are the best qualified to judge. A lot of the differences between studios lie in 'feel' or atmosphere – something you have to have experienced to recognize.

If you can't get any word-of-mouth recommendations, you're going to have to do a little research.

Check out the music press by all means – but don't be tempted simply to pick the studio offering the cheapest hourly rate. Call a few studios and compare costs. Ask them how many tracks they offer – studios can be anything from four-track to 48-track – and what facilities. What other bands have worked there?

Once you've hit upon a studio where everything seems right, book your session. But don't relax – your work has only just begun.

PREPARATION

FIRST, DECIDE on the songs you want to record. Go for the ones with the most instant appeal, the ones that really leap out and grab the listener's attention. Whatever kind of music you play, memorable melody lines and catchy 'hook' phrases carry a lot of weight when it comes to demos. Remember, the person who's going to listen to your tape is probably going to do so in a hurry – fast forwarding through your carefully crafted epics, trying to get an instant fix on what it's all about. Make sure your tape is full of solid 'meat', and save the atmosphere-building intros and extended solos for live gigs.

Unless someone already has an interest in your band and has specifically asked for a longer tape, don't plan on demoing more than four or five songs. But once you've decided on them, make sure you *know* them. Rehearse them again and again until you can all play your parts in your sleep – and remember that faults which might go unnoticed live will become glaringly obvious during a recording session.

Having made sure that the band is

"I met Dave Gilmour of Pink Floyd through a friend of my brother, and he used his name and money to enable me to make a proper demo tape. I couldn't have done it on my own—I'd go round the record companies, but nobody wanted to know." KATE BUSH

musically perfect, you should make sure that all your equipment is in equally good shape. Check all your instruments, leads and amps, bearing in mind that any stray buzzes and hums are going to sound horribly worse in the studio.

One other thing – when the day of your session dawns, get there early. The studio will have allowed a period before your session for you to set up your equipment – much better to use that than waste precious recording time.

IN THE STUDIO

HOPEFULLY YOU will have been able to take a look at the set-up before arriving for your session, so you will know roughly what to expect. However, if you've never seen the inside of a studio before, this is what it will look like.

There will be a control room where the tape machines and ancillary equipment are situated. The room will be dominated by a control 'desk' – size depending on the number of tracks – covered in switches, dials and fader controls. The engineer sits at the desk and looks out through a soundproof window into the studio itself, communicating with those in the studio via a speaker system. (Incidentally, even in the most elaborate studios control room accommodation tends to be cramped – it isn't a good idea to ask friends along to your session.)

The studio itself will be lined with soundproof material and cluttered with mikes, mikestands, headphones and all the other paraphernalia of recording. A portion will probably be screened off to accommodate the drums, to avoid them overpowering other instruments during recording. All except the smallest studios will have a piano. Many will also have synthesisers and drum machines, though you may have to pay extra to use them.

Once you've set up your gear – generally positioned by the engineer or assistant – you'll all be 'miked up', particular concern again being paid to the drum set. Then the engineer will ask you each to play a few runs to get a recording 'level' – and you're ready to go.

Well, some of you are anyway. Recordings are made by building up layers, track by track, and you invariably start by laying down the rhythm track. To keep everything together, the lead vocalist will normally sing a 'guide vocal' along with the rhythm section – this will be scrubbed out later.

Once the rhythm and bass tracks are completed to everyone's satisfaction, the next step might be to record, say, keyboards and guitar. Finally, the finished vocal is added and vocal harmonies, if any, layered on. The vocalists generally have to peform on their own in the studio, with the rhythm track being relayed through headphones – a slightly daunting task if you haven't done it before!

However, recording should be an enjoyable process – provided you know your material and you don't try and do too much in one session. You don't have to get everything right first time. If you're not happy with anything, do it again – and again, if you want. If your vocals were perfect until the last chorus when you forgot the words – no problem. The engineer can 'drop you in' so that the final result will be seamless – a perfect vocal from beginning to end. There's all sorts of studio trickery that can be used to correct imperfections, from strengthening vocals to speeding up the entire finished recording, and the more sophisticated the studio you hire, the more facilities of this type will be available.

Don't forget, the engineer is there to help you. If this is your first demo session, you don't know all the ins and outs of production technique, but you do know what you want the final result to sound like. However inexperienced, you and your band are paying for the studio and you are the producers – so keep on until you get it the way you want it.

This particularly applies when you have finished laying down tracks and are ready to 'mix' – that is, integrate all the tracks into the final finished product. The 'mix' is one of the most important parts of the whole recording process – to a large extent it determines what your demo is actually going to sound like.

Unfortunately it's also the area at which you, first-time recording artists, are likely to have least experience. There's no easy answer. You have to ask questions, absorb the processes which go into putting together a mix, and be insistent about the result you want.

But remember this is a demo, not an

"The industry is looking for hit singles. I got so many letters saying the tracks on our demo weren't commercial enough and were too long, we should do three-minute singles. We had to build up a live following to get signed." FISH, MARILLION

album. You needn't bother with some of the enhancing effects which are available at this stage. Managers and A&R men know that anyone can add echo and reverb – they want to hear what you've basically got to offer, unhindered by extraneous technical wizardry.

THE END RESULT

AT THE end of it all you should have a master tape and a number of cassette copies – cassettes rather than reel-to-reel tapes or discs are the accepted medium for demos. You've spent a lot of time and probably quite a lot of money getting to this stage, but you've now got a shop window for your talents, a calling card that can open the door to all sorts of possibilities. With a good demo to your name you're up and running – and ready to stop the rock business in its tracks. . .

IF YOU want to take things a stage further, the next step has got to be performing in public – to an audience of paying customers. But remember, playing in public is a quantum leap away from playing for your friends. The public at large don't care whether you're a nice guy or not, they just want to be entertained.

So how do you set about getting those all-important first gigs, the gigs that will transform your band into a semi-professional if not a professional outfit?

As a means of getting some sort of track record, you might find it worthwhile to play for nothing – or expenses only – to begin with. For example, charities often mount benefit concerts for one good cause or another, and they're generally only too glad to add another band to the bill.

By the same token, local clubs are always promoting talent nights, usually on a slack night of the week. On those nights they will present two or three bands on an expenses-only basis, charging low door prices to attract custom. Again, the benefit is mutual – they cover a slack night and you get to play in public, with the chance, if you impress, of getting a real paid booking at a later date.

THE RIGHT PEOPLE

WHEN IT comes to real, paid bookings, you won't find it easy. You're probably going to have to rely on your demo tape – the good old 'calling card' of the music business.

Needless to say, you shouldn't simply send it out to every venue in your area. Club owners, like record companies, get demo tapes arriving by every post, and they have even less time to listen to them.

Instead, do your homework first. Visit all the likely venues in your area. Check out which ones would be right for your kind of music. See if you can find out who does the booking. Make the acquaintance of other musicians, and ask their opinion. Find out which places have a policy of trying out new talent.

Don't send your demo, give it to the booker personally. Make sure it's well packaged and presented, with the name of your band and a contact number.

Choose your moment. Don't approach a club owner during a gig, for example. He's going to be far too worried about how *this* evening's going to think about some future occasion involving your band. On the other hand, if you're around after a successful gig, when everyone's celebrating a good night and the club owner's looking forward to a big take, it might be worth approaching him. It's all a question of psychology.

You should let him know if there is any time when he can check you out in person – if you rehearse nearby, for example, or if you have any kind of a performance lined up.

Having said all that, nothing is going to help you if your band isn't up to scratch. So don't try and get gigs before you're ready. You'll simply make it doubly difficult for yourself when you are ready to take the plunge.

READY FOR ANYTHING

IF YOUR music is good enough, and you're prepared to put in the legwork, sooner or later you'll land a gig. But don't think your troubles have ended, because they've only just begun.

As with any other performance, a good rock show depends largely on preparation. Assuming that you're already well-rehearsed, that means preparation of your equipment.

Make sure it all works. If it doesn't, get it fixed, or hire or buy some more. Always make sure you carry spare leads, strings and so on.

MAKING YOURSELF HEARD

THEN THERE'S the question of the PA (public address) system. If you've managed to raise the money to buy your own, then you've no problems – although you should make sure it's powerful enough to fill the venue you've been booked into.

"I saw The Who at Live Aid, when Pete Townshend fell over on his back—and Roger Daltrey immediately fell down next to him. That's what being in a band's all about. You can't laugh at a member of your own band, you have to pretend it's part of the show."

PAUL YOUNG

If you haven't got an adequate system, you're going to have to hire one. There are plenty of equipment hire firms where you can rent PA suitable for venues ranging from a small club to a major stadium. Ask other musicians which is the best place to go to, ring round and get quotes, and make sure you know exactly what you are going to get for your money.

Depending on the venue, it is possible that a house PA system will be available to you. Check this out beforehand. Similarly, you may be able to borrow the PA of the headlining group, if there is one. Again, you're going to have to get in touch with the other band and find out beforehand.

Whatever you do, don't just wait until the night and hope for the best.

Speaking of equipment, you should consider insuring yours. Also, make sure your stuff is clearly identified as yours: stencil your name or logo on your amps and speakers.

ONE TWO THREE TESTING

ON THE day of the gig, your 'be prepared' philosophy should apply even more. Set out early – better to have to kill an hour than arrive late and have to rush setting up your equipment.

Make sure you know what time you're supposed to be playing, and what time your soundcheck is. If you're playing second fiddle to a headlining group, you probably won't be given much time for a soundcheck anyway.

However long you get for a soundcheck, remember that the idea is to balance your live sound, not rehearse your set. If you have a sound mixer and someone who knows how to operate it, so much the better. If not, you're going to have to get a balance by ear. Either way, it's the last chance you'll get to iron out any unexpected glitches in your sound.

IF AT FIRST YOU DON'T SUCCEED

AS TO the gig itself. . . well, as ever, how you go down largely depends on how talented you are and how much work you've put into your act. But don't be too disappointed if you don't get three encores. When it comes to playing live, nothing improves a band like playing live – the more gigs you do, the tighter and more professional you'll get. In the early days, you're doing well if you just get asked back.

Trial and error is the name of the game, but there are nevertheless a few points you should bear in mind when you're playing to a live audience.

RUNNING ORDER

OBVIOUSLY YOU should have a running order, so that you all know what you're going to play next without massive onstage conferences. But don't be afraid to change the order if necessary, depending on how your stuff is going down. If the audience wants to bop, let them bop with some hard rock – don't slow them down with mournful ballads.

Whatever kind of music you play, and whatever order you play it in, try and avoid clichéd announcements on the lines of "are you having a good time?" Unless one of you is a real comic talent, it's best to avoid long announcements of any kind – and in-jokes are definitely out.

As for the music, give your act some sort of shape, pacing it so there is a good balance between fast and slow, loud and soft. Make sure you save a couple of your best numbers for the end, and have a real 'hit-'em-between-the-eyes' number standing by for an encore – just in case!

THE PAYOFF

FINALLY, WHEN the gig's over and the customers have gone home, there comes the moment of reckoning when you actually get a cash sum thrust into your hands, the moment that makes all the sweat and hustle, the cramped van and the even more cramped dressing-room seem worthwhile. You're on your way to becoming professional musicians.

IT SOMETIMES seems as though half the population under thirty is in a band. Yet at the same time, there are fewer opportunities to play live, and even the mighty record business is feeling the pinch.

Despite the record-breaking sales achieved by megastars like Michael Jackson and Bruce Springsteen, sales overall are down.

So currently the supply of bands is somewhat outstripping the demand, and the result is that it's harder than ever to get the break that will turn your outfit from a working semi-pro band into a collection of rock stars.

Having said that, there's always room at the top for someone new, original or just plain lucky. If you've got talent and, even more important, sheer determination, you can still make it in the music business.

However, you've got to be prepared for rejection. With very few exception, there is no such thing as an overnight success. When it seems that a new star has come from nowhere, it usually turns out that he or she has been slogging away obscurely for ten years, gaining experience and refining their craft.

A WORD IN YOUR EAR

AS WE discussed previously, contacts are important. Of course if the band's no good, it's not going to help if your uncle is the managing director of a major record company. But if you have got the potential, you need to start off a ripple of word-of-mouth appreciation, a buzz, which is eventually going to reach the ears of the right people in the business.

So whenever you're gigging, try and get people to come and see you – anyone whose opinion is worth something, like local journalists (who sometimes also freelance for national publications), other musicians (particularly those in more established bands) and people on the periphery of the music business proper, like record store and music shop owners. Find out whether record companies have representatives living locally, and ask them along too.

As we've said before, a recommendation, however remote, can make all the difference.

For example, the person who reviews your gig for the local paper might also review records – in which case they're probably on the mailing list of several record companies, and known to their press officers. If you can get that reviewer to submit your demo for you, or even just make a call to the press office before you submit it, you're in with a much better chance.

When you're trying to make these first few contacts, don't forget that the music industry is a small world. Journalists know publicists, managers hang out with record company execs, A&R scouts drink in the same places as agents. So if someone receives your tape and is impressed by it, even if they're not interested in taking matters further themselves, they'll pass it on to someone who might be. So a tape sent to an agent could eventually land you a management contract.

DON'T GET TIED DOWN

TALKING OF management, you'll probably find out quite early on that there's no shortage of so-called 'managers' at a minor league level. Typically, these are small businessmen – sometimes on the periphery of the music business – who for one reason or other want to get involved with a band. *You* have to make up your mind whether you want to get involved with *them.*

Obviously, a locally based manager can be useful if he (or she) can hustle gigs for you. A manager with funds might be a help in getting hold of equipment, transport and so on. At best, he could help you make those first important contacts.

On the other hand, there's probably not a lot he can do that you can't do yourself, and he is likely to try and tie you down to some sort of contractual agreement. This will probably be bad news if you do start to make some headway in the music business, as record companies generally prefer new bands to come unencumbered by advisers of any kind. They prefer to place new bands with management companies of their own choice. Likewise, heavyweight management companies are generally not keen on having to buy out some smalltimer before they can handle you.

"We don't have a manager, so we discuss all decisions among ourselves. But the more successful we become, the harder it gets—on tour it's a real strain. I wouldn't advise any young group to do it our way. You need a manager if you're looking for a deal."
DAVE GAHAN, DEPECHE MODE

On the whole, it's probably better to stay clear of the smalltime local manager. But if you do come across someone who looks as if he can genuinely do something for you, don't sign anything. Keep your relationship on a 'gentlemen's agreement' basis. If he insists on some form of contract, two golden rules apply.

First, you must take the advice of an independent lawyer (something you should do at all important junctures of your career anyway). Secondly, if you must sign, it's the length of the contract that's important. Keep the period down to a year, or two years at most. That way, if the worst comes to the worst, you can always just sit out your contract before making your next move.

JOINING THE MAJOR LEAGUE

WHETHER YOU have a relationship with a local manager or not, when you make your first approaches to the music business you may do well to try management outfits first, rather than record companies.

There are several good reasons for this. In the first place, record companies have a higher profile, and tend to get swamped by hopefuls who have copied down their addresses from record sleeves. What's more, they prefer acts who are immediately recordable. Management companies, on the other hand, work at the coalface of the music business. They are to a greater extent in the business of finding and developing raw talent, and are sometimes prepared to take time and trouble over an act that a record company would regard as simply not ready.

If you're courting, or being courted by, a management company, try and find out as much as possible about them – who their other artists are, the kind of reputation they have, their track record. Music business managers are a notoriously tough breed, and many of them are legendary for their uncompromising business methods. But if you do come up against any types who are reputed to hold those who displease them out of upper storey windows, don't let it necessarily put you off. Such types are often fiercely protective of their artists' interests, and people who receive the window treatment are usually those who owe the act money.

IN THE BUSINESS

WHETHER YOU sign with a management or record company first, the moment you put your signature on the dotted line, you're in. You've joined the music business, become part of the powerful machine that can open the doors to radio, TV, headlining tours and eventual fame and fortune.

Your management team and record company will set you up with all the other experts that a promising young band needs on the road to stardom.

Take a look at the chart on the next page and you'll get some idea of how it all works. Naturally this is only intended as a rough guide to the business, as the functions of the various departments and companies often overlap.

We've depicted a typical major label, with numerous different departments. Many independent record companies consist of no more than a handful of people, each of whom does whatever has to be done at any given time. But even a small label will have to fulfil all the functions on our diagram.

Any band coming into the business can expect to have dealings with most or all of the different outfits shown on the diagram.

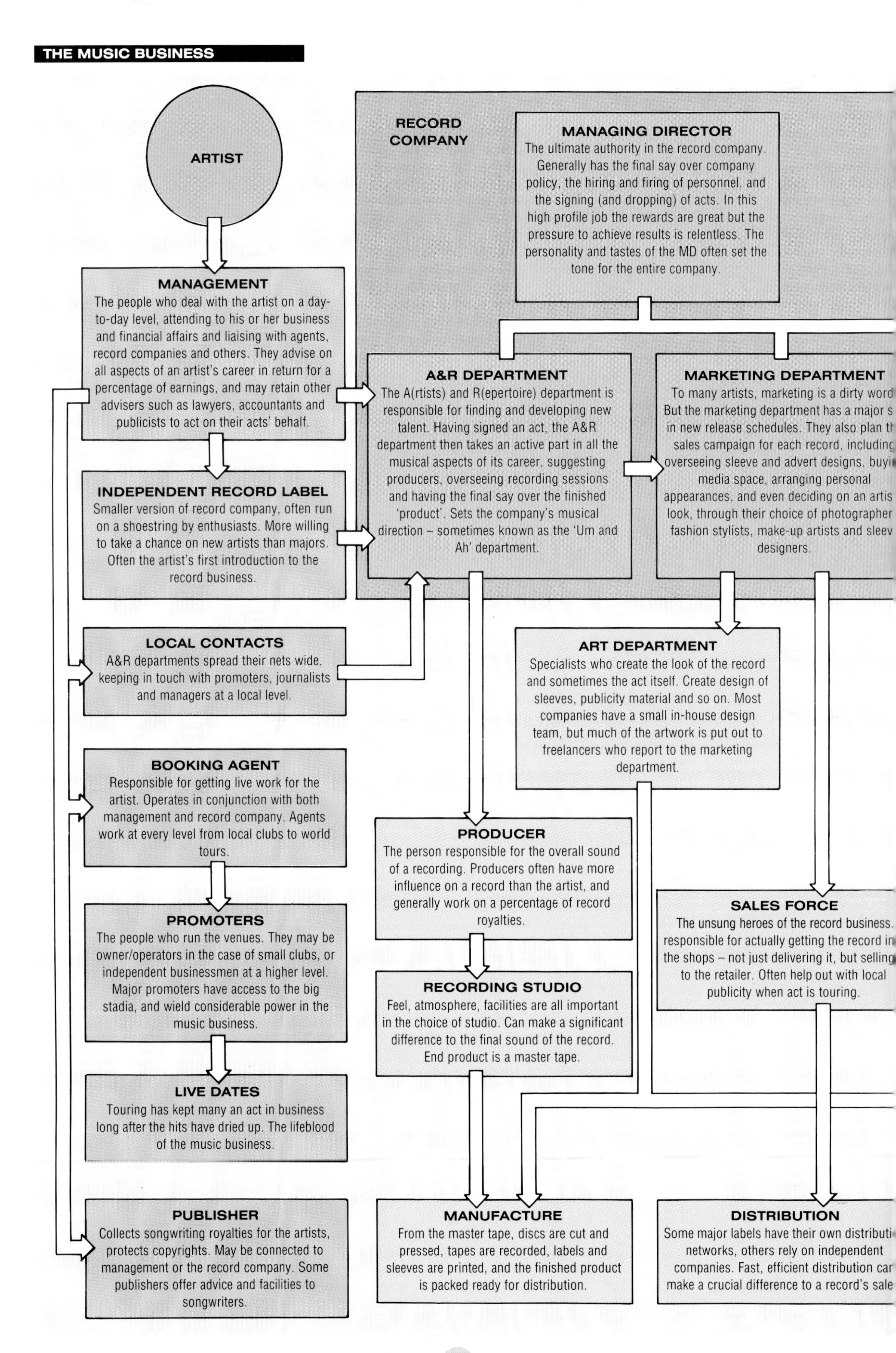
ARTIST
MANAGEMENT
The people who deal with the artist on a day-to-day level, attending to his or her business and financial affairs and liaising with agents, record companies and others. They advise on all aspects of an artist's career in return for a percentage of earnings, and may retain other advisers such as lawyers, accountants and publicists to act on their acts' behalf.
INDEPENDENT RECORD LABEL
Smaller version of record company, often run on a shoestring by enthusiasts. More willing to take a chance on new artists than majors. Often the artist's first introduction to the record business.
LOCAL CONTACTS
A&R departments spread their nets wide, keeping in touch with promoters, journalists and managers at a local level.
BOOKING AGENT
Responsible for getting live work for the artist. Operates in conjunction with both management and record company. Agents work at every level from local clubs to world tours.
PROMOTERS
The people who run the venues. They may be owner/operators in the case of small clubs, or independent businessmen at a higher level. Major promoters have access to the big stadia, and wield considerable power in the music business.
LIVE DATES
Touring has kept many an act in business long after the hits have dried up. The lifeblood of the music business.
PUBLISHER
Collects songwriting royalties for the artists, protects copyrights. May be connected to management or the record company. Some publishers offer advice and facilities to songwriters.
RECORD COMPANY
MANAGING DIRECTOR
The ultimate authority in the record company. Generally has the final say over company policy, the hiring and firing of personnel, and the signing (and dropping) of acts. In this high profile job the rewards are great but the pressure to achieve results is relentless. The personality and tastes of the MD often set the tone for the entire company.
A&R DEPARTMENT
The A(rtists) and R(epertoire) department is responsible for finding and developing new talent. Having signed an act, the A&R department then takes an active part in all the musical aspects of its career, suggesting producers, overseeing recording sessions and having the final say over the finished 'product'. Sets the company's musical direction – sometimes known as the 'Um and Ah' department.
MARKETING DEPARTMENT
To many artists, marketing is a dirty word
But the marketing department has a major s
in new release schedules. They also plan th
sales campaign for each record, including
overseeing sleeve and advert designs, buyi
media space, arranging personal
appearances, and even deciding on an artis
look, through their choice of photographer
fashion stylists, make-up artists and sleev
designers.
ART DEPARTMENT
Specialists who create the look of the record and sometimes the act itself. Create design of sleeves, publicity material and so on. Most companies have a small in-house design team, but much of the artwork is put out to freelancers who report to the marketing department.
PRODUCER
The person responsible for the overall sound of a recording. Producers often have more influence on a record than the artist, and generally work on a percentage of record royalties.
RECORDING STUDIO
Feel, atmosphere, facilities are all important in the choice of studio. Can make a significant difference to the final sound of the record. End product is a master tape.
SALES FORCE
The unsung heroes of the record business.
responsible for actually getting the record in
the shops – not just delivering it, but selling
to the retailer. Often help out with local
publicity when act is touring.
MANUFACTURE
From the master tape, discs are cut and pressed, tapes are recorded, labels and sleeves are printed, and the finished product is packed ready for distribution.
DISTRIBUTION
Some major labels have their own distributi
networks, others rely on independent
companies. Fast, efficient distribution car
make a crucial difference to a record's sale

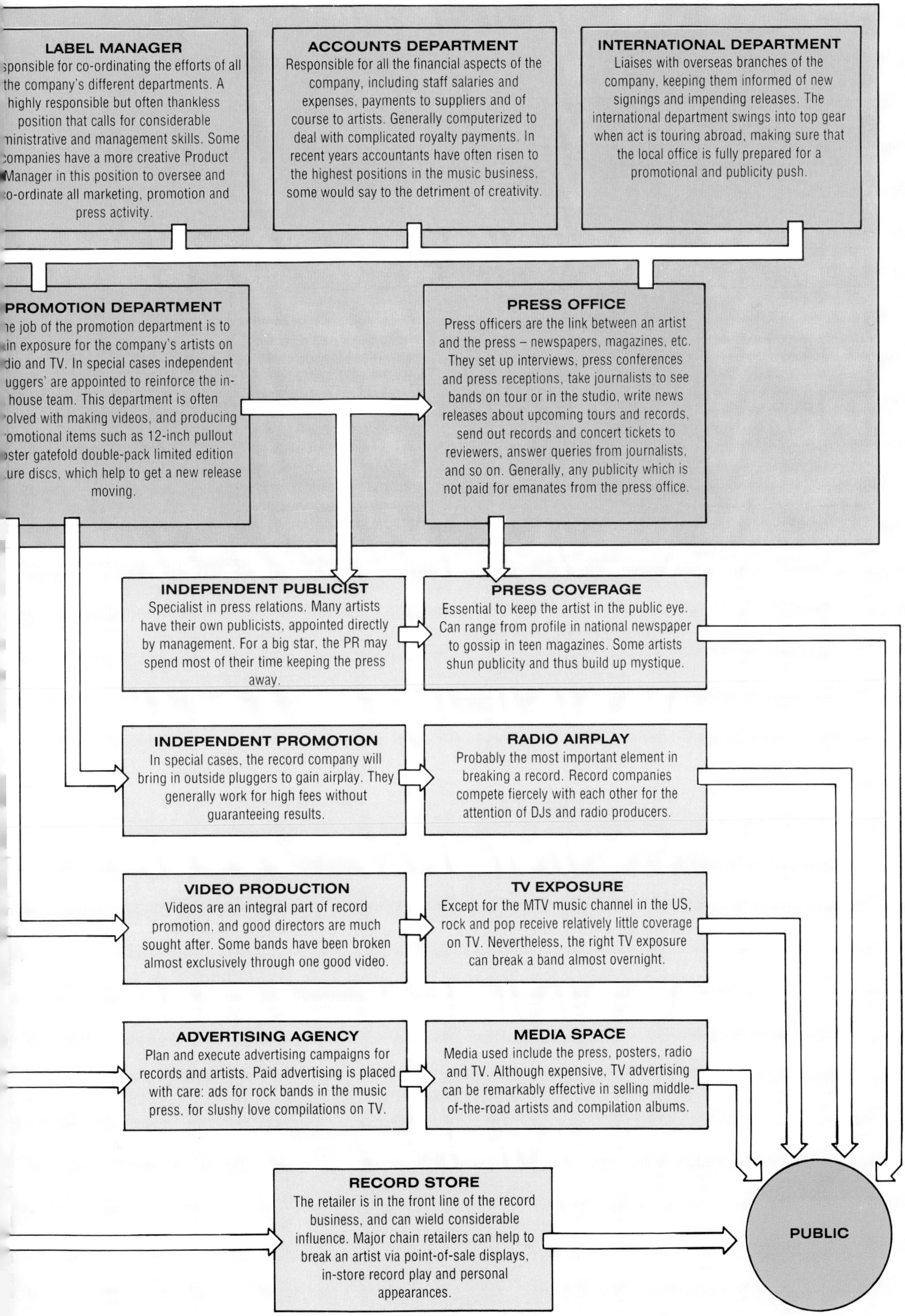

LABEL MANAGER
sponsible for co-ordinating the efforts of all the company's different departments. A highly responsible but often thankless position that calls for considerable ninistrative and management skills. Some companies have a more creative Product Manager in this position to oversee and o-ordinate all marketing, promotion and press activity.

ACCOUNTS DEPARTMENT
Responsible for all the financial aspects of the company, including staff salaries and expenses, payments to suppliers and of course to artists. Generally computerized to deal with complicated royalty payments. In recent years accountants have often risen to the highest positions in the music business, some would say to the detriment of creativity.

INTERNATIONAL DEPARTMENT
Liaises with overseas branches of the company, keeping them informed of new signings and impending releases. The international department swings into top gear when act is touring abroad, making sure that the local office is fully prepared for a promotional and publicity push.

PROMOTION DEPARTMENT
ne job of the promotion department is to in exposure for the company's artists on dio and TV. In special cases independent uggers' are appointed to reinforce the in-house team. This department is often olved with making videos, and producing omotional items such as 12-inch pullout ster gatefold double-pack limited edition ure discs, which help to get a new release moving.

PRESS OFFICE
Press officers are the link between an artist and the press – newspapers, magazines, etc. They set up interviews, press conferences and press receptions, take journalists to see bands on tour or in the studio, write news releases about upcoming tours and records, send out records and concert tickets to reviewers, answer queries from journalists, and so on. Generally, any publicity which is not paid for emanates from the press office.

INDEPENDENT PUBLICIST
Specialist in press relations. Many artists have their own publicists, appointed directly by management. For a big star, the PR may spend most of their time keeping the press away.

PRESS COVERAGE
Essential to keep the artist in the public eye. Can range from profile in national newspaper to gossip in teen magazines. Some artists shun publicity and thus build up mystique.

INDEPENDENT PROMOTION
In special cases, the record company will bring in outside pluggers to gain airplay. They generally work for high fees without guaranteeing results.

RADIO AIRPLAY
Probably the most important element in breaking a record. Record companies compete fiercely with each other for the attention of DJs and radio producers.

VIDEO PRODUCTION
Videos are an integral part of record promotion, and good directors are much sought after. Some bands have been broken almost exclusively through one good video.

TV EXPOSURE
Except for the MTV music channel in the US, rock and pop receive relatively little coverage on TV. Nevertheless, the right TV exposure can break a band almost overnight.

ADVERTISING AGENCY
Plan and execute advertising campaigns for records and artists. Paid advertising is placed with care: ads for rock bands in the music press, for slushy love compilations on TV.

MEDIA SPACE
Media used include the press, posters, radio and TV. Although expensive, TV advertising can be remarkably effective in selling middle-of-the-road artists and compilation albums.

RECORD STORE
The retailer is in the front line of the record business, and can wield considerable influence. Major chain retailers can help to break an artist via point-of-sale displays, in-store record play and personal appearances.

PUBLIC

INDEX

All figure references which appear in **bold** type relate to captions to illustrations.

THANKS

Our thanks to the following people for their help on Play Rock Keyboards:

PAUL CROCKFORD MANAGEMENT
for their help in getting material to and from Mike Lindup

ROGER SEARLE AND PAUL SELWOOD
and the rest of Level 42's stage and lights crew, for their help in setting up the picture on pages 4/5

SASHA STOJANOVIC
for interview material

In selecting and assessing keyboards, we are indebted to Julian Colbeck, author of the annual keyboard buyer's guide *Keyfax*, which details practically every electronic keyboard released since 1970.

PHOTOGRAPHS

LONDON FEATURES INTERNATIONAL
All pictures, except where credited to other agencies or record companies

MIKE PRIOR
All instruction pictures, covers, inside covers and title pages

STEVE RAPPORT
Pages 4/5, shot at Brighton Conference Centre using Level 42's stage set-up

FRONT COVER PICTURES
Stevie Wonder Robin Kaplan
Howard Jones Phil Loftus
Elton John Ebet Roberts
Nick Rhodes Eugene Adebari

6 **Jean-Michel Jarre** Richard Young (Rex)
6 **Kraftwerk** Ilpo Musto (Rex)
6 **Lionel Richie** Ebet Roberts
6 **Daryl Hall** Ebet Roberts
6 **Mags Furuholmen** Eugene Adebari
6 **Genesis** Ilpo Musto
6 **Devo** Elisa Leonelli (Rex)
6 **Pet Shop Boys** Peter Mazel
6 **Billy Joel** Sam Emerson
8 **Mike Lindup** Polydor Records
8 **Level 42** Geoff Swaine
9 **Level 42** Mike Prior
10 **Little Richard** Phil Loftus
10 **Bryan Ferry** Anwar Hussein
10 **Howard Jones** Phil Loftus
17 **A-Ha** Sam Emerson
19 **Sting** Michael Ross/A&M Records
21 **Eddie Murphy** Ken Regan
23 **Human League** Simon Fowler
24 **Stevie Wonder** Phil Loftus
25 **Booker T** LFI
25 **Billy Preston**
25 **Jan Hammer** Richard Aaron
27 **Rick Wakeman** Gary Merrin
30 **Billy Joel** Nick Elgar
31 **Elton John** Philip Ollerenshaw
34 **Harold Faltermeyer** MCA Records
34 **Jon Bon Jovi** Ross Marino
35 **Terri Nunn** Tom Sheehan
35 **Jean-Michel Jarre** Paul Cox
35 **Tornadoes** LFI
35 **Emerson Lake & Palmer** Neal Preston
39 **Roxy Music** LFI
40 **Mike Barson** Paul Cox
41 **Stevie Wonder** LFI
42 **Doobie Brothers** Gary Merrin
43 **Tom Cruise** Rick Mikels
49 **Keith Emerson** Michael Putland
50 **Costello and Naive** Adrian Boot
51 **Eno** Island Records
57 **Peter Gabriel** LFI
58 **Soft Cell** Eugene Adebari
59 **Vince Clarke** Paul Cox
63 **Herbie Hancock** Ann Summa
86 **Mike Lindup's keyboards** Steve Rapport
87 **Pet Shop Boys** Peter Mazel
89 **Devo** Ebet Roberts
90 **Franklin and Richards** Ross Marino
93 **Grammy show** Sam Emerson
94 **Stevie Wonder** Clive Dixon (Rex)
95 **Erasure** Steve Rapport
97 **OMD** Michael Putland
98 **Duran Duran** Paul Cox
98 **Mick Talbot** Ebet Roberts
100 **Tony Banks** Ilpo Musto
102 **Paul Hardcastle** Ilpo Musto
102 **Jean-Michel Jarre** Paul Cox
104 **Anne Dudley** Lynn McAfee
104 **Booker T & The MGs** LFI
105 **Devo** Ebet Roberts
105 **Ray Charles** Cinzia Ganzinelli
105 **Depeche Mode** Andrew Catlin
106 **Vince Clarke** Adrian Boot
106 **Tom Dolby** BBC/LFI
107 **Duran Duran** Eugene Adebari
107 **Keith Emerson** Michael Putland
107 **Eno** Tom Sheehan
107 **Doors** LFI
108 **Aretha Franklin** LFI
108 **Genesis** Ilpo Musto
109 **Paul Hardcastle** Fons Van Rooyen
109 **Human League** Paul Canty
109 **Herbie Hancock** Sam Emerson
109 **Christine McVie** Neal Preston
110 **Jean-Michel Jarre** Richard Young (Rex)
110 **Billy Joel/Randy Newman** Ken Regan
110 **Kraftwerk** Ilpo Musto
110 **Little Richard** LFI
110 **Jerry Lee Lewis** LFI
111 **Elton John** Michael Putland
111 **Billy Preston** Paul Cox
112 **Howard Jones** Linda Matlow (Rex)
112 **Level 42** Ilpo Musto
113 **Michael McDonald** Sam Emerson
113 **Yellow Magic Orchestra** Paul Cox
113 **Pet Shop Boys** Frank Griffin
113 **Dave Greenfield** Paul Cox
114 **Scritti Politti** Carole Segal
114 **Steve Porcaro** Sam Emerson
115 **Roger Powell** Sam Emerson
115 **Vangelis** Polydor Records
115 **Prince** Neal Preston
115 **Yello** George Dubose
116 **Rick Wakeman** Michael Putland
116 **Edgar Winter** Henry Diltz
116 **Stevie Wonder** Robin Kaplan
118 **Alison Moyet** Derek Ridgers
119 **Eurythmics** Ilpo Musto
120 **Morten Harket** Eugene Adebari
121 **Kate Bush** Phil Loftus
121 **Marillion** Ilpo Musto
122 **The Who** Frank Griffin
123 **Depeche Mode** Steve Rapport